WHY CAPITALISM SURVIVES CRISES: THE SHOCK ABSORBERS

RESEARCH IN POLITICAL ECONOMY

Series Editor: Paul Zarembka
  State University of New York at Buffalo, USA

RESEARCH IN POLITICAL ECONOMY   VOLUME 25

WHY CAPITALISM SURVIVES CRISES: THE SHOCK ABSORBERS

EDITED BY

PAUL ZAREMBKA

State University of New York at Buffalo, USA

Emerald

JAI

United Kingdom – North America – Japan
India – Malaysia – China

JAI Press is an imprint of Emerald Group Publishing Limited
Howard House, Wagon Lane, Bingley BD16 1WA, UK

First edition 2009

Reprints and permission service
Contact: booksandseries@emeraldinsight.com

British Library Cataloguing in Publication Data
A catalogue record for this book is available from the British Library

ISBN: 978-1-84855-586-0
ISSN: 0161-7230 (Series)

Awarded in recognition of
Emerald's production
department's adherence to
quality systems and processes
when preparing scholarly
journals for print

INVESTOR IN PEOPLE

CONTENTS

LIST OF CONTRIBUTORS

Guglielmo Carchedi	Faculty of Economics and Econometrics, University of Amsterdam, Amsterdam, Holland
Shūichi Kakuta	Department of Economics, Ritsumeikan University, Kusatsu City, Japan
Victor Kasper, Jr.	Department of Economics and Finance, Buffalo State College, Buffalo, NY, USA
Dimitris Paitaridis	Department of Economics, University of Macedonia, Thessaloniki, Greece
Simon Stander	Free lance writer, formerly of the UN-mandated University for Peace, Costa Rica
Lefteris Tsoulfidis	Department of Economics, University of Macedonia, Thessaloniki, Greece
Paul Zarembka	Department of Economics, State University of New York at Buffalo, Buffalo, NY, USA

PART I
WHY CAPITALISM SURVIVES
CRISES – THE SHOCK ABSORBERS
BY SIMON STANDER ☆

☆Simon Stander taught for many years at Middlesex University in London and more recently at the UN mandated University for Peace in Costa Rica. He now lives in Costa Rica.

INTRODUCTION

Included in this volume is a 200-page monograph that provides a provocative challenge to the traditional Marxist view of the role of the working class in social change. For Marx, the role of fundamental social change is centred on the leadership of workers who as the exploited class would have the greatest motivation for change. In developed capitalism they would represent one of the two most important classes. As per Marx, the classes are defined in terms of how groups of people related to the means of production. For industrial capitalism, this means capitalists – those who owned and controlled the means of production – and workers – the direct producers who were required to work for wages.

Stander has a view of society consisting of three basic classes. They are capitalists, workers and a shock absorber class. His concepts of capitalists and workers are not necessarily identical with those of Marx. His shock absorber class does not directly appropriate surplus value or directly produce it. They serve to ensure that the surplus output produced by an expanding economic process is sold at a profit that keeps the system operating as a whole. As the economy experiences periodic crises, the shock absorber conceptualization is that the shock absorber class must respond by altering consumption patterns in a stabilizing manner. Stander seems to understand that this class would find the constant drastic fluctuation in their standard of living and community and social relations increasingly intolerable. This would provide a primary motivation for reform.

We see Stander's monograph as raising a number of issues that those with more Marxist views have been confronting for some time but he raises these issues within a more systematic framework. He challenges the view of the working class as the primary motivator for social change. He supplements the Marxist analysis of class. He challenges the need for fundamental change. We do see, however, precedents for his class concept.

CHALLENGING THE VIEW OF WORKERS AS MOTIVATORS FOR CHANGE

For Marx, workers would be the prime motivators for a fundamental change toward a new economic system. They produce the output of the economy but have little control over their working environment, the product or the direction that economic change would take. They are alienated although often without a consciousness of the systemic source of their alienation. The social system results in workers having to work longer than necessary to reproduce their socially defined needs as workers. The surplus product, taking the form of surplus value, generates property income in the form of rents, interest and profit. Those holding ownership of the means of production claim the results of the workers' labour. The existence of wage labour creates a necessary condition for means of production becoming capital. This concept of capital is different from both chattels and personal property. Stander notes such a difference between these two and capital, but he does not note the difference between means of production and capital which seem to be identical for him.

Industrial capital, in a Marxist understanding, is a social relationship that requires the development of wage labour. The direct producers are exploited because they directly produce the output but exist under a set of social relations that allows others to take a large share of what they produce. This share is used to reinforce that set of social relations. Direct workers, thus, find themselves both exploited and alienated. They are primed for change and resistance but it would only be through class political struggle that fundamental change could be made possible. The twin burdens of exploitation and alienation can result in ineffective venting through crime, depression and/ or apathy or reactionary patterns. Still, the possibility of a coherent political force emerging based on the working class is enhanced by their double burden. In addition, there is a philosophical view that as human beings they are not mute beasts of burden forever bowing docilely to the direction of capital and its minions. As human beings, the possibility for resistance and struggle for fundamental change, revolutionary change, is always a possibility. This double burden provides the basis for the coherence of workers, a coherent political force based on common interest that could lead a broader coalition to fundamental social change. There might be other classes and contradictions among workers and within capital but the most fundamental contradiction is between capital and labour. The periodic crises endemic to capitalism would further stoke the conditions for an emergent class consciousness that could become a growing and effective engine of social change.

Stander implicitly suggests that this picture is not reflective of present conditions. Empirically the working class as motivators for social change has not happened on a sustained basis. He seems to adopt the position that workers accept alienation and exploitation and see their lot tied to the success of capitalism as eternal and themselves inferior subordinates, in the class sense, to capital. This seems consistent with the view of workers being the object of economic activity moved to act by the subject or active mover, capital. There is only room for worker resignation. Stander is led to develop what he sees as a new source of change rooted not in the exploitation in production but in requirements related to adjustment to shocks within the framework of capitalism. He ignores the social relationship in the very nature of capital. In this he is consistent with some of the literature that he cites that focuses on exchange relations.

The term shock (of shock absorber) could be argued to resonate with the more traditional neoclassical-based macroeconomic theory schools of thought such as the New Classicals and New Keynesians. These schools see the system as basically sound but subject to periodic exogenous (outside) "shocks." The market economy requires adjustment to these shocks. The shock absorber concept can invoke the image of a well-built automobile (economy) running on a rough road and needing good shock absorbers. Stander's shock absorber class goes through the most wrenching adjustment to these crisis events. They are, thus, more motivated to seek and struggle for reformist change. They do not want fundamental change. Fundamental change would seek to eliminate the exploitation and alienation of the direct producers. A good analogy would be to envision insurance agents facilitating the slave trade who are motivated to see it operate more effectively. Many in the middle classes, re-conceptualized by Stander as the shock absorbers or absorptive class, see their lot tied to the surpluses expropriated from the direct producers. They do not seek to overturn the source of what provides them with their source of comfortable, or at least tolerable, livelihood in periods when the system is exhibiting exuberance. Stander sees the socioeconomic system as creating wants, perceived differently from needs. These new wants create instruments by which the absorptive class fulfils its role.

SUPPLEMENTING THE MARXIST CONCEPT OF CLASS

Stander's concept of class and surplus is not well defined. He seems to imply that active workers cannot adjust much to the economic downturns if the system is to survive. Marx would argue that workers have to struggle to maintain given social wages. This social wage may rise or fall over a longer run due to victories or defeats in political struggles. Short-run declines in the market wage would result in the decline or degrading of the working class. Capitalists – because of their wealth and power as a class – will adjust to downturns while maintaining their comforts. Many people in between, however, will be called upon by the needs of adjustment to significantly alter their standard of living and endure relatively severe privation. These groups, at least following one interpretation of the classical Marxist perspective, may swing in a manner to coalesce into a political movement possibly led by either the working class or by capital.

The middle groups (professionals, retired workers, some academics, clerics, the armed services, etc, those chronically out of work etc, crafts people, small capitalists and unproductive workers (in the Marxist sense)) would become the explicit and implicit targets of the system during crises. These middle groups taken together constitute Stander's shock absorber class. Many would find their standards of living and mode of living markedly altered by shocks. Stander sees as new the absolute magnitude of the class in its modern form. There is, therefore, a need to recognize their new potential as a political force. The size of this grouping, being deeply integrated into the system, does provide a strong social basis for why fundamental social change may not be in the cards.

CHALLENGING THE MARXIST VIEW OF THE NEED FOR FUNDAMENTAL CHANGE

Stander's implicit position is that the desire for revolutionary or fundamental change is outmoded. Workers may momentarily provide a basis for change but historically this does not appear to have been sustainable. He implies that either the exploitation and/or alienation of direct producers – which may be reflected in apathy and acceptance – are not of fundamental importance. The implication seems to be that imperfect labour or product markets generate the surplus. In any case, he seems to abandon some important insights of Marx. He seems to imply that monopoly power is the basis of the surplus, rather than exploitation. In his discussion of the commodity, Stander does recognize some aspects of the nature of labour power, but he also gravitates to more mainstream interpretations of value.

Stander's shock absorber class is a composite set of diverse economic interests. This economic interest approach is similar to a more mainstream approach that sees the government as a neutral arbitrator between competing interests. Again, Stander's approach is different from that of Marx. He sees a coalition of these different economic-interest groups as a coherent force for leading a reform of capitalism. Their uniting interest is the need for stabilizing their standard of living. They need to ensure social safety nets (social security, unemployment insurance, welfare, etc). Workers are, however, called upon to support this composite grouping in spite of costs they themselves must bear.

Worker-led coalitions that take a more Marxist approach often call for similar reforms. However, they do so while trying to bring attention to the underlying contradictions in the system and pointing to the exploitation and alienation upon which it is based. Stander's approach suggests that such a progressive grouping might jettison the baggage contained in the Marxist approach of highlighting the contradictions of productive relations. Instead, reform of the system is fine. Workers that generate the surplus are cogs who do not perceive exploitation and alienation, or they do not care. Even if they did, Stander would argue that they see no better alternative. The best that can be done is reform.

Stander uses a concept of surplus that is not well defined but appears to be linked to the concentration of capital. There appears to be an appeal to the pure economic interests of his coalition that will wrest some of the monopoly power related gains from those currently appropriating the surplus. These monopoly-related gains would implicitly include both that arising from corporate power and from unions. The concepts used in Stander's approach are a bit eclectic and sometimes vague. This is to be expected with a set of ideas in the process of development. Yet, his concept of surplus has to be kept vague. Otherwise, the source of the surplus generates a moral and very strong political issue.

WHY IS STANDER'S CONCEPT NEW?

Stander's monograph presents an argument that the shock absorber class is now so large that its potential for achieving reformist change is readily apparent. In our understanding, his definition of the shock absorber class is not, in fact, so transparent. Even though the constituents of this class have a common economic interest in keeping the system stable and in redistributing the surplus, they harbour diverse and conflicting interests. Their main common interest is in wresting control and distribution of the surplus from the original appropriators. Yet, this idea in itself is not new. Malthus at the dawn of industrial capitalism had a view of the landed aristocracy as a realization outlet for the surplus. The workers would only consume at subsistence, or temporarily above it until the population increased. Capitalists were busy making money and accumulating. For Malthus there would be a surplus that these two groups would be unable or unwilling to purchase. The landed aristocracy filled the role as the ultimate purchaser to prevent a glut of output. But this placed the renters of land as the surplus absorbers. Stander's grouping is larger and includes what Marx would call unproductive workers, small capitalists, the unemployed, etc.

Stander's absorptive class is motivated and united by a desire to maintain the share of the surplus. Presumably, this class would also like to increase the surplus. If they are not challenging capitalism, this means they want to increase the rate of exploitation either of workers at home, abroad or both. This means maintaining social programs at the expense of workers with workers not having much control over the process. Workers would have to produce the social surplus required for those unable to work.

Workers would find themselves subordinated to the requirements of the broader absorber class. Workers' focus and energy would be devoted to ensuring the social welfare of the shock absorbers at the workers' own expense without demanding that the very structure for the system of surplus generation and expropriation be questioned. This would channel the energy of workers away from changes that would more directly address exploitation and alienation. In fact such a diversion would implicitly ask workers to deny or ignore the existence of the exploitation.

THE HISTORICAL CONTEXT

The existence of the Soviet Union, regardless of what were major flaws in its system, created a bargaining chip for workers and progressives in the west during the cold war. Concessions were made in social programs and for unions because of its existence. With the end of the cold war, the social programs that were developed supporting what Stander would call the absorber class were no longer required for co-opting either workers or this absorber class into acceptance of a system based upon exploitation. As a result, there was an increased attack on the social safety net and the unions throughout the west. Using Stander's concept, the absorber class found itself in need of an intellectual justification for progressive reform as opposed to fundamental change. The political card of fundamental change could no longer be plausibly used in the new environment.

The Soviets, despite mismanagement, a less-developed society and unfavourable historical circumstances, had devoted a larger effort at ensuring employment, advancing education, medical insurance initiatives and the rights of women than capitalist societies at comparable levels of development under better circumstances. This served as an example of what could be done for a broader mass of people even under unfavourable circumstances. The Soviet advances in science also spurred the need for increased investment in education in the West. The absence of the Soviet rivalry opened up to renewed attack what social initiatives that had been enacted in the west. Welfare, social security and unemployment insurance came under increased assault.

WHY HAS THE WORKING CLASS BEEN DEMOBILIZED?

Stander's monograph ties into a long-term discussion. Why has the working class in so many countries been so demobilized? This question has been raised and answered in a variety of ways:

1. insufficient class consciousness (highlighted by Gramsci);
2. the enormous impact of Stalinist political practices;
3. the adverse circumstances under which the socialism has been attempted;
4. ethnically and racially divided working classes;
5. the changing nature of the work environment; and
6. government infiltration of militant unions.

If one would have a hopeless view of the capacity of the working class to lead a social revolution (ignoring some evidence to the contrary, perhaps most well-known in Latin America currently), then Stander's work could be seen as a possible outcome. Thus, if one does not have a Marxist view of capital as social relation, then one has less of a need to see the importance of the working class in generating the social surplus product that manifests itself under capitalism as surplus value. For Marx, however, direct workers (physical or intellectual in the Marxist sense) make possible both the existence of industrial capital and the generation of the surplus value. There will be contradictions within capital and within labour. Nevertheless, the most important one is between capital and labour.

Stander's work is well researched and thought provoking. Persons of various persuasions within progressive thought will find it worthy of serious engagement. His review of the literature on class is impressive. We must remember that none of us has a magic formula for moving forward and we learn as new approaches are explored.

Victor Kasper
Paul Zarembka

CHAPTER 1

THE ABSORPTIVE CLASS

...political economy offers this advantage ..., that though it is an organic science (no part... but what acts on the whole, as the whole re-acts on each part), yet the several parts may be detached and contemplated singly.... I had been led in 1811 to look into loads of books and pamphlets on many branches of economy; I saw that these were generally the very dregs and rinsings of the human intellect; and that any man of sound head, and practised in wielding logic with a scholastic adroitness, might take up the whole academy of modern economists, and throttle them between heaven and earth with his finger and thumb, or bray their fungus heads to powder with a lady's fan. At length, in 1819, a friend in Edinburgh sent me down Mr Ricardo's book: I said, before I had finished the first chapter, "Thou art the man!" Had this profound work been really written in England during the nineteenth century? I supposed thinking had been extinct in England. Could it be that an Englishman, and he not in academic bowers, but oppressed by mercantile and senatorial cares, had accomplished what all the universities of Europe, and a century of thought, had failed even to advance by one hair's breadth? (Thomas de Quincey, Confessions of an English Opium-Eater, 1821 edition, pp. 99–100)

1. OBSERVATION OF CRISES AND THEIR REOCCURRENCE: EXPLANANDUM

There have been times in recent years when it has seemed that the US economy, in particular, has defied economic gravity. This was certainly the case in the late nineties of the twentieth century. Many heaved a sigh of relief when the Nasdaq and the Dow responded to the pull of economic gravity and fell to earth in the early part of the twenty first century. The Earth at the time, in 2002, appeared to be indices of around 8,000 for the Dow and 1,250 for the Nasdaq. These measures still indicated huge wealth in terms of saleable bits of paper as well, indicating the underlying huge capacity of the real economy for creating surpluses. Both indices climbed back, though the Nasdaq was a long way from its astronomic former heights before the next (2007) crisis hit. True to the cyclical record of modern capitalism, however, by 2006 the US and the world stock markets were booming again. The nominal value of shares traded worldwide in 2006 by some estimates was nearly $70 trillion (Bogle, 2005). In 2007, another crisis appeared, ushered in supposedly by the collapse of the sub-prime mortgage market in the United States; subsequent events took their toll in economic and financial terms not only in the United States but worldwide in most of the major economies. The terms "credit crunch" and "sub-prime" had become so pervasive within a few weeks of the onset of the latest economic crisis that by July 2008, the *Concise Oxford Dictionary* provided definitions for them. While these terms are now embedded in the language of economics and everyday speech, inevitably the affected economies will recover from the crises and continue to grow. While there is no shortage of reasons posited for the latest crisis and those preceding it, far fewer explanations have been forwarded to tell us why economies survive economic shocks and, despite dire predictions and expressions of gloom, recent crises have not been as disastrous as was once the case, notably as in the Depression years of the 1930s. During the Depression of the Thirties, production fell by a third between 1929 and 1933, unemployment reached 13 million and even by 1938 one person in five were unemployed. No economist has predicted these dire consequences even for the crisis of 2007–2009. In 1999, Paul Krugman published his short book: *The Return of Depression Economics* in which he not only reminded us of the 1930s Depression but suggested that the then economic crises bore an "eerie resemblance to the Great Depression."[1] He retreats within a few pages and describes the events as the Great Recession because the global damage has been "well short of Depression levels" (Krugman, 1999). A decade later, Krugman, by then a Nobel laureate for economics in 2008, began his 2009 revised edition of *Return of Depression Economics* thus: "The world economy is not in depression: it probably won't fall into depression (though I wish I could be completely sure about that)" (Krugman, 2009). By early January 2009, he surprised other economic commentators by using the term "depression" in his *New York Times* column.

In 2001, it was reported that rich investors on both sides of the Atlantic had lost $2.6 trillion, or 6% of their total wealth. According to a report by the Boston Consulting Group, that was the equivalent of the entire private banking assets of Switzerland. Certainly, in the late nineties, disbelief manifested itself in many circles at the prolonged soaring bull market in the United States, and the dire predictions of collapse bore a superficial resemblance to those of 1929. The collapse, when it came, did relatively little damage to the US economy as a whole, despite the fact that, according to John Bogle, over $2 trillion were lost to shareholders (Bogle, 2005). By 2006, the United States was supposedly on track again for rapid growth. A report by Bush's Council of Economic advisors was predicting in February 2006 that US growth would be 3.4% for the year and much the same in 2007. As we now know, however, another crisis emerged and the US economy had to face up to the prospect of recession again; at the same time fears grew quickly regarding a credit crunch, replaced by fears of falling interest rates Keynesian style, followed by a sharp fall in the dollar against other hard currencies. The dollar subsequently recovered as other economies faced recession.

The 2007 crisis appeared to begin with the collapse of the sub-prime mortgage market in the United States; this was followed by a number of uncertainties which included the collapse of Northern Rock, an important mortgage lender in the United Kingdom. Other banks displayed serious wobbles or posted huge losses and there was trouble at Citigroup and other financial institutions including mortgage lenders, insurance companies, and merchant and commercial banks. Central Bankers, especially the Fed, European Central Bank and the Bank of England, were generally acclaimed for their actions by economic journalists for providing stability in a situation that was seen as one where the key question was to expand or restrict credit through the manipulation of interests rates and other devices. All this was conducted against the background of the US dollar sliding down against other hard currencies, notably the Euro and the UK pound sterling. The underlying issue was clear. Restrict credit and risk serious economic recession, or expand credit and allow certain economies to overheat. There was too much money (surplus) sloshing around. Even as far into the crisis as January 2009, *The Economist* was reporting that "there are huge amounts of money sloshing around."[2] As Gordon Brown, the UK prime minister, announced further credit for the banking system, a similar comment came from Norman Lamont, a former Chancellor of Exchequer under Thatcher, who suggested that the problem was too much cash, not too little. Those that believe in the iron laws of supply and demand would say that the price of money (interest rates) being at rock bottom would indicate that there was too much money around, not too little.

Thus, the capitalist system had reached a point only a few years after the crisis of the 1990s where the surplus was too great; the capitalist system needed to burn it off; policy makers were caught between the need of the system on the one hand to slow down and the need of political and business interests, on the other, with its requirement to maintain the levels of production and the rate of profit. While economic recession was seen as the main problem, it was and is the solution to the problem of the capitalist system as a whole, that of overproduction.

But, as with the recession crisis of the post-Clinton years and those preceding it, the remarkable phenomenon has not been the recurrent economic and financial crises but US resilience, and that of other advanced economies, in the face of crisis. The explanation for this lies at a deep level and is *intimately connected with new class formation*. This book sets out to explain why capitalism, despite these ever recurring crises, which have been endemic to capitalism for 250 years or thereabouts, fails to collapse, and the explanation for the resilience of capitalism is presented in the context of class analysis.

2. CLASS AS EXPLANANS

Class analysis, once central to social science debate, has fallen into decline since 1990 and the fall of communism, though hopefully not into disrepute. This book puts class analysis back into its previous pivotal position in a unique way.

First, it identifies the existence of the absorptive class, the shock of absorbers of the title, and defines this new class in terms of its economic functions. Its key function is to absorb the commodities that are over-produced by the capitalist system. Also, it functions, in conditions where finance capital increasingly has come to dominate all other forms of capital, to absorb the economic crises that occur in the process of burning off excess capital by absorbing the shock of the decline in the value of financial instruments, while allowing the real economy to survive, more or less intact, through the continued purchase of commodities produced by the capitalist system for profit.

Second, to see clearly the existence and functions of the absorptive class, some of the ideological accretions associated with orthodox economics have to be removed, the most important being the concept of scarcity. Economic activity under capitalism (indeed any economic activity, capitalist or not) revolves around the production of a surplus. Thus, in the discussion of the absorptive class, it is of central importance to keep in mind that the class of absorbers has been produced to deal with what capitalism has done only too well, produce massive surpluses. Surplus absorption and its importance has been noted by David Harvey "Surplus absorption is the central problem ... The incredible expansion in capitalist surplus-value absorption coupled with another destabilizing round of technological innovations have simply led to the production of even more massive surpluses ... Capitalism ... has also invented all manner of new forms of speculation in asset values that suck massive quantities of capital surplus..." (Harvey, 2006, pp. xxiv–xxvi). It was, however, Baran and Sweezy (1966), whose contribution is discussed in Chapter 6, who first developed the concept of absorption (see also Lippit, 1985).

Third, my approach to class differs because it isn't "neo" anything, though it is of course heavily *indebted* to all the founding fathers of sociology and economics and modern political thought: Marx, Weber, Durkheim, Smith, Ricardo and Mill. Later commentators, despite their worthiness, such as Baudrillard and Bourdieu, serve mostly as useful foils in the fencing match that has produced this exposé of the absorptive class.

Fourth, my analysis differs from most contemporary discussions of class as exemplified for instance by the several authors in Erik Olin Wright (Wright, 2008) because my starting point is the threefold integrated "complex" of state–economy–class where class functions to maintain the coherence of the state–economy unity. This makes reformism a central concern rather than class conflict or the concern for the detailed examination and empirical revelations of the stratification of classes, which now seems to be the current concern of some class analysts.[3]

Fifth, the empirical nature of the investigation of class and class strata *a la*, say, Goldthorpe et al. (Goldthorpe et al., 1969), is rejected on the grounds that it is hidebound by acceptance of the existence of the individual as defined by the capitalist system itself (and probably by all systems, in fact). To understand the existence and functions of the absorptive class we have to review the nature of the individual. Just as classes exist and can be seen to function as fractions so too individuals consist of ill-fitting fractions so that each one is more like, as it were, not a sleek horse but a rather lumpy camel. I am a university teacher located clearly in a vague stratum that could be labelled in a number of ways: socio-economic group II for instance, but what is my real economic place in the world? In my analysis, I am a commodity because education itself is a commodity and I have been produced by the system to be that commodity but I am also a clear member of the absorptive class, absorbing everything from a house to a car to a pension plan to medical insurance. However, it is possible that I might also be a consultant and be a link person for other consultants, in which case I am also probably a small capitalist, being involved in both extracting a surplus and absorbing it. Alternatively, I may also be a wage slave, and thus a proletarian. The fact that I cannot locate myself exactly simply indicates that I do indeed consist of ill-connected fractions. But the sum of fractions makes up the class, which functions independently, systemically, as a class independent of the individuals within the class. This line of thought is wholly consistent with the Durkheimian view that society is a thing in itself and pervades sociological discussion. This view is not only Durkheimian but pervades sociological theory: "...psychologists and sociologists have recognized that groups are not at all identical with the sum total of their members, but develop a character and form of their own. A group behaves very differently from its members" Erich Kahler (1957, p.6). Thus, we can argue that class is a thing in itself as is the capitalist system.

Six, I take the approach that class is about class formation in the way Aronowitz explains, employing the insights of Adam Pzeworski, though class formation and class struggle is seen somewhat differently (Aronowitz & Paul, 2002, p. 9. 11 et seq., pp. 63 et seq., p. 141 et seq.). Hopefully, the reader will be able to "see" how the absorptive class has come into being, matured, and is finding its particular form of consciousness during the time–space specific process of formation.

Seven, reform and reformism becomes one of the primary concerns rather than class conflict in the arguments in this volume. The contracted proletariat, supposedly to be the driving force of change, does conduct residual struggles. However, the proletariat has been relegated by many commentators to the state of the "underclass" and as such, very much in the role of the new *lumpenproletariat*, is assumed not to be a major actor on the stage of history. In reality, reform is, however, very much an issue and the absorptive class does have a key role in this process, thereby maintaining the viability of capitalism. Major class conflicts remain but are fiercest (whether we see it clearly or not) between fractions of class. For instance, between the petty-bourgeoisie and the Labour movement in Britain at the outset of the Thatcher era or between industrial capital and finance capital as is the case currently in the process of so-called globalization, are examples of conflicts of interests between fractions of class. While Marx and Engels regarded the peasantry as essentially conservative and excluded them from the revolutionary struggle, we can now regard the agricultural worker as part and parcel of the working class, though constituting an identifiable fraction.

While Marcuse's *One Dimensional Man* stands as a shining object lesson in analysis, I sense one-dimensional society is not quite as one dimensional as all that. Marcuse did think that the power of technology could be harnessed potentially to the purpose of freeing man from dominance by all forms of totalitarianism and capitalism, though he does not pursue this point. He is more concerned with showing how man is euphoric in his unhappiness under a system marked by toil, aggressiveness, misery and injustice, and where men had lost their powers of critical judgement and independence of thought (Marcuse, 1991, pp. 1–3). "Free election of masters does not abolish the masters or slaves," he wrote (Marcuse, 1991, p. 7). Indeed, he goes on: "One dimensional thought is systematically promoted by the makers of politics and their purveyors of mass information" (Marcuse, 1991, p. 14). In such circumstances, the scope for reformism seems somewhat limited. Thus, while I adhere very much to Marcuse and his interdisciplinary method and his theoretical approach, an important point of departure for me is that reform of a substantial nature is possible as the absorptive class will "realize" its historical role, not only of absorbing commodities, and absorbing the shocks of economic and political crises, but also preserving itself, not, of course, through revolution, but through the only way open short of sheer decay: reform.

Eight, the shrinking proletariat obscures the fact that there are essentially three big classes rather than the traditional two of the bourgeoisie and the proletariat: to these two "big classes" should be added the major new class of the absorptive class born from the historical processes of the last 100 years, but especially of the last 50. Generally speaking, this book, when it refers to class, refers to these three big classes, not to Weberian style strata or occupational groups. Identifying three big classes helps us to escape from the continued problem of seeing the working class as the prime movers in history, and arguing whether so-called middle classes are really proletarians.[4]

Nine, the class picture would not be complete without asking the question: what constitutes the capitalist class? The answer to that is not so straightforward since ownership of stocks and shares does not necessarily constitute being a capitalist any more than being a senior executive in the system does. Undoubtedly Warren Buffet and George Soros are capitalists. So, too, is the owner operator of a corner shop. Capitalists are just as fractionalized as, say, the proletariat or the absorptive class itself. One of the developments that, in a sense, have turned the world upside down is the fact that capitalists increasingly are not individuals but corporate bodies or legal entities that operate for profit. While science-fiction writers may have envisaged robots that make, distribute and serve, the real "robots" are corporations that behave with mentalities of their own, taking on and rejecting human beings as the profit process succeeds, proceeds or fails.[5] These corporate bodies *qua* "robots," like the metallic or plastic ones of science fiction, however, are prone to date, malfunction, rust, melt-down, or grinding to a halt. But the capitalist system goes on and may be even stronger as a result of the robotic wastage, and, of course, the reformist pressure exerted by one of its major products, the absorptive class.

3. CLASS ANALYSIS: A BRIEF HISTORY

Needless to say, with the fall of totalitarian regimes, class analysis has fallen into decline in the apparently mistaken belief that those regimes were socialist and that class analysis should be cast out along with socialism in its various forms. The attempts at the identification of so-called civil society lying somewhere between the economy and politics within the nation state, and thereby, the separation of, say, NGOs from their class base is probably a disaster for understanding real social processes. There are those who cling to the view, nevertheless, that class analysis is still valid for explaining how things work in modern nation states. Some, even, would claim that a new class has arisen in the international sphere. One proponent of this is Leslie Sklair whose relatively recent volume *The Transnational Capitalist Class* claims to have identified the existence of a new class (or at least a significant fraction of class) both theoretically and empirically (Sklair, 2001).

He claims the following four features for the class:

- The Transnational capitalist class is more or less in control of the processes of globalization.
- The Transnational capitalist class is actually becoming a dominant class in some spheres.
- The globalization of the capitalist system reproduces itself through the profit-driven culture-ideology of consumerism.
- The Transnational capitalist class works consciously to resolve contradictions produced in this process, notably growing inequalities and the problems associated by unsustainability. In other words, it is consciously reformist.

The concepts used in the analysis such as class, fractions of class and class dominance and hegemony are all familiar, though they have fallen partially into disuse and, mistakenly, out of favour. The problem in Sklair's formulation is that it is hard to argue that a class exists independent of state and economy. Given that the global economy is not as developed as a model national economy nor is there anything like a global state, it seems premature to argue for a Transnational class. This is despite the fact that we can see self-evidently the existence of considerable accretions of strength as a result of the concentration of capital and may well mistake certain common actions and opinions as indicating the existence of class. Moreover, the interpretation of the empirical evidence provided by Sklair may be distorted by the weaknesses of the underpinning theory.[6]

Though Sklair's analysis may be somewhat premature given the inchoate nature of global capitalism, his concern for restoring class analysis in the social sciences is clearly justifiable. French academics have been prolific in the reinterpretation of class in the last 30 or 40 years: Bourdieu, Baudrillard, Derrida, Deleuze, Guatarri, Althusser all have made their contributions, but overall, though important insights remain, definitive analysis of a convincing nature remains elusive from their work (Corlett, 1998).

One of the main problems with class analysis is its unfinished nature in the history of the social sciences. The way Chapter 53 of Marx's *Capital* runs into the dust is only one example of the elusive nature of the concept of class and of subsequent class analysis. Both in theoretical and empirical terms, class has been difficult to define with precision despite the fact that classes are there to be seen. On the other hand, not everyone has yet been able to see them whereas "civil society" has become a universally visible, though a thoroughly misleading, concept. The issues surrounding civil society and the way that concept has obscured class analysis are developed more fully in Chapter 2.

Class analysis, to all intents and purposes, began in the modern sense with the statement in the *Communist Manifesto*:

> The history of all hitherto existing society is the history of class struggles.... The modern bourgeois society that has sprouted from the ruins of feudal society has not done away with class antagonisms. It has but established new classes, new conditions of oppression, new forms of struggle in place of the old ones.... All previous historical movements were movements of minorities, or in the interest of minorities. The proletarian movement is the self-conscious, independent movement of the immense majority, in the interest of the immense majority.

History, however, has moved on. In none of the OECD countries, for instance, does the proletariat form an immense majority. Something of great fundamental importance has happened in these countries, but classes have not disappeared. What, in place of the proletarian and bourgeois struggles, now exists? History may have moved on, but does the assertion remain true that "history is the history of class struggle?" If so, in the absence of a revolutionary proletariat, have new classes been formed out of the old and what are they and what functions do they perform?

It is possible to keep much of Marxist methodology and utilize a number of concepts such as class, state, fractions and consciousness while moving on substantially from being bogged down in the nineteenth-century versions of class war. Rather than focus on the issue of revolution, placing reformism at the forefront of the analysis may offer a better approach. The meaning of this term, reformism, and its importance in relation to the absorptive class will be discussed later, but for the moment it needs to be stated here that the concerns of many early revolutionaries lay heavily in hastening revolution to pre-empt reformist movements which, it was thought, and feared, would destroy the revolution forever. The absorptive class has not only become the class that absorbs shocks and commodities but is also the very class that carries with it the contradictory possibilities for continuous reform of the capitalist system, thus sustaining capitalism into the foreseeable future. If, writing in 1848, Marx and Engels claimed the process of history and the bourgeois-feudal struggle had created new classes, is it equally possible, given that history is the history of class struggles, that new classes have been generated? Assuming new classes have been generated, what are they? How do they function? What do they function for? What has brought them into existence? Poulantzas in the 1970s identified fractions of class as being of great significance. In this case, his interest lay in the fractions of the bourgeoisie. Fractions in the working class had already been identified, for instance, and their role delineated. The aristocracy of the working class had been identified, not only by Marx, Engels and Lenin in particular but by British labour historians also as being crucial in the process of reformism in the United Kingdom and was a major explanation for the non-revolutionary attitude of the British proletariat. By the sixties, the work of Goldthorpe and Lockwood (Goldthorpe et al., 1969) had identified the "affluent worker" and this led to widespread discussion of the process of embourgeoisement which further explained the lack of revolutionary intent among the skilled UK workers employed in industry. By the 1970s it was clear, or should have been clear, that key fractions had appeared within capitalism in, say, the United Kingdom that could explain all kinds of policies and developments such as the conflict between industrial and financial capital. This, in turn, would explain the dominance of the City (of London) and the process of de-industrialization as well as the appeal to the "silent majority" giving a role to the petty-bourgeoisie and its support of Thatcherism and the attack on the Welfare State. However, while commentators such as Will Hutton (Hutton, 1995) have noted the growth and dominance of finance capital to the detriment of the economy as a whole in the United Kingdom, he makes no observations about the relationship between the changes in the nature of capitalism and changes in class structure.

On the question of what is and what is not a capitalist there is also a considerable degree of uncertainty which has emanated from the observed distinction between managers of large corporations and their separation from ownership of capital (Marx, 1972, Vol. III). Thus, the identification of "managerialism" was another obfuscation that occurred in the sixties and seventies. The growth of the mixed economy with huge concentrations of capital in both the public and private sectors supposedly ushered in the age of the manager, the technocrat and the meritocrat. These elite groups appear to assist in the separation of management from ownership of both public and private capital. It then began to be unclear who the capitalists actually were as the ownership of capital (in the form of financial instruments) had become diffuse whereas real nineteenth-century capitalists like Lever, Rockefeller and Ford, while still remaining in the persons of newspaper magnates, oil millionaires and more recent computer and knowledge age wizards like Larry Page and Bill Gates, very generally speaking were much smaller in relation to the seemingly huge amounts of shares traded on the world's markets. Instead of capitalists we hear of more references to the super-rich which obscure the differences between a capitalist and a rich absorber. One socialist-oriented web site in discussing the general election in the United Kingdom in 2005, refers to the 1,000 top super-rich whose wealth amounted to $43.4 billions. This group is not allocated a class but are referred to as a narrow layer of those (6% of the population) who have more moderate wealth and who are described as upper-middle-class having benefited from the speculative boom in the stock market.[7] Reinforcing this, John Bogle points out: "driven by mega grants of stock options, the total pay of the average CEO soared from 42 times that of the average worker in 1980 to 280 times in 2004" (Bogle, 2005, p. xx). This confuses the capitalist with a rich CEO who is more likely to be a rich absorber than a true capitalist. As the twentieth century progressed toward the twenty-first, the class struggle came to be seen by academics and journalistic commentators less as a struggle between capitalists and a proletariat conscious of its historical mission to bring down the capitalist system prone to crisis, than as a battle between bosses and workers over short-term gains in an economy based on sectional interests and short-sighted managerial decision-making. Fractions of one class, skilled workers about to be deskilled fought industrial capitalists about to be de-industrialised (as with car workers and print workers and miners in the United Kingdom). This struggle seemed to end the phase known as Fordism in which mass production had to find mass consumers. As the absorptive class developed out of these fractions of workers, small capitalists, occupational and professional groups, birth pangs of the formation of the absorptive class became noticeable as the "smug" fifties of early mass consumption gave way to the angst and dissent of the 60s. This point is noted in David Horowitz's biography of the underrated Vance Packard who did more than anyone in his own special style to observe new class formation, though he did not create an economic analysis to go with it (Horowitz, 1994).

As Lasch notes: "Only a handful of employers at this time [early twentieth century] understood that the worker might be useful to the capitalist as consumer: that he needed to be imbued with a taste for higher things; that an economy based on mass production required not only capitalistic organization of production but the organization of consumption and leisure as well" (Lasch, 1979, p. 72). However, in fact, it was perceived by many at the time that what mass production required was a culture of consumption, which, a 100 years later, is now fully in place. To many commentators, this is a matter of economic determinism: "When economic necessity yields to the necessity for limitless economic development, the satisfaction of basic and generally recognized human needs gives way to an uninterrupted fabrication of pseudo-needs" (Lasch, 1979, p. 72).

The culture of consumption is, thus, manufactured, or, better, produced. The culture of consumption does not determine production but is produced by the producer society. So, "Fordism" refers to this policy of winning the loyalty of workers to benefit from a high-wage economy, by producing commodities for the masses as cheaply as possible through the application of assembly-line techniques. It was this policy which brought the United States to the position of the dominant capitalist power by the end of World War II. The difficulty with Fordism was that while it depended absolutely on the loyalty of the workers it offered no room for innovation or worker participation, and the low price was achieved at the price of mind-numbing uniformity and indifference to market demands: market demand was the *result not the driving force of production*. As the international economy slowly became a more global economy in the 1960s and 1970s, the "national bargain" that had characterized labour–capital–state relations since World War II began to fray at the edges. Fordism did not disappear overnight; indeed many aspects of Fordism are still with us to this day. However, the perpetuation of Fordism from the late 1960s was becoming increasingly difficult as the international economy began experiencing a series of qualitative changes as a result of time–space compression, technological changes in production (and especially the pace of change), market changes, rising foreign competition and a generalized crisis of consumption. The concepts of "post-Fordism," sometimes called "neo-Fordism," "flexible specialization" and "Toyotism" (since so many of the principles were developed in Japan), are used as broad and abstract tools to describe the multiplicity of changes in the organization of labour that began in the late 1970s and intensified in the 1980s and 1990s.

Thus, we can see the origins of the absorptive class as stemming partially from the aristocracy of the working class to Fordist workers to the affluent worker and colliding and merging with the managers required for the running of all forms of commodity production and all the professional services and teachers and so on as well as the multitude of employees of the "big state." These constitute the body of people cast into the class of absorbers created by the system of production and functioning to maintain it and reproduce it. Elements remain within the class that echo its origin, however, so that individual absorbers within the class are partly proletarian and partly something else, maybe petty bourgeois, maybe commodified professionals. The consequence for the individual is profound because that individual is rarely whole but is split into fractions. The essence of the individual, of course, is to be whole. This "split" is one of the causes of malaise and violence in advanced countries.

A typical confusion on the identification of class is hinted at by Lasch: "Much of what is euphemistically known as the middle class, merely because it dresses up to go to work, is now reduced to proletarian conditions of existence" (Lasch, 1979, p. 68). He goes on to talk about the "glorification of the individual in his annihilation" (Lasch, 1979, p. 70). I discuss the individual in more depth in Chapter 5, but for the moment we can note simply that commentators have over time veered from observing and describing angst in relation to the disintegration of the individual under capitalism-consumerism to the degradation of the middle class and their reduction to the ranks of the proletariat. The Labour movement in Britain claimed to recognize this process of the proletarianization of the middle class in its appeal to workers by hand and *by brain* to extend their electoral support to as wide a section of the populace as possible. The weakness of this observation is that the middle classes (so-called) have not become proletarianized but are in fact incorporated into the absorptive class.

The Goldthorpe and Lockwood (Goldthorpe et al., 1987) extension of the aristocracy of the working-class theory to the theory of embourgeoisement began to coincide with the confusion felt by commentators such as Lasch who see the middle class as proletarianized. Together the proletarian middle class might, one would have thought, coincided with the embourgeoised proletariat to form a moderately revolutionary force in Western Europe and North America. Interestingly, there have been times when these combined "cultures" show some fight. The anti-Vietnam movement in the sixties and seventies, student rebellion, trade union demonstrations, fights over civil rights or abortion, environmental protection, abolition of hanging, gay and lesbian rights, legalization of cannabis and demonstrations against weapons of mass destruction and arms expenditure specifically and world peace generally all seem to elide at certain points. Recently, the large number of peace demonstrations associated with the war and so-called liberation of Iraq may be eliding with anti-Davos, WTO and other instruments of global economic governance. Are these signs of revolutionary movements? Well, pretty certainly, no. Are they signs of reformist movements? Yes, of course. But what exactly are the dynamics of these movements and what (not who) do they represent? My contention is that it is class *malaise* caused by the essentially fractionalized nature of class, the fractionalized nature of the individuals within in it and basically the growing pains (class formation) of the absorptive class itself.

The grand claim of Marx and Engels that all history is the history of class struggle may seem a little far fetched. Nevertheless, let us assume this holds some truth. Let us assume that modern bourgeois society (*a la* nineteenth-century Britain, France, Germany, Holland and Belgium) did spring from the ruins of feudal society. Could it be that the modern absorptive class has sprung from the ruins of nineteenth-century bourgeois society and economy? Marx and Engels observed that the proletarian struggle involved not the struggle of a minority but of the immense majority. The absorptive class is now the immense majority in OECD countries but one that serves the interest of the capitalist producer class through its dedication to consumption and thereby maintaining the social order through necessary concomitant political, cultural and social processes. One might consider the prospect of the inevitable contradictions in the system that might lead to that very absorptive class shifting its functions so as to serve the genuine interests of its constituent members in such a way as to vastly improve the quality of life through developing major reformist tendencies in order, if nothing else, to shed the angst and malaise of its constituent members (Horowitz, 2004; Easterbrook, 2003).

The productive forces of capitalism based on the division of labour and private ownership of property has created the absorptive class out of the material at hand: workers above the poverty line at all levels of skills, middle classes and commodified professionals of all kinds. It would be odd to expect a new class to be born painlessly. After all, the modern bourgeois classes have been in continual fractionalized conflict. Industrial capital sought to depose finance capital in Nazi Germany with the industrial bourgeoisie backed by the petty-bourgeoisie and the lower middle class. The City of London triumphed over industrial capital based largely in the Midlands and the North shifting wealth from the former industrial North to the South East in the process. Today global capitalism is a process whereby finance capital struggles to dominate all other forms of capital.

It is not unreasonable to suppose that the absorptive class would manifest its existence not simply by quietly performing the functions required of it but also at times coming into conflict with other forces coexistent within capitalism. After all, nothing remains unchanged and while the absorptive class exists to ensure that the system performs effectively it also exists to promote change. Hence it is a matter of great importance to recognize that conflicts and contradictions move society forward (or at least to new positions). The system is far from harmonious as Adam Smith would have it.

The observations and responses, therefore, of Lenin, the Labour Party, the Fordists and Goldthorpe and Lockwood and the managerialists are, in fact, observations that note the formation and consolidation of the absorptive class. There is not a fixed moment of birth or clear time of pubescence. The class has been in formation almost from the moment that capitalism began its march over the planet and, in many parts of the world is in the process of formation or expansion or consolidation, but we can see it clearly and definitely in Western Europe and North America and Australasia and Japan, though most clearly in the United States as presaged by Vance Packard writing in the 1950s and Christopher Lasch in the 1970s.

This then brings us to the question of class consciousness. To use the Marxist approach we would have to say that the absorptive class lives normally in a state of false consciousness (discussed in Chapter 7): its functions are defined for it largely in terms of consumption and maintaining the political system in a largely reformist mode. What then is the real, as yet, unrevealed historical role for this class? The role of the proletariat was to end capitalism and replace it with a socialist, moneyless society and end politics through the administration of things rather than the state acting as some sort of glorified agent of the capitalist class. Could the historical role of the absorptive class be to bring enlightenment, save the planet, bring peace and end exploitation through the full development of democratic societies? (This is discussed further in Chapter 7).

4. WEBERIAN SOCIAL STRUCTURE AND SOCIAL CLASS

While the end product of Weberian class analysis, that of social stratification, obscures the way in which big classes function in the economy, the

Weberian analysis does, in its historical, legal and economic perceptions and conceptual analysis, help in the identification of the absorptive class and in the uncovering of its importance for analysing the functioning of modern economies. By big classes, I refer to the key underlying commitment to the existence of three major classes: proletariat, absorptive class and capitalists: other classes have to be seen as fractions of these three main classes. The effect of the Weberian analysis happens for several reasons.[8]

First, as Weber writes: classes are not communities; they merely represent possible, and frequent, bases for communal action.

Second, he has a clearer definition of class than Marx does. He recognizes the existence of class when a number of people have in common a specific causal component of their life chances, in so far as this component is represented exclusively by economic interests in the possession of goods and opportunities for income and is represented under the conditions of commodity or labour markets.

Third, he stresses the fact that arguments regarding class under capitalism refer largely to the state of being either propertyless or the state of owning property under market economy conditions.

Fourth, he is aware of fractions of class when he, for instance, recognizes rentiers and/or entrepreneurs. For instance, he writes "... class situations are further differentiated: on the one hand, according to their kind of property that is usable for returns; and, on the other hand, according to the kind of services that can be offered on the market" (Gerth & Mills, 1958, p. 82).

For Weber "class situation" is ultimately "market situation." Class exists unambiguously out of economic interest, and, indeed, only those interests involved in the existence of the "market." (Gerth & Mills, 1958, p. 183). Weber argues, however, that though class is a matter of economic interest, the action of an individual with or without other fellows in a communal action is highly ambiguous because economic interests will differ for different individuals or groups or the capacity to act as between groups and individuals will differ. He recognizes the force of communal action as being capable of great variations: "... the direction of interests may vary according to whether or not *communal* action of a larger or smaller proportion of those commonly affected by a 'class situation', or even an association among them, e.g. "trade union," has grown out of the class situation from which the individual may or may not expect promising results" (Gerth & Mills, 1958, p. 183).

Thus we see in Weber

- The clearly underlined difference between class and community. If class is treated conceptually as having the same value as "community," the analysis of class conflict becomes distorted.
- The tendency of the class to act more or less in average union. "That men in the same class situation regularly react in mass actions to such tangible situations as economic ones in the direction of those interests that are most adequate to their average number is an important and simple fact for the understanding of historic events."
- The relation between economic conditions and class formation. These conditions are those that provide for class conflict: that is, in the context of late nineteenth century and early twentieth century class struggle as represented by the capitalist/worker struggles (Gerth & Mills, 1958, pp. 184–185).
- The difference between the action of an individual man or group and the action of the class as a whole.
- The fact that class exists within a specific economic context.
- All classes are fractionalized and Weber gives examples in respect of both the bourgeois class and the working class.

5. THE ABSORPTIVE CLASS

The absorptive class is not a fraction of class and it is not a stratum. It is a whole class. One recent Weberian approach, adopted by Richard Florida, provides a misleading concept of what a class is and it is illustrative to compare his view of class with that of a "big" class. Richard Florida's two books identify a segment of the working population in the United States as the creative class and is essentially Weberian in that he has identified a social stratum, actually strata, identified by their occupational position in the economy. He erroneously identifies these strata as creating wealth. The creative class does participate in the productive process, and as individuals are clearly clever people who may do a good job. But these diverse groups of men and women have themselves been created by the capitalist system. The vast majority of human beings have the capacity to be creative: they have high intelligence, highly capable hands and have the capacity to benefit both from education and training. There is nothing special about the human beings who inhabit the United States. What they have, all human beings have as natural endowments. On the other hand, what advanced economies have is the capitalist system to produce "creative people." He writes, "..the Creative Class has shaped and will continue to shape deep and profound shifts in the way we work" (Florida, 2003, 2005). A more correct formulation would be: *the large numbers of people who earn their living in what might be loosely termed creative occupations is an outcome of the capitalist system based on the production of commodities and their distribution. These groups "benefit" from the surpluses created by new technologies and the deskilling of older ones in the process of absorption.*

Typical of his analytical weakness is the way in which he skates over the history of one of the most symbolic inventions/innovations of the English industrial revolution, the steam engine. He writes: "... in the late 1700s James Watt developed a vastly improved steam engine, and its use quickly spread to other applications. The combination of automated machinery and a system for using it efficiently unleashed a wave of creativity by kicking off a long-running bull market in mechanical innovation." I can feel my old professor of economic history turning in his grave.

The (false) impression given by Florida is that the sheer creativity of James Watt produced a steam engine which somehow led to a lot of other inventions that somehow came to be innovations. James Watt was a technician in the science laboratory of Professor Joseph Black in Glasgow University and there he learned basic theories and the latest ideas in a subject now called physics, particularly concerning latent heat. Early in the 1760s, Watt was asked to repair a Newcomen steam engine. While doing so he realized that it could be massively improved. At the time Watt was engaged in assisting Black incentives were high for the first entrepreneurs to invent machinery to speed up the production of cotton yarn as weavers used up yarn at a greater rate than it could be produced by hand. Richard Arkwright, a barber, managed to steal or plagiarize an invention he heard about while cutting hair and shaving customers, and succeeded in raising the finance to have the machines made which were placed in a single building and powered by water mills (Hence the word mill for a textile factory). This meant cotton-spinning factories had to be built and operated in a specific kind of location where there was regular rainfall, fast running streams and in the countryside.

A huge incentive (the chance to make, in modern day equivalent, millions of pounds) offered itself for the invention and introduction of an alternative source of power for machinery, which would allow factories to be built in towns where labour could be had and transport would be available for both the raw materials and the finished product. The person who came forward to provide the funds to back Watt went bankrupt and Watt eventually turned to the man with the experience and who was willing to take the risks in perfecting such a machine in the interest of profits, Matthew Boulton, a Birmingham entrepreneur and manufacturer with a history of working with metal and machines. He knew of both the Newcomen steam engine that had been used for half a century to pump water from ever deeper mines and of Watt's progress in developing a separate condenser. It was his ability to draw on resources for investment and drive for greater riches that was responsible for the establishment of the Boulton and Watt partnership that eventually produced the steam engine, with a separate condenser to make the engine use the coal economically and be capable of converting the machine to rotary motion so that it could power textile machinery. The important point, therefore, is that it was the capitalist system (expressed *through* Richard Arkwright and Matthew Boulton) that produced Watt as inventor, who in turn, assisted in the production of the steam engine with a separate condenser and capable of being linked to rotary motion and fuelled by coal.

I have laboured this point a little, but it does establish what is generally speaking wrong with Florida's analysis. Thomas Homer-Dixon succinctly makes the point: "Modern markets and science are an important part of the story of how we supply ingenuity. Markets are critically important, because they give entrepreneurs an incentive *to produce* knowledge" (Homer-Dixon, 2000, p. 5). Potential creative people are everywhere. The capitalist system identifies that creativity which is required in the drive toward profit via commodification. Nathan Rosenberg further reinforces this point to the extent that he sees that science itself is a product of the economic process: "... technological concerns shape the scientific enterprise in various ways."[9]

Creative ideas that cannot be commodified and turned to profit have great difficulty in flourishing. The musical creativity in the geographical area known as Germany in the eighteenth century was the result of the fact that there were several hundred German states of all sizes and the patronage of the absolute rulers of these states lead to a huge outpouring of musical composition: the same is true in relation to music and art in Italy, also composed of scores of states, in the sixteenth and seventeenth centuries. In these pre-capitalist countries or proto-capitalist countries and city states, much creativity was determined or produced by the nature of the patronage exercised by absolute sovereigns. Philanthropy performs that function in the age of capitalism and all sorts of donors like Carnegie, Guggenheim, Rockefeller, Getty, Mellon, JP Morgan, Hearst and many lesser-known people have seen it fit to donate some of the surpluses produced to apparently non-commodified creative activity, but true non-commercial patronage remains very, very low in relative terms. Indeed the huge sums spent on art by say Mellon or Hearst or J.P. Morgan were spent on buying in accepted art works and by no means made any real contribution to the creation of new art (Rubinstein, 1980). Andrew Mellon spent $30 million on art work and Randolph Hearst over $50 million, and JP Morgan's art collection was valued at $50 million when he died but their dabbling in the art market made more of a contribution to simply inflating the market price for art works along with their egos.

The individual members of the creative occupational groups (erroneously described as the creative class) are themselves commodities produced in the interests of producing other commodities or for their own reproduction. For instance, the economy produces let us say computer software designers in universities to work in industry producing software and at the same time produces a small number of professors of software design to produce more software designers. It is rare for capitalism to produce creators or a genuine space for creativity that is not part of the process of producing a surplus that has to be absorbed.

At the root of creativity in advanced economies is knowledge. In these days of the so-called knowledge-based society, many relevant questions have not yet been posed or, if so, not adequately answered. Whose knowledge? Knowledge for whom or what? Where does knowledge come from? What other kinds of knowledge are possible? What knowledge is rejected or destroyed? If some of these questions were answered we would probably discover very quickly that creativity is manufactured, that what we judge to be creative may well be destructive of truer forms; that creativity is relative; that much creative activity is mere absorption of the surplus, while other creativity is production of the surplus.

And, as to the creative sub strata, some will have a role to play once they realize that they are, in reality, in the absorptive class. But at this point in the argument the most important point to stress is that the absorptive class is not a Weberian stratum.

We now turn to where the absorptive class is to be found geographically. Clearly the class is largest within the national boundaries of the advanced nation states. Theoretically, given that capitalism is international (even global), we might expect some possibilities for the class, were it to become conscious, to be international (or global). The absorptive class functions in the interests generally speaking of national capital in the first instance. However, the absorptive class absorbs worldwide. There is clearly an absorptive class in, say, Costa Rica. It absorbs not only the surplus created in Costa Rica but surpluses created by the advanced industrial nations and mass-producing economies in waiting. Increasingly it absorbs books, wine, cheese, household goods, producer goods, cars, boats, computers and other electronics. Much more important are the growing absorptive class in India and China. For instance, *The Economist* reported in respect of India the following under the heading of "Maharajahs in the Shopping Mall": " ... in 2002 Louis Vuittton made a triumphant return to India" and other luxury purveyors soon followed including Dolce and Gabbana, Hermes, Jimmy Choo and Gucci. India has fewer than 100,000 dollar millionaires but the number is growing fast, possibly at the rate of over 12% per annum, but the middle income groups will expand to 583 million by 2025.[10] India thus welcomes the absorptive class!

The Chinese economy, which has received considerable attention by commentators over the last decade or so, is seen as having a huge potential not simply as a producer, and thus feared because of its demand for raw materials and energy sources and for its potential military dominance in Asia and elsewhere: it is also seen as a possible saviour as an absorber of commodities. The Chinese economy has grown nine times in the last 30 years with its per capita income increasing sevenfold making its actual and potential absorptive capacity enormous both as a result of private consumption and state expenditure, given the need not only for huge infrastructural projects but also military expenditure. China is now probably set to become the second-largest military power in the world. Though in terms of GDP, China is ranked fourth behind the United States, Japan and Germany, some commentators judge that it is already the second-largest economy in the world based on real purchasing power of what it produces (Hutton, 2007, p. 5).

Much recent literature on China has pointed to the instability in China which will lead to the slowing of growth and the need for considerable restructuring of various kinds. The socialist market system and sheer pragmatism of political decision-making along with accusations of corruption and the like give the impression that China is about to be hit by some sort of dire nemesis. However, the Chinese economy will continue to grow; it will be an uncertain path as is the case with burgeoning and mature capitalist style countries experience alike. The bottom line, however, is that a huge part of the Chinese people will join the absorptive class and assist in the stabilization of crises within China and within the global capitalist system as a whole. Never mind that China does not have a fully developed capitalist system, or that the state intervenes too much, or that China does not as yet have multinational enterprises or internationally recognized logos.

The United States and Europe have benefited from cheap goods emanating from China and from cheap labour applied to US and European manufacturing. In due course, the massive expansion of Chinese disposable income will keep the US and European economy at least partially protected from the regular crises that will arise after the current one has passed and the next one becomes due. Still to come are the Russians, the Brazilians and the Indians. The absorptive class lies in wait well into the foreseeable future.[11]

Identifying the individuals making up the absorptive class empirically is bound to be elusive just as attempting to put individuals into social classes always has been. Classification requires identifying both characteristics and function. In terms of economic characteristics we would have to say that the class is composed of individuals (and their families) who receive remuneration for their activity greater than their labour power or, in other words, they have some share of the surplus available to them in the form of wealth and income that can be disposed of more or less at will. On the other hand, they do not own capital or land beyond what might be called chattels. This would include large quantities of things and one or two dwelling places. Within the same family there may be both capitalists and absorbers since a wife may run a small business and the husband may be a school head teacher and the son and daughter may own a fledgling dot com business. A husband may own stocks in a company as part of his pension provision whereas a wife may own stocks and be active in the business of that same company. At one extreme an individual may be in the absorptive class one day and, by way of inheritance, be in the capitalist class the next. Such fluidity and lack of precision is of no account because the important thing is the mass of those who, generally speaking, belong to the absorptive class, which *qua* class, performs the functions in reality that we have identified theoretically.

The important distinction between the individual and the way in which the individual is fractionalized is dealt with in Chapter 5. This explains why it is possible to identify the absorptive class theoretically and less easy to do so empirically.

6. ABSORPTION ON A VAST SCALE: A NOTE

There is a tendency at times to focus too heavily on the super-rich, probably because they make good, even outrageous, copy in the media. In June 2008, Merril Lynch in association with the Capgemini Group announced the outcome of their recent research into millionaires. They announced there were now 10 million dollar millionaires, their combined wealth being $41 trillion. These assets excluded housing. A large and growing percentage was in China, India and Brazil. What they buy or do with their surplus is seemingly always fascinating. For instance, in February 2002, the obituary pages of the world's press noted with much affection the death of Stanley Marcus whose flourishing business rested on the custom of both the capitalists ridding themselves of some of their personal surplus and of the excesses of the absorptive class. He helped create and identify something called the "best" (extremely expensive) recognizing consciously the importance of *wants* rather than *needs*. "I've never found a man who needs a necktie, but he may be fascinated with the colour or the design, and he wants it." Neckties, of course, were not enough and so he created wants for his and her aircraft, matching camels and his and her submarines.[12] It is also true that the super-rich are not only gaining in numbers but are getting even richer in relation to the merely rich. But the real absorption is done across a wide spectrum and, in sum, on a gigantic scale, surpassing what is remotely possible even by the super-rich alone.

Over 10 years ago, Alan Thein Durning observed in his identification of a "consumer class" that it took home 64% of the world's income (Durning, 1992). The same author also noted that measured in constant dollars, the world's people have consumed as many goods and services since 1950 as all previous governments put together. He also noted that each generation shifts the threshold of needs. He argued that the consumer society has impoverished us by raising our income. For instance though, he claims, people living toward the end of the twentieth century were four and a half times better off than their great grand parents at the beginning of that century, they were not four and a half times happier. It is, of course, equally possible to agree or disagree with such a moral judgement based on empirical observations. The point, however, is less to make moral judgements and more to identify the process and nature of the class. It is thus contended here that labelling and identifying the absorptive class is more important analytically than complaining about the collective actions of a so-called consumer society.

Simply consider the social worker who eats out once a month at an expensive Italian restaurant, the professor of chemistry who takes a holiday in Florence, the Canadian accountant who sends his child to a private school in Switzerland, the surveyor who buys thick pile wool carpet, the actuary who has a year's subscription to the ballet, the estate agent who buys his wine directly from a French vineyard, the airline pilot with a

passion for his CD collection, the hospital administrator with an equal
passion for antique type-writers.... None shop at Nieman Marcus and
none are capitalists but multiplied millions of times over, they form a class
that functions beyond simply being consumers.

7. CAPITALIST, CAPITALISM AND
THE CAPITALIST CLASS

This section discusses briefly the capitalist class, but relocates huge segments
of supposed capitalists into the absorptive class. Having insisted that there
are three main big classes in advanced capitalist countries, capitalist,
absorptive and proletarian, it would be wrong to proceed without a
discussion, however brief, about the capitalist class.

From the 1840s onwards until the last 20 years, the perception of the
capitalist class has been very largely in relation to the working class. The one
defines the other. Much argument has looked to the way in which capitalism
might or might not give way to socialism of one kind or another in an
organic and non-violent manner.[13] And, of course, there is a huge amount
of Marxist literature that discusses the possibilities for revolution. The
collapse of the totalitarian versions of socialism, the emergence of global
capitalism and the apparent shrinkage of the proletariat, especially of urban
industrial proletariat, in the advanced economies, and the concentration
of capital and of political power have left the impression that capitalism is
triumphant.

This leaves a number of issues to be contemplated. What is a capitalist?
What is the capitalist class? How uniform is the capitalist class? What is
capitalism? What is the (or a) capitalist system? How have any of these
changed over the last 100 years? What is the significance of the answers
for understanding the nature of the absorptive class and the relation of the
absorptive class to the capitalist class? Here is a way of summing up the
general position. A capitalist at the most primitive level is someone who
owns the means of production and employs wage labour, and seeks to make
profit and accumulate capital to produce more as efficiently as he knows.
In doing so, he competes with other capitalists until he finds that not
competing suits his own interests. As capitalists become a class they
dominate the state and prevalent ideas. The state mediates conflicts among
the capitalist interests while whenever possible repressing all other ideas that
might threaten capitalists. In other words, a capitalist *system* emerges within

a nation state and beyond because the capitalist, and his drive for profit, prefers to know no frontiers. Capitalisms may differ from nation state to nation state as between Germany and Japan and the United States but they are bound together by common aims and processes. While conflicts do emerge because of the competitive nature of capitalism, the systems can function together in the right conditions to produce greater and greater productive capacity, even though the surpluses produced may be shared out unevenly.

In this simple theorization we have capitalist, capitalist class and capitalist system, and it is all too easy, for the sake of the convenience of argument, to slip from one to the other. In the nineteenth century, the individual capitalist was easily recognized. Today he is recognized when we see him listed in rich lists in *Forbes* or *The Sunday Times*. Or is he? (There are very few women listed in rich lists). Haseler claims that the top 400 billionaires in the world in 1998 were characterized by being white, American or European and male. Most started with inheritances. Doubtless most would qualify as capitalists (Haseler, 1999, pp. 4–7).

Capitalists as a class hold to minimizing paying taxes, maintaining economic growth and stability, resisting both inflationary pressures and deflation, ensuring that the rate of profit does not fall and, if it does, at least ensuring that the mass of profit continues to increase, protect laws pertaining to private property, and, especially, maintaining law and order where it is in their interest to do so. They also argue for what they call the market and small government. However being rich, oddly, does not necessarily make an individual a capitalist since many very rich people, below the level of the mega-rich, do not own capital in the way the model nineteenth-century capitalist-owned capital. For instance, many CEOs of major corporations are rich, but, even though they may hold to the position held by capitalists listed in the paragraph above, they are closer to being rent takers, i.e. absorbers of the surplus that is produced in the system. Nor are they secure: "in recent years ... we have seen how vulnerable top executives are, as boards of directors dismiss them after a few quarters of low profitability" (Aronowitz, 2003, p. 4). Thus the capitalist has been progressively replaced by the corporation on the one hand and the capitalist *system* on the other.

First, consider the corporation. Corporations are set up to make a surplus. Much of that surplus is translated into profit and some into capital to make more capital. No individual is able to prevent that without forcing the corporation out of business. Researchers into business operations do find wide discrepancies among corporations about how efficient they are

and despite great variations in success, still stay in business. The circumstances under which corporations operate change, sometimes suddenly and
unexpectedly. All business is uncertain and risky. But corporations have a life
of their own. Bad management and/or bad luck may force them out of
business or into the arms of a competitor. But increasingly the corporate body
is able to take evasive action. It is the CEO or the Directors who may be paid
off and dumped. The corporation becomes the thing rather than the human
beings who run it...at any level. And the corporate robotic life is constantly
being infused with new managers and new forms of competitive techniques
and fierce drives toward greater efficiency, innovation and maximized output
and profit. In the last 30 years, the advanced economies have seen the steady
thrust of Japanese-inspired corporate changes. In the next thirty we will see
the Chinese shaking up corporations. Chinese capitalism is now ravenously
hungry to take over major western conglomerates. The attempted takeovers
a few years ago backed by the Chinese state of Unocal and Maytag were
eventually averted as US capitalism fought a strong defensive battle. But the
Chinese will succeed one way or another because the system itself encourages
the strong move toward mergers and acquisitions. The Economist, April 8,
2006, noted "The value of European companies acquired in the first three
months of this year was almost 130% greater than in the same period a year
ago. In this wave deals are getting bigger..."

Second, consider the capitalist *system* in which the corporation is located.
Just what are the motor forces that drive it? Liberal commentators in the
United States or leftist ones in Europe will say that it is driven by profit.
Though this is true, the corporations do not operate in a clear field. The
system contains other forces that resist the drive for sheer profit: the system
is simultaneously driven toward profit but is circumscribed by class forces.
The system thus tends in certain directions and attempts to self-correct in
the face of obstructions, inept policy by politicians, severe class confrontations or in the face of a myriad of other contradictions. In sum, *the
overwhelming tendency of all capitalist systems is survival in the face of any
process that tries to inflict on it serious damage. That is why, at certain
historical moments, capitalism is susceptible to reform.*

8. THE SURPLUS

At this point we need to depart from this issue and to discuss what the
absorbers absorb. They absorb "the surplus." What is the surplus?
To discuss this we turn to the very nature of the discipline of economics.

In most orthodox textbooks we find the following, more or less: "economics is the allocation of scarce resources among diverse competing ends." Orthodox economics has it that resources are scarce and that economics is about the allocation of resources through the price mechanism. The orthodox economist claims (disingenuously) to be happiest as a positivist scientist;[14] he is not concerned with judgements, but only with the purity of the laws that govern the process of allocation. In the classical system, supply equalled demand at a particular price level; it was price, determined by market conditions of supply and demand that determined optimal allocation of resources and, generally speaking, it was interference with this process that caused disturbances in the allocation of resources. Despite many ifs and buts this law of supply–demand–price still holds sway as a central tenet of orthodox economics. Any nation's government, then, when in doubt, is urged to return to market forces as the best means of dealing with resource allocation.

The alternative system of allocation of resources is through centralised "planning." In other words, the political process has to deal with procedures that orthodox liberal economists would regard as inevitably distorting the "natural" economic system. It is now possible to point the finger of failure at the Soviet system, quite rightly, and say that it did not deal with the allocation problem properly. However, what liberal economists are unwilling to admit wholeheartedly is that some sort of mixed system of resource allocation is the only system that has ever worked because the "pure" market exists only in a limited number of very special circumstances. Positive economics, therefore, has severe limitations as an applied discipline because as soon as the liberal system is mixed with the "planning" system a myriad of normative decisions are made requiring political devices for arranging the allocation of supposedly scarce resources. In actual fact, therefore, nowhere in the world is it possible to see a liberal economic system without a state that exists substantially for the purpose, one way or another, of determining tax levels, collecting the revenues, spending them, protecting the currency, picking up on some of a number of market failures and so on. A key policy prescription is to bring the real world closer to the model by maintaining the mobility of the factors production and assisting generally capital accumulation.

What happens, by contrast, if we view economics as really being centrally concerned with the production, extraction and distribution of a surplus? If we take the factors of production: land, labour and capital we find that by putting them to work we produce a surplus. A piece of land, some capital such as a plough and some seed plus some labour can be made to produce a surplus of food to be fed to more human beings other than those who ploughed, seeded and harvested the land and brought the produce to the buyer. Some fixed capital such as factory and machinery located on a piece of land and some raw cotton with the addition of labour will produce far more cotton yarn than can be consumed by the individuals who make it. A surplus is created from those factors of production. This is what has taken large parts of the world from self-sufficiency to surplus. In the early history of modern economic thought, David Ricardo (1772–1823) demonstrated, in developing his theory of rent, how the landowner extracted the surplus that derived from the differential fertility of land; it was the expropriation of this surplus that "artificially" depressed both profits and inflated wages and led at times to unemployment. Marx took this as one of his key starting points in developing his own theory of the surplus but he argued that it was the capitalist, too, who expropriated a surplus from labour power which, in the form of profit, was split between himself, the commercial capitalist and the *rentier*.

Generally speaking, the concept of the surplus is not much discussed outside Marxist theorising in relation to surplus value, though the Ricardian theory of rent is making something of a comeback in relation to monopolistic and oligopolistic practices. This involves concern with exchange value, use value and theories of exploitation, productive and unproductive labour and capital as dead labour. Typical is a piece by Jon Beasley-Murray. In a critique of Bourdieu, who it has been claimed has obscured the economic and the primacy of productive forces in capitalism, he argues that Bourdieu obscures the understanding of the importance of the forces of production and, so, most crucially the surplus and so calls for a the reintroduction of the concept of surplus. He continues thus: "As the commodities produced ... are sold by capitalists to realise" the "surplus, the labour they incorporate is alienated from the workers, presented to them (in the market) as an object of consumption: the total value of the commodities is measured in terms of the amount of dead labour time they incorporate. Hence the labour theory of value. It is this abstraction that both enables the extraction of the surplus, and its mystification as an alienated fetishised relation."[15]

Here, for the time being, we are not concerned with this argument as such. The labour theory of value is something for the pure and even less pure Marxist to argue about one way or the other. The surplus for the purpose of this argument in this book is what is actually produced in the form of commodities over and above the level of need loosely defined. It is clearly the case that when the factors of production are put together in certain ways the outcome is the production of goods and services on a vast scale, and ever more efficiently (i.e. using fewer factors of production to produce more and more units of production). While it may well be that the theory of surplus value overlaps a little with this cruder conception, our establishment of the existence of the absorptive class does not depend on the minutiae of proof of the labour theory of value. All that matters is that there is an enormous surplus rather than any real shortage in the capitalist system. Later (both in this chapter and in Chapter 6 more fully) we do explore the nature of the surplus more closely particularly in its relation to profit.[16]

Scarcity, of course, does exist and economists make use of this obvious fact in a number of ways most of which have their uses. Let us take a typical text book, *Economics* by Baumol and Blinder, Dryden 1994, Sixth Edition, for no other reason than it has been used by several generations of under-graduates and I happen to have a copy. It is clear, readable, to the point, thoroughly orthodox and includes the normal number of graphs, illustra-tions and diagrams regarded as *de rigueur*. Thus a national economy will have a "production possibilities frontier" for instance which will demon-strate at any one point in time the range of choices that can be made. In their words we have:

> "The position and shape of the production possibilities frontier that constrains the choices of the economy are determined by the economy's physical resources, its skills and technology, its willingness to work, and how much it has devoted in the past to the construction of factories, research, and innovation." (Baumol & Blinder, 1994)

They are in fact discussing the age-old choice as between guns and butter. The production of one will affect the other, and "even a rich and powerful nation like the United States or Japan must cope with the limitations implied by scarce resources." However, there is a ready solution to the problem, according to Baumol and Blinder: the nation (the national economy) is not a static phenomenon, but a dynamic one; therefore, the solution is "economic growth." Shortages are dealt with by making more! More of what might be asked. More of everything it is supposed. Their first definition of economic growth is apparently highly egalitarian: economic growth means that the average citizen gets larger and larger quantities of goods and services. In other words, the production possibilities frontier is simply pushed outwards. And they answer the question how by suggesting "many ways," among which are more skilled labour, more producer goods instead of consumer goods and more inventions (by which they mean innovations). They summarize the position thus: "An economy grows by giving up some current consumption and producing capital goods for the future instead. The more capital it produces, the faster will its production possibilities frontier shift outward over time."

We now turn about 800 pages very quickly and arrive at Chapter 34 to find out more about economic growth and we find that economic growth is almost totally about "productivity" (Baumol & Blinder, pp. 852–871). This means using the same factors of production to produce more. In other words, the economy is devoted to maximizing the surplus. Old shortages are pushed aside and new ones found but only to be conquered. There are a few ifs and buts, but they conclude: "Though we do not know whether long-run US productivity growth has declined, for the past few years it has fallen below its historical levels. Failure to recoup threatens to hold back the growth in US living standards... Productivity growth is indeed the stuff of which prosperity is made. In the long run, nothing is more important than productivity growth for the economic welfare of the country and the world."

A number of issues are clear from this orthodoxy. Scarcity occurs but it can be overcome through increases in productivity (getting more from the factors of production or substituting one factor for another), slowing up of productivity growth affects living standards (consumption) that reduces the quality of life and so by implication recessions must be conquered.

Pointing up scarcity demonstrates why the perfect competition model is valid. In a static situation, with many suppliers and consumers, prices allocate shortages. This part of economic theory gives primacy to the market in respect of allocation of scarce resources. *However, the real objective of economics is to conquer shortages and produce surpluses.* Economic theory thus simultaneously promotes the idea of scarcity and the importance of the market while identifying the importance of productivity and economic growth (more of everything) as the key motor force of the economic system.

These massive surpluses are absorbed partly by the state in both civilian and military expenditure; they are partly absorbed by both the capitalist class and the proletariat. But the absorptive class has also been produced, virtually unnoticed, for the precise job of absorbing much of what has been produced and in such a way as to protect the capitalist economies from the full shock of depression when the system hits crisis proportions as is now the case as I write in 2009. It is empirically observable that the capitalist system has been enormously successful at producing surpluses. Thus much is admitted by David Dollar, for instance, who is known for his belief in the beneficial effects of globalisation: "it now takes only 2–3 years, for example, for the world economy to produce the same amount of goods and services that it did during the entire nineteenth century... Human productivity has increased unimaginably"[17] (Dollar & Kraay, 2001). The capitalist class have been able to accumulate this capital to invest and to create an even greater surplus. The system, therefore, suffers from a permanent condition of overproduction because it is in the nature of the capitalist to continuously engage in the production of a surplus (in the dual interest of profit and capital accumulation). This means that absorbers must be available to engage in the consumption of the outpouring of commodities and commodified services that result.

However, the absorptive class now keeps that very system in place by not only absorbing commodities but also purchasing and holding financial instruments and other "risk" assets (see Chapter 7) and, thereby, buffering the system against collapse through the dissipation of ownership of such fragile instruments. Thus in the United States the massive reduction in value of stocks as the decade of the roaring nineties ran its course was absorbed on a broad front by this class either directly, through absorbing the fall in value of the stocks which they have purchased or through their savings or through their pension arrangements. Similarly during the growth period under Clinton in the United States of the 1990s, this class maintained the system through purchases of financial instruments and massive consumption of commodities underpinned by these financial instruments and by credit, the source of which is derived from the massive surplus that is being constantly created even during so-called periods of recession. In the crisis that began in 2007, the story is the same. By April 2008, for instance, the credit crunch, according to the IMF, was likely to be $1 trillion worldwide. What the IMF did not report is who or what exactly absorbs this crunch. The bearers of risk are now overwhelmingly the absorptive class. But this is a small beer against the $5.2 trillion lost in falling share prices estimated by G7 analysts earlier in the year.

One of the main weaknesses of the Marxist analysis is that it saw society as being increasingly divided into the bourgeois class on the one hand and the urban, landless proletariat on the other. It was this class struggle that would provide the motor force for change. However, given that the capitalist class cannot consume everything and that the proletariat would become increasingly impoverished, who was going to do the consuming of the commodity? The answer traditionally has been that capitalism expands outside the capitalist countries generated by the international monopolistic forces of capitalism. The latest neo-Marxist arguments of Antonio Negri and Michael Hardt accede to this analysis in developing the concept of Empire as it relates to a replacement of Imperialism. However, for all their elegant development of neo-Marxism, they seem somewhat hidebound. "Indeed capital does not function within the confines of a fixed territory and population, but always overflows its borders and internalises new spaces" (Hardt & Negri, 2000, p. 221). There is no objection to the fact that this happens. Nor is there objection to many of the observations concerning the process of globalization, its range and its impact for good or ill. However, we do assert that this focus on globalization, Empire, economic imperialism and the like has obscured what is happening *within* the political national boundaries of all capitalist economies, particularly in relation to new class formation.

While in identifying the importance of the absorptive class I accept the position described by Hardt and Negri when they quote Fernand Braudel: "capitalism only triumphs when it becomes identified with the State, when it is the State" (Hardt and Negri, 2004). My analysis departs from Hardt and Negri's adherence to the proletarian/bourgeois class struggle and from their discussion of the nature and description of the triumph of the capitalist system. In other words, Hardt and Negri, reluctant to abandon the proletarian–capitalist class struggle, search for the possibilities for social change with the proletarians as the main actors. I see the change as related to reform, not as a result of the revolutionary forces associated with new class formation leading to capitalist overthrow from below but see change in the nature of the reformist tendency of the absorptive class which has come into being. The relationship between reformism and the absorptive class is dealt with in Chapter 7.

In the next chapter, we look at the nature of the capitalist state and, importantly, the way in which the term civil society has obscured some crucial realities.

NOTES

1. (Krugman, 1999). Economic historians usually describe the 1930s as the "Depression" (of the 1930s) because they had already allocated the title Great Depression to the period 1873–1896. This may seem pedantic but the point is that depressions, great or otherwise are endemic, to capitalism. So are economic crises. For a short clear historical survey see Charles Kindleberger (1976). The Depression of the 1930s continues to fascinate, no doubt because of the cyclical nature of the capitalist system. See Ben S. Bernanke (2000, p. 34): "..we have learned and will continue to learn a great deal from the inter war economy."

2. *The Economist*, 3–9th January 2009 in a comment entitled "Subject Wall Street."

3. Wright (2005). See also Carchedi (1987). The discovery of the existence of the absorptive class makes a contribution to solving the "problem of the middle class" as expressed in the following comment "At the heart of ... Marxist theorizing on the

problem of class has been what might be termed the 'embarrassment' of the middle class" Wright (1989, p. 3).

4. Zweig (2004); Aronowitz (2003); New York Times (2005). Locating the middle class has been one of the pre-occupations of those concerned with class analysis: cf. "The twentieth century witnessed the emergence of a new class of salaried managers and trained scientific and technical intellectuals, none of whom can be credibly described as either traditional proletarians or capitalists" (Aronowitz, op. cit, 2003, p. 3). Such tomes as Lawrence James's *The Middle Class: A History* published by Abacus in 2006 helps reinforce the acceptance of the term middle class and so obscures the existence of the absorptive class and its place in historical processes.

5. See, for instance, the documentary, *The Corporation*, written, directed and produced by Mark Achbar et al. (2004) which shows the corporation as having the characteristics of a psychopath.

6. Strength is used deliberately rather than power. The people still have power if they could use it. See Arendt (1970).

7. http://www.wsws.org/articles/2001/may2001/uk-m17.shtml Downloaded 8 March 2005.

8. These points are paraphrased from Weber in Gerth and Mills (1958, p. 180ff). See also Bendix and Lipset (1966).

9. Rosenberg (1982), Chapter 7 "How endogenous is science?" See also Kamien and Schwartz (1982) for an assessment of Schumpeterian theories on innovation and economic growth.

10. *The Economist*, 2 June 2007. See also Panagariya (2008).

11. Hewitt (2008); Fenby (2008); Yasheng (2008). US consumers constitute only about 4.5% of the world's population; they bought $10 trillion worth of goods in 2008 whereas China and India combined constitute ten times as many people but only consumed $3 trillion of goods in 2008. The scope for the expansion of the absorptive class to deal with the huge possible surpluses of the future seems considerable.

12. Cf. *The Economist*, Feb 2, 2002, p. 82. *The Telegraph*, Stanley Marcus, obituary pages, 6 February, 2002. The firm was taken over in May 2006 by two private equity firms, Texas Pacific Group and Warburg Pincus LLC., for $5.1 billion.

13. In the last 50 years we have a number of "classic statements": Strachey (1957), Chapter XIV "Democracy and the last stage of capitalism"; Sweezy (1972a), Chapter on "Theories of New Capitalism": Bottomore (1980), Chapter 6 "From Capitalism to Socialism". See also Schumpeter (1950). Infra is discussed in Chapter 5.

14. Richard G Lipsey et al., *Economics*. Refer to any of many editions and authorial combinations over the last thirty years.

15. See Jon Beasley-Murray, www.radicalphilosophy.org

16. Proving that labour is the source of most value is actually justificatory ideology since, once established, the case for the proletarian revolution is justified.

17. By "human productivity," the authors seem to mean capitalist productivity.

CHAPTER 2

STATE THEORY AND CIVIL SOCIETY

Given that the capitalist system tends to produce huge surpluses, there needs to be an extensive arrangement by which the state deals with such surpluses. Understanding the nature of the state and its relationship to the economy is of great importance. However, theories of the State have gone into decline along with class theory. Instead we have been presented with the nebulous construct of "civil society."

The term civil society, it has been commonly accepted, has been dragged into prominence for two reasons: first, the collapse of the Soviet system appears to have left the "people" without a voice so that turning the concept of the people into "civil society" has its usefulness both for discourse and an acceptance of a kind of common meaning. Second, and in an associated way, the problems of so-called collapsed states calls for the re-invention of a concept such as civil society to express a way for the masses to express their views as part and parcel of the process of finding new ways of introducing functioning government or "governance." However, the route forward for them may still be cabinet government, political parties, lasting and protected constitutions and a civil power in control of military power (Biljana Vankovsa et al., 2003). Otherwise the form of civil society power will simply reflect the corrupt and authoritarian regimes based on force and repression. The polity, will until fundamental change occurs, be based on a strange modern mix reflecting finance capital, primitive and pre-capitalist accumulation and mercantilist style accumulation through taxing trade and population movement and local means of extraction of surpluses (drugs, cobalt, diamonds, coltan, fuel, gold, timber and so on).

It is not the main aim of this book to pursue the problems associated with failed states or the problems associated with rebuilding a polity deformed by many decades of totalitarianism. We are concerned with the implications of new class formation in the advanced industrial spheres. However, simple observation would indicate that the pressure of so-called globalization, or, more accurately, global capitalism is in precisely the same direction as historic capitalism. Primitive accumulation–commercial capitalism–industrial capitalism–financial capitalism, now exist, not as stages of development as such but as side by side realities, sometimes competing and sometimes assisting in the process of creating capitalist classes on the one hand and proletariats on the other. The road to what appears now to be a final destiny, absorption by the masses in the interests of the few, is somewhat accelerated by the visibility of the blessings of capitalist surplus creation, the shopping malls, the electronic equipment, apparent plenty in terms of food, shelter and education. The downside is shrugged aside, not unnaturally, since life in the suburban United States does on the face of it seem preferable to living on the pavements of Calcutta.

Nevertheless, it is important to shrug off the ideological implications of civil society and return to an earlier form of state theory if class analysis is to be properly restored in the realm of political economy. The story begins with the importance of the reality of the unity of state and economy and the way in which ideology has separated the two.

1. UNITY OF ECONOMY AND STATE

Adam Smith, it is generally acknowledged, founded the modern discipline of political economy with the study entitled *An Inquiry into The Wealth of Nations* (1776) which he built upon the ethical system he presumed to exist in his *Theory of Moral Sentiments* (1759). Ricardo took Smith's observations somewhat further with his publication of *On the Principles of Political Economy and Taxation* (1817). When John Stuart Mill wrote his *Principles of Political Economy* in 1848, his considerations of economic processes were intimately connected with the political. By the time Marx published *Das Kapital* as a critique of political economy in 1867 the term was entrenched in both academic life and in common parlance and political circles. The study of economics was an integral part of the study of the state. Ironically, however, political economy was about to be upstaged by the development of economics as a separate and positivist discipline. William Stanley Jevons had published his "Brief Account of a General Mathematical Theory of Political Economy" in the *Journal of the Royal Statistical Society* in the previous year. This was much more widely read at the time than *Das Kapital*. By 1890, Alfred Marshall had published his *Principles of Economics*. The book began with these words: "Political economy or economics is a study of mankind in the ordinary business of life." The great tradition of seeing economics as an integral part of politics and vice versa was disappearing. However, though economists were anxious to convert that part of political economy known as economics and see it as a scientific discipline, the reality, that is the integrated nature of the state and the economy, remained. Simply because certain ideologues decided to separate politics from economics did not mean that the state in any sense disentangled itself from the economy or the economy from the state.

This division of labour between economists and political scientists has led to a perpetual series of misunderstandings of processes within the apparent twin domains. The reality is that economics is less about the allocation of scarce resources and more about creating a surplus. However, orthodox economics demonstrates that scarcity is dealt with by price (requiring, ideally, a small state) whereas the creation and distribution of a surplus actually requires considerable intervention by the state because the state has the legitimate right to levy taxation (seize as well as to protect property) and re-allocate wherever and whatever it thinks fit. Market economics concerned with reaching equilibrium through price of demand and supply is supposed to require the small state but the capacity of economies of high productivity to expand its capacity to produce surpluses requires a big state.

Cloward and Piven put the position well in respect of the United States. "To foist the doctrine of the separation of politics from economics on a people is a remarkable feat. In the United States it was especially remarkable, for it persuaded Americans (sic) that the most pressing issues of their daily lives had nothing to do with democratic rights for which they had fought... This extraordinary feat was not accomplished by propaganda or mere sleight of hand. It was accomplished by nothing less than the construction of a world in which the doctrine was made real, a realm of lived experience in which democratic rights mattered, but from which economic grievances against property were barred" (Richard Cloward & Frances Piven, 1982). It would seem that all capitalist states manage to achieve much the same to a greater or lesser extent.

2. THE STATE AND OWNERSHIP OF PRIVATE PROPERTY

The state is also required for the protection of the private ownership of property. The protection of property or capital takes precedence over the preservation of human life. In an extreme case, a starving family may attempt to take food from a retail shop or wood from a farm to provide heat in the winter. If caught, that family will be prosecuted by the law and may be imprisoned. The owner of the food or of the wood will not be prosecuted for failing to provide for a starving family nor will the politicians and administrators employed by the state. As a last resort, the individual must take his or her chances within the economic and state system that exists under private ownership of property. The failure of the Soviet system to provide commodities and its failure to provide freedom from daily oppression is renowned but what was commendable was its prioritization of providing the essentials of life free or nearly so to everyone (in principle): above all the free or nearly free provision of housing and heating and education and health and employment as a right was an apparent goal of the system. Such a goal is not true in the same way under capitalism. Under that system the market is thought to provide while the State will consider safety nets of various forms differing from country to country if the market happens to fail. Thus blame can always be laid at the individual's door for his or her own failure to benefit from the system. While, therefore, much is said about equality, human rights and the eradication of poverty, the fundamental obstacle to achieving these outcomes remains: private ownership of property is a fundamental necessity for the proper working of the capitalist system. Among the key reasons why the State is intimately and permanently connected with the Economy is because of the need to protect property rights, and to direct both the production of the surplus and its distribution, including the surplus itself and as part of that process helping to produce the absorptive class.

As a point of clarification, there is an important distinction between property *qua* capital, the factor of production required in the process of production (often put simply as plant and machinery) or land, on the one hand, and chattels on the other. While the law does protect chattels (the house you live in and the things in it) strictly speaking these are non-productive and are simply things owned privately and the ownership of them does not make the possessor a capitalist. Capitalists own the means of production (capital in the strict sense) which potentially makes possible the accumulation of more capital. The absorptive class absorbs things (goods and services) which are protected by the law more in the interests of law and order rather than in the interests of capital or capitalism directly. Therefore, the right of ownership is unproblematic and any state is correct in protecting the right of ownership, not only the right of state institutions to ownership, but the right of associations (trade unions, NGOs, Boy Scout troops, private clinics) to own and the right of individuals to exclusive ownership of chattels. In this sense, as has been argued, property is a right and not a thing.[1]

When the state protects property rights it is protecting overwhelmingly the right of the owner of the means of production (landowner and owner of capital) to exclusive individual ownership, including the right to pass the right of ownership to heirs at his own discretion (minus whatever tax the state requires in its own interests and that of the capitalist state in general). The state also protects the right of individuals to own non-productive commodities and chattels, but this is in the interests of law and order, and is effectively Hobbesian in origin. From time to time when the interests of capitalists are strongly at odds with that of the state, the state may win. One such classic case is the Accumulation Act or Thellusson Act which was passed by the British Parliament in 1800. Peter Thellusson, a banker and one of the richest men in England was obsessed by the legend of Croesus and the dim prospects of immortality (He is believed to have once said: "I would give my whole fortune to come back as a coachman"). He left his whole estate, apart from a few baubles, to his as yet unborn oldest surviving great-grandson. It was estimated that this person would be enormously rich, probably worth 14 million pounds (In 1844 the whole sum of printed notes of the Bank of England was limited to 7 million). The State was alarmed since that person would be an *imperium in imperio* and able to exercise enormous political strength through his economic strength. The Accumulation Act, which has also had the force of law in the United States, prevents wealth being left to accumulate for more than 21 years after the death of the settlor. As a matter of historical record, the legal disputes in the Thellusson case soaked up so much wealth from the estate, the final inheritors (there were two) received not much more than the original sum bequeathed, but the State made its case clear. No single individual could be allowed to be more powerful than the state itself. This Act was reinforced by the Rule Against Perpetuities. However, both legal provisions were enacted at a time when the capital class was still less than dominant. Currently, both provisions are perceived to be outdated as far as modern capitalist activity is concerned and we see in the United States, in particular, an erosion of the principles against accumulation since such provision is contrary to the interests of the concentration of capital. Twenty states in the United States have abolished the provisions against accumulating resulting in at least $100 billion in trust assets pouring into those 20 states (Robert, 2005; Sitkoff, 2005).

Industrialization in the nineteenth century led Proudhon and Marx as well as T.H. Green and John Stuart Mill to consider the problem of labour, also a factor of production and consider the rights of labour to own the means of production since labour, at least for Proudhon and Marx, was the major source of value, capital being considered as dead labour. The extent to which the origins of property lies within the individual right to property in themselves (a Lockean and Marxist view), then what is most denied under capitalism is those fundamental property rights to own one's labour, that is to benefit from the direct result of exercising one's own muscle and brain power. This view is still alive. For instance John Christman writes: "I have shown...that the natural right to one's body and labour, one's self-ownership, amounts to the right to (authentically) control access to and use of one's body and labour" (John Christman 1994, p. 161).

Modern capitalism and the capitalist state, therefore:

- protects the right of capitalists to own capital in the interests of individual capitalists and to use that capital for purposes determined by capitalists minus whatever taxation is thought necessary by the capitalist state;
- supports all members of the constituent populations to own as many chattels as they are able to acquire (though not on an equal basis);
- denies labour the right to the full fruits of its labour;
- denies labour the right to work as an automatic right (though fullish employment is necessary for the stable development of the system).

For the purposes of establishing the importance of the way in which property rights are recognized under modern capitalist systems in relation to the formation and development of the absorptive class, the important observation to note is that the perceptions currently held clearly serve the interests of maintaining a false consciousness among the burgeoning absorptive class. The class is led to believe itself to be part of a "property-owning democracy" in that its members are led to believe that they own property whereas in fact they own chattels. Driven to own more chattels they believe themselves to be even stouter members of the property-owning democracy, believing that to be middle class and, therefore, an integral part of the capitalist or ruling class. They own, however, little property in the sense of owning and controlling the means of production. They do not have, despite all the talk of stakeholders and civil society, any significant access to power. And until they become part of a social or political movement that will ever be the case. The chattel most mistaken for property is the house, one of which most members of the absorptive class own. The house, sometimes called a home, is in fact normally a non-productive repository for storing a vast array of commodities which he or she has been induced to own. Part of this repository contains a storage space labelled garage in which a vehicle is kept to ensure that commodities can be regularly transported to the personal storage facility otherwise known as the home. Significantly, while garages used to be, like stables, separated from the house, they are now integrated into the house, and, significantly, now contain, not only the vehicle(s) for transportation, but also those commodities that can no longer be contained inside the actual living quarters from which they have overflowed. In the United States, "despite fewer people per household, the size of houses continues to expand rapidly, with new construction featuring walk-in closets and three- and four-car garages to store record quantities of stuff. According to my estimates, the average adult acquires forty-eight pieces of new apparel per year" (Juliet B Schor, 2004).

This redefinition of the term property is too important to be passed over as do many writers. Aronowitz observes: "the term property has been expanded to mean ownership of any kind of house, patents, savings accounts, small stock and bond holdings" (Aronowitz, 2003, p. 16). This redefinition is a matter of common usage and constitutes an unfortunate obscuring of an otherwise rigorous definition that distinguishes between property as a reproducing means of production and mere commodity.

Having, hopefully, established the paramount importance of the unity of the state and economy without which class analysis would make no sense, we turn to the current ideological fad for hiding behind the concept of civil society.

3. ECONOMICS IN OR OUT?

The current conceptualization of the term civil society obscures fundamental truths about the way in which societies are ordered. As one commentator has put it succinctly: "It is perhaps time for us in the West to tell a few home truths about capitalism, instead of hiding them discreetly behind the screen of 'civil society'."[2]

The crucial approach to the nature, role and functions of civil society depends on whether you leave in the economic dimensions in the theorization of civil society or take them out.[3] *The theorization of civil society makes absolutely no sense with the economics left out.* Moreover, within this approach of "keeping economics in" it is argued that we have to reject pluralist theories of the democratic state. It should not, however, be supposed that we are simply making a plea for the return of Marxism. We are not, but we do accept a crucial reality, that of the empirical observations that see the economy and the state as indissolubly unified. We may have a range of labels for the institutions of the state and the economy that might appear to separate political institutions from the economic and the social, but, in reality, there is still such a phenomenon as capitalist rule exercised through these institutions with the functional support of the absorptive class. Civil society is managed through the absorptive class on behalf of the capitalist classes generally or, to put it another way, civil society exists as a set of institutions through which dominance, change and stability is managed by the capitalist state and supported by significant fractions of the absorptive class.

In essence, the analysis of civil society in the post-Soviet world has replaced that of class analysis in the years preceding the collapse of totalitarianism as if class (a) had never existed and (b) the state stood as a separate identifiable set of institutions which could be influenced by a citizenry organized into ever changing associations for a myriad of purposes, thus supposedly giving democracy greater meaning than did mere representative local, regional and national elected bodies of councils, assemblies or parliaments.

Attempts to explain the nature of civil society as a purely political pheno-menon and with the economics left out do not make any sense whatever. Civil society with economics put in was not the work of Marx originally, of course, but, as Ehrenberg points out, the work of Adam Smith.[4] John Ehrenberg has carefully discussed the Smithian contribution in this respect. He points out that what is now central to introductory economics, the description of the working of land, labour and capital in the process of production, was first formulated by Smith and Ricardo; it is this formula-tion which, in effect, also describes civil society. In other words, the functions of the main classes in industrial society, their relationship to each other and their relationship to the state, indeed how the landed interest and the bourgeois classes together came to form both the government and the state are shown to be determined by the very nature of economic organiza-tion and distribution of rewards in the form of wages, rent and profit.

The very foundations and principles of the market-based civil society are determined by the requirements of the system for production: "Civil government, so far as it is instituted for the security of property, is in reality instituted for the defence of the rich against the poor, or of those who have some property against those who have none at all" (John Ehrenberg, 1998, p. 104). Adam Smith is quite clear. Civil society is bound and defined by the needs of the system to produce. Liberty is a matter not for the individual but is determined by the needs of the capitalist-based producing economy. Smith also knew that the productive process resulted in the "debasement" of workers but that this would have to be controlled by government rather than through a mass class confrontation. Civil society, or class, would always have to be under the control, one way or another, of the government.

On whose behalf would that government be acting? This is as we have seen clearly answered by Smith and is in the work of Marx, of course. To the latter the state is nothing but the executive committee of the bourgeoisie for managing its common affairs. This may have the characteristics of an assertion and may not have been "proved" empirically in every respect of every "bourgeois" government for every form of capitalist formation. Proof or not many find the assertion instinctively convincing. "The state's formal separation from the economy could not conceal that it was an instrumentality of market society. Smith had no desire to pretend that either sphere stood on its own" (John Ehrenberg, 1998, p. 108).

Given that in the earlier stages of capitalism the masses presented a potential threat to the development of this new society, the development of pluralist theory helped divert attention toward the benign effects of capitalist processes and provide a role for the masses redefined as a collection of interest groups which appeared to mirror the market forces of capitalism based on self-interest.

> If mass society threatened to create an empty space between individuals and the state, pluralism populated civil society with a multitude of interest groups that could tame popular passions and turn individual interest to the service of stability. (Ehrenberg, 1998, p. 201)

However this can only work, it was argued, if there are certain agreed rules of the game, notably the rule of law, that losers will not resort to violence and that there is a modest degree of egalitarianism. While capitalism clearly produces a particular class formation, pluralist theory argues that consensus, non-violence and the way in which public policy is formed from interest group politics, displaces class as the analysis of social order and social change. It follows from this that in the pluralist model social protest takes the form of extra class action based on diverse non-class interest. Protest loses its class nature and becomes one based on narrow sectional interest. Protest has, by contrast, become commodified and has led directly and indirectly to an expansion of the absorptive class. Feminists, gays and lesbians, blacks, Hispanics and so on have all simply been converted into absorbers of the surplus. Hence we hear, for instance, of the "pink pound" whereby marketing executives discover new spending groups who become targets for the disposal of the surplus: thus pink restaurants, pink holidays, pink clothes, pink interior design, pink entertainment can all be forged for newly created wants in new ghettoes. Similarly we also hear of the grey pound of seniors or the black dollar in the USA (Heath & Potter, 2004).

4. POLITICAL PARTIES VERSUS CIVIL SOCIETY

It may well be that the term civil society will be increasingly treated with greater circumspection, though not much hope is held out for that. One possible sceptic is Neera Chandhoke (Chandhoke, 2003). She writes that "today there is much more restraint, hesitancy, ambiguity and scepticism amongst those who write about it [civil society]. This, it seems to me, is a welcome change." The trouble is that those who write about civil society in a critical fashion are less significant than those who write about, talk about and assume its importance in everyday life and among journalists and politicians who welcome the obfuscations and sloppy thinking that it offers. Chandhoke reinforces the importance of economics by throwing in Smith's contemporary Adam Ferguson into the debate who, she argues, saw civil society as interchangeable with commercial society and is "intimately linked to the emergence of the market economy." She goes on: "He, and later classical political economists, regarded civil society as the fulcrum where individual and collective energies come together in a market economy based on the legal recognition of private property as the root of freedom" (Chandhoke, 2003, p. 3). Of course at the end of the eighteenth century, philosophers knew what to say in this regard because the clash between the old regimes based on absolute monarchy was at its height, and economic changes demanded a new look at the role of the citizen and at property rights as stronger forms of capitalism emerged to challenge the power and authority of the aristocracy. Vast new territories were being opened up. The East India Company defeated the French in India. Huge fortunes were being made in the slave trade. And it was from the successes of commercial capital and the mercantile system that industrial capital emerged so strongly.

Whereas Hegel might have seen the need of the state to crush such new developments, in England and the Low Countries commercial and industrial capitalism demanded a new kind of citizen to change the state in the interests of the new economy. The state had increasingly to be composed of the property owners other than landowners. Subsequently political action developed in the context of representative democracy, expanding franchises and political parties. Such developments provided the associations for political action in the context of developing forms of parliamentary government. We need to ask ourselves has this political process given way to "civil society" as the main supposed focus for democratic expression? Just as many have argued (wrongly) that the nation state is now an antiquated form, we have to ask ourselves whether obituary notices for political parties are much ahead of their time. Here is a current point of view, also taken from Chandhoke: "Parties are in a state of collapse with falling member-ships, low electoral turnouts and the replacement of ideologies by managerial spin...working on a research project in five cities – we found that people we surveyed had lost hope in the political party to represent their interests; nor did they repose much hope in the capacity of civil society organizations to do so." She refers to big cities in developing economies in the Indian sub-continent and South America. But how true is the general proposition, that civil society is (filling or failing to fill) the gap left by the failure of the party system to deliver a share of power and a fair share of the surplus?

If we take one criterion about the importance of political parties and representative democracy, we can turn to the figures from IDEA and look first at Western Europe which examined the 15 member states of the EU before 2004 plus Iceland, Malta, Norway and Switzerland. The table shows the overall position that looks pretty healthy taking the period as a whole, "but has come to be much more extensively debated during the 1990s. Examples of declining turnout are brought up at one national election after another, with particular concern being expressed after spectacular drops such as the 12% drop in the United Kingdom between the general elections of 1997 and 2001. But, as Richard Rose asks in his chapter, do these elections provide evidence to support a general theory that turnout in Western Europe is falling? If so, is it then valid to infer that public interest in democratic participation has declined, or even that the general public's commitment to democracy is waning?" If there is a shift in Western Europe then it is a little early to tell, and coincides with, but is not related to the discussions relating to civil society in the former Soviet Union. What we seem to be getting is "noise" rather than any solid information that a long-term shift is taking place in Europe away from political parties. Many factors seem to be at work. As IDEA reports: "There are, however, con-sistent findings that turnout is related to political systems, frameworks and institutions: for example, proportional representation systems tend to be associated with higher turnout, while the call for citizens to visit the polling station 'too frequently' to participate in elections and/or referenda may depress turnout" (IDEA, 2004).

On the other hand, election watchers cannot fail to notice the low turnouts in US elections. In the year of presidential elections it has been around the 55% mark which compares unfavourably with Europe.[5] In the non-presidential years the turnout is an abysmal 30% or so. The first country with a mass vote, the United States, does not vote *en masse*. There may well be a relationship between the most advanced capitalist society + false belief in civil society + acceptance of pluralism + narcissism + poor response to political parties + apathy + existence of large absorptive class. That would take some working out. However, at this stage, the claim that representative democracy and political parties have been replaced by an alternative form of governance embracing "civil society" is very much premature. It may well be that if there is a decline of the political party system, the decline is a result of the relationship between the ever growing concentration of capital and the concentration of power within the state. Civil society associations (like NGOs) therefore are expressions to a considerable extent, not of democratic power, but of fractions and narrow interests of the power holders, plus an element of dissent which may be in a few cases the expression of new class formation. It is certainly the case that researchers and commentators have noted the way in which the relatively low voter turnout has grave dangers for US democracy. The tendency toward concentration of power and of capital is accentuated by the low turnout in two major ways. One is clearly that the political agenda can be skewed according to the turnout, and the other is that what purports to be "civil society" is in fact the working out only of narrow interests among the power holders.

The problem of low turnout, as expressed by Ruy Teixeira, "may be accentuated by the well-publicized activities of organized groups lobbying for particularized agendas (so-called political interests). These activities should be thought of as a form of political participation by these organized groups – participation, moreover, that has been growing over time ... and because this participation has a relatively high impact, attempting as it does to directly influence the agenda set by policymaking elites through extensive personal contacts and the dispensation of favours, the need for a democratic counterweight to special interest participation seems compelling" (Teixeira, 1992). Though at the last presidential election in the United States in 2008, the expectation of a huge turnout in favour of Barack Obama was high, voter turnout was not that much greater than in 2004. It proved to be just 1% higher than in 2004, and 2% lower than in 1960, but both these years were a marked improvement on the presidential election turnouts between 1972 and 2000.

Teixeira also claims as a result of his empirical research that turnout decline has "not been the responsibility of any one demographic group, no matter how these categories are defined (by income, education, occupation, race, age and so on)" (Teixeira, 1992, p. 104). And that, in his opinion, this disconnection with politics of the American (sic) people should be reinstated through political reform (Teixeira, 1992, p. 182 et seq). This call for reform, for democracy to do its work by taking on corporate influence is strongly expressed in the arguments and the rhetoric of Cloward and Piven.[6] "Big business," they write cleverly, "has no votes; it cannot win elections by mobilizing votes in its own interests, and it never could." In the interest of the poor and the weak, the people of the United States do certainly need to "reconnect" to politics. They stress in a later work when the US voter turnout had declined even further: "The right to vote is the core symbol of democratic political systems" (Cloward & Piven, 1998, p. 3). The fact that voter turnout is so low in the United States (and the United Kingdom is following the trend) means that the lobbyists, special interest and personal connections, now with a handy label, crony capitalism, have a much freer hand than ever before, and since voting turnout is symbolic of the health of democratic life, one assumes the rest of the democratic system at all levels is equally weakening in the United States.

The huge expansion of NGOs and the frequent talk of civil society hide this clear development: democracy and the capitalist economy/state are in direct conflict. As far as I know no thorough analysis has been conducted on the numbers of NGOs and their financing or on assessing their adherence to specific political agendas. However, there is plenty of anecdotal, journalistic comment and partial enumeration to allow me to venture, with a good degree of confidence, that the well-funded political right with its pro-corporate and pro-religious agendas far outweigh the more leftist or, even, reformist elements. In 2001, I did a short survey of internet sites that concerned themselves with nuclear weaponry. Assuming anti-nuclear sites are leftist and reformist and pro-nuclear sites are right of centre, I found that the leftist and reformist sites were outnumbered and outweighed. I do not think many would argue against the assumption that most think-tanks in the United States are sponsored more from the right wing interests than leftist or reformist ones despite the sham that such think-tanks are supposedly bi-partisan (to qualify for tax exemption).

Currently, neither in the United States nor in the United Kingdom do political parties represent "big classes." This has never been the case in the United States but the British Labour Party did for a time grow out of the bowels of the trade union movement and out of the working-class movements generally. The scope for the working class to adopt parliamentary reform as a road forward helped create the non-revolutionary, non-Marxist working-class movement in Britain. Much the same is true in France, Italy and Germany, though proportional representation led there to much more fragmentation and varieties of electoral alliances. In 2008, the struggle to gain the nomination for the Democratic presidential candidate in the USA does not represent any kind of struggle among the three big classes but a struggle among fractions of classes pursuing their own narrow interests. Even though the main issue became the so-called economy rather than militarism and the health provision, the outcome will not affect the fundamental nature of US capitalism one iota. The prospects for change remain entirely located within a limited reformist agenda. Both Barack Obama and Hillary Clinton offered more rhetoric than the prospect of change to their fractionalized absorbers.

Many commentators and activists attached with various degrees of firmness to the Marxist tradition in the post-sixties era have tended also to obscure the political process, especially in their advocacy separating the state from the economy in the interests of praxis to which issue we now turn.

5. THE DISSERVICES OF NEO-MARXISM TO POLITICAL THEORY

The various forms of Marxism that developed after 1945 were concerned with developing strategies and tactics for "seizing" power as were other socialist and social democratic movements. Generally speaking, social democratic or democratic socialist movements were committed to gradualism or increment-alism (and, where they exist, still are). Euro-Communists, a mongrel mix of Marxists and Democratic Socialists, were committed to faster movement while remaining within the parliamentary processes that were open to them. The problem for these movements was, and is, to separate economics from the state. To command state power, you would need to see it as existing as a set of separate institutions that could be captured. However, such an approach is to ignore the obvious. The state, whatever it is, does not make decisions outside the fast-moving economic–political system. Even the early pioneers of the far from revolutionary Labour Party in Britain knew this to be the case: hence their famous Clause 4 designed to control the commanding heights of the economy through nationalization of the major industries and the major financial institutions, and thereby developing a strategy to enable the state and the economy to establish a non-Marxist socialist society. One commentator concludes clearly: "In defining civil society so that it no longer includes the economy, however, these post-Marxists effectively eliminate economic power and economic position as a basis for political change" (Hall, 1995). It is unfortunate that Gramsci, Althusser, Poulantzas and Habermas developed intellectual commitments to see the state in some measure or another as having a separate existence, at least sufficiently to be able to capture it through parliamentary processes, welfare statism and the redistribution of income and wealth. However, what is convincing is that the system, the integrated economy and state, makes shaky decisions or compromises that result in a perpetual series of conflicts, debates and differences among competing interests. These competing interests are reflections of the fractionalized nature of capitalists and other participating classes involved in the process of determining the directions that society takes.

Similarly, the current stress on civil society weakens the real importance of the political process as exercised through parliamentary forms as is argued in the next section.

6. NGOs, CIVIL SOCIETY AND SOCIAL MOVEMENTS

Despite the fact (or perhaps because of it) the number of persons involved in NGOs, as calculated by the UNDP in 1994, was about 250 million, it is difficult to claim that NGOs in any sense really reflect "civil society" acting on behalf of the citizenry nor can NGOs be seen as constituting genuine social movements acting in the interests of the mass of the people against the encroachments or repression of the state or of governments. Alex Demorovic summarizes the position reasonably succinctly:

> NGOs enhance the rationality of national and international political institutions in two ways: by creating democratisation and by contributing to a consensus-based domination. The price for this is that the NGOs become bureaucratised and apolitical and lose much of their self-organisational and critical significance, and, finally, also of their efficiency. It is for this reason that NGOs do not constitute a social movement. ... they do not consolidate different practices of social protest and social identities in order to articulate an antagonism between the movement and an opponent impeding progress or emancipation ... NGOs disarticulate protest into a wide range of negotiation and implementation processes.[7]

While there may be some democratizing virtues that spin-off associated with NGO activity, generally speaking NGOs and their participants tend to serve to ameliorate protest, provide compromises for the class factional struggles, provide employment for commodified middle class professionals, and provide a channel for government and state funds aimed at the production of compromises and the maintenance of a conservative hegemony.

Similarly, Ehrenberg writes:

> It is no accident that accelerating inequality is proceeding hand in hand with a historically unprecedented concentration and centralisation of economic power and wealth...the New York Times recently reported ...last year alone a record of $1 trillion in mergers involved American companies... The economy...is an extraordinarily powerful set of social relations...No conceivable combination of PTAs, soup kitchens, choral societies, or Girl Scout troops can resist it. (Ehrenberg, 1998, p. 248)

Another critic, George Soros, summarizes the argument more succinctly: "The main enemy of the open society is no longer the communist but the capitalist threat" (Ehrenberg, 1998, p. 250).

Further criticism comes from Negri and Hardt who are unequivocal in their view that civil society, far from active, has withered away (Hardt & Negri, 2000, pp. 328–329). They explain this in relation to the decline of the dialectic between labour and capital. This is a point of great importance because civil society was never stronger than when there was a clear struggle between capital and labour. Indeed, it was this struggle that produced representative democracy in its modern form. Capital would never, on its own, have conceded the degree of voice for the mass of the people that now exists in the OECD countries. However unsatisfactory representative democracy may be, it is superior as a form of civil society than the hodge podge of NGOs which are now supposed to represent the genuine interests of the population at large.

A relaxed view of the absence of civil society can be taken if we learn, in our assessment of the usefulness of Marxian analysis, to escape from the future. The capitalist fear of the mass proletarian revolution should now have subsided. The absorptive class is seeing to that. For instance, while trying to explain the failures of the proletarian movements, Gramsci observed a civil society that behaves precisely as it is now suggested the absorptive class functions:

> Wedged between the state and class – structured economy – these fortresses and earthworks normally protect the outer ditch of state power and shield the ruling class from the shock waves produced by economic crises. (Keane, 1998, p. 15)

A key problem, felt most heavily by the left, is that the collapse of the worker–capitalist dialectic leaves a huge vacuum as far as the much-valued "praxis" is concerned. Action is severely circumscribed. "The concerns of these new social movements are not the material questions of economic production and distribution, but the forging of new collective identities and political cultures that are not based on class" (Hall, 1995). Thus, as we have seen, they are not social movements at all. The absorptive class is doing its job well, absorbing both the surplus in the economic sphere of production and absorbing the shocks in the political sphere as well as the economic.

One current text dealing with social movements which attempts to make sense of the fact that conflict occurs but seemingly outside the theoretical framework of class struggle is by Donatella della Porta and Mario Diani.[8] For instance, they write: "the general relevance of the capital–labour cleavage has been, in various countries, supplemented by others" (della Porta & Diani, 1999, p. 27). In other words, it is reasonable to suppose that tension is still very much a part of the underlying reasons for conflict but that there are all sorts of other sources: ethno-territorial, church and state, urban–rural. They have three criteria for analysing the relationship between social change and conflict. Social change may:

- Facilitate the emergence of new social groups.
- Increase the resources that facilitate collective action.
- Modify patterns of relations between people.

They then discuss the above in relation to production, the state and the relationship between public and private spheres with the aim of assessing how "new" movements "affect our understanding of concepts like class conflict and class action" (della Porta & Mario Diani, 1999, p. 28). In their highly useful survey of the analyses of structural transformations, new conflicts and new classes, they identify a number of reasons why the arguments presented by a variety of authors[9] lead to differing outcomes: authors "move from different points of departure, and use the same terms in quite different ways. To begin with, we must note the difference between a 'historical' and a 'structural' or 'analytical' concept of class...A number of scholars have stressed...the so-called 'new middle class' ...this class is able...to play a central role in new conflicts" (della Porta & Diani, 1999, p. 47). Interestingly, they conclude "that it is still doubtful that a new political cleavage...has emerged, let alone been consolidated."

I feel pretty sure that as we develop our awareness of the existence of the absorptive class we can see more clearly why a new cleavage, on the proletarian-bourgeois pattern has not occurred; the role of the absorptive class is precisely to prevent structural changes leading to the kind of political confrontation that would seriously threaten capitalism and the capitalist state. Overall, despite the good intentions of della Porta and Mario Diani, the analysis of social movements leaves me with a lingering feeling of dissatisfaction. For a moment I have to abandon the academic approach to the discussion and use this paragraph to go back to the impressions of protests at Seattle, Bologna, G8 and World Economic Forum meetings and the Peace Marches (rarely reported in the mass media), and, like many others, wonder exactly who the protestors are and whether they form the essence of any future effective social movement. In recalling these more-recent demonstrations, I recall two decades of my early years from the end of the fifties to the end of the seventies and try honestly to perceive what a CND (Campaign for Nuclear Disarmament) rally meant, what an anti-apartheid vigil achieved, what my personal boycott of Chilean apples meant to anyone, what pro-abortion marches were about, what I was doing as a union activist marching in the seventies for higher pay and better conditions for lecturers and teachers. I wonder not *why* did I give money to striking miners in the eighties when Margaret Thatcher organized the last of the big confrontations between unions and the state in the United Kingdom, but *who* was I? Protest and dissent on its own is not enough: protest and dissent must be rooted in class action as we discuss further in Chapter 7. For all my protestations I was not a proletarianized member of the middle class in the sixties and seventies. I was not and I am not a worker of the brain. I was not an intellectual preaching revolution. Now, I am sure I am a member of the absorptive class, writing a book calling on my class to work toward moving the capitalist system to reform itself, pretty drastically, and spending my pension accumulated in the United Kingdom in a low-cost country in Central America.

7. PLURALISM VERSUS STATE THEORY

The noise relating to civil society has drowned out to a considerable extent the debates in relation to the form of the state that were current prior to 1990. The main line of the arguments at that time were contested by those who insisted on the description of the neutral state under capitalism in the context of theories of pluralism against those who argued for the base-superstructure analysis of Marx and Engels (and a vast array of subsequent variations) (Jessop, 1982; Aronowitz, 2003). One of the leading theorists of pluralism was Robert A. Dahl who in the company of Charles Lindblom set the tone for several decades in establishing an analysis that was essentially pluralist in nature. That is, they were able to establish to their satisfaction that, essentially, democracy and capitalism were compatible. More recently, Dahl has retreated from that position and sees capitalism as a drag on democracy to such an extent that wider forms of democracy than now exist in advanced economic nations are unlikely to occur. He writes:

> Democracy and market-capitalism are like two persons bound in a tempestuous marriage that is riven by conflict and yet endures because neither partner wishes to separate from the other.... (Dahl, 2000, p. 168)

On the plus side he argues that, as a matter of historical observation, market economies have only existed in polyarchal[10] democracies: and that this is so because certain basic features of market-capitalism make it favourable for democratic institutions. Conversely, some basic features of a predominantly non-market economy make it harmful to democratic prospects. Generally speaking the market economy, he claims, leads to economic growth, and such growth is "favourable to democracy".[11] Democracy and the market system reduces poverty and social conflict and "provides individuals, groups, and governments with surplus resources to support education and thus to foster a literate and educated citizenry" (Dahl, 2000, p. 168). Dahl, like other commentators (Lasch, Braverman, Miliband) referred to in Chapter 6 infra, notes the large middling stratum of property owners (meaning in reality owners of chattels) who typically seek education, autonomy, personal freedom, property rights, the rule of law, and participation in the government. "The middle classes, as Aristotle was the first to point out, are the natural allies of democratic ideas and institutions." Unfortunately, Dahl does not really give this middling stratum or middle class any economic function or functions. Nevertheless, Dahl then goes on to say that the market economy does not need a powerful authoritarian state. Thus, having established the happy symbiosis of market economy (by which he means capitalism) and democracy, Dahl proceeds to the less happy. First, there are certain built-in conflicts. Government intervention is required to establish and maintain the necessary institutional structure within which the market can operate: moreover the market economy, unfettered, can be responsible for severe damage to persons and groups and further government intervention is thereby demanded. And he gives a page-long list of necessary government intervention with the addition of "and so on and so on."

Second, the market economy distributes certain kinds of resources unequally, in fact highly unequally. Dahl then makes a devastating indictment of capitalism. "Because of inequalities in political resources, some citizens gain significantly more influence than others over the government's policies, decisions and actions. These violations, alas, are not trivial. Consequently, citizens are not political equals – far from it – and thus the moral foundation of democracy, political equality among citizens, is seriously violated" (Dahl, 2000, p. 178).

Finally, he argues that the market, though it dissolves authoritarian regimes, may not be able to proceed beyond the particular forms of polyarchy that exist in nation states on the "western" pattern and democracy must therefore be always limited to its current particular form.

Dahl, for so long, the ideologue and proponent of the pluralist formulation of the state under capitalism, has abandoned that position to note what in a sense we all know in our hearts. Capitalism does bring benefits, but it limits the development of full democracy. Capitalism tends toward the concentration of political and economic power to the benefit of the power holders generally speaking and resists the dissipation of power which would otherwise be the end of democracy. Dahl admits of all kinds of associations and interests who will be involved in the process of polyarchical "rule" but he has no need in his analysis for civil society. It is a total irrelevance. He can easily discuss, analyse and describe the workings of democracy without any reference to such a totality as civil society. In other words, the term would hinder the critical position he has taken over the limits to the growth of democracy under the market system. By contrast to the pluralist model, the most general Marxist formulation would have the state and the economy as a unity, with the dominant class, the capitalists, controlling both economic development and state power in the common interests of the fractions of the ruling classes. (The capitalist class as an emerging power may be in alliance with the former dominant class as in eighteenth and nineteenth century England where the capitalist class merged to considerable degree with the former dominant class, the aristocracy: remnants of this class remained within the Thatcher government. She disposed of them.)

The link that connects state and economy is class formation and to that extent I am here accepting in very general terms a Marxist formulation. As far as I can make out the particular variation that I would be closest to is that of Joachim Hirsch, as outlined by Jessop under the heading of "political economy, political sociology and class domination" (Jessop, 1982, pp. 103–104). Hirsch's arguments conclude that the capitalist state needs both a pluralistic structure and specific processing mechanisms to ensure that the demands of various class forces can, nevertheless, serve the purposes of capital accumulation and political domination. This is because of the threefold economic function of securing the process of economic reproduction, ensuring that the dominant class remains so through coercion, concession and ideological primacy and unifying the fractions of the dominant class. A number of issues arise from the bare bones of this analysis, one of which is the role of crisis and the special importance of the Tendency of the Rate of Profit to fall which is explored further in Chapter 6. "Hirsch refers to the important role of crises in steering the activities of the state. He argues that serious failures of market forces and state intervention to reproduce those conditions needed for capital accumulation and/or political domination threatens the 'governing groups', stimulates demands for action, class forces and imposes new priorities on the state" (Jessop, 1982, pp. 105–106). The tendency of the rate of profit to fall is important in the analysis but, so, too, are the political repercussions.

While I do not adhere to the reductionist view that the state is nothing more than the executive committee of the bourgeoisie for managing its common affairs, I am convinced that attempting to separate the state from the economy is misguided as is taking either politics or economics out of any form of social science analysis. In sum, the use of "civil society" is a poor anodyne substitute to the vitality and importance of these earlier debates about the nature of the state under capitalism.

8. BIG STATE/LITTLE STATE/WELFARE STATE/WARFARE STATE

Generally speaking the modern big state has its origins, it is claimed, in the development of industrial economies of the nineteenth and early twentieth centuries.

One contradiction regularly noted by economic historians of nineteenth century Britain has been that, to get an efficient small state required by classical economics who also subscribed to Benthamite utilitarianism, you needed to have laws enforced relating to the orderly conduct of business and labour: this created the modern civil service as evidenced by such pieces of legislation as the Reform Act, the Factory Acts, Poor Law Amendment Act and Bank Charter Act. The modernization of the tax system meant the end to farming taxes and the creation of a government-owned service and so on. Each piece of utilitarian legislation led to the expansion of the state at national, regional and local levels from which there was no retreat (John Gray, 1998). Thus, despite the theory of both classical economists and neo-classical economists which argued for the existence of small government, the state began to grow and with it also the local and regional state with urbanization, municipal government and free education. The economic theory simply did not match the political practice.

A second pressure for the big state was the trend toward the Welfare State which was also driven in part by the need for social control. Rapid urbanization with its vast pool of concentrated, impoverished workers, was too unstable for political reasons. Germany and Britain thus responded by introducing the Welfare State not simply because of the need to offer reformist policies to the working poor but because of the perceived manpower needs of military and imperialist aggrandizement and hegemony prior to the First World War. Subsequently Keynesian Welfare Statism arose to stabilize the economy in the face of recurrent crises as we see in more detail in Chapter 6 infra. Thus, it has been argued the Welfare State and the Warfare State owed its origins to the competitive struggle among nations for markets and raw materials beginning noticeably also with Anglo-German rivalry. In addition, it has been argued, the pressure from the working class helped produce policies of public housing in the period immediately after the First World War and for more comprehensive provision which included the 1944 Education Act and the introduction of the National Health Service in 1948 in the United Kingdom. The price the working class exacted for participation in the total war economy (1939–1945) was an extensive Welfare State (security from cradle to grave) plus nationalization of coal, steel and transport industries. The big state became common place in Western Europe in Germany, the United Kingdom, Scandinavia, Holland, Belgium, Italy and France. Despite the fact the United States did not pursue a Welfare State provision on the same pattern, the size of the state grew and public expenditure has remained high despite the ideological position that a small state and low taxation is the preferred policy. The Warfare State also accounts for high levels of government expenditure and a big state. As a result of the fact that economies have grown enormously and that the pattern of international security has changed, the proportion of public expenditure in many national economies going on arms has declined but nevertheless remains high in absolute terms especially in the United States. The role of the Warfare State however has been important.

The weak absorptive class was obvious in the United States of the 1930s. Whereas the United States benefited enormously from the First World War in that its productive capacity and financial power in the world grew enormously but in the thirties the collapse of the industrial sector was equally substantial. When the decision came to re-arm, the US economy scarcely noticed the process to begin with. As Paul Kennedy writes "Even these rearmament measures scarcely disturbed an economy the size of the United States. The key fact about the American economy was that it was greatly underutilized. In 1938, the United States produced 26.04 million tons of steel, well ahead of Germany's 20.7 million, the USSR's 16.5 million, and Japan's 6.0 million; yet the steel industries of the latter three countries were working to full capacity, whereas two thirds of the American steel plants were idle" (Kennedy, 1987, p. 331). The docile nature of US imperialism can be recognized in the fact that despite a National Income of $68 billions, defence expenditure was only 1.5% compared with that of the British Empire where defence expenditure represented 5.7% out of a national income of 22 billion: Germany spent 23.5% of its NI of 17 million on defence while the USSR spent 26.4% of its national income of 19 billion on defence.

While the Second World War helped expand US industry, the United States also was poised for a post-war period of expanded private consumption. This could only take place if an absorptive class was produced to add to the absorptive capacity of the civilian and military state. We discuss this further by reference to the work particularly of Baran and Sweezy and military expenditure (see Chapter 6 infra) as well as noting the issues relating to government civilian expenditure in the work of Galbraith in his book, *The Public Purpose*.[12] It is also worth remarking upon, however, the contradictions in the ideology of the so-called free-market. For instance take this statement from a public web site that seeks to educate the general public about the virtues of private enterprise:

> The American belief in "free enterprise" has not barred a major role for government, however. People in the US rely on government to address matters the private economy overlooks, from education to protecting the environment. And despite their advocacy of market principles, they have used government at times to nurture new industries, and at times even to protect American companies from competition.[13]

The built-in contradiction is that the market is required for allocation of resources or solving scarcity and this requires a small state, but economic growth, producing surpluses, requires the big state. Historically this contradiction is seen by Fernand Braudel, the French economic historian, as part and parcel of historical development of capitalism: "What I personally regret, not so much as a historian, but as man of my time, is the refusal in both the capitalist world and the socialist world to draw a distinction between *capitalism and the market economy*" (Braudel, 1977, p. 114).

The contradiction created by the coexistence of the big state for dealing with the surplus and the small state for allowing the market to operate is observed but not analysed. For instance Stiglitz writes: "Abroad America (sic) preached a version of capitalism, based on a minimalist role for the

state, which America (sic) had itself rejected... America (sic) never bought
the myth that big government is bad" (Stiglitz, 2003, p. 277).

My argument, then, is that the reasons given for government intervention
are valid but do not go far enough. Again, the point is that *the big state* is
required not simply to pursue war (supposedly for defence), put in place
welfare (to protect internal security) but to help produce the absorptive
power required by the capitalist system of production. The absorptive class
has to be consistently expanded through the creation of public servants of
all kinds at all levels of government (local, regional, state, central): immigration officials, inland revenue officers, teachers, forest rangers, actuaries,
accountants, lawyers, advisers, planners and so on. The tension between
public expenditure by governments and the belief in the market and the
small state is continuous and, as things stand, irresolvable. At times the
balance will be seriously challenged as under the Thatcher governments
in the United Kingdom in the interests of the rate of profit but at the end
of the day, commentators found that very little change in the balance
between public and private expenditure had been "achieved." Rather than
cutting substantially public expenditure, her governments had made the
public sector more "efficient" and helped keep up the rate of profit or at
least minimized its fall.

We now move on from establishing the unity of the state and the economy
to the next central feature of the argument, the commodity.

NOTES

1. Cf. Macpherson (1978), Chapter 12. Christman (1994), Ryan (1984), Proudhon
(1966).
2. Keane (1998, p. 70), quoting Ellen Meiksins Wood.
3. This point is clearly made in by Martin Shaw www.sussex.ac.uk/users/hafa3/
cs.htm and "Civil Society" in Kurtz (1999, pp. 269–278); also in Ehrenberg (1998),
Chapters 4 & 8.
4. Neera Chandhoke makes a claim also for Smith's Scottish *enlightenment*
contemporary, Adam Ferguson. www.opendemocracy.net, 17 March 2005.
5. The voter turnout in the United States in 2008 was, however, 62% and in 2004
was 61%.
6. For example Cloward and Piven (1982), Cloward and Piven (1998).
7. Demirovic (2000, p. 5) to be found at http://userpage.fu.berlin.de/~mayer/
mm/courses/WS0203_docs/PS_NGOs_Demirovic2000.SocialMovements/GlobalOrder.
doc Doubts about the contradictory functions of NGOs are also expressed in Eade
(edit.) (2000).

8. See della Porta and Diani (1999); Goodwin and Jasper (2003); Crossley (2002); Bandy and Smith (edit.) (2005).

9. They refer to Touraine, Lash and Urry, Melucci, Eder and many others.

10. For a full development of the concept, theory and description of polyarchal democracies see: Dahl and Lindblom (1953). Polyarchy, a term introduced by Dahl and Lindblom, exists where the following political institutions exist and operate: elected officials; full, fair and frequent elections; freedom of expression; alternative sources of information; associational autonomy; inclusive citizenship.

11. Dahl does concede that economic growth can take place without democracy or with the aid of planned economy: examples of the former being the Tiger economies and of the later second world wartime Britain and the United States.

12. Galbraith (1973); cf. "The procedure here described reaches its full perfection in the case of weapons and weapon systems, where the sequence of innovation and obsolescence has been fully systemized. Successive generations of aircraft, missiles, submarines, helicopters and main battle tanks are formally projected with the approximate dates in the future when the particular item will be made obsolete by further innovation and, accordingly, will require replacement" (p. 153).

13. www.EconomyWatch.com/world_economy/usa downloaded 10 May 2005.

CHAPTER 3

THE COMMODITY

The commodity exerts a fascination, to say the least, over the lives of all of us. Some, like Guy Debord, might go as far as claiming that society *is* the commodity. To others the commodity is non-problematic. Work hard. Get paid. Spend the bulk of it on commodities in satisfying wants in the form of goods and services. Defining the difference between a need and a want is simply a waste of good absorbing time. Exposing the real meaning of a table made of wood seems hardly worth the paper and ink required to do so. However, Marx supposed, referring to the wooden table, that there was a difference between a need and a want, and it was this difference that was crucial in the understanding of the capitalist process, and, in identifying this difference, it was vital to understand the nature of the commodity.

While the section on commodity fetishism in *Capital* is central to the whole story of how capitalism works, it actually appears as what seems to be an afterthought tacked onto the end of Chapter 1 of the first volume of *Capital*. It is here that Marx wrote:

> The form of wood, for instance, is altered by making a table of it. Yet, for all that, the table continues to be that common, every-day thing, wood. But, as soon as it steps forth as a commodity, it is changed into something transcendent. It not only stands on its head, and evolves out of its wooden brain grotesque ideas, far more wonderful than "table-turning" ever was.[1]

In continuing, Marx, economist, then resorts to a strange mystical explanation, choosing suitable language to accompany it.

> In order...to find an analogy, we must have recourse to the mist-enveloped regions of the religious world. In that world the productions of the human brain appear as independent beings endowed with life, and entering into relation both with one another and the human race. So it is in the world of commodities with the products of men's hands. This I call Fetishism, which attaches itself to the products of labour. So soon as they are produced as commodities...[2] (Karl Marx, 1972)

The implications of not knowing what we are doing as human beings in the system means, to Marx, and to others who are not Marxists, that the

71

individual lives a life akin to the hero in Greek tragedy. "We are unable to create social institutions to alleviate poverty and meet basic human needs, despite our immensely expanded powers of production, because the pressure of market competition makes us believe we are too poor. Parents wind up overworking themselves to make money to give their children a better life, all the while depriving the children of the direct comfort and love they crave and substituting alienating gifts of money and commodities for direct company" (Foley, 1997, p. 94). The individual produces her or his own personal tragedy; the seeds of failure as a human being are contained in the success accomplished as an absorber of commodities. What Marx is anxious to show is that the commodity is the labour power embodied in it, but, significantly, because of the system of division of labour (so eloquently discussed by Adam Smith) the production of commodities and their distribution is a collective act involving the generality of persons involved in the process. The whole of society is involved in what appears to be individual acts. The commodity itself has value only because it embodies human labour power. Labour power is an important concept as it enabled Marx to make a distinction between exploitation that ensured the *reproduction* of the working class so that it would continue to be exploitable, and spoliation of labour which would result in the *destruction* of the working class (Marx, 1972, Vol. I, Ch. 10, passim). The capitalist system as a whole has no intention of destroying the geese that lay the golden eggs (though individual capitalists may do so). Thus, the commodity is apparently a thing but is, in fact, a social relation. Interestingly, for those with a concern for etymology, if we go back to sixteenth century England, commodity meant greed and self-interest as in Shakespeare's *King John* when the Bastard son of the late Richard the Lion Heart concedes to the (alleged) usurper thus:

Commodity, the bias of the world....
This sway of motion, this commodity
This bawd, this broker, this all-changing word...
Why rail I on this commodity?
Since kings break faith upon commodity,
Gain, be my lord, for I will worship thee!

However, the common belief is that the market system and the capitalist mode of production treats the commodity as if it were somehow a *fetish*, a religious object to be consumed as an act of worship. In consuming a commodity, we are led to believe that it is an act analogous to religious duty. We do not, for instance, understand that, at least to some extent, we are consuming our fellow man. When we buy a car we are purchasing the men and women, in part, who made it, as well as perpetuating the system whereby such an act is possible.

1. EDUCATION AS COMMODITY

In Marx, a commodity is a thing brought to the market for sale at a profit where it satisfies a want rather than a need and embodies labour power and is purchased by the consumer as if it were a fetish. The term commodification did not come into usage until late in the 1970s but is now thrown around with some frequency, sometimes casually with imprecise meaning, sometimes more pointedly. Frequently it is used to indicate the shift of social activity previously conducted outside the market or commercial world generally, into the world of trade, money or exchange. Typical are these resolutions emanating from the headquarters of the ESIB, The National Unions of Students in Europe. The ESIB resolves to:

> Promote on an international level increased consciousness as to the current and possible future negative implications of *commodification*.
>
> Analyse in further detail the implications and consequences of *commodification* of education as well as the manner in which ESIB may positively contribute towards ensuring that education remains a public good.
>
> Encourage student unions and decision makers in higher education to involve themselves in the discussion relating to the *commodification* of education.[3]

Thus, it comes as no surprise, for instance, that commodification has become an increasingly common-place phenomenon. For instance Marx wrote in the Communist Manifesto (1848): "The bourgeoisie ... converted the physician, the priest, the poet, the man of science into its paid wage labourers." When ESIB students complain that education is commodified, they are not discovering anything new. Whenever a teacher offers his service and is paid for it, the service embodies labour power and is a commodity. Students are in reality complaining about something else. They are in effect complaining about the commodity itself: that of an educational qualification being more expensive than it was, of poorer quality and satisfying wants at a lower level. Given that education, and a particular education delivered in particular institutions, determines in large part the chances of an individual to enter the absorptive class at a relatively high level of potential as absorbers, students in Europe, already part of a distinctive elite, are demanding a bigger share of available commodities during their lifetime for themselves and their putative families. Thus consumers will generally argue for what they regard as better commodities. This is, after all, their "job," or function, as shock absorbers. These attempts to acquire better commodities for a given price will not halt the over-production of goods and services: on the contrary, they will lead to further production.

From the teacher's point of view there is some despair and even resistance to both being commodified and offering the educational commodity as inevitably the end product in both cases leaves much to be desired. Christopher Lasch in his discussion on narcissism, a term that we use extensively in Chapter 5, also links education with commodification by arguing that in modern conditions (1970s) the university is a "diffuse, shapeless, and permissive institution that has absorbed the major currents of cultural modernism and reduced them to a watery blend, a mind emptying ideology of cultural revolution, personal fulfilment, and creative alienation" (Lasch, 1979, p. 151). Rightly or wrongly, he argues that general education is despised and students are urged to see their education largely in terms of their future employment. General education is reduced to a mindless, soulless and meaningless eclecticism. When Dorothy Parker, the wit, writer and reviewer, took a job as a distinguished professor in literature for a year at California State University in the 1960s she was bitterly disappointed by her students:

> Dorothy's students were there to obtain three credits. Many of them failed to get much pleasure from reading... She found their political conservatism and their narrowness of mind to be disgraceful... it only stood to reason that their writing skills would disappoint her. She discovered only three of them [out of 72] were able to put together a sensible English sentence. (Meade, 1989, pp. 389–390)

In return Dorothy turned up for only two thirds of her classes, but never gave a bad grade. It may well be that teachers of undergraduates are still facing much the same kind of problems that Dorothy Parker and Christopher Lasch encountered several decades ago.

2. RECYCLING AND THE COMMODITY

While students and teachers object to the commodification, overtly or latently, others complain about waste and they turn, ironically, to the commodification of waste recycling. In this case, the process of production simply concentrates on utilizing a different raw material; the capitalist productive process is not arrested one jot, let alone altered. Most recycled products are used as raw material for the products of a capitalistically organized private enterprise company operating on the basis of profit and responsible to their shareholders. For instance, if the firm that utilized the recycled raw material did not make a profit, it would not exist. Normally, therefore, the market price of the product composed of used products as its raw material wholly or in part, is higher than products that use primary raw materials. This is so for several reasons. Take paper as an example. Used paper is more expensive to collect, sort and purify than wood pulp; and manufacturers can trade on providing a "morally" superior product, which, in terms of quality and utility, is normally inferior to paper made from wood pulp from freshly cut trees. This ability to sell an inferior product at a higher price is made possible through the marketing process (which we can count as part of the manufacturing process) and through the existence of the absorptive class, which has been educated to consume at even higher levels of unit price. Manufactured political correctness overrides market forces in the interests of profit takers. Waste, as we mention later, is impossible under the capitalist system since all production is for profit; therefore, the production of a commodity, wasted or not, serves its purpose under capitalism once it has garnered profit. If we lived in a society organized on the satisfaction of needs rather than wants then waste would become an issue.

3. COMMODITY, PRICE AND THE ABSORPTIVE CLASS

The relationship between price and the commodity brings us to a crucial departure from popular belief or conventional wisdom. Consumers tend to equate price with quality. Thus fully fledged members of the absorptive class will tend to seek out higher priced goods rather than lower priced goods. Of course, many goods and services entering the market must be competitively priced. That is so, but it is even more so that all goods will tend toward a price that the market will bear. In addition, the tendency toward the concentration of capital reduces the number of producers, and this, on occasion, is associated with both latent and covert cartelization. So, for instance, if marketers are able to generate a demand for vitamins at high prices, leaving the producers vast profit margins, those prices will hold, more or less. The supply–demand–price model in orthodox economic theory only works as a model: none of the assumptions in the orthodox model hold very true in the real world: perfect competition, mobility of factors of production, perfect knowledge, time scale, huge numbers of consumers matched by large numbers of suppliers and so on. Thus in the real world, with its tendency toward the concentration of capital, we know for sure that the absorptive class can be led to consume at higher price levels rather than lower ones. In this pattern, the competition works only at the very edges. Thus a shock absorber will say: "Look I got these vitamins for $24.99 instead of $29.99. I saved $5!" In fact the cost of producing the vitamins (excluding the marketing) may have been as little as a dollar or two. The purchaser should say: "I was ripped off but only $20 this time instead of $25 like I was last time." Power and status are linked to spending, whether directly or vicariously. Producers know this. While the buyer can to some extent compare like with like, they cannot effectively distinguish between a vitamin and a packaged vitamin. Sadly, moreover, for hopefuls wanting to prolong their lives, vitamin supplements to diet may well be counterproductive and actually damage health according to a recent study published by Copenhagen University in April 2008. This might have been bad news for the global market worth around $2.5 billion, though to date the news of these research findings by the Cochrane Collaboration does not seem to have dented global sales.

4. PROTEST AS COMMODITY

As we have seen, any kind of objection or protest or campaign against the commodity is simply itself commodified (Heath & Potter, 2004). Consumption serves as an *alternative* to protest or rebellion. Lasch argues that consumption turns alienation into a commodity. This is certainly the case, though not quite the way Lasch suggested. The general malaise and emptiness[4] created by the lack of real purpose leads to all kinds of faddism, yoga in several forms, Buddhism, organic foods, veganism, reflexology, many forms of massage, aromatherapy, water cures, psychotherapy, meditation, all of which, effective or bogus, are turned into commodities. Thus contemporary man, tortured by self-consciousness, turns to new cults and therapies not to free himself or herself, according to Lasch, from obsessions but to find meaning and purpose in life, to find something to live for, precisely to embrace an obsession, if only the *passion maitresse* of (psycho-)therapy itself. These observations have been further pursued by Oliver James in his chatty walk about *Affluenza* (James, 2007). However, in the end he elevates psychotherapy into a special and useful category of need. Rather than seeing such activity as little more than the commodification of a doubtful service to the individual that, on the whole, does little to alleviate the mass *malaise* of the age that Oliver James himself identifies, he continues to believe, not surprisingly, in its efficacy in providing solace to those sickened by the disease of affluenza.

The contradictions inherent in the recycling process are repeated in the area of protest, and though glimmered, they are not fully understood. For instance, in a letter to Detritus, a website devoted to recycling, one devotee hesitates: "The way *Adbusters* magazine treats 'culture jamming' seems like the magazine is helping in the worst way possible by turning rebellion against consumption into another consumer device."[5] This is absolutely right except that the writer might have noted the rebellion should be against production not against consumption. Only then might there be a realization that all protest becomes another form of production. There is always an entrepreneur who will seize upon the possibility of producing a good or service, and where the objection can be turned into a commodity for profit this will be done. The commodified medical practitioner, for instance, if unable to provide a satisfactory therapy or if he causes additional iatrogenic disorders through side effects of his pharmaceutical prescriptions, may play a part in stimulating "alternative medicine." In other words, the commodified medical profession plays a part in bringing into being competing commodities. Yet, alternative medicine is notorious for the way in which (i) it is largely ineffective, (ii) it is untested, (iii) it may be actually life threatening by diverting desperately sick patients away from orthodox medicine,[6] (iv) it is always incredibly expensive when the amount of money spent is measured against results and (v) the actual substance may be harmful. The best that can be said relates to the advantages that may accrue through the placebo effect on the sufferer. The expensive packaging of cocktails of vitamins and minerals and their marketing result in terms of countless miles of supermarket shelves stacked with such products plus countless specialist shops selling such products at obviously outrageous prices when compared to the price of simple unadorned products containing the odd mineral or vitamin that might just possibly be absent from your diet. It is far better to eat a simple but varied diet, including meat, in as many forms as possible, though not to excess. That way you will not have to bother with all those soy products, vitamins, minerals, herbal remedies and similar alternative substitutes, which cost far more, and return super-profits to the huge conglomerates that are involved in the production and marketing of them.

The best current example (unlikely to go away for some time) relates to protest over government action or inaction regarding climate change with all the associated commodification around that movement. Everything has been commodified from scientific punditry to tree hugging. Al Gore, the climate change guru, now makes his living from it to the extent that he can sustain a 22-room home and private jet in his high-carbon-energy lifestyle. The overall position has been nicely stated thus:

> This was the year [2007] that we began to believe in global warming – not in the abstract science of the prospect... but in the fact that there was money in it, power to be won and lost... profit to be wrung from crisis. (Funk, 2007)

5. LEISURE, FOOD, EXERCISE AND THE COMMODITY

Perhaps the most symbolic commodification is that of physical exercise. The United States and the United Kingdom can claim some of the fattest people in the world; the greater part of their populations eat too much; or, to put it another way, producers are successful at ensuring the absorptive class eat and drink a substantial part of the surplus produced by the outstandingly efficient industrialized agricultural system. The United States in particular has been enormously successful at industrializing agriculture. A little over 1% or so of the working population can produce enough to feed and water the rest of the nation, and more besides. The cost of this food and liquid is, in relation to average earnings, extremely low so that the average person is free to eat and drink until he or she bursts. In addition, the average citizen in the United States is obsessed with convenience, that is easy and labour-saving access to food and drink. One aspect of this convenience involves staying in, or as close as possible to, their motor vehicles, at all times. Another is to spend as little time as possible in the preparation of meals.

The result of high level of food consumption plus a tendency not to move from their personal motorized transport, as we all know, is that a high proportion of citizens are less healthy than they might otherwise be through obesity and lack of exercise. The answer to this relatively unhealthy state is, of course, to commercialize exercise through the provision of such facilities as gymnasiums, exercise machines at home and even such services as massage whereby the overweight client who lacks exercise can be led to believe that he or she can get exercise by being pummelled by a complete stranger with greasy hands. Even where the individual seeks to jog regularly or take aerobics walks or whatever, the activity is commodified through the availability for sale at a profit of suitable clothes from baseball caps to lycra shorts to the "proper" walking or running shoes. To look at fully fledged members of the absorptive class taking exercise in London, Paris or

New York is to look at human beings more concerned with their commodified appearance than with the real result of an activity purportedly designed to improve health. Moreover, the acts of so-called exercise, which are becoming so common, are taking on increasingly ritualistic forms, supplanting, for instance, the walk to and from church in Sunday best clothes of previous generations. However, it makes no difference whether producers supply Sunday suits and shiny leather shoes and polish to shine them with or, on the other hand, sun visors or shorts with reflector stripes or sweat suits and trainers: it is all surplus to be absorbed. And whether we go to church or not, we now no longer have the foggiest idea of what is sacred and what is profane.

Leisure might at first thought to be an alternative to work, an antidote to both production and consumption. In fact, leisure is quite the opposite. The size of the leisure industry is enormous and growing rapidly. As people take more of what is described as leisure, they spend more money. This is true of going to sporting fixtures; participating in sports; manufacturers relentlessly discover new sports such as snow boarding and kite-boarding; cinema, dancing, musical events, theatre, travel to ever more distant and exotic places, casinos, night clubs, educational class of all kinds, and so on seemingly endlessly. In short, any activity, including non-activity, will be turned by the producer into something that can be purchased for money.

6. THE DISSERVICES OF CULTURAL STUDIES

The clear existence of the absorptive class which we see emerging from the circumstances we have described is obscured, not highlighted, by the sloppy term consumer society and by the emergence of the development of cultural studies out of more rigorous sociological theory. Two books were published at the outset of this century with identical titles. One was *The Consumer Society Reader* edited by Schor and Holt, *The New Press*, 2002 and the other by Martyn Lee published earlier by Blackwell in 2000. Both contain similar, and in some cases, identical readings and both were clearly well intentioned, setting out to understand, critically assess and attack the value system of so-called consumer society. However, it seems to me both collections carry out a disservice by accepting the term consumer society and with that term a basically "cultural" approach, despite the fact that Schor, at least, is an economist. Though eventually diverging from Martyn J. Lee's position, our starting point is much the same as his. An initial observation must lie in the nature of the commodity, and a *leitmotif* must be what is the truth (of anything)? To Marx, as Lee notes, the point of the discussion of the nature of the commodity is that it reveals the exploitative nature of capitalism, and exposes production and the productive process at the root of the system. Unfortunately, at this early point, Lee directs our attention to Baudrillard who, he claims (not entirely accurately because of the sometimes elusive nature of Baudrillard's work), shifts the "centre of gravity" from production to consumption by challenging the supposedly artificial distinction between use and exchange value, there being nothing natural about human needs. Therefore, he argues, on behalf of Baudrillard:

> In the twentieth century this sign-value [the value-form] which attaches to commodities is increasingly determined by the powerful institutions of advertising, motivational research, and commodity promotion generally. These institutions grant consumer goods their meanings within a self-referential system of cultural meanings, calculating and recalculating their "worth" (their cultural meaning) according to the precise conditions of the (symbolic) "market"... With Baudrillard we have the clear and unequivocal assertion that consumption is as much a cultural activity and process as it is an economic one. (Lee, 2000, p. xiii)

I am uneasy about such a wholesale retreat to cultural arguments. Of course, at one level one can say glibly that there is a culture of consuming. But that is mere description. One can say advertisers are enormously powerful in designing that culture, and social explanations will enlighten us about how that culture is created. However, such arguments do not explain how it is that production remains as the primary force. The cultural arguments do what precisely Marx wanted to get away from and that was hiding the truth. To Marx, the truth revolved around the fact that commodities were composed of labour power. As far as I am concerned, the truth revolves around the way in which the producers have produced a new class, the exponents of the culture. However, I do agree with Lee's acceptance of the need to reject the "consumer is king" nonsense that has been propounded by those who seek to assure us that this is sheer observable common sense (Lee, 2000, p. xiv).

The reference to Bourdieu, largely uncritically represented by Lee, is no more helpful in uncovering the truth. The inequalities in what individual's consume are not a result of class fractions as they are of inequality which is persistent in the absorptive class. Some individuals are capable of more consumption of commodities than others. Airline pilots consume more than hospital nurses. Both, however, are well and truly in the absorptive class. Both absorb as much as they can. Both absorb the shocks that capitalism is heir to through their pension arrangements since both will most likely have a retirement plan funded through the financial sector. In the final paragraph of his introduction when he is forced to some sort of conclusion to the collection of interesting and thoughtful and wrongheaded essays that compose the volume, Lee writes: "whatever their primary focus, all the selections chosen for the *Consumer Society Reader* ultimately emphasize that consumption is first and foremost a political category..." (Lee, 2000, p. xxiv). That is a pity because if there is a first and foremost at all it is that that consumption is an economic category.

7. THE SACRED

While Marx has given us a peg on which to hang a discussion of the commodity in terms of fetishism, other sociologists have also given consideration to religious, quasi-religious or mystical concepts to discuss human responses to the commodity. The language of religion, as we have already noted, pervades much of Marx's discussion of the commodity. He introduces the notion of the sacred and profane in the *Communist Manifesto*: "All that is solid melts into air, all that is sacred is profaned, and man is at last compelled to face with sober senses his real condition of life..." It is this kind of statement that connects Marx significantly with Durkheim (Durkheim, 1995) to whom the concept of the sacred and profane was of central importance, probably as important as commodity fetishism was to Marx.

Durkheim arrived on the scene a couple of generations later than Marx, and at a time when the concern for the decline of religious belief was marked in Western Europe and when philosophers debated whether God was dead. Marx had already pointed out that Man made God rather than vice-versa and Darwin had finally pronounced himself at least an agnostic. Modern science required by technologically based industrial capitalism sat uneasily with religion, or, at least, the Church (in its various forms). "We must discover the rational substitutes," argued Durkheim dispassionately. He also brought to bear a number of interlocking ideas which support our main arguments, notably:

- Society is God
- Society is a thing in itself
- Society involves a conscience collective
- A person becomes human through society
- A human being is body, desire and appetite
- Poverty is a form of social control
- Nothing is sacred or profane unless made so by society
- Sacredness is "contagious," which generates restrictions to keep the sacred apart from the profane

- When the clan gathers the individual is transported from the profane to the sacred
- The more one has the more one wants.

This array of ideas took many books for Durkheim to spell out and we do not intend here to establish the arguments in full. Instead, what follows is a short discourse in the context of the relationship between the commodity, society and religion that explores whether the sacred–profane dichotomy helps in understanding the way in which the commodity is produced, promoted and received in society, and to what extent the commodity dominates the society in which it is produced.

Durkheim claimed that society was a thing in itself: society is considered to be a massive synthesis made up of countless interactions. While the individual obviously lives in society, and without society there is no humanity, he or she poorly understands the complexities that are involved and the consequences of actions are likely to be unintended. While Marx had introduced the idea of false consciousness on the part of the proletariat as a whole under conditions of capitalism, he believed the truth could be revealed. Durkheim by contrast believed that the "phenomenon of society is not dependent on the personal nature of individuals." Society dictates very generally speaking the context and the rules that determines the common behaviour of all. One of the key elements in the cohesive process was religion. In a world in which religion appeared to be fading, or where religion contributes to disintegration rather than cohesion, society requires some alternative cement. Current arguments connect Islamic resistance to a westernization that would be imposed as a result of the expansion of global capitalism, and Islamic resistance to the commodity is by implication a resistance to the way in which the sacred (the Koran, Islamic religious way of life, Islamic values, Sharia law) is attacked by commodity-based capitalism which threatens to become the all-pervading new religion. Other interpretations would have the resistance rooted in petty bourgeois opposition to big capitalism. For instance the support for current Turkish Islamic fundamentalism is funded to a considerable extent by small capitalists who are resisting, among other elements, foreign manufacturers, franchised retail operations and the like. Clearly, Islamic resistance to westernization, western imperialism and global capitalism comes from many sources, but religious-based resistance to the commodity is certainly of considerable importance.

Another feature of commodity-based capitalism is reinforced by the link with worship, which in most mass religions practised today is communal. Collectivities have for centuries gathered at prearranged dates and times to worship together, guided by the sun or moon or by man-made calendars or bonfires or church bells or carvings in the desert. The worship may also involve literally the consumption of fellow human beings as with the Mayans or Aztecs or by the symbolic consumption of the blood and body of Christ. In these processes, a class of people become significant and dominant not only in respect of the spiritual beings of men and women but over their temporal lives too. Now it is the temporal power that has with varying degrees of success striven to be the representative of all that is holy on earth. The fact that consumption may be part and parcel of the process of believing is of great importance (Veblen, 2001, Chapter XII). We have always consumed, or more accurately, absorbed our deity or deities, and we do it best in the company of our fellows. Sacred acts are collective ones. It is possible, therefore, to link this whole process with capitalist society which has essentially communal features because it requires considerable division of labour among its members to produce efficiently, even though capitalism appears to be the exact opposite: individualistic. Theories of individual action are essential to the misleading notion that society under advanced industrial capitalism is based on the individual: for instance, the so-called Austrian School of economists has been committed to promulgating this view through the work of Von Mises[7] and Von Hayek and lesser acolytes since the earlier part of the twentieth century. Of course, individual human action does take place, but production and distribution cannot occur without immense co-operation among human beings. For Durkheim this process is made possible by the existence, not of the individual's consciousness, but of the collective conscience that exists in every individual. Thus we have a similarity between economic behaviour and religious behaviour: they are communal, collective or cooperative acts that arise out of the needs and wants of the individual.

Durkheim argues that society is God apotheosized. This can be juxtaposed with the statement referred to at the outset of this chapter: society is the commodity. We can run together these assertions: society is God = society is the commodity = the commodity is God, despite the fact that the suggestion that the commodity is God seems outlandish to many. However, further arguments support a general line of argument that provides a significant place for seeing the way in which modern producer society has taken advantage of the deep-seated sacred tendencies that are entrenched in human existence. A helpful analysis is located in the work of the Romanian author on the nature of religion, Mircea Eliade. He calls the act of (religious) manifestation *hierophany*. Anything, he claims, can become sacred. It is all a matter of manifestation.

> By manifesting the sacred, any object becomes *something else*, yet it continues to remain
> *itself*, for it continues to participate in its surrounding cosmic milieu; a sacred stone
> remains a *stone; apparently* (or, more precisely, from the profane point of view), nothing
> distinguishes it from all other stones... the man of the archaic societies tends to live as
> much as possible *in* the sacred or in the close proximity to consecrated objects... the
> *sacred* is equivalent to *power* and... to *reality*. (Eliade, 1959, p. 12)

The preferred cosmos of man is the reality of the sacred. Eliade sees the
modern world as profane: "It should be said at once that the *completely*
profane world, the whole desacralized cosmos, is a recent discovery in the
history of the human spirit" (Eliade, 1959, p. 12). I am suggesting, however,
that the producer economy has (unwittingly) utilized the tendency that exists
within human societies to revert to the sacred. The commodity, therefore,
though apparently profane, increasingly manifests itself as sacred. The
atomization of society in the context of the ideology of individualism has
also led to the sacralisation of the home (or the individual's cosmos)
and coincides nicely with the increased tendency toward the narcissism of
the individual. In this way, the ultimate reductionist tendency is that the
individual narcissistic ego in the context of his home and possessions (his
cosmos) becomes God. It is seemingly within man to tend in this direction
no matter the kind of economy he inhabits. As Eliade puts it:

> "... beginning at a certain stage of culture, man conceives himself as a microcosm. He
> forms part of God's creation; in other words, he finds in himself the same sanctity that he
> recognizes in the cosmos... as a divine work, the cosmos becomes the paradigmatic
> image of human existence". (Eliade, 1959, p. 164)

Thus, it is not unreasonable to suppose that while human beings have
a strong tendency to revert to a sacred cosmos and, as individuals, to
suppose themselves to be sacred and to suppose their home to be an *imago
mundo*,[8] as Eliade puts it, the problem lies with the individual's perception
of the "other." His narcissistic tendency makes it almost impossible for
the individual thus produced to feel or act for the community except as
a largely narcissistic act to improve his own mirror reflection. To Eliade
the real modern tragedy is somewhat similar but sufficiently different to be
worth a mention. Eliade writes: "modern nonreligious man assumes a tragic
existence and that his existential choice is not without its greatness... but
he is also the work of religious man... he is the result of the process of
desacralization." This former world is always present to him and he is
"haunted" by that former world: "... that behaviour (of the former world)
is still emotionally present to him, in one form or another, ready to be
reactualized in his deepest being" (Eliade, 1959, p. 204). The producer
society has reinforced these deep-seated tendencies and the world of the

commodity is now the sacred world. However, this world is produced only by an economic process that reduces the sacredness of human life and renders it profane. This is the personal crisis of the individual within the absorptive class which blocks and/or distorts action.

We do not have to look far to find expressions of the sacred–profane dichotomy in a range of literature and observations. Roland Barthes wrote that now classical description of the Citroen DS which entered the automobile market in the late 1950s. He described the car as a cathedral. It was as if drivers no longer merely possessed wheeled transport but actually entered the house of God, not merely a church but a cathedral no less. Other commentators have noted this observation by Barthes. For instance, Dick Hebdige has noted that Barthes, referring to the Citroen, describes:

> "how the 'tangible' is made to intersect with the 'ethereal', the 'material' with the 'spiritual' through the convention of the annual motor show... He refers to the mystique of the object: the dual mystery of its appearance..to religious myths and stereotypes..to the transubstantiation of labour power into things, the domestication of the 'miracle' in use". (quoted by Schor & Holt, 2000, p. 118)

Barthes goes even further to suggest that the DS Citroen is the Goddess brought to the "heaven" of the Metropolis (Schor & Holt, 2000, p. 120). More recently, Eduardo Galeano, the Uruguayan polemicist, has written thus of the car (Galeano, 2001). "Cars are like Gods. Born to serve people as good-luck charms against fear and solitude, they end up making people serve them. The church of the sacred car with its US-based Vatican has the entire world on its knees. The spread of the car gospel has proven catastrophic, each new version deliriously multiplying the defects of the original." He continues: "Ferocious volleys of lead penetrate the blood with utter disdain, attacking our lungs, liver, bones and soul" (Schor & Holt, 2000, p. 204). Is he saying that we literally absorb our car-God? If we do, the appetite is enormous. Susannah Cullinane a BBC correspondent has noted a trend in the United Kingdom (let alone the United States) of the three or even four-car family despite 24 million cars already on the road. "One in five of British homes with 17–21-year olds living at home is classified as a four-car household," she claims. God is everywhere.

Essential to religious belief is the concept of the soul: an inner self, which guides the individual through life, informing behaviour and living on into the "next world." Marcuse wrote in 1962 in his celebrated philosophy of the age that attacked both capitalism and Soviet Communism, *One Dimensional Man*, that man's soul had become the commodity. "The people recognize themselves in their commodities; they find their soul in their automobile, hi-fi set, split-level home, kitchen equipment" (Marcuse, 1964/1991, p. 9). He goes further and points out that protest against the commodity even when it takes on religious appearances is simply digested or absorbed by the system.

> There is a great deal of "worship together this week," "why not try God," Zen, existentialism, and beat ways of life etc. But such modes of protest and transcendence are... the ceremonial part of practical behaviourism, and are quickly digested by the status quo as part of its healthy diet. (Marcuse, 1964/1991, p. 14)

It has long been the case that objects have been required to reify the concept of the holy or sacred or God: a crucifix, the Turin shroud, the bones of saints. Now commodities represent the sacralization of the producer economy.

For some time, on one of the worldwide cable channels ESPN, specialising in sport, viewers were invited to watch football (soccer) matches by entering the Temples of Football, that is the major stadiums around the world of such popular teams as Real Madrid, Manchester United and Bayern Munich. The events of commodified football are not mere games where young people show their prowess but have become places were the collectives meet either literally or via the television at prearranged times and ritually worship their Gods as ancient Greeks worshipped their deities. As we saw, Durkheim has already noted that the sacred becomes contagious. Moreover, when the family and clans meet together we have the most-intense religious moments of all. The advertising agency that designed the Temple of Football need not have read Durkheim to have identified the mass appeal of turning football into what is in effect a prayer meeting that reverses what the event once was, a profane hour or so of fun kicking a ball around. Nor is it surprising that at the games where most is at stake like cup finals or international matches, the mass singing of hymns and anthems precede the start of play. Nor is it surprising that such teams as Manchester United have successfully commodified the sport not only through the fees charged to spectators and through turning the players themselves into saleable, highly priced commodities, but also through the sale of such commodities as franchised shirts and boots and flags and other paraphernalia purchased by fans, which are sources of much greater revenue than attendance at live matches. Brazil, the almost perpetual world soccer champion, is seen as having the temple of temples by some commentators, notably Eric Hobsbawm who refers, in respect of Brazilian football, to visiting football matches as "pilgrimages" to "places of public ritual like Rio de Janeiro's Maracana Stadium (two hundred thousand seats), where Cariocas worship the divinities of futbol" (Hobsbawm, 1996, p. 294).

The modern Cathedral and sacredness is most evident and is most contagious is in the modern mall. Such texts as *The Malling of America* by William S Kowinski (1985), and Egotopia by John Miller (Miller, 1997), especially the first chapter on "Dark Satanic Malls," have drawn attention to the shopping mall, which to some is the most appalling outcome of modern society. The mall exemplifies the architectural and cultural desert where many of the malls have come to be located (Underhill, 2004). This is a long way from the original elegant mall, the shady broad boulevard that runs from Admiralty Arch to Buckingham Palace in London. Nevertheless, though in design shopping malls are a long way from The Mall in London and even further from the grandiose cathedrals and basilicas in Paris, Reims, Rome and Moscow, the modern shopping mall does have much in common with Cathedral architecture. The sheer space of the walkways, the enormously high ceilings, the chapel like boutiques, the fawning sales persons, many uniformed like priests, all treating the crisp new artefacts as if sacred objects to be carefully packaged and carried home to one's own private chapel in the sacred car...all reminiscent of the medieval Cathedral reaching to the heavens to glorify God. The modern Cathedral, on the other hand, is oddly unembarrassed in turning itself into a shopping arena where the consumer finds the sacred and profane apparently inextricably linked. For instance, at the Washington (DC) National Cathedral one can purchase, among many other mass-produced artefacts, the following:

- Tibetan Sceptre and Bell: essential to the ritual practice of Tibetan Buddhism. Price: $37.95
- Qiblah Compass and Prayer Rug: a handsome prayer rug and specially equipped compass – age-old tools of traditional Islamic spiritual discipline: $59.95
- Personal Labyrinth with Stylus: this personal labyrinth offers a tool for meditation that fits in the palm of one hand, while the other traces its way with the smooth wooden stylus. $30.95

Many religions have utilized the burning light in the form of a candle, or as with the temple light in Judaism, an eternal flame associated with the holiest of scriptures or the Hindu festival of lights. Now the flames burn in every home in the form of the television, which even when switched off, retains a vivid light indicating that electric power is still available: the same is true for the computer, the stove, the microwave, the telephone answering machine. The eternal flame guards our holiest commodities. (Most electricity is created by burning oil.) Of course, these connections demonstrating the new alignments and differentiations between the sacred and the profane may simply be fancy literary polemic, and will to some readers appear to be stretching matters through mere artful language. To them the deeper meaning suggested by this use of language may actually be absent. Semiology, indeed, does have its adherents as judged by the work of Barthes, Baudrillard and Eco, though it tends to be more Continental than Anglo-American. Nevertheless, to return to Durkheim we note that his contention was that sacred objects were so because they symbolized society. Thus, in modern times, we would expect the vast range of commodities as symbolizing society and, therefore, at least, from a sociological point of view, society would regard them as sacred. The next logical step, deriving from Durkheim, is that when men worship sacred objects, they, unwittingly, celebrate the power of their society. What is that power exactly that is being unwittingly worshipped? It is not the power to consume. It is the power to produce. What is sacred then is the producer, but not the direct producer, the labourer by hand or brain, but the owner of capital. This point is of the greatest importance in understanding why, in the society most dominated by capitalists, the USA, the capitalist and their associates can adopt, for instance, imperialist and profiteering activities, for instance, and be openly accepted rather than condemned.[9]

While some of these suggestions as to the religious nature of commodities may appear to be far-fetched, it is no more far-fetched than the suggestion to an atheist that Christ was the son of God or that there is a God or Gods of any sort. It is absurd to suggest to a Muslim that the Roman and Greek belief in a whole range of deities cavorting in the heavens could possibly be credible. On the other hand the atheist, while not believing in the existence of a God or Gods, may acknowledge that men and women who have become aware of their own mortality, may need a God, and where the faith in the existence of God has weakened, the commodity may fill a vacuum. Under capitalism, therefore, men and women are inclined to satisfy themselves by absorbing their God, the commodity, much as they have absorbed the body and blood of Christ for the last 2,000 years (It has been Christian-based societies that first produced the industrial revolutions that have led to huge quantities of commodities requiring absorption).

8. THE PROFANE

Durkheim argues that there is nothing in this world that is either sacred or profane. Society turns things, institutions, systems and processes into one or the other. My argument is that society reverses the recognition that was once held in pre-industrial societies (and is still the case in those societies). The human being is sacred in the sense that we worship the human race: Jews, Christians and Muslims believe that God made man in his own image. In many other religions across the globe from China and Japan to the native Americans, humans are worshipped via their ancestors. Under capitalism two changes have occurred. The human being is reduced to profane labour power while what he or she produces becomes sacred as we have seen. On the other hand, the pretence that the individual is at the core of market processes has led to the elevation of the ego, which, in essence, is the ultimate profanity. Chapter 6 dealing with the tendency of the rate of profit to fall deals with why human life has become profane, and the capitalist is himself rendered profane. Chapter 5 deals with the profanity of the ego.

NOTES

1. See I.I Rubin, www.marxists.org/subject/economy/rubin/1ind.htm "The theory of fetishism is, *per se*, the basis of Marx's entire economic system, and in particular his theory of value." See also Pilling (1980).

2. Also for *Capital* see Karl Marx internet edition: www.econlib.org/library/ YPDBooks?Marx/mrxCpC13.html#VolI

3. ESIB www.esib.org

4. Sennett (2006) calls this emptiness "uselessness".

5. detritus.net/contact/rumori/2/000067.html Also Heath and Potter (2004), Chapter One.

6. Orthodox medicine leaves much to be desired and is hugely commodified with doctors, insurance companies, pharmaceutical corporations and the like in prime position to benefit more than their patients. Nevertheless, modern medicine can list many triumphs over disease that cannot be similarly ascribed to considerable areas of so-called alternative medicine.

7. von Mises (1963). See Chapter VIII in particular "Human Society", p. 143 et seq. As with Adam Smith who had already provided the underpinning of the *Wealth of Nations* with his *Theory of Moral Sentiments*, so von Mises had underpinned his seemingly outrageous views expressed in *Human Action* with *Epistemological Problems of Economics*, first published in German in 1933; see von Mises (1960). See also Chapter 5 infra.

8. Eliade (1959, p. 179). "The 'house' – since it is at once an *imago mundi* and a replica of the human body...."

9. The invasion of Iraq was driven to a significant extent by the chance of profit associated with oil interests: electricity is created by burning oil, and it is oil that provides "eternal" light for our homes and its appliances: this would be far-fetched if it was not for the underlying Christian fundamentalism that drives much of US foreign policy.

CHAPTER 4

PRODUCTION OF THE CONSUMER SOCIETY UNDER CAPITALISM

1. PRODUCTION VERSUS CONSUMPTION[1]

Capitalism has proved to be by far the best society at producing surpluses. Other societies at particular points in history have been effective, too. For instance Ancient Egyptians were obviously good at it, directing their surplus into building pyramids and great monuments. The Mayans, Incas and Aztecs were good at it too, in the same way as were the Neolithic builders of Stonehenge in England, the Callinish stones in the Hebrides and Carnac in Britanny. Capitalism, however, is unique in the sense that its capacity to produce surpluses far exceeds that of any other period or system. In addition, the capitalist system involves a threefold possibility for the utilization of the surpluses: consumption by individuals, consumption by the state for civil and military purposes and reinvestment by capitalists to produce more surplus. The balance among these three determines the stability of the system and the pace of growth. Consumption by the state is the least new phenomenon; here again, the pyramids of the Aztecs, Mayans and Egyptians are examples. What is new, and certainly new on the scale we now observe, is that the capitalist system is dependent on those individuals who collectively make up the absorptive class, and on the host of small and medium capitalists and the huge corporations to reinvest the surplus to make more capital. However, the *system as a whole serves to destroy the surpluses* when capitalist processes are such that the capacity to consume diminishes in relation to the quantities produced.

Thus, in this section, we deal with a number of current perceptions and conceptions of the consumer, consumer society and consumption to demonstrate how ultimately all these approaches obscure a concrete reality. That reality involves accepting that overproduction lies at the heart of the injustices, inequalities and angst associated with consumption, and that the consumer is not sovereign. The system of production is sovereign. There are many important implications following from restoring "production" to its dominant position over "consumption" (Harvey, 2006, pp. 80–81).

For instance when we read this commonly held view: "Consumption had become a weapon in the cold war" (Reynolds, 2001) we can read more correctly: "The cold war was used as a weapon to expand consumption by the productive forces of the capitalist system." The route to a greater understanding of the capitalist process is to identify the relationships that exist at the simultaneous political, economic and social levels between production and consumption. Other examples include the ways in which governments and the state operate to win ideological dominance to protect what in the United States are called "special interests," to keep the ground as clear as possible for the concentration of capital and the minimization of controls over corporate power and for generating the overall impression that mass consumption is more or less the "end of history." Nevertheless, there remains a core of literature that identifies the fact that producers produce the drive to consume quite apart from those with a Marxist orientation where the theory demands a perspective based on the primacy of production.

> Influential representatives of the middle class and of the business community eventually realized the importance of matching mass production with mass consumption...Faced with excess productive capacity, industrialists and others realized that as consumers, workers should not be self denying...In the twentieth century, commodity consumption emerged as a way of life, a basic force that shaped American culture. (Daniel Horowitz, 1985, p. xxiii)

While the angst concerning the moral dangers of consumption are deeply entrenched in US cultural history (cf. Daniel Webster, Henry Thoreau and Francis Wayland), the critics of consumption have been steadily drowned out. The producers maintain their double lie: mass consumption is good and gets better, and the consumer is sovereign, not the producer.

The fact that economic growth is based on the sovereignty of the consumer is largely erroneous. The economy based as it is on production produces consumers. Establishing this is a major point of this article. However, the advertising industry, journalism, conventional wisdom, common parlance and much else convinces us that the consumer is king. Of course, simple observation of individual behaviour would instantly lead us to believe that the consumer is dominant in the market because of the apparent nature of choice. However, ever since Vance Packard's popular "sociology" of the fifties, the power of the "hidden persuaders" indicates that the consumers have their strings pulled by the marketers on behalf of the producers. Despite Packard's shock horror style he has done a service to critics of mass consumerism by demonstrating the way in which the advertising industry not only boomed in the 1950s but how the advertisers used all kinds of current "science" including especially psychology to ensure that consumers would buy and buy (Packard, 1958; 1961).

Missing in terms of emphasis is, of course, that the advertisers were only hand maidens of the producers and that the consuming power that was present had to come from somewhere. Nevertheless, Packard noticed early on that the consumer was far from sovereign and was being duped or persuaded by hidden forces to consume on an ever greater scale. In doing this, he was mounting a massive personal challenge to the standard ideological position, which remains largely unchanged to this day. For instance, *The Economist*, though not entirely uncritical of what happens in the world of orthodox economics, proudly announced on the front page of their issue of April 2–8, 2005, "POWER AT LAST, *How the internet means the consumer really is king (and queen): 14 page special report.*" It is odd, however, that the consumer can ever be considered as dominant in the market because orthodox economists argued early on in whatever text book you take to hand that demand, supply and price are intimately connected (theoretically). In the model where no single buyer dominates and no single supplier dominates, demand always tends to equal supply through the medium of price. Were the consumer to really dominate, the model would cease to operate. Consumers can be no more powerful, no more kinglike, than producers. Should the consumer be really kings and queens in the market, *The Economist* would have to help redraw economic theory (Their 14-page supplement does not deal with this issue). The reason for their headline is that the internet, it is claimed, is changing the process of consumption so that the consumer can gain knowledge and super awareness to such a level that producers must accede to this power provided by the information available on the World Wide Web. In short, the information revolution, it is falsely claimed, enthrones the consumer.

Many observations have been made about selling on the internet. The expansion of the market through the internet is no different from the opening of vast new shopping malls, re-establishing main streets, distance selling through catalogues and the rest. It is simply an expansion of the space for market operations. The fact that consumers may believe themselves to have more choice of products and to be more knowledgeable about products or to pay lower prices is neither here nor there. Simply because you allege the market to be more efficient does not make the consumer king. The market expands, more goods are sold, more goods are produced, new technologies and new techniques and experts (themselves commodified) come into existence. The internet is an expansion of the market place, and at the same time, the techniques and technologies are consumed. All this is dominated by producers, not consumers. It is a mystery why anyone, least of all *The Economist*, would want to see it as anything else unless it is simply its continued ideological obfuscation, an activity much practised in its 150 years of existence.

Indeed as we look closer at the content of the supplement we see the discussion departing from the headline. For instance in the section on Motoring Online, the article points out that Ford in the United States has shifted its expenditure on marketing so that 20% now goes on the internet rather than as in previous years (some 2%). "A website works like a living brochure. For example, Ford's F-150 pick-up truck, of which some 900,000 were sold last year [2004], is shown in graphic detail. There was even a series of videos in which rival trucks were cut apart and their components compared with the F-150. Users can check models and prices, browse through the inventory of local dealers or get a quote for the one they have designed for themselves using Ford's build-your-own option."[2] Quite clearly this is simply more advanced marketing with the sellers using ever more appealing techniques,[3] but using nevertheless the same techniques fundamentally that Packard pointed to in his *Hidden Persuaders*. Significantly using the internet to allow buyers to personalize their vehicle is all aided by and contributes to the narcissism which we discuss in more detail in the next chapter, and reinforces the argument expressed at the way in which the production of narcissistic personalities reinforce the whole process of consumption of commodities. In the case of cars, then, do the consumers buy cars over the internet? Well, no, according to *The Economist*. In fact nothing has really changed other than selling that has become more high-powered (turbo-driven!) "The dealership is more important than it used to be. People want to touch the vehicle, to smell the inside, to kick the tyres and to take it for a test drive." The dealership thus is unchanged, but new skills emerge. For instance one company (Edwards) can tell by the way car websites have been accessed whether buyers are simply interested or are actually going to buy. The development of software is in hand so that agencies can project up to a month ahead what demand will be made on their stock of cars. The internet is not making the consumer king: it is simply expanding the market in the interests of existing producers (car manufacturers) and generating new products (internet sales-forecasting software.)

Similarly, as *The Economist* points out, one outcome it discusses in "Target Practice" (the way in which advertisers are responding to technological changes) is the use of yet another associated new technology. "Satellite radio, which suddenly turned up in America in 2001, now has around 4 m. subscribers, providing a small but potentially interesting alternative audience." Producers, through their advertisers and marketers, leave no stone unturned, no new technique unexplored.[4] Thus, a more accurate headline than "Crowned at Last" would read: the consumer is not king, he is a hunted man! *The Economist* knows this only too well because the same article carries the following fact: "The average American (by which it means USA resident) is now subjected to some 3,000 marketing messages every day... Two-thirds of consumers feel 'constantly bombarded'."[5] This means advertisers, according to the same source, will find backdoor methods such as advertisements dressed up as editorials. However, it is true that many people can spot these tricks "and, if they can't, there are hundreds of news groups and bloggers on the web who will happily point it out to them. Today's consumers have plenty of champions."

Someone needs to point out the superficial shift of ground taken by *The Economist.* The text unequivocally points to the fact that, though consumers have a great deal of knowledge, that information is given to them by producers via their marketers and the consumer overall is no more powerful than he ever was. Bloggers are merely individual narcissists who are led to believe in the power of their views which are essentially, in the face of the power of capitalist system, entirely negligible. Maybe one day the contributors to *The Economist* might like to take a long think about their own 1843 mission: "to take part in a severe contest between intelligence, which presses forward, and unworthy, timid ignorance." *The Economist* becomes increasingly ignorant, if not so timid.

What is happening, this "consumer king" supplement tells us, is that there is a constant pressure to expand and find new ways to segment the market for all kinds of new products, bringing into being new technologies, new techniques and new occupational groups. The producers produce the media for sales and the consumers are produced for the whole process. Is the producer economy concerned about the expansion of the internet? Of course, not. While individual producers and distributors may be anxious and lose in the process, the producer economy clearly welcomes the change in the sense that the market is expanded as is the absorptive class itself; also reproduced is the ideological obfuscation that the consumer decides not the producers; further outcomes include the tendency toward the concentration of capital, increased productivity, de-skilling and the introduction of new skills and further occupational stratification.

The Economist writes "Having achieved power, consumers will not give it up." And then goes on to quote a Dell spokesman thus: "There's clearly no turning back. The market will get more fragmented, customers' needs will get more diverse, and sophistication and empowerment will continue to grow." Yet, *The Economist* has proved the opposite: the whole consumption business is dictated to by the producer economy. The quote should read: "There is clearly no turning back. The success in continuing to find new markets for our products through fragmentation and playing to the consumers' wants through their narcissism and image will continue with even greater effect. And the pretence of consumer sovereignty will aid us significantly in this struggle to produce more and keep up our rate of profit. We thank you at the offices of *The Economist* for supporting us in this endeavour by lending your 'reputation' to this ideological subterfuge that the consumer is king and queen and no amount of surface gender correctness will alter the situation." The argument, then, is that producers have produced consumers and continue to do so. I am not proposing anything particularly new as the literature on consumption abounds with arguments that forward the position that capitalist producers dominate the market rather than atomized individual consumers who are readily manipulated. Dick Hebdige quotes Paul Sweezy thus: that the need of modern capitalism is expressed by "the profound need of the modern corporation to dominate and control all the conditions and variables which affect viability."[6] Or, as Hebdige continues "the element of risk was to be eliminated through the preparation and control of the market."[7]

The history of the proposition that producers produce consumers has a long and respectable history as we can see from the work of Veblen and Galbraith and their heirs.

2. VEBLEN, GALBRAITH AND THEIR HEIRS

The founding fathers of the idea of a consumer society are Veblen and Galbraith[8] and their arguments and observations have been further developed by a number of others among whom are Alan Durning, Juliet Schor and Jean Baudrillard to whom reference will be made in due course.

Much has been written about Thorstein Veblen as an angry man and maverick economist. Times and observations have changed in very many ways in the last 100 years or so. But Veblen's analysis of *The Leisure Class* is helpful in the understanding of the way in which the absorptive class has been formed and currently functions. Certainly reading his work is irritating because he mixes his history and anthropological references in a seemingly random and in any case largely unreferenced way so that one is never sure what time or place he is writing about. Equally irritating is that though the word class pervades the work, it is never defined nor is it used consistently. Moreover, Veblen is concerned with the Leisure Class not directly with consumption despite the fact that the Leisured were becoming increasingly known for their consumption and owned the capital that produced the surplus. Nevertheless, several key points can be extracted which point to the formation of the absorptive class. Veblen argues that consumption generally speaking is linked to power, and wealth is an element in establishing and maintaining power: "In order to gain and hold the esteem of men it is not sufficient merely to possess wealth or power. The wealth or power must be put in evidence, for esteem is awarded only on evidence" (Veblen, 2001, p. 29). For our part we can take this statement further. While the rich and powerful must demonstrate both their wealth and power through consumption, we should also be able to say that if a person can make a show of wealth he may believe that he is esteemed as if he possessed wealth and power even though he does not possess either. In other words, the appearance or semblance of wealth and power can be had through the purchase of commodities. Such motivation thus becomes important in the regular storms of purchasing required to maintain advanced economies in the style to which they have become accustomed. And such a phenomenon is recognized by such contemporary critics as Juliet Schor (infra). Again, the much underrated Packard demonstrated the relationship between perceived self-esteem and the uses made of it in *The Status Seekers*, which, though dated and odd in places, is still worth reading.

Veblen deals at some length with the role of women in the extension of new markets, and this gives us the clue to understanding the processes that extend from production to consumption, and we shall see later how one key to expanding production has been the discovery of new consuming groups and the encouragement of their expansion. Veblen claimed that in some societies, past and present, women were kept as chattels and numerous wives indicated wealth in the same way as owning sheep or cattle. However, industrialization saw women as reproducers of labour, providers of labour power and, in post-industrial society, as consumers. To this extent women are increasingly allowed a degree of liberation or apparent liberation in that they serve more as consumers and less as reproducers of labour as the absorptive class is more visibly created. Whereas their earlier function was in terms of consuming vicariously for the head of the household, women increasingly consume in their own right as well as continuing their vicarious function not only on behalf of the head of the household but on behalf of the nuclear family as a whole (Veblen, 2001, p. 142). The "liberation" of women marks the turning point in the creation of the absorptive class whose key function is to keep the forces of production going through consuming. Here we are making the observation that the mobilization of disparate groups into homogenized groups (mass consumption) is as vital a development as is the contradictory development of the creation of specialized, disparate and niche groups in the interests of expanding markets for the ever hungrier producers. (In the more advanced societies supplying labour increasingly becomes a secondary function because this function is exported to the less developed countries.) Gender differentiation makes possible a form of specialist consumption which is compatible with the simultaneous need for homogenization of markets. Thus, it is not that boys and men have by nature a set of spending priorities: toys of war, clothes for soccer and dangerous sports, cars, tools for carpentry and metal work and that similarly women have a natural penchant for paper flowers, carpets and a demand for domestic-labour-saving machinery. The gender differentiation is promoted and exacerbated by the processes of production. Galbraith also picked up this point and took his cue directly from Veblen's observations:

> "In few other matters has the economic system been so successful in establishing values and moulding resulting behaviour to its needs as in the shaping of a womanly attitude and behaviour ... Without women to administer it, the possibility of increasing consumption would be sharply circumscribed. With women assuming the tasks of administration, consumption can be more or less indefinitely increased." (Galbraith, 1973, p. 37)

What we note, therefore, is a constant tension between homogenization of the market in the interests of mass consumption and the persistent search for new markets and extending production through the exploitation of new markets that have to be constantly created through the forces of advertising, marketing, design and technology. In the United States new social groups are constantly being transformed from such formerly repressed segments and groups or lower-class elements as gays and lesbians, Afro-Americans, Hispanics and so on. For instance if you look at www.wict.org, a site that is devoted to women in cable and telecommunications, you can click on such headings as "People of Color as an Economic Force" and this page will tell you about the spending power of minority groups that appear to be emerging as consumers with such comments as "From 1995 to 1998, people of color increased their spending on motor vehicles by 37.2%; the increase for Caucasians was only 13.4%." These kind of figures abound in the marketing and sales world, and contribute to the ever-increasing pressure by producers on consumers in every nook and cranny of the economy.[9] In fact the first attempts to cash-in on black liberation came very soon after the successes in the civil rights movements in the 1960s. Take this absolutely up-front statement in a book designed to identify ways to exploit the purchasing power of the liberated black communities:

> "The distinctive nature of the Negro revolution is that it is not a revolution to overthrow the established order as much as it is a revolution to achieve full membership of that order. Because material goods have such an important symbolic role in American society, the acquisition of material goods should be symbolic to the Negro of his achievement of full status."[10]

George Joyce calculated in 1971 that for the period 1968–1980 the black population would account for one quarter of the increase of population in the United States, and, what is more, calculates increasing disposable income by looking at employment trends (Joyce, 1971). Welcome to the absorptive class! By 1975, black consumers were well-known targets and there were those who were suggesting using the marketing techniques that were used to attack the black consumer to attack the female consumer (despite the fact that Galbraith and Veblen before him had recorded the importance of the female consumer in absorbing commodities). Marketers were finally seeing that the so-called liberation of women (women's lib in the 1960s) could be an inspiration for marketing strategy. Under the heading "The Negro and The Woman," Rosemary Scott wrote in 1975:

> The advertiser can learn a lot from the fact that the woman today is facing the same problems of advertising and media representation that faced the black a few years ago. The stereotyping, the incidence of representation in general media, all follow a similar pattern. Nevertheless, while the image of blacks as a cultural minority has tended to become more accurate and realistic in line with their emancipation, for women this has just started. (Scott, 1975)

The marketers were just getting round to make sure they had a clear target. It took a little longer to identify gays and lesbians as target markets, but sure enough the time has come and been around for 20 years or so. "Likened by some advertisers to a market that is 'upscale and cutting edge', gay and lesbian consumers have achieved a visibility unthinkable a few years ago." Indeed, as the juiciness of the market is referred to, you can hear the ring of cash registers:

> Increasingly, marketing specialists have found the demographics of gays and lesbians attractive. In a study sponsored by major gay newspapers, Simmons reported (for 1988) gay incomes well above national average, generated by high proportions of managers

and other professionals .... A readiness by gays to travel, use charge cards, and drink wines has not only attracted the trendy travel industry and vintners but the old guard of banking and tele-communications as well. More basic characteristics – high level of self-employment, concentration in top markets, heightened concern with well-being and stress – suggest a consumer group that is open to new technologies, health care, and self-improvement.[11]

While the author questions this picture a little, and suggests that the market is not all that easy to identify, the picture he paints is generally speaking now commonly accepted. In fact, gays and lesbians are just like anyone else in the absorptive class, but the marketers have an interest in segmentation to maximize their impact on chosen targets. Once out of the ghetto or the doll's house or the closet, the marketers will embrace you warmly assuming you have the capacity and they ensure that you generate the will to absorb. Gay and lesbian marriage will catch on in due course as there is massive absorptive power in weddings and setting up home.

Clothes for the couple, flowers, food, ceremony, music, photography, presents, hairdresser, cake, alcohol, accountant, postage, cards, advice and counselling, travel and lodgings for guests, hire of tuxedos or morning dress and honeymoon may not represent not a full list but already an expensive one.

The urbanization of consumption and the "privatization"[12] of consumption has become of vital importance in the context of the small nuclear family. Each family must have its own dwelling place with several rooms, each of which has to be filled, a garden or yard that requires its own lawnmower and gardening equipment and increasingly a car for every member of the family. Sub-urbanization is even better because everything can be placed at greater distances with greater consuming possibilities with a myriad of shopping innovations. The government will happily subsidize the building of roads but not the running of public transport. The individual may spend many hours of his life in queues and traffic jams and frustrated journeys but the economy continues to benefit. The individual consumes more by travelling by car than by sitting at home and moreover diversifies consumption by doing so. The reason public transport takes second place to private transport is that it serves the producer who produces more vehicles and extracts and refines more oil, it is not simply that the individual wants to keep up with the Jones's by buying a new car (though that helps but it is secondary). It is here that we can see clearly the playing out of the specialist versus homogenized markets. The car becomes mass produced, and then new brands develop the market possibilities until the new versions become mass produced. In the United States, the phenomenon of the pick-up truck and the SUV are examples of how the niche markets move to homogenization. Again, note that this process derives its dynamics from the producers (and their salesman) rather than from the consumer. There is nothing more ridiculous than large numbers of over powered, heavy weight four-wheel drive vehicles vying for city parking space.

One way in which it is apparent that production takes precedence over consumption is in the context of waste. If we believe that the economic system is about surpluses then there can never be waste. All consumption and production serves the system. Only if we believe that there is such a phenomenon as scarcity can we believe in waste. Technically, for our purposes, therefore, there can be no waste. Veblen is interesting on this issue. Waste, trash, rubbish and recycling worry us a lot because of concern with non-renewable resources and issues related to so-called sustainable development. Veblen, however, was keen to describe the rational nature of waste. : "waste . . . is not to be taken in an odious sense." He argues that once a convention has been formed in relation to the usefulness of starched linen or tapestries or tablecloths, the expenditure ceases to become waste. The interesting point is that this conversion of waste to useful expenditure must "conduce to the particular consumer's gratification or peace of mind." Clearly if no such full gratification is afforded, the individual consumer will become uneasy as he becomes aware that the expenditure on the commodity has been a "waste." Much angst, therefore, doubtless accrues to those who are uneasy about their expenditure on commodities that do not appear to them to be of use any longer. Hence, the individual will live in a state of repressed or only partial uneasiness, constantly having to find ways of justifying expenditure, disposing of commodities to "poorer" people (which merely encourages his expenditure on other commodities), actually describing commodities from time to time as waste and discarding them before their "usefulness" is over and so on. Even worse some people hoard commodities and can scarcely be persuaded to empty their attics, cellars or storage units, keeping their commodities as the skeletons of the dead labour that is incorporated in the commodity.

The important thing is that the bulk of commodities have no or little or only partial[13] use value; therefore, the owner may keep them or destroy them. It really does not matter which he or she does. What does matter is producing them. Junking commodities is not wasteful because more can be purchased from the producer. Waste is functional because it maintains the system of production. This is not a new observation in that much has been written on the concept of planned obsolescence and first came to greatest prominence in the work of Vance Packard (Packard, 1960) in the 1950s and 60s. Of course, there is more to waste than planned obsolescence.

Waste is all around us and is contained in the goods and services that are provided solely to satisfy wants. There is also the concept of waste in production rather than wasteful expenditure by the consumer. This is, for instance, discussed in Baran and Sweezy. They point out that, though observers and critics like Packard are worthy in their aim of criticizing the behaviour of large corporations in respect of their apparently wasteful processes of manufacture, packaging and sales, they have little interest in true comprehension of the economic system, and they remind us of the limitation of such an approach by quoting Marx: "the strength and the weakness of that kind of criticism which knows how to judge and condemn the present, but not how to comprehend it."[14] Thus, consumer groups are marked by good intentions, poor understanding and impractical solutions.

Baudrillard's response to waste is partially Veblenesque, and tends to the social rather than the economic. Thus: "All societies have always wasted, squandered, expended and consumed beyond what is strictly necessary for the simple reason that it is in consumption of the surplus, of a superfluity that the individual – and society – feel not merely that they exist, but that they are alive" (Baudrillard, 1998, pp. 42–47). Consumption takes place because of the nature for instance of gaining esteem through destruction of commodities. He also does keep sight of the "economic" only seemingly to dismiss its importance. For instance, he goes on:

> " ... a definition of consumption as consummation i.e. as productive waste – begins to emerge, a perspective contrary to that of the 'economic' (based on necessity, accumulation and calculation) and one in which, by contrast, the superfluous precedes the necessary, and expenditure takes precedence in terms of value of accumulation and appropriation ...." (Baudrillard, 1998, pp. 42–47)

His summary is in the form of a semi-rhetorical question: "does not affluence ultimately have meaning in wastage?" But he does not answer the question in terms of production but in terms of consumption so that Baudrillard, who one might have thought would resist the consumer is king ideological pressure, does the opposite. In the West, at least, the impassioned biographies of heroes of production are everywhere giving way to biographies of heroes of consumption (who are further described as great wastrels) who "fulfil a very precise social function: that of sumptuary, useless, inordinate expenditure." It is his concern for the *social* function of wasteful expenditure that dominates Baudrillard's thought and the acceptance of this kind of thought disguises the real process which is the economic function where there is no waste, only production. The consumers, whether it is Richard Burton buying a ring for Elizabeth Taylor, or Michael Douglas and Catherine Zeta-Jones throwing a million dollar wedding breakfast, are mere products of an economy based on production of surpluses. The "economy" does not "care" that much how the consumption takes place: it simply has to happen on a vast scale. Baudrillard tells us *how* it happens, not *why*.

One of Veblen's starting points is to say that in earlier societies or more primitive societies conspicuous consumption was intimately related to religious practices. In discussing the consumption of commodities in the modern period, he frequently seems to ascribe to the commodity an ability to fulfil spiritual needs " . . . the conspicuously wasteful honorific expenditure that confers spiritual well-being may become more indispensable than much of that expenditure which ministers to the 'lower' wants of physical well-being or sustenance only" (Veblen, 2001, p. 77). He refers to the wealthier classes as performing "quasi-sacerdotal office." He argues that the purchase of clothes, in particular, fulfils some "higher" or spiritual need.

Among some of Veblen's most acute observations are those that relate to smaller family size and its development of ever higher per capita consumption. Thus falling family size does not reduce but increases consumption both in total and per capita. Interestingly, therefore, the historical trend runs from increased consumption to smaller families to higher consumption per capita to higher gross consumption. Again, there may be some long-term benefits if the planet were able to sustain this process whereby eventually the world population would decline but the productive capacity would increase for a time and then the potential might develop for its gradual stabilization. The decline in the number of children in the more affluent parts of the world as well as elsewhere (especially in the former Soviet Union and satellites) is now more than ever clearly observed. Many authors see this as a crucial turning point in world history, some pessimistically, others less so. Emmanuel Todd believes for instance that a decline in the size of the family plus increasingly literacy is a sign that the future of the world is more less safely assured (Todd, 2003).

On the face of it the effect on the absorptive class of a declining birth rate might be supposed to be catastrophic: fewer rich people, less capacity to absorb. The opposite is the case. The decline in the size of the family simply leads to high levels of consumption by the absorbers per capita and nowhere is this truer than in the case of children. Underpinning this argument is the extended observation by Juliet Schor, for example, that details the way in which children, diminishing in numbers, become special targets for the producers. The producers of commodities simply redouble their efforts to ensure that, echoing the title of Schor's book, children are born to buy.[15]

"The architects of this (consumer) culture – the companies that make, market, and advertise consumer products – have now set their sights on children." Schor claims that in recent years the magnitude of the shift of attention of manufacturers and their lackeys to children has been enormous. "The typical American (sic) child is now immersed in the consumer market-place to a degree that dwarfs all historical experience" (Schor, 2004, p. 19). Susan Linn, writing in 2004, puts the advertising budget devoted to mani-pulating children at $15 billion in the United States. Despite the Children's Advertising Review Unit, the self-regulating body of the advertising industry, advertising directly to children has, she claims, "exploded" in recent years (Linn, 2004, p. 195 et seq.). Two-thirds of children have televisions in their bedrooms in the United States and the average child sees about 40,000 commercials per year.

3. JOHN KENNETH GALBRAITH AND THE DOMINANCE OF PRODUCTION

Galbraith not only brought the attention of the world to the existence of *The Affluent Society* he did so by stressing the importance of production. Unhappily those that have some recall of what he did say seem only to remember that he bemoaned the nature of a consumer society. Galbraith was cleverer than that.

It is in Galbraith that we find a number of arguments that take us closer to the discovery of the absorptive class. Above all, while Galbraith might be supposed by the casual reader to be discussing the so-called consumer society or consumerism, he is in fact hammering home the fact that produc-tion takes precedence over consumption in any serious economic analysis. Nor was he afraid or embarrassed at the mention of Marx. His admiration for Marx in Chapter 6 and in Chapter 9 which is actually entitled "The Paramount Position of Production" plus the emphasis also in Chapters 12, 16 and 20 all stress unequivocally that capitalism is driven by the forces of production. Consumption is the outcome of production. Moreover, consumers are not too sure of what they are doing. Indeed, the opening words of the book are: "Wealth is not without its advantages ... but, beyond doubt, wealth is the relentless enemy of understanding." Galbraith never loses sight of the fact that the capitalist system is about produc-tion: "The trouble was (according to Marx) that the purchasing power of the workers did not keep abreast of what they produced"

(Galbraith, 1958/1996, p. 57). And he recognizes that in the analysis of capitalism Marx is always holistic. "No one before, or for that matter since, has taken so many strands of human behaviour and woven them together... On class conflict, or imperialism, or the causes of national war, Marx was bound to be influential, for he was the only man who had offered an explanation which was all integrated with the rest of human experience" (Galbraith, 1958/1996, p. 59). Moreover he recognizes the importance and visibility of class: "Yet classes obviously existed" (Galbraith, 1958/1996, p. 61). These attributes make Galbraith one of the most important economists to have criticized the capitalist system in the twentieth century and well worth acknowledging. Despite his efforts (and perhaps because he did not resort to equations) economists were unwilling to concede the existence of class or of the importance of the primacy of production or of the need to avoid separating economics from political analysis. This is still true, more so than ever. High levels of production are universally applauded, argued Galbraith, adding cynically that "it is a relief on occasion to find a conclusion that is above faction, indeed above debate" (Galbraith, 1958/1996, p. 99). Moreover, it is universally conceded that increases in production and productivity are driven by technological changes, and that the bulk of people applaud investment whatever the outcome. Few voices argue that investment could be more rational or useful or effective at solving social problems. Generally, therefore, we applaud what presents itself but rarely criticize what we do not have. Few of us have any idea of what is missing. It is only in certain kinds of crisis that we might break out from the constraints imposed by conventional wisdom. For instance: "there is an interesting proof of the point in the increase in production which, in the past, we have regularly achieved during the war or under the threat of war" (Galbraith, 1958/1996, p. 107). Indeed, economists studying economic history are able to identify many occasions where war has appeared to have been beneficial to particular national economies, possibly ignoring the detrimental effect simultaneously to others. In peace time we regard some frivolous production with pride and others with regret. Always, however, private production takes precedence over publicly produced goods and services in contrast with war economies when public production takes precedence over private, though the public production of goods are largely destined for destruction. We are "persuaded of the dire importance of the goods we have without our being in the slightest degree concerned about those we do not have. For we have wants at the margin only so far as they are synthesized. We do not manufacture wants for goods we do not produce" (Galbraith, 1958/1996). Writing in 1959, Galbraith could argue that the "widely accepted" theory of consumer demand was based on two propositions:

1. "that the urgency of wants does not diminish appreciably as more of them are satisfied"; indeed wants can never be satisfied.
2. "that wants originate in the personality of the consumer". (Galbraith, 1958/1996).

Moreover, as society becomes increasingly affluent, wants are increasingly created by the process of production in a society of increasing expectations. Galbraith calls this the Dependence Effect. However, he observes that the general theory of consumer demand is "peculiarly treacherous" because it hides the fact that it is production which creates consumer desires. The individual psychology that brings about the dependence effect is itself produced by the system of capitalist production. Increased production is dependent (generally speaking) on the contrivance of demand. He is thus led to observe that: "the attitudes and values which make production the central achievement of our society have some exceptionally twisted roots" (Galbraith, 1958/1996, p. 131). It follows, he argues, that we should take account of the "Vested Interest in Output." Or put another way, it is clear that the individual with greatest stake in the present economic goals is the businessman. We can conclude that while the capitalist system of production remains in being in its present dominant position, production largely determines the nature of our society and of our daily lives. Advanced economies appear to be dominated by the drive to consume, but this drive itself is the outcome of the process of production. Nowhere is this better stated in Frederick Pohl's satire set in the futuristic Midas world.[16] The story pictures a society where the poor are bound by law to consume vast quantities of goods and services whereas the rich can spend time working and are privileged by not having to consume. Interestingly enough Frederick Pohl wrote his pivotal and perceptive science-fiction story which presaged the formation of the absorptive class in 1954. The story opens with a tearful wife who is desperately unhappy at being poor and longs to be rich. The rich have very few possessions and even talk in clipped sentences. The poor are required to consume huge amounts of commodities in the form of things and services. She is absolutely fed up with her 22-room house, new clothes every day and holidays almost every week. The poor are required to spend almost every hour of their lives consuming and wearing out products as fast as they are produced and complain bitterly about the quotas that have to be consumed by the robot manufacturing system. The individual ceases to be a human and becomes as robotic as the robotic producers.

To Galbraith the fact of a producing society is not the problem, however. The problem is *what* is produced since there is an "implacable tendency to provide an opulent supply of some things and a niggardly yield of others." More specifically private goods and services take precedence over public goods and services (except those required by the warfare state). This correct emphasis on the primacy of production over consumption in economic analysis has become somewhat attenuated more recently as we shall see in the next section.

4. OTHER COMMENTATORS

Galbraith has not been followed by other economists in the sense that the primacy of production has been obscured by an over concern with consumers and the so-called consumer society.[17] One example is the work of Juliet Schor whose books include *Born to Buy: The Commercialized Child and the New Consumer Culture*, Scribner, 2004 and *The Consumer Society Reader*, *The New Press*, 2002. The problem with her well-intentioned approach is the heavy reliance on what she calls new consumerism in her analysis. While she briefly refers to production, the bulk of what she has to say is concerned with consumption. For instance, in terms of prescription she argues that we "should" aim to consume differently as if the consumer is able to be in control of anything much; neither size nor quality of appetite seems to be under control, and this is true of such things as cars, appliances, furniture and furnishing, leisure, pharmaceuticals as it is of food and drink given the horrendous degree to which US citizens tend toward obesity. Juliet Schor talks about "competitive consumption" and about the sacrifice of human lives to longer hours of work to find the resources to consume more and to live a debt-burdened lifestyle.

In other words the thought process goes: the nuclear family (the main consuming unit) is pressed to work longer hours, encourage multiple wage-earners in the family, consume goods and services, including so-called education and in the process experience a permanent angst of dissatisfaction. As these arguments proceed, however valid they are, we are noting the *effects* on the consumer of having contrived wants being produced as part of the producer society. The danger, then, is to see the solutions as being in the hands of the individual: consume differently (this is still consumption), work less (this means consuming leisure), save more (consume financial instruments). None of these "solutions" are solutions at all because the producing society simply produces new wants. Juliet Schor proposes solutions that stem from the consumer *qua* consumer: "The basis of a new consumer policy should be an understanding of the presence of structural distortions in consumers' choices, the importance of social inequalities and power in consumption practices, a more sophisticated understanding of consumer motivations, and serious analysis of the processes that form our preferences."[18] However, none of this will make one jot of difference to the producer for, as we have seen, if you block the producer in one way he will emerge in another place. Also, as we have seen, if the consumer as worker works fewer hours he will be induced to buy leisure or relaxation or therapy: leisure time will be attacked by travel agents, real-estate agents offering second homes, producers producing more fishing tackle or surf boards or hammocks; there will be more classes in foreign languages, Tai-Chi, flower arranging; there will be more cable channels and electronic gadgets and games; more home-improvement stores and more cook books and so on seemingly endlessly. The claim that the consumer is sovereign is arrant nonsense. The claim that the market is remotely perfect is, like-wise, manifestly wrong. The imperfections of the consumer are only to be expected because consumers are being manufactured in much the same way as the commodities are for purchase. The whole ideological hegemony within capitalism is aimed at producing perfect consumers but the system is not perfect. This does not matter as long as it produces so-called effective demand, which tends, generally, to maintain the system. (Why should we expect perfection in the consumer? Isn't this an application of the tendency toward narcissism?) Where she is stronger is on the issue of work, at least in identifying the importance of the fact that despite higher and higher living standards, measured by a combination of ownership of things, access to services and increased longevity and better health provision. As she observes the typical tendency in the United States is for adults to work more rather than less, and the same tendency is being observed in the United Kingdom. Historical trends would have the affluent working fewer hours. In nineteenth century conditions in Britain and elsewhere during the industrialization process, factory workers would typically work 12-hour days for six days per week, and that was following the Factory Act provisions. As time progressed, the working day and the working week shortened, partly as a result of working-class pressure, but largely as a result of rising levels of productivity, increasing economic efficiency and technological change. The gross income levels available in any one national economy needed to stay in balance with the capacity to produce goods and services. Productivity levels are now so high (and nowhere as high as in the United Staes), yet the working day, which one might expect to be shrinking, is expanding.

Writing in 1991, Juliet Schor remarks: "In the last twenty years the amount of time Americans (sic) have spent in their jobs has risen steadily. Each year the change is small, amounting to about nine hours ... [but] ... the accumulated increase over two decades is substantial." This is followed by the observation that most people in the United States are driven by the work-and-spend cycle. Aronowitz, among others, has also observed the odd phenomenon that US workers spend more time at their workplace: "because people can't earn a living by performing only one job or by working eight hours a day, more and more take on two jobs; industrial workers accept all the overtime they can get just to pay the bills, so life is experienced as work without end ... We have become a nation of pill poppers because many of us suffer from severe stress owing to overwork born of mounting bills amid job insecurity ... We are in the throes of 24/7 ... This is the era of the twenty-four hour supermarket" (Aronowitz, 2003, p. 214). The United Kingdom is not far behind where the day has also been extended into night. Seven million workers in Britain have night jobs and this is due to double in the next few years; workers in the United Kingdom now work longer hours than those in Continental Europe where welfare capitalism in a number of countries is making a last ditch stand. New technologies like Blackberry and the ever-present cell phone extend the working day. All this is in the interest of making the shock absorbers more effective. To Emmanuel Todd this tendency toward long hours and overwork is also part of a worldwide absorptive process thathas become an especial burden for the US "middle class." "A declining and indebted middle class (in the USA) cannot serve much longer as the market of first resort for countries trying to export their way to prosperity" (Todd, 2003, p. xi).

What is being observed is the process whereby the absorptive class is being produced. The answer is not as is frequently suggested simply to find ways of taking "leisure time" because the way in which leisure is conceived is a trap in itself.[19] As we have seen in the previous chapter, leisure itself becomes commodified. If I trade work for not working I must be sure of being totally uninvolved in the process of absorbing commodities. Cycling, running in specially designed shoes or other apparel, playing tennis, reading a book or magazine I have specially purchased for my leisure time, taking photographs, painting a canvas on an easel, digging a pond and filling it with bought plants and goldfish, travelling to Machu Pichu or the Great Wall of China, eating out instead of at home, going to the cinema or bowling, watching Chelsea win at the Champions League or Andy Murray win his first Grand Slam – all are part of the process of absorbing commodities or absorption of the surplus. Genuine leisure that does not involve absorbing the surplus is hard to find. Leisure in the form described requires a share of the surplus, and we members of the absorptive class usually have to work for it. Genuine leisure involves not absorbing and not acquiring the wherewithal to pay for commodities in the form of goods or services. The producer economy does not want you to do that. That's why the system demands longer hours and indebtedness to maintain the stick of work rather than the carrot of more or less non-existent leisure.

Sadly, one of the few things that the producer economy cannot manufacture is true, unadulterated leisure.

5. JEAN BAUDRILLARD

Baudrillard became for a time the doyen of analytical and theoretical analysis of the consumer society. Important in his approach is the concept of surplus and the relationship of that concept to needs and wants. He asserts strongly that there have never been "societies of scarcity"[20] or societies of abundance for that matter because whatever the perceived case the production of the surplus regulates the whole (of society) and that the thresholds of abundance and scarcity are always regulated from above. Indeed, adopting standard economic concepts he argues that in fact production is not the point, but productivity is because this makes possible the surplus. Interestingly, Baudrillard, in a footnote drifts off into a science-fiction reverie. "Robots," he writes, "remain the ideal phantasm of a total productivist system. Still better, there is integrated automation," but this, he insists "amounts to the aim of all productivity, which is a political goal." Oscar Wilde, in the *Soul of Man Under Socialism*, thought that machines would free men if used properly under socialism. It was not that the machines were good or bad but the political system under which they operated. To Baudrillard the marked feature of the modern day man is that he is not so much surrounded by other "human beings but by objects ... and we live at the pace of objects." The explanation for this, however, is not always convincing. For instance at one point he writes: "All societies have always wasted, squandered, expended and consumed beyond what is strictly necessary for the simple reason that it is in the consumption of a surplus, of a superfluity that the individual – and society – feel not merely that they exist, but that they are alive." However, it is not clear how Baudrillard knows this to be the case. Nor does he explain the link between the individual and that vaguest of terms "society." The point, as we repeat often, is that under capitalism it is really the class, not the individual, which is constructed to consume. The absorptive class is functioning on behalf of the capitalist class that has created it for just that purpose.

However, class does enter Baudrillard's analysis. For instance, he claims: "Consumption, like education, is a *class institution:* not only is there equality before objects in the economic sense (the purchase, choice and use of objects are governed by purchasing power and by educational level, which is itself dependent on class background etc) – in short, not everyone has the same objects, just as not everyone has the same educational chances – but, more deeply, there is a radical discrimination in the sense that only some people achieve" (Baudrillard, 1998, p. 59). His conception of class in this somewhat inelegant sentence is the old conception of class referring no doubt to lower-income groups (proletarians) and higher-income groups (bourgeois elements). All this is to miss the point. The enforced consumption of goods by producers has unified former disparate elements to form a unified class, the absorptive class, and this process continues daily and is ever more widely and deeply consolidated. Baudrillard's concern for inequality has hidden from view what unifies what might be called "the not rich" from the better off: their capacity, to a greater extent, and enforced willingness to consume the products of the capitalist system. The affluent worker or his slightly less-affluent co-worker is in terms of function absolutely no different from the airline pilot or chartered surveyor. Baudrillard also attacks the concept of scarcity, which as we have seen is so erroneously at the centre of the modern economic theory. He writes for instance of the "obsession with scarcity characteristic of the market economy" (by which he means neoclassical orthodox economists) and goes on to observe, correctly: "Since what is satisfied in a growth society, and increasingly satisfied as productivity grows, are the *very needs of the order of production,* not the 'needs' of man (the whole system depends indeed on these being misrecognized), it is clear that affluence recedes indefinitely: more precisely, it is irrevocably rejected and the organized reign of scarcity (structural penury) preferred." He repeats this idea of misrecognition elsewhere as one might expect as false consciousness is crucial to all Marxist writing on the proletariat. "Overall, then, consumers as such are lacking in consciousness and unorganized, as was often the case with workers in the early nineteenth century" (Baudrillard, 1998, p. 86). Issues related to the consciousness or otherwise of the absorptive class are discussed in Chapter 7 infra.

In many ways that position of Baudrillard's brings this work closer but not nearly identical with Baudrillard's position on at least two grounds: that of misrecognition in general and the other on the question of how the overt concern with scarcity disguises the covert centrality of the surplus. It is thus also easy to agree with a further point. "The truth is, not that 'needs are the fruits of production' but that the system of needs is the product of the system of production" (Baudrillard, 1998, p.74). This leads to the position I do have in common with Baudrillard: "...all is clear if we accept that needs and consumption are in fact an organised extension of the productive forces." However, where I part company is on *how* the individual is differentiated from the class and the existence of the class (the absorptive class) that functions to produce the individuals within it. The scale and differentiation between individuals who consume is not the important issue: what is important is that the class consumes: it is this mass which is of importance just as what Marx and Engels saw at one historical moment, the proletarian mass, which they considered to be the motor force of history in the nineteenth century. Of course, Baudrillard does not abandon the differing conceptualization as between the individual function and the collective function. In the process of discussing the process of enjoyment he says: "The truth of consumption ... is that it is a ... function of production ... not an individual function but an immediately and totally collective one" (Baudrillard, 1998, p. 76). He does not explain however how the collective function is manifested, how it coheres, or how it has been formed. While the concept of class is precise, the concept of the collective is not. Nor is this acceptance of the collective extended much beyond the enjoyment process. Nevertheless, it is important always to make this distinction between individual behaviour and individual responses on the one hand, and, on the other, the generality of the function of the class as a whole.

It is Galbraith, writing in the 1970s, who is the clearest and most instructive on the importance of production. He writes in *Economics and the Public Purpose:*

> How economic resources – capital, manpower, materials – are allocated to production, both in the public and private sectors of the economy, depends, and heavily though not exclusively, on producer power. And, with the development of the economy, it depends increasingly on that power. This is the basic tendency of the economy. In the neoclassical model production is controlled by consumer and citizen choice...(but) in the modern reality the equilibrium reflects the power of the producer...Production is not great necessarily where there is great need...Discussion of the practical issues associated with this overproduction – and the underproduction of other things – can only be avoided if it is agreed that the consumer and citizen are resistant to the power of the producer...if advertising and salesmanship are the froth and not the substance of economics....
> (Galbraith, 1973, p. 144).

In other words, in reality the producers hold power while the neoclassical economists obscure the truth with their insistence on consumer sovereignty.

Before leaving the issues raised by the dominance of production over consumption we need to look briefly at the key theory in modern economics that sets out to prove the opposite, the theory of effective demand.

6. THE THEORY OF EFFECTIVE DEMAND

Intimately related to the discussion of the consumer is the question of "demand" which can be traced in its modern form to Britain as it experienced the first industrial revolution, during the years 1770–1830 or thereabouts, and also the point at which modern economics began with Adam Smith, Ricardo and James Mill. It is also the case that modern economic fluctuations begin in Britain from the last quarter of the eighteenth century onwards, and that early debates revolved around both the causes of such fluctuations and around possible policy solutions to them. In the process of industrial production three classes were identified by Ricardo: landlords, capitalists and labourers. If there were gluts (unconsumed goods) causing economic crisis and, therefore, social unrest, the causes needed to be discovered and remedies sought. In the immediate period following the end of the French Revolutionary and Napoleonic Wars in 1815, Britain experienced high levels of unemployment, slowing up of industrial activity and trade generally which appeared to give rise to such spontaneous outbursts of protest as the Peterloo massacre in Manchester and the Cato Street conspiracy aimed at assassinating the prime minister and the whole of his cabinet. To the ruling class(es) in Britain, it seemed that they had spent two decades setting Europe straight after the French Revolution, and it was clearly important to ensure economic stability in the interests of achieving social stability at home. While the cause of the social unrest was laid at the door of economic crisis, what could be the causes of the failure of the economy to perform satisfactorily? One answer came from Thomas Robert Malthus. He raised the question of effective demand: that is, he argued that there should be an increase in consumption. This could not be done by labourers as their wage levels needed to be maintained at a low level in the interests of production and capitalists were required to save to provide the necessary capital for investment. This meant the income of the *rentier* landowners should be boosted and would be the source of consuming power to sustain a buoyant industrial economy. His friend, David Ricardo, however, argued that boosting or protecting the landowner was, in effect, exploitation of the industrial classes, the labourers and capitalists. In practical policy terms, this meant protecting

British agriculture, especially the producers of wheat, from foreign competition to maintain the level of rents and sustain the wealth of the aristocracy which owned most of the best agricultural land. The protection for the landed class did stay in place for a generation and not finally repealed till the 1840s; thus Malthus's view did remain for some time as the primary justification for the maintenance of the economic and political power of the old aristocracy. Hence, apart from the development of economic theory that was occasioned by this Ricardo-Malthus debate, we do see the fact that much of economics is used to justify ideological positions in support of those in power. In that sense it was a nineteenth century equivalent of the Keynes-Friedman policy arguments that marked the last quarter of the twentieth century and have continued through the crisis of 2007–2009. Though it took some time for policy to match the theory when it came to tariff protection for the aristocracy, orthodox economists took it that, as we shall see, supply creates its own demand. This important theoretical position subsequently came to revolve around the importance of "effective demand"; it was the crises of the 1930s that put the discussion of demand, and therefore, consumption by individuals and the state, as being much more central than ever before, especially in terms of economic policy analysis and formation.

The discussion of effective demand becomes a matter of concern to economists at a point where the capitalist economy is slowing or in actual decline. The earlier theories of demand assumed that supply created its own demand, assuming continuous capital accumulation and labour mobility (and non-interference by government in regulating the economy as far as wages or prices were concerned). This theoretical position is usually ascribed to the remarkably successful manufacturer and university professor Jean-Baptiste Say (Harvey, 2006, p. 75 et seq.) whose law was viciously attacked by Marx. This story of how the theory of equilibrium in classical economists held some sort of sway until it gave way to the Keynesian theories of aggregate demand has been told many times in a variety of versions with varying force (Keynes, 1936/1973). For our purposes, the important early position of Say states the reductionist case: supply creates its own demand. This classical doctrine had held sway for the whole of the nineteenth century and into the twentieth, and was also very much part of the Anglo-Saxon tradition, despite its French origins. James Mill, the father of John Stuart Mill, and popularizer of Smith and Ricardo wrote categorically in 1820: "...men consume for the sake of production" (Mill, 1963, p. 221). This insight early on put the producer in prime position, but has since been lost. At a crude level it also appears rather obvious. Consumers do not conceive of, design, manufacture and market iPods or Hollywood movies or digital cameras or cell phones. Suppliers do that and then create the demand (with varying degrees of success).

So-called effective demand comes in two ways: first, it may be created by policy or arises out of the interests of the producer class and through their political processes, and secondly it is created by the capitalist system that "knows" the importance of effective demand, or put another way, under capitalism and in favourable circumstances, supply, indeed, does create its own demand. Keynes in re-drawing economic orthodoxy in the face of the failure of most capitalist economies, those of United States, Germany and the United Kingdom, to maintain high levels of employment and world trade in the 1930s, challenged Say's Law on the grounds that simple observation seemed to indicate that supply was not creating its own demand and the consequence was high unemployment. He argued: "Thus Say's Law, that the aggregate demand price of output as a whole is equal to its aggregate supply price for all volumes of output, is equivalent to the proposition that there is no obstacle to full employment." However, he goes on, if this is not true, a "vitally important chapter of economic theory" remains to be written (Keynes, 1973, p. 26). Keynes then produces what is overwhelmingly an under-consumptionist theory. The community (the mass of the people plus the government) need to consume more and this involves analysing what Keynes calls the "propensity to consume"; as well as the marginal efficiency of capital, and, thirdly, the rate of interest. This would "fill in the gaps in our existing knowledge." Keynes points the finger at Ricardo for misunderstanding the nature of effective demand. Ricardo as with Jean-Baptiste Say and James Mill, were confident that supply would find its own demand (If this happened, then the unemployment problem would not have occurred). In filling in one of the key gaps he has identified, Keynes writes: "consumption – to repeat the obvious – is the sole end and object of all economic activity." Keynes thus produces his new orthodoxy and dismisses James Mill, Ricardo and Say at the stroke of a sentence by writing: " ... every weakening of the propensity to consume regarded as a permanent habit must weaken the demand for capital as well as demand for consumption" (Keynes, 1973, p. 106).

Keynes' proposal is well known. Governments should spend their way out of economic crises when unemployment occurs on a sufficiently large scale. He is, of course apologetic in saying so because he is by inclination, background and intellectual bias a "conservative" and not (in the US sense) a liberal. He regards his theory, and the policy prescriptions that follow, as "moderately conservative." Government intervention as a policy measure was to circumscribe the free-market system only to a limited extent and he shows earnestly his concern for staying well within economic orthodoxy: "But if our central controls succeed in establishing aggregate volume of output corresponding to full employment as nearly as is practicable, *the classical theory comes into its own again from that point onward.*" This is a perfect reformist statement, and a model for the reforms that are produced daily during periods of crises in capitalism as is the case in the policy prescriptions for solving the 2007–2009 crisis when for the first time for several decades Keynesianism is being openly invoked.[21] Some of the more hysterical commentators in the United States have even referred to these policies as socialism in the making.

Keynes provided the theoretical response that guided policy for several decades, and despite protestations to the contrary, is still alive and well in many respects. The way out of the crises was seen to be through spending (and is maximized through the multiplier effect). The stimulation through policy means of both public expenditure and private expenditure is supposed to lead to economic recovery and full employment. Full employment, i.e. maximum ability to consume, became the answer to crises and this approach seemed to serve policy makers in good stead in the period 1945–1980 until the emergence of monetarist policies that were supposed to curb consumption and conquer stagflation, the bugbear of the economies of the 1970s. Monetarism had its observable shortcomings even within Reagan and Thatcher style economic policy, and gave way, in turn, to supply-side economics, tax cuts and the failed hopes for trickle-down. In any case, policy is one thing. The way the system responds is quite another. Counter-systemic and counter-productive policies may be forced on governments or governments may implement short-sighted and damaging policies for all sorts of reasons, but, unless the outcomes are really devastating (such as leading to a nuclear holocaust) the capitalist system will tend to do what all systems do, and that is make a systemic response in the direction of survival. The systemic response in this case is the creation, expansion and strengthening of a class of shock absorbers. Thus at this point I make two observations: one way the capitalist system of production generates effective demand is through the creation of the absorptive class whose main economic function is to absorb commodities; second, thanks to Keynes contribution to ideological domination, the consumer is now erroneously thought to be sovereign, whereas in the classical economic theory the producer was seen to be the prime mover. The ideological root of this is probably the fact that capitalism needs to be seen as being synonymous with democracy whereas the reality is that democracy (the dispersal of political power) is incompatible with modern capitalism (the concentration of economic power).

It is now time to turn to the way in which individual consumers are socialized into the belief that they are politically liberated to consumer commodities as well as themselves becoming commodities, creating an ugly society based on the repressed aggression of the narcissus.

NOTES

1. Marx discusses the relationship between production and consumption at some length in the *Grundrisse* and sees a unity of production and consumption but he does write that: "The important thing to emphasise is only that production and consumption appear as moments of one process in which production is the real point of departure and hence also the dominant moment."

2. *The Economist.*

3. One freeconomics utilized by Google, Skype and Yahoo who appear to offer "free lunches" but in fact look for enormous markets, happy to give 99% away to make a killing on the lucrative 1%. Not that much different from the loss leaders of supermarkets except the scale is different.

4. *The Economist.*

5. Ibid.

6. Hebdige op. cit., p. 131 quoting Sweezy (1972b).

7. Hebdige, ibid. The discussion of this form of risk is continuous, sometimes taking the how to? approach: Chatterjee (2004); Gilad (2004); McCarthy and Flynn (2004).

8. There are many other writers who have made important contributions including Nader, Packard and significantly Riesman's *The Lonely Crowd* should not be neglected.

9. See also Joyce (1971), Nevaer (2004).

10. Bauer et al.

11. John E Bowes, "Out of the Closet and into the Market Place: Meeting Basic needs in the Gay Community", in Daniel L Wardlow (Wardlow, 1996, p. 220). The author makes no apologies for using the term needs instead of wants.

12. By privatization, I mean that individuals or at most the nuclear family avail themselves of the private use of commodities that are for their personal or private use. Thus we have, of course, televisions rather than cinemas and washing machines rather than public laundries, cars rather than public transport.

13. Obviously some commodities can be partially useful. A car that will get you from A to B reliably may well be useful, depending on your reason for travel but may be unnecessarily large or powerful or comfortable or adorned. Such a car can be described as partially useful.

14. This is drawn from *Capital*, Volume 1, Chapter 15, section 8e. Baran and Sweezy (1966) op. cit., 1966, p. 128n23.

15. Schor (2004), See also Barber (2008).

16. Pohl (1982, pp. 167–231).

17. Some Economists seem to want to explain how everything else works in the world apart from economics. See: Frank (2008); Harford (2008). These recent works are counter balanced by Marglin (2008). He regards Economics as more dangerous to our health, however.

18. http://bostonreview.mit.edu/BR24.3/schor.html, p. 5

19. This trap is sprung frequently for the unwary. See for instance Gini (2003).

20. Baudrillard's italics. The discussion of this point is taken from "The ideological genesis of needs" reprinted in Schor and Holt (2000) op. cit., p. 56 et seq.

21. Despite all the hype around so-called monetarism, Friedmanite economics made no serious progress in policy terms in the advanced economies as a solution to stabilizing economies. In fact when Friedman himself was interviewed by the *Financial Times* in 2003, he admitted that monetarist policies had run into the sand: "the use of the quantity theory of money as a target has not been a success."

CHAPTER 5

NARCISSISM AND THE FRACTIONALIZATION OF THE INDIVIDUAL

1. THE COMMODITY NARCISSIST

This chapter discusses the extent to which the absorptive class has been created as essentially narcissistic in character by the system of capitalist production. Guy Debord, an early critic of a post modern capitalism, argued that capitalism had gone so far in the production of the commodity that society is turned into a mirror or spectacle that represents the kind of void in existence felt at the core of the individuals within it. He also laments the way in which the economy exists for its own sake, rather than for those that live within it and as part of it. In his somewhat incoherent work, *The Society of the Spectacle*, he writes of the commodity as spectacle, and we find such assertions as (Debord, 1983):

"The spectacle aims at nothing other than itself."

"The spectacle subjugates living men to itself to the extent that the economy has totally subjugated them. It is not more than the economy developing for itself."

"The spectacle is capital to such a degree of accumulation that it becomes an image."

Debord sees the world turned into a huge spectacle that reflects the commodity-dominated world. While I do not agree fully with his perception of the nature of the spectacle, it is not hard to see that a huge angst exists in relation to what the commodity appears to be doing within the context of the modern capitalist system. "The (capitalist) economy transforms the world, but transforms it only into a world of economy." This is what we now explore a bit further in the context of the individual and what he or she has become or is becoming.

119

Before I embark on the exercise of discussing the new or commodity narcissist, I am not suggesting everyone is a narcissist. If you think you are not, however, you probably are. This is the problem with dealing with feelings of individual subjects. I realize I do talk in the most-general terms. I cannot prove how general is the presence of narcissism in the sense of how many individuals are narcissistic and how narcissistic they might be on a scale of 1–5, not having embarked on empirical work. Nevertheless, I present sufficient rational argument to make what I believe to be a convincing case from a variety of generally accepted sources.

The New Narcissist is a term already coined and so we are faced with the temptation of attempting to coin another name for the sake of clarity. It may simply be easiest to refer to Commodity Narcissism by which we refer to the narcissism promoted in advanced societies by the production and consumption of the commodity. It affects, therefore, both producers and consumers though producers and consumers may be the same individuals. Let us, for the sake of being reasonably precise, call the individual members of the absorptive class "commodity narcissists" who will in due course be defined by function and by the personal characteristics of the individuals and fractions of individuals who make up the class. The commodity narcissist is a product of the more advanced societies, and is linked inextricably with the process of production which is manifested through the mass consumption of commodities. This discussion provides a picture of what the absorptive class has become in terms of the individuals within it. However, the individual personalities form a kind of collective personality that is encroaching on everyday life in a way that echoes the despair of Herbert Marcuse in *One Dimensional Man*, and this collective personality, having been formed, impacts on society and economy so that it reinforces all that is dangerous and unacceptable, accounting partially, at least, for the public acceptance of the unacceptable. It also, possibly, accounts for the acceptance of what is irrational in the name of rationality, to use Marcusian terminology. In other words, we have to be able to explain individual motivation as it amounts collectively to mass acceptance of commodity absorption to the exclusion of sympathy for the bulk of the rest of humankind.

Our very thought processes, even when they are well intentioned, are distorted by this egocentricity. For instance, we heard very soon after the September 11 attack on the Twin Towers that poverty bred violence and that we should eradicate poverty to stop poor people attacking us. The poor were to blame and rich people could prevent international terrorism by making the poor people rich because rich people do not presumably cause violence, whereas some might think that is rich people who are behind violence. It is rich people who have an interest in both attacking others to become richer or prevent themselves from being attacked so to hang on to their wealth. It is wealth and the desire for it that is a major reason for violence. It is called greed (Berdal & David, 2001).

One important beginning for the preparation for a peaceful world is to understand the nature of the narcissistic and dangerously aggressive world that has been created: the world of the absorptive class, made up ironically of individuals who on the whole do not personally want to kill but who support unconsciously, for the most part, the system that perpetuates a world of killing. The people of the United States experience a great deal of violence which indicates a society beset by malaise and repression, but as a whole the society is not bellicose in that as US military intervention expands, recruitment to the military declines or is difficult to maintain.

Though much of the literature dealing with narcissism talks about the Freudian origin of the narcissistic personality and discusses the supposed significance of the birth and nurturing process, I make little comment on the validity of the origins of narcissism but see the commodity narcissist as manufactured or produced by his or her existence within the absorptive class. Narcissists may well be products of nature, but the commodity narcissists who appear to have elements and characteristics in common with Freud's description are certainly featured in the absorptive society. The world of the narcissist is made by the mirror. The mirror and the image reflected back is everything. Producers of commodities, as we know only too well, sell with the aid of mirrors. Advertising, the promotion of the celebrity, the personification of power (the way in which political and economic power is presented in the form of charismatic individuals), the protagonist-hero, the personification of evil are all presented in the mass media as mirrors. It was Vance Packard who first called the attention of the public to the power of the advertiser's appeal to narcissism. "Studies of narcissism indicated that nothing appeals more to people than themselves: so why not help people buy a projection of themselves? That way the images would pre-select their audiences, select out of a consuming public people with personalities having an affinity for the image... the image builders could spark off love affairs by the millions." This approach worked especially well with cars and cigarettes but, as one might expect best of all, with women's lingerie. These products sold best, not when the buyer was observed by a third party, but when the woman in the advertisement was seen to view herself in a full-length mirror.

Christopher Lasch called our intention to narcissism in the 1970s in making a sweeping critical attack on US society and commenting on a lost past, which, to him, was worth lamenting. There is no class analysis of any significance in his work on narcissism and, while narcissism is seen to be widespread, it is seen to be a matter that affects large numbers of US citizens as individuals but he develops no particular economic analysis from his observations. In addition there is a problem with his not separating out the individual narcissist from the response of a class of such people. Indeed, his concern is much more with the individual and what has become of him or her as a single person. Nonetheless, his observations make for an excellent and perceptive starting point. Lasch states clearly that the (individual) narcissist depends on the other for self-esteem (Lasch, 1979, p. 10). Any seller of commodities one can assume is delighted with such a person. The need for admiration would lead to such a person becoming a peacock. The need for more and more admiration would lead such an individual to develop the equivalent of a huge decorative tail to the detriment of his being able to fly in the most effective manner (Richard Dawkins, 1996, *passim*).

Whereas the peacock is "driven" by the process of sexual selection, the commodity narcissist is not a product of nature. He and she are products of the system of production. There is nothing natural in a human peacock however much we convince ourselves that packing our dwelling places, our wardrobes and fancying up our SUVs and pick-up trucks is in any sense a response to human nature. In producing commodities, the capitalist system produces those who will compete on the basis of demanding more and more admiration from his or her neighbour. This long-recognized process of keeping up with the Jones's develops out of this tendency toward mass need for self-esteem through the purchase of the commodity.

Closely related to this need for finding self-esteem through the other, it is claimed that the narcissist has a void within; this makes him/her more vulnerable to existence mediated by reflected images of the exterior being (Lasch, 1979, p. 21). In other words, the mirror process works in both directions. Everyone, it would appear, is looking at everyone else at the same time as absorbing his or her own image. Important, however, is the observation of the existence of the void within. Where does the void originate? Of course, it could be explained in Freudian terms: that is, in terms of the individual in his or her own development from infancy and in universal terms, thus affecting every individual more or less. The narcissist is, of course, self-absorbed in Freudian terms and into that empty self-absorbed existence commodities would seem to fit perfectly. Lasch argues that the primary narcissist, the infant, takes time to discover that the source of need is within but that the source of gratification is without and that is the explanation for the void (Lasch, 1979, p. 38). However, my argument is that such a void is a consequence of it being manufactured and arising out of the disintegration of the individual To this extent, I depart from other explanations in the mainstream: it is not alienation from the means of production any more than an anomic society that produces the void but it is the effect of manufacturing the absorptive class composed of disintegrating and fractionalized individuals that has produced the emptiness and also a consequence of the division of labour and what follows from it as part and parcel of the productive process. Staying with the concept of the mirror for the time being we find that Lasch develops his arguments further in a number of ways. The whole process of hero-worship, which is, of course, not in any way a new phenomenon in itself, is put to particular use (Lasch, 1979, p. 84 et seq). Endless examples can be quoted from the everyday press in almost any advanced country in relation to a range of heroes, though sport offers the best examples. Not only does the tabloid press urge admiration of the sportsman whereby the readers identify with goal scorers, winners of Wimbledon, Olympic gold medallists of all sorts and so on, but in the UK, still prone to shadow medieval practices, especially successful sportspeople are awarded with knighthoods, reminding the British public at least of some past Arthurian heroic age, with its connotations of heroism and derring-do. This hero-worship of sporting personalities and many other celebrities is utilized by producers in the sale of all kinds of commodities as sports heroes and others "endorse" sporting products, clothes, cosmetics, cars, soft drinks and the like.

Lasch seems, however, not to have got sport quite right as he follows the work of Huizinga (Huizinga, 1971). Lasch argues that athletic events, for instance, lose the element of ritual and public festivity (Lasch, 1979, p. 108). By contrast, however, "sport" soaks up surplus: attendance at games, travel to games involving hundreds or even thousands of miles, eating and drinking at games, purchase of sports equipment of all sorts from golf clubs to football socks. Huge amounts of sport are consumed in many forms. For that to succeed, the ritual element is of great importance. On the other hand much effort is spent to turn the sports event into a religious ceremonious occasion with the venue treated as temples, the victors as Gods or superhuman beings overcoming obstacles that would have floored lesser mortals. Lasch does connect sport and consumption in his discussion of leisure as an escape. "The appearance in history of an escapist conception of 'leisure' coincides with the organization of leisure activities as an extension of commodity production" (Lasch, 1979, p. 123). Sporting organizations, leagues and competitions of all sorts, tend toward the concentration of capital as do all production processes. Thus while there are more competitions than ever, the big teams and the big names predominate. Lesser mortals will just not do; only Gods serve the process of absorption of commodities. Concentration of capital means for sport fewer teams at the top end in more competitions. However, the sport is played by human beings as mortal as the rest of us who are subjected to more and more injury and, therefore, shorter and shorter active life spans. While it thus appears that the sporting heroes and celebrities can command more and more money, they have shorter lives at the top and become mere disposable commodities. This concept of winner as mirror has its exact flipside in the concept of the loser and this is the point made by Maccoby and also quoted by Lasch. Maccoby's argument is that the qualities that make the top managers are provided by the narcissistic personality whose deepest fear is that of being a loser, and, again, this makes such people vulnerable to demands to consume.

Moving from sport to movies, we see the same process. The standard plots and stories of movies involve one protagonist and a limited number of sub-plots. Even anti-heroes are designed to engage the identification of individual audience members in their use of the cinema as a narcissistic mirror. In Lasch's words: "the narcissist cannot identify with someone else without seeing the other as an extension of himself, without obliterating the other's identity" (Lasch, 1979, p. 86). It is not too difficult to extend these short observations of hero-worship and modern pop culture and confirm that the commodity narcissist is a key driving force in consumption patterns. As Lasch also observes, the celebrity is also part and parcel of commodity narcissism. But, overlapping with the highly paid sports person, all forms of celebrity not only feed the narcissist observer but also consume the surplus. Thus the consumer narcissist by insisting on a celebrity-based society[1] creates the conditions whereby the surplus can be consumed by the celebrity. This is fully justified in modern orthodox economic theory in that grossly highly rewarded celebrities, including sports personalities, TV celebrities and pop singers receive not a "wage" for their performance but, after Ricardo's theory of rent as a surplus, rent.

Now we are only on a short journey before we develop the analogy of the theatre. Thus, associated with the mirror is the concept of theatre, performance and acting for the observer in that all narcissists need to exist only for the performance. Lasch now asserts: "all of us, actors and spectators, live surrounded my mirrors" (Lasch, 1979, p. 92). Clearly, the sellers on behalf of production-driven capitalism, use this narcissistic tendency to full advantage. Sociological theory, to the extent that it has developed as a justificatory ideology, underpins the view that life, or reality or real life, is in fact a series of actions taken on the stage; hence the sway held by role theory in the sociology of the 1960s and still a key theoretical underpinning in gender and feminist analysis of social relations and dynamics. The term role model is, of course, now used with as much frequency, if not more, than "Freudian slip" or "avoidance technique" or "in denial" or "attention deficiency syndrome" or other dime store sociological or psychological sound bites. Later in this chapter another implication of role theory not hitherto fully explored is the way in which role theory indicates that the individual is not whole but in a state of more or less permanent disintegration as he or she tries to fill a number of roles. The important issue at this point of the argument, however, is that associated with role modelling, the audience are led to imitate the "Gods." It is this mimetic society that Marcuse so tellingly attacked at the very time in the 1960s when certain streams of sociological and psychological theory were used by the mirror makers, the advertising industry, to expand their markets in the first real decade of modern style mass consumption of cars, household goods, gadgets, services and entertainment. Along with the dictum that sex sells went the general belief in offering a mirror to the shock absorbers.

The "atmosphere" of everyday life is now no different from that 30 years ago. Lasch writing at that time could well be saying the same now: "Today almost everyone lives in a dangerous world from which there is little escape. International terrorism and blackmail, bombings, and hi-jackings arbitrarily affect the rich and poor alike. Crime, violence and gang wars make cities unsafe and threaten to spread to the suburbs" (Lasch, 1979, p. 68). In the sense that he goes on to talk about the "glorification of the individual in his annihilation," he is heir to Marcuse's view on rationality:

> "...the insanity of the whole absolves the particular insanities and turns the crimes against humanity into a rational enterprise. When the people, aptly stimulated by the public and private authorities, prepare for lives of total mobilization, they are sensible not only because of the present Enemy, but also because of the investment and employment possibilities in industry and entertainment. Even the most insane calculations are rational: the annihilation of five million people is preferable to that of ten million.... It is hopeless to argue that a civilization which justifies its defense by such calculus proclaims its own ends." (Marcuse, 1964/1991, p. 52)

To Marcuse, then, we owe a perspective that gives us a conception of rationality, technology, commodities, the state, government and bipartisanship and the human condition and what the state fears most, which is not an external enemy, but the liberation of its own people.

Enslavement is achieved through the educational system. Thus, Lasch laments what he sees as the decline of educational standards particularly in respect to the decline of critical thought and the erosion of intellectual standards. It is possible to argue that, given that this assertion is true (he provides no real evidence), it is linked to the creation of the herd like nature of the absorptive class in its response to the process of production and consumption. The educational system is devoted to conformity in the interests of social control, and specialist education to aid the division of labour. Society requires a "stupefied population, resigned to work that is trivial and shoddily performed, predisposed to seek its satisfaction in the time set aside for leisure" (Lasch, 1979, p. 126).

But what is also the case about education, given its endless expansion, is its commodity like nature. Education is consumed so that in terms of qualifications the absorptive class is at one level over-qualified, performing jobs and tasks for which their education is excessive in quantity but largely irrelevant to the tasks that need to be performed. Thus education when provided cheaply or free by the government, local, regional or central, soaks up the surplus and, at the same time, when provided by the private sector is simply another commodity. Educational qualifications are nailed to walls of hallways and dens and offices more as commodities than as signs of intrinsic usefulness on the part of their collectors, but they are also employed as mirrors reflecting back the perceived value of the individual.

Lasch goes on to argue, probably more or less correctly that "while modern society has achieved unprecedented rates of formal literacy, at the same time it has produced new forms of illiteracy" (Lasch, 1979, p. 126). He argues, with almost vicious contempt: "People ... find themselves unable to use language with ease and precision, to recall the basic facts of their country's history, to make logical deductions, to understand any but the most rudimentary written texts, or even to grasp their constitutional rights." The production of a post modern (meaning unaware of the past and its relevance), uncritical, largely apolitical mass of irrelevantly educated mass is ideal for the manipulation into a class whose main functions relate to the absorption of commodities and the shock inherent in capitalist "progress." This view is reinforced by Hobsbawm's comment:

> "The extraordinary growth of higher education which, by the early 1980s, produced at least seven countries with more than 100,000 teachers at University level, was due to consumer pressure...the scale of the student expansion far exceeded what rational planning might have envisaged". (Hobsbawm, 1996, p. 296)

In other words, the need for a highly educated labour force for economic expansion was required by planners and politicians, but the outcome was to produce far more than required. It was a case of overproduction in the form of over-commodification of the educational output. What can be the explanation for this overproduction? The answer lies in the creation of this huge number of educated people to serve the function of absorbing the surplus through the production of irrelevant commodified educational instruments of low value, and also produces the collective mind-set to consume in an increasingly apolitical atmosphere of ignorance, apathy and commodified unfulfilling leisure. The very short-term outcome, it is true, was to produce a significant section of students who were instrumental in the raising of loud voices against the ravages of capitalism, and generally pro-leftist attitudes to ending war, promoting peace and demanding justice. The movement, however, was short lived in historical terms and largely confined to the period of most rapid expansion of higher education in the second half of the sixties and early seventies. A rough analogy would be with the creation of the proletariat in the nineteenth century which also produced considerable conflict and leftist tendencies. However, this modern student movement petered out, partly because of its commodified nature. Rather than, in the longer run, turning out to be radical, the expansion of higher education, and all forms of education in its wake, has produced not a radical thinking society but a passive, narcissistic conventional mass miserably and largely unquestioningly absorbing the surplus in the interests of the producers rather than the consumers. Historians other than Hobsbawm, naturally enough, have noted similar tendencies but report the phenomenon less dramatically. Take for instance David Reynolds. He argues that after early industrialization "in due course, the service sector expands, reflecting and enlarging consumer demand. Children become one of its prime targets – not only for clothes and goods, but also for education, which becomes a status symbol as well as a job qualification" (Reynolds, 2001, p. 301). Here my contention is that the status symbol, the narcissistic element, is crucial in the conversion of education into a commodity rather than an element that is useful both to the individual as well as to society as a whole. The job qualification aspect is of use to many and to society up to a point, but the bulk of education is of limited direct use to the individual and most of it is mere commodity.

Demographic change linked to education also increases the tendency toward narcissism. Historians and others have not failed to notice that birth rates generally speaking in advanced economies have fallen: this accelerates narcissistic tendencies in that families concentrate heavily on attention given to children, shower them with commodities, including that of educational opportunities. Thus, the fall in the size of families does not lead to a fall in consumption of commodities but in an increase of them.

After Disraeli had given the urban working class the vote in the 1860s, he turned to the question of education and this led to his exclamation: "We must educate our masters!" It has been clear ever since (as well as earlier) that the role of the state is to provide the education that the state considers favourable for its ends. What Disraeli really meant was: "we must educate our slaves to accept us as their unchallenged masters". As the state and the economy are perceived to be aspects of the same unity, then Disraeli's exhortation has since been manifested in the provision of an education system that generally favours the creation of commodity narcissism, rather than a system that is aimed at genuine self-fulfilment for the individual.

2. JOHN MILLER AND THE MEGASELF OF EGOTOPIA

John Miller's somewhat vicious attack on the aesthetics of consumer United States and the narcissistic New Man, helps us bridge the argument between class and the individual. "Today," he writes "a New Man is being born ... Over the past fifty years the concept of the individual, defined as part of the social whole, has devolved, some might say mutated, into the concept of the megaself. This powerful megaself perverts the notion of individualism by negating moral, religious, and ethical constraints on individual behaviour. Instead, the megaself postulates a worldview in which self-autonomy is the preferred means to achieving private ends." He goes on, even more vehemently: "Today's consumer-driven, comfort obsessed, rights-promulgating, self-gratifying way of life is hardly life within a society. Rather, it is the life of a loose confederation of autonomous and anonymous individuals interacting in the market place of commodities, lovers and therapies" (Miller, 1997, p. 32–33). While the malaise of Miller is instantly recognizable and heard from a number of directions, the malaise requires some explanation. Of course, commodities and markets are at the centre of the whole process, and, of course, individuals appear to be amorphous and not fully connected. The point of this chapter is to show how the individual is necessarily disintegrated and disconnected and produced as narcissistic beings by the producers of commodities. However, while the disintegrated individuals are in that state, they are a class. What unifies them are the economic functions as specified earlier in this book. The disintegrated individuals that form the class are in as much a state of regular and imminent crisis as the system of producer capitalism itself. As Miller notes, the process of steady disintegration of the individual has been taking place for "the last fifty years."

To Miller the outcome has been that the bulk of the inhabitants of our global village have been produced as village idiots, measured not just by their illiteracy, but by their autonomy and atomism. Moreover, Miller recognizes the way in which the pursuit of a better life is nothing more than the narcissist or megaself soaking up all kinds of commodities for profit. One of his major targets is the (psycho) therapist who urges getting "in touch with feelings" rather than a "sense of ethics." Self-esteem (of the megaself), he claims, takes precedence over genuine intellectual pursuits (Miller, 1997, p. 34). In a despairing conclusion to his chapter on the New Man he concludes that "education clearly demonstrates that we are less members of a culture than members of an economy" (Miller, 1997, p. 37). It is at this point that this author connects with my main arguments. When he says that individuals in the United States are members of an economy, we can see the possibilities of transferring our attention from individual to class. The individuals are driven to act in a particular way because in doing so they assist the class in performing its key functions, to absorb effectively. A few pages later, Miller gets even closer to the concept of class when he connects "society" and "self." "The entire society must become literally a perpetual, omnipresent, round-the-clock market. The consuming self must be free to pursue self-creation, self-renewal and self-redemption through the unfettered act of spontaneous consumption" (Miller, 1997, p. 35 et seq).

3. BAUDRILLARD AGAIN

This is reinforced by Baudrillard. Narcissism is for Baudrillard (see also Chapter 4 supra) of crucial importance in the understanding of how individuals behave. He cites the following examples:

> "What mother has not dreamt of a washing machine specially designed for her alone."
> (Quote from an advertisement); and, similarly, "The body you dream of is your own."

This kind of observation allows Baudrillard to summarize narcissism, the consumer and society in the following way:

> We shall see how consumer society conceives itself as precisely a society of consumption, and *reflects itself narcissistically* in its own image . . . Like violence, the forms of seduction and narcissism are laid down in advance by models *produced* industrially by the mass media . . . " (Baudrillard, 1998, p. 95–98)

This narcissism reflects back to the producer-based economy in that production becomes directed to more and more trivial commodities. In Baudrillard, this tendency is categorized under the headings of, for instance, the ludic and the kitsch.[2] Clearly it is in the discussion of the "body" that the issue of narcissism arises as being of key importance. Baudrillard's summary in his Chapter title for Chapter 8 is "The Finest Consumer Object: The Body." It can be argued, as Baudrillard appears to do, that sexual liberation is entirely linked to the producer's drive to profit from this close association of the body, sex and commodities. We see nothing less than the commodification of sex–body. In order for the producer to maximize this process, the more narcissistic is the consuming class the better. This position, the "sacralization" of the body,[3] brings out an apparent major contradiction. The argument in this book is that the human being is rendered profane while the commodity becomes sacred. We appear, then, in current society to have to render sacred our bodies to be narcissistic enough to purchase all those commodities based on the body: clothes, health products, medicines, holidays, keep-fit, spas, participative sport and similar activities, perfume, deodorant, hairdressing and hair products, and so on seemingly endlessly. Baudrillard recognizes this contradiction in a way. In discussing responses of modern women to the pressures of consumption he says: "The functional and the sacred are inextricably intermingled." For functional it may be possible to read profane. In this case, however the profane and the sacred may be conceptually separated: the body becomes commodified and in reality is profane: it is there as part of the process of conception. However, the souls of men and women are rendered profane in the sense that the real purpose of life is consumption and not real self-fulfilment. The narcissist sacralization of the body, therefore, is apparent and not real. Despite the belief of the narcissist, the person is profane whatever the body (a mere physical thing) has become.

A further feature of narcissism is the sincerity/insincerity phenomenon. Selling to the narcissistic involves what Baudrillard has described as "solicitude." Customer service, have a nice day, smiling, apparent frankness occur as part of self-conscious training in the delivery of goods in actual market places. While individuals may well be open and honest and smiling, the consumer is perpetually flattered and made to feel as single individuals the single most important consumer. It is no coincidence that many nationalities feel the "American" (citizens born and brought up in the United States) are insincere and complain if the "service" they receive in the market place fails to live up to their expectations. Both features are the outcome of narcissism. In addition and less happily, narcissism and violence is part and parcel of the same social phenomenon. This is well argued by Baudrillard as well as others concerned with relationship between the repression and violence (cf. Marcuse). Baudrillard summarizes his position: "The consumer society is at one and the same time a society of solicitude and a society of repression, a pacified society and a society of violence" (Baudrillard, 1998, p. 174 et seq). The narcissist is able to push the violence into separate and often ludic categories.[4] The violence is repressed internally (personally) and externally (by society). Violence always happens "elsewhere". Finally before we leave the general appreciation of Baudrillard as expressed in *The Consumer Society*, we note that the word absorption or absorber does not appear in the index. However, he does use the term absorption toward the end of the book. He asks: "can the schema of alienation still be operative in a context in which the individual is no longer ever confronted with his own split image?" the process of consumption "is no longer one of labour and self-surpassing, but a process of absorption of signs and absorption by signs . . . in the generalised process of consumption, there is no longer any soul, no shadow, no double, and no image in the specular sense."

While my overall argument in this book is to establish the existence of the absorptive class and argue for its distinctiveness from such vague concepts as the consumer society, Baudrillard has proved to be instructive: reviewing the importance of the concept or schema of alienation, discussion of narcissism and mirrors, and reference to such concepts as soul, profanity and sacralization, all of which provide an important link to uncovering the existence of the absorptive class and the process by which it is produced and nature of its current existence. Though the work of Baudrillard is challenged here as being somewhat missing the mark, there is much that remains still of value despite the fact that *The Consumer Society* was written in the late 1960s, since which time the producer economy has become more transparent.

4. THE INDIVIDUAL AS FRACTIONS UNDER CAPITALISM

The individual shock absorber, as I suggest in Chapter 7 infra, is as potentially fractionalized as the class itself. It is not entirely new to argue the point. Marx was aware of this "dismemberment."

"Marx had spoken of the dismemberment of the human body in the social machinery of industrial capitalism. Labourers coupled to the productive process only has hands that assemble on assembly lines, or has legs and backs that bear burdens, or has arms that stoke furnaces. It is only the hands and eyes of clerks in offices that are paid for . . . The capitalist is the calculating brain disconnected from the capitalist's own taste and caprice. The industrial enterprise is the whole body upon which the part-organs are attached."[5]

Lingis, the author of this extravagant rendering continues:

"Marx conceptualized, as alienation, the dismemberment of the body ... and invoked the idea of integral man, the man whose body parts would belong to himself."

Lingis does admit that such a notion, that man can be an integer, is a utopian thought. To put it another way, as expressed by Bertell Ollman:

"What occurs in the real world is reflected in people's minds: essential elements of what it means to be a man are grasped as independent and, in some cases, all powerful entities, whose links with him appear other than they really are . . . . The whole has broken up into numerous parts . . . This is the essence of alienation." (Bertell, 1971, p. 135)

To Marx, however, the solution to the re-assembling of the broken whole, is not utopian: the solution lies in the establishment of a scientific and rational socialist society that will provide the social framework for individual self-fulfilment. Indeed, the problem of how "whole" is the individual has been a recurrent issue since raised by Marx and somewhat repressed since the end of ideology apparently presaged after 1990. Take this confident statement by Erich Kahler written in 1957: "Our survey has furnished us ample evidence of a powerful trend toward the disruption and invalidation of the individual." In *The Tower and the Abyss* he set out to show the following, partly through a multi-lingual literary analysis that draws out the existential angst of the 1940s and 1950s:

"In the course of this study we shall see the evidences of *disintegration* of the individual in all fields of contemporary experience, from social, political and economic processes to those in learning, art and poetry. They are but different aspects of one vast, comprehensive transformation that has come to affect the very inner structure of man and threatens the human values which were inherent in him as an individual." (Kahler, 1957)

Finally, as a result of his survey Kahler is satisfied that he has discovered what has "split the individual *from without*" and the "corresponding movement *from within* the human psyche and the human mind . . . worked toward fragmentation of the human being and of his experience" (Kahler, 1957, p. 184). This existential angst that was so strongly felt in the 1950s is no less strong 50 years later. Take this comment from a professor of psychology: "this book attempts to make sense of the growing number of people who play by the rules, do everything right, get everything they think they want, and end up profoundly dissatisfied and confused." There may well be any number of approaches to answering these questions. However, Barry Schwartz 's book is called *The Costs of Living* and he connects the downsides of the market economy with the angst of the generation entering the twenty-first century (Barry Schwartz, 1994). His Chapter 6 is called "Consumed by Consumption." He wanders through possibilities: addiction, scarcity, happiness (using much the reference points as those of Alan Thein Durning), relative economic position, moral restraints, doing the right thing or not doing the right thing, commercialization of social relations. These are all descriptions of the angst that, no doubt, we all of us more or less recognize, and probably lay at the door of living "affluent" lives absorbing as we are manufactured to do. His descriptions are fine: his explanations a little more elusive.

I am not intending here to rehearse all the arguments concerning man as individual, man in relation to the other, man in peer-groups, man and schizophrenia,[6] the individual versus the collective, man and "cascades", versions of alienation, man and responses to the division of labour and so on. However, there are sufficient studies in the social sciences as well as a plethora of literary sources to suggest that the fate of the members of "society" generally under capitalism is one of a sense of disintegration. However, the human animal in the very nature of a living organism has "a tendency to the integer." He or she simply wants to feel whole. Where this feeling is greatest is not so much felt generally by society but among the constituent members of the absorptive class who seek for integration in many ways, not least in so-called holistic therapies or holistic diets; and through weak attempts to reject their disintegration by crying in their individual wildernesses to become whole again. Needless to say such cries and apparent wants (that may really be needs) are rapidly commodified, leading the disintegrated individual into a further labyrinthine wilderness from which there appears to be no return or escape.

5. NARCISSISM, IDEOLOGY AND CLASS

Capitalism was exposed to the greatest weight of criticism, probably, in the fifties and sixties and seventies of the twentieth century at the very moment it was moving most rapidly to the point of creating massive surpluses, as well as producing an expanded absorptive class to deal with these surpluses. It was at this moment that critics across a wide spectrum (they were by no means all Marxists) gained the greatest attention: Marcuse,

Arendt, Galbraith, Sartre, Camus, Fanon, Brecht, Packard, Riesman (Riesman, 1950/1961), C Wright Mills and so on. Much of the criticism focussed on the individual and his alienation in a world of plenty; similarly attention focussed on such issues as class and classlessness. Much of this debate has weakened in recent years. Fukuyama's *End of History* has sought to replace Daniel Bell's *End of Ideology*. However, much of the fifties and sixties material is still relevant even if it requires updating. Certainly a steady output of contemporary and *post-hoc* work exists which reviews that period as a time of turmoil and protest, and seemingly came to an end with Thatcher in the United Kingdom and Reagan in the United States.[7] Interestingly, much of this work rejects the protests of that "sixties" generation. For instance, Collier and Horowitz (1996) "admit how profoundly the God of Leftism has failed us and our country (USA) alike." The post-Soviet collapse and the identity problem for the so-called Left, have to run their course so that a new-new left might appear. This new-new left will based on the appearance of a narcissistic absorptive class, and will be reformist in nature. But reformism still involves conflict and protest; and working-class action, it should be noted, is not as dead as might be supposed by reading the smug assessment of Peter Clecak, for instance:

> "In spite of gains in the democratization of personhood and a corresponding rise of selfishness, real and fancied, most Americans (sic) remained quite bounded by economic needs, occupational requirements, social position, and personal obligations. One might go as far as to suggest that there was not enough selfishness and not nearly enough genuine concern with the self in the sixties and seventies." (Clecak, 1983)

The sixties and seventies, a time of educational expansion and youthful idealism, appears to have been a time when the whole economic and social and political process which put the individual at the centre of so-called progress was being called into question. Those movements may have failed and may have been overtaken by the weight of narcissism or selfishness or individualism or atomization of society or fractionalization of the individual or disintegration of the individual. On the other hand the creation of an absorptive class in this period and the decades that have followed may yet balance the angst of the new generation and manifest itself in the kind of reformist movement that will at least ameliorate the worst features of capitalism.

While much of Lasch's work on narcissism has helped point to the narcissistic nature of the absorptive class, we also find the same confusion about the real nature of class forces when we look at a contemporary work of Richard Sennet. He claims: "Some writers attempt to portray this change by speaking of a transformation of the bourgeois classes into the middle classes, the *classes moyennes*. They point to the fact that it is no longer possible to speak of the shadings from accountant to banker as differences of tone within one class...One must conceive of a class structure within the white-collar world, they say, with its own proletariat, *artisanat*, petite bourgeoisie, and managerial class." He quotes Daniel Bell, Alain Touraine, Andre Gorz and Serge Mallet in support of this view. While I have earlier rejected neo-Weberian arguments about class formation, and I would argue that all these white-collar workers are in the same absorptive class, I agree wholeheartedly with the arguments that point to the development of narcissism among these hugely expanded occupational groups. Sennet connects the angst of the individual with narcissism thus:

> "...the belief in one's work, unstable and protean as it is, is an expression of one's personality ..., the reflection of that process in the consciousness of the worker himself. This image of work position as a mirror of the self, yet a mirror in which nothing fixed can ever be reflected, is the first stage in the induction of narcissistic feeling..."
> (Sennet, 1977, p. 330)

Sennet goes on to claim that narcissism is the protestant ethic of our time since the individuals in the "new class" see their identities tied up in their work. To this extent (though I would have to reject the relationship between asceticism and narcissism proposed by Sennet) there is a connection between the development of the overworked American of Schor and the way in which the workaholic sees himself reflected in his job.

Before we leave this subject of the individual it is important to deal with the major ideologue of individual action, which is at times latent and at times covert in the ideology of everyday life under the capitalist system. Ludwig von Mises and his views and arguments on the individual and the *primacy* of individual human action underpin modern capitalist ideology.
  He asserts:

> "...we must realize that all actions are performed by individuals. A collective operates always through the intermediary of one of several individuals whose actions are related to the collective as the *secondary* source...the hangman, not the state, executes a criminal. It is the meaning of those concerned that discerns in the hangman's action an action of the state." (Von Mises, 1963/1949, p. 42)

This feels very much like the statement from the National Rifle Association in the United States that guns don't kill, people do. Von Mises goes on to assert forcefully: "There is no social collective conceivable which is not operative in the actions of some individuals...Nobody ever perceived a nation without perceiving its members...It is illusory to believe that it is

possible to visualize collective wholes." In this way he is able, and it is a
position held consciously or unconsciously by the mass of people living
under capitalism, to put the ego in the foremost position in the strongest
possible assertive language. Here is a man without doubts or concerned with
ifs and buts:

> "The Ego is the *unity* of the acting being. It is unquestionably given and cannot be
> dissolved or conjured away by any ... quibbling. The We is always the summing up
> which puts together two or more Egos... The We cannot act otherwise than each of
> them acting on his own behalf." (Von Mises, 1963/1949, p. 44)

The individual, in real life, is clearly torn by the tension created by the
reality of material conditions and by what is ideologically imposed. We are
constantly taught directly and through the process of ideological domination that we are responsible for our own actions. As for "creative genius"
this is the ultimate individual series of actions and a gift of nature. Creative
genius "is by no means the result of production in the sense in which
economics uses this term" (Von Mises, 1963/1949, p. 42). For von Mises, in
general, "action, if successful, produces the product." He claims that
productive forces are not material at all, but arising from the human mind
are spiritual, intellectual and ideological phenomena. Marx turned Hegel
on his head, and von Mises seems also to have this Germanic tendency and
attempts to turn Marx on his head. It is not surprising that today's individual
may feel he lives in a topsy-turvy world. For most of the time the individual
thinks he knows how the world works, but the world is full of contradictions.
For instance, modern man and woman think themselves to be sovereign as
consumers, yet, at another level, they sense themselves to be powerless in a
feeble weakened democracy, marked by capitalist domination.

For Joseph Schumpeter, von Mises's Austrian contemporary, capitalism
did not have such a bright future and would, in due course, decompose. This
would arise for several reasons but, for our present purposes (our interest
in the individual and his or her relationship to capitalism) Schumpeter's
point about the internal weakness of the capitalism system arising from the
disintegration of the bourgeois family requires some examination. He argues
that the decline of (Victorian) marriage as measured by the rise in number of
divorces and the reduction of the number of children produced was a sign of
the disintegration of the bourgeois class as a whole. He considered, as an
old-style Victorian might, that the bourgeois drive was intimately connected
with the establishment of a bourgeois family dynasty. Without that dynastic
attitude the drive for profit would be diminished, there would be fewer
wants to be satisfied and bourgeois culture would concern itself with other

matters than profit. As he puts it "the desirability of incomes beyond a certain level is reduced" and without the need for large bourgeois homes the apartment house and the apartment hotel would "represent a rationalized abode and another style of life" (Joseph Schumpeter, 1950).

Schumpeter refers here to what was widely observed as the fate of Victorian style capitalist families, seemingly going into decline as represented so vividly in German literature in the Buddenbrokes' syndrome after Thomas Mann's book of the same name or as dramatized in John Galsworthy's English novel(s) the *Forsyte Saga* and has since been expressed from time to time in social history as "rags to rags in three generations" (Perkin, 2002). The error in this Schumpeterian analysis is one that we are now trying to avoid by making a distinction between class and the individual. As the forms of capitalism changed so did the nature of the capitalist change, but the overwhelming point is that capitalism is a *system* and the system now produces the individual capitalist. In any case, capitalism proceeds, despite as much as because of the individuals within the capitalist class. Moreover, though the capitalist class has expanded round the globe in China, Brazil, India, former Soviet Union and so on, the capitalist class has shrunk in size in the traditional advanced economies leaving the system to be run by the inner drive of corporate entities. Of course, I exaggerate to some extent, since clearly individual capitalists exist who are driven by profit. But capitalism now exists for its own sake more than the individual capitalists that constitute it. Frequently when policies are adopted to satisfy fractions of the capitalist class, the system as a whole may show serious cracks and tensions. One historical example has been the way in which finance capital has taken on industrial capital (and usually has won) and this has led to rust belts and industrial wastelands and the like. A good example of such tension is on the issue of capital movements versus labour movements across national frontiers which we discuss in Chapter 6.

6. CONSCIOUSNESS AND CLASS

This brings us to the issue of consciousness and whether or not there is a role in history for the class of shock absorbers as a whole. Of the three big classes discussed earlier, the working class, the absorptive class and the capitalist class, the absorptive class is the one that largely lacks consciousness. The genuine working-class man has a degree of consciousness. He knows himself to be at least relatively poor, deprived of power without class action, excluded from ownership of wealth, limited as to his range of chattels and may seek redress through one area of class action he has knowledge of trade unions, despite the limitations of union action, but may also resort to parliamentary methods for redress through participation in the activities of political parties. The hundred years or so of socialist thought and communist experimentation around the world and the regular debates setting socialism and capitalism as alternative systems as well as the actual material conditions and rise of a proletariat in the advanced industrial nations, have served to reveal to the proletariat some essentials features of their condition and to help set the agenda for political action. But the proletariat does lack revolutionary consciousness, and it looks as if, to be Hegelian, history has written them off.

The capitalist, when we are talking of human beings rather than corporate entities, knows even more clearly than do individual members of the working class about his role and that of his class in relation to economic and political power, personal liberty, and his motivation for profit. Von Mises even gives him, as producer, spirituality. He claims that the producer or capitalist in his creative power tends toward the sacred. He says quite directly and unequivocally: "the material changes are the outcome of the spiritual changes" (Von Mises (1963/1949, p. 141). The individual embedded in the absorptive class has no such certainty because:

- He or she is not aware of the existence of the absorptive class or his or her own membership of it.
- Though the individual is aware of direct class action, this collective action has hitherto been really working-class action and the individual needs to perceive of himself or herself as somehow being proletarianized to participate; thus, for instance, to participate in street demonstrations requires a substantial shift of mind-set; regular issues and action in relation to specific issues have to be a regular feature of life to politicize the individual.
- There are no institutional arrangements for collective action among the absorptive class; no equivalent exists of trades unions[8] for instance and political parties are not normally suited for direct demonstrations, only parliamentary action.
- No political party *consciously* represents the interests of the absorptive class in parliamentary democracies.[9]
- Though the techniques for direct collective action are developing, they are still in their infancy; these techniques, rather than mobilizing large numbers of individuals over the internet, need to mobilize

organizations; existing organizations, however, are too loosely connected in their aims.

- Individuals have to escape from the anodyne and superficial features of the dominant media outlets to feel compelled to develop institutions for action, including alternative media outlets to aid in the construction of political agenda and see them through.

The angst is felt in many quarters and is expressed in diverse ways. One researcher and trade union activist has expressed this in *The Impact of Economic Anxiety in Postindustrial America* (Nancy Wiefek, 2003). Despite the continuous growth of the US economy, she sees this anxiety as being related to subjective interpretations rather than economic categories, that overall things are not going to improve for many people, their way of life is under threat especially in relation to health provision, debt and costs of education and there is a high degree of political frustration. Her empirical research deals with assessing the "political impact of fears and anxieties built upon long-term economic decline following a period of sustained economic gains" (Nancy Wiefek, 2003). In this process she also claims that "the rumours of the death of class in America (sic) may have been greatly exaggerated." Unfortunately she, like other commentators have a problem with trying to conceptualize what they mean by "middle class" and her discussion is bogged down in social stratification rather than class. Nevertheless, she does perceive a relationship between economic change–class–anxiety and connects that to political frustration, especially in relation to controlling the apparent juggernaut of capitalist "progress". She puts it in this way:

> "The problem lies in the fact that there are so few forces to balance the market forces and take the heat off those who are left insecure by this turbo-charged capitalism. In other words, what lies at the centre of these fears is not the distress of experiencing this dynamic economy that can make many feel like they are walking on a tightrope, but rather the absence of a safety net." (Nancy Wiefek, 2003, p. 113)

The response she believes may lie in the potential for "progressive politics." The barrier she believes to achieving progress in this area lies in the fact that politics has become a dirty word. And she feels that addressing the anxiety and inequality in the US involves developing non-elite politics by combining the forces of labour unions, political parties, community groups, public schools, and she points to the importance of forming alliances and the ripeness for doing so: "at this point in America's (sic) history there exists a potent potential for coalition-building." While I believe generally that this is a worthy sentiment, it is not a programme or an agenda and is not built on sufficiently sound theory of class. The perception of middle class is too vague and the acceptance of social stratification does not necessarily point to the right kinds of alliances. Nor is it clear exactly what is progressive politics in her terms. However, the general point should be received. Fractions of class can form alliances, in the context of an ill expressed malaise, to produce outcomes that would reform the capitalist system. This is discussed further in Chapter 7, but first we turn to our major explanandum, economic crises and why they do not bring down capitalism.

NOTES

1. Barack Obama, on the eve, of his nomination as the presidential nominee of the Democratic Party was seen at one stage to be more a celebrity than a politician with a serious political manifesto.
2. Ibid cf Chapter 7 passim. In the strange movie, The Matrix, the central character is called Neo. Neo keeps his play discs in a hollowed out copy of The Simulacrum (another work by Baudrillard). In the *Consumer Society*, the first cross-head of Chapter 7, entitled Mass-media Culture is The Neo. See also Chapter 3 supra on the Commodity.
3. For the relationship between the sacralisation of the body see Mircea Eliade (1959), Chapter 4.
4. 29 Jun 2005 a 19-year-old who killed his parents in the United States was able to plead diminished responsibility as he was found to be suffering from a "rare" mental disorder, narcissistic personality disorder.
5. Alphonos Lingis, "The Society of Dismembered Body Parts", in Boundas and Olkowski (1994, p. 299).
6. Schizophrenia is used here to mean the disintegration of the individual, the loss of rationality, problems with action and understanding. Kahler uses the term somewhat differently: the failure to connect one apparently rational action with another apparently rational action, the two being quite contradictory.
7. Lyons (1996); Cloward and Piven (1972); Collier and Horowitz (1996).
8. Marx lamented that the working class would be a "plaything" in the hands of the ruling classes unless it is "trained by continual agitation...to undertake a decisive campaign against the collective power, i.e the political power of the ruling classes." Quoted by Harding (1996, p. 34).
9. Tony Blair's "New" Labour Party probably comes closest as measured by policy agendas, excluding its militarist nature.

CHAPTER 6

ECONOMIC CRISES AND THE THEORY OF THE TENDENCY OF THE RATE OF PROFIT TO FALL

1. CYCLES AND ABSORPTION

One of the main functions of the absorptive class is to minimize the impact of economic crisis within a given national economy and where possible to shift the impact of economic crisis to less-developed or developing economies or indeed to another advanced economy. Hence the absorptive class displays the same feature of capitalism: it is simultaneously both national and international. This process of absorption is not done consciously, of course. It is the way the system has come to operate. Had the system not done so, capitalist economies would have lost a great degree of its capacity for resilience in the face of recurrent crises. Since the industrial revolution gathered momentum in England in the eighteenth century and spread rapidly to a limited number of countries in the world, economic crisis has been commonplace, threatening the very fabric of the economies created by the system. Economic crisis is taken to mean a severe disjuncture between production and consumption, marked by a reduction in economic growth. Depending on one's theoretical position economic crisis is caused by over-production or under-consumption or by some combination of the two. Adam Smith who published *An Enquiry into the Wealth of Nations* just about at the onset of the industrial revolution in England believed that any disjuncture between glut and scarcity was an effect of wrong-minded intervention by government. Left alone market forces would always tend toward the elimination of gluts. Thus, want of employment (the word unemployment was to be invented a 100 years later), so dangerous to the social fabric, would be avoided and capital accumulation would take place steadily in an unimpeded way. However, by the early nineteenth century, the British economy seemed to fluctuate ever more wildly than it had done in less industrial times, and as the urban population grew, such instability was especially feared by the ruling classes in Britain and, later, in Germany, the United States, France and Italy. Clearly, policy intervention by governments took place to manage such crises and the governments sought increasingly to achieve financial and price stability, and in Britain for instance this culminated in the Bank Charter Act of 1844, having 10 years previously introduced legislation aimed at achieving labour mobility with the infamous Poor Law Amendment Act.

As time went, on the re-appearances of crises did not diminish and statisticians and economists discovered many more forms of economic fluctuations or cycles.[1] By the end of the 1930s we have Schumpeter's business cycle, Kitchin's inventory cycle, Juglar's investment cycle and Kondratieff's long cycle or wave as well as Keynesian explanations for so-called depressions. Later we have Kuznets's infrastructural investment cycle, and Rostow's analysis of cyclical growth during the industrial revolution and much else. All of which added to the non-statistical observations by Marx, Engels and Lenin that crises are endemic to capitalism and at some point when crises arrive one upon the other, the proletariat will assist the system to fall under its own weight. For some time this Marxist phantasm was highly influential, especially when the United States, Western Europe and other connected parts fell into a massive crisis in the 1930s. The war that resulted in September 1939, presaged by military intervention by Germany, Italy and Japan, appeared to be largely a result of this economic crisis. Hence after the Second World War much effort was taken to ensure that economic crisis would be averted. The Bretton Woods institutions, the IMF and the World Bank and the WTO descendant of the GATT, all attest to this historic international policy response. As the crisis of 2007 proceeded there were many calls for a new Bretton Woods. Policy prescriptions and outcomes are held to have been thus responsible to some considerable degree for averting the crises. For instance the general acceptance of the Keynesian domestic economic policies as well as the international institutions that were Keynes's brainchildren appeared to provide until the 1970s the much sought after stability and economic growth with only milder so-called recessions to disturb the thought processes of policymakers. By the end of 2008 the overt policy prescriptions of Keynes were again becoming current demands.

While economic policymakers in advanced economic nations strive toward stability, they also pursue economic policies not entirely favourable to the well-being of the capitalist system as a whole for a variety of reasons. The invasion of Iraq has promoted all sorts of outcomes not foreseen. Some outcomes assist growth, others impede it. Generally for the US the intervention has been good for parts of its economy in the sense that the intervention led to a fall in the dollar on the foreign exchanges for a time thus increasing US industrial competitiveness while the military expenditure helped burn up the capacity of the United States to produce massive surpluses that would result in the even more massive production of yet more surpluses. In mid-2006, the US economy was judged to be booming and exceeding growth forecasts despite dire predictions caused by the unduly high price of oil.

However, explanations for the rapid recovery from crises have not been entirely satisfactory and are, as one might expect, couched in conventional economic terms. For instance this comment was taken from an internet article in 2005 in the space between crises:

> Another potential depression-level crisis occurred in the fall of 1987, when the American stock market crashed deeply again. The then new chief of the Federal Reserve, Alan Greenspan, protected the financial system by providing large amounts of money for the banking system. This action was very necessary at the time, as the potential for a general depression was very great. Nobel economist Paul A. Samuelson believes that the crash could have led into another Great Depression: "On every proper Richter scale, the 1987 crash rivaled that of the 1929 crash. By contrast with journalists, mainstream economists correctly computed that the late-1987 25 percent erosion of worldwide asset values was prone to reduce by about 1 percent per annum the likely 1987–1989 growth in global output. Had you told those economists to factor into their IS-LM diagrams [econometric charts] the worldwide acceleration of the money supply induced by the October 1987 crash, their regressions [econometric statistical equations] would have projected the continuance of the 1982 recovery that history has recorded in 1988–1989."[2] Samuelson seems to believe that the accelerated money supply in late 1987 probably was the difference, *but that accelerated money supplies will not always work to resolve a crisis* – as when a crash occurs against a backdrop of previously existing stagflation [emphasis by author of the article].[3]

That is not surprising. One orthodox response to crisis is to provide money and credit on the Keynesian model. The other orthodox response is to allow the crisis to take its course up to a point on the grounds that the economy is "over-heated" in some way. The point I am making is that the crisis can be allowed to take its course if the absorptive class is in a position to absorb, i.e. take financial losses without the real economy suffering unduly in the short run because burning off capital is good for the medium term. This commentary above might well serve as a summary of the 2007+ crisis, too, in many ways. Certainly the fear of a depression is there in exactly the same way as it exists in the circumstances of 2007–2009. It is astonishing the way memories dim in relation to past crises despite their regular occurrence.

While this essay sets out to explain why capitalism is resilient and, despite recurrent and inevitable crises that beset its seemingly inexorable growth, the issue has been discussed on many occasions but usually with the cart before the horse. For some Marxists, the question has been will capitalism collapse as a result of the combination of its own contradictions and the proletarian struggle? And what has caused the delay and what is the economic analysis underlying the arguments to explain this delay? As we shall see the debates by orthodox economists have been what can be done to avoid crises, and much argument surrounds the question of effective demand. For Marxists, who began the arguments about the collapse of capitalism, Marx's Volume II of Capital is critical. A good discussion can be found in Meghnad Desai's book, *Marx's Revenge: The Resurgence of Capitalism and the Death of State is Socialism* (Desai, 2002). Two chapters (6 & 19) deal with the specific debates about how near is the end of capitalism. He points out the importance of the analysis contained in Volume II of capital as well as the important modification made by Rosa Luxemburg in *The Accumulation of Capital* (published originally in 1913). It was Imperialism, it was argued in the early twentieth century by Marx–Leninists, that provided the absorptive power for capitalism that was otherwise lacking, and this extended the life of capitalism through recurrent crises. It was Rosa Luxemburg who provided what at the time was regarded as a brilliant extension of Marx's analysis much to her own vilification within the movement (Luxemburg, 2003). Desai provides a succinct account of Luxemburg's contribution to extending Marx's own analysis.

> The other theme Luxemburg introduced was the addition of a 'third Department' to Marx's scheme. This Department's role was to absorb the surplus output, and produce output for which the demand came not from workers, or from any other consumers, but from governments. This was the armaments industry. Thus the armaments industry could absorb surplus machinery from Department I and make armaments which governments could buy. (Desai, 2002, p. 95).

Desai then goes on immediately, reporting on Luxemburg's arguments: "So the perspective here is that capitalism needs a 'sink' which can *absorb surplus* output of machines sector." Metaphors such as absorption and sink indicate that the problem is all about what is to be done about the surplus one way or another, though "sponge" might be a slightly better word than sink. Desai confirms that at this historical point in time (prior to the First World War) "the continued survival of capitalism was a puzzle to be solved.

Luxemburg explained it by linking the core countries with the periphery. Imperialism here did not mean political domination: it was an exchange relationship in which the core sold machine goods and bought raw materials" (Desai, 2002, p. 96). This process could not go on forever, it was supposed so that capitalism must cease at some point to be able to reproduce itself. A review of a new edition of *The Accumulation of Capital* (published in 2003 by Routledge) also provides some insights that help take the absorptive arguments further. The reviewer, Judy Cox, in the *International Socialism Journal*, explains in clear language both the position laid out by Marx and Luxemburg's modification. Marx, according to Luxemburg, did not explain where increased demand would come from. Cox explains what Marx had to say in this way.

> After starting with this model of simple reproduction, Marx moved on to describe a model of "expanded reproduction." In this model the surplus produced is not simply consumed by the capitalists. Rather, the surplus is divided between what the capitalists get for their luxury consumption, what workers get to consume, paid in the form of wages, and accumulation for further production, spending on new materials and machinery for example.[4]

Cox then has an interesting quote from Luxemburg.

> The essential difference between enlarged reproduction and simple reproduction consists in the fact that in the latter the capitalist class and its hangers-on consume the entire surplus value, whereas in the former a part of the surplus value is set aside from personal consumption of its owners, not for the purpose of hoarding, but in order to increase active capital, i.e. for capitalisation.

The flaw spotted by Luxemburg and reported to us by Cox is simply that the workers could not provide sufficient consuming power. But Luxemburg refused to accept the argument that capitalists could be each other's consumers: "we have before us a merry-go-round which revolves around itself in empty air... production for the sake of production, thus, from the standpoint of capital, utter nonsense."[5] Thus Luxemburg's logic was that effective demand must lay outside the capitalist system: "capital cannot accumulate without the aid of non-capitalist organizations..." As Cox points out, capitalists (that is, the capitalist class) are only interested in profits not in bringing consumption to society, only in accumulation. Consumption is a by-product of the capitalist process.

Where I depart from Marx and Luxemburg is in arguing that capitalism has solved its problem quite unconsciously, that is individual capitalists have no conscious awareness of the outcome whereby they have produced the absorptive class to absorb the surplus. In other words while there is a relationship between imperialism and the continuance of capitalism more or less in its present form, the capitalist system has developed an endogenous or immanent process for absorbing surplus: that is, it has produced a class to do it. Clues for its existence lie in the work of Luxemburg and in Marx. Let's, for instance, return to this quote referred to above:

> The essential difference between enlarged reproduction and simple reproduction consists in the fact that in the latter the capitalist class and its hangers-on consume the entire surplus value, whereas in the former a part of the surplus value is set aside from personal consumption of its owners, not for the purpose of hoarding, but in order to increase active capital, i.e. for capitalisation.

Who are the hangers-on? Is it conceivable that the hangers-on who were so insignificant in earlier stages of industrial capitalism in Britain, Germany, France and the United States become in due course not merely hangers-on but a vital key element in itself? In other words, the so-called hangers-on become a key part of the embryonic material for the absorptive class. Similarly Miliband in his path-breaking analysis in the *State in Capitalist Society* was thoroughly bemused as to what do to with the "large and growing class of professional people – lawyers, accountants, middle-rank executives, architects, technicians, scientists, administrators, doctors, teachers etc. – who form one of the two main elements of the middle-class" to which he later added "cultural workmen," writers, journalists, preachers, poets and later he mentions the professionals who run the state: judges, civil servants, politicians, military men.[6] Lasch also found it difficult to locate the middle class. "Liberals and conservatives alike have assumed that the middle class is growing and that its standard of living is steadily rising. In fact it is shrinking, and its standard of living is deteriorating...." He goes on to quote Harry Braverman's 1974 comment that "the most common occupational combination within the family is one in which the husband is operative and the wife a clerk." Lasch draws the conclusion that this represents, rather than embourgeoisement, proletarianization (Lasch, 1991, p. 479). In fact it is neither. What we see is the growth of the absorptive class in exactly the fractionalized way that I suggested in Chapter 5 of this essay and developed further in Chapter 7.

Placing these endlessly growing middle-class professionals in their massive variety into a single class that has meaning has never been easy. It is not good enough to say that they are mere hangers-on, or that they are distinguished by their values or as lieutenants of the bourgeoisie or by their "consciousness." The discovery of the absorptive class, therefore, fills this gap as well as deals with the confusion found in the work of such authors as

Luxemburg, Miliband and Lasch. Capitalism thus has produced the class, the absorptive class, missing in Department I and II in Marx and missing, too, in Department III identified by Luxemburg (Desai, 2002). In other words, the capitalist class shares out the surplus to the absorptive class, which is formed and extended through transfer payments and fiscal policies of the "big state." Luxemburg argued it was not possible for "third persons" who are neither capitalists nor workers to take up the demand. "Priests, civil servants, landowners were also invariably paid out of the pockets of the capitalists or, via taxes, the pockets of the workers."[7] However, we are saying precisely the opposite. As capitalists cannot possibly consume everything produced, and as there are political limits for state consumption of armaments, as the developing world fails to expand its capacity to consume sufficient amounts of commodities, as civil expenditure fails to keep pace with production and in any case helps less to sustain the rate of profit than other forms of consumption, the absorptive class is constantly expanded. And, as we underline several times, the class not only absorbs commodities, but also thereby absorbs excess capital and shocks to the capitalist system itself and absorbs political discord.

2. CRISES 1959–2000: THEORY AND POLICY

The post World War II boom, it is generally agreed, lasted from 1945 to around 1973. There were cyclical fluctuations and in some countries like the United Kingdom serious structural adjustments were taking place. The crises were much more of a cyclical variety than a secular or long wave, though the whole period may be considered a Kondratieff upswing. The couple of decades after the oil shocks appear to be the most unstable to economic historians. For instance, Robert Brenner writes "an era of slowed growth and increasing economic turbulence from 1973 onwards, was marked by deeper recessions and the return of devastating financial crises absent since the Great Depression" (Brennner, 2006, p. xix). Hobsbawm, writing about the short twentieth century, begins his chapter entitled the crisis decades, 1973–1991, unequivocally: "The history of the twenty years after 1973 is that of a world which lost its bearings and slid into instability and crisis." Yet, as he goes on to examine this period, despite the obvious and undeniable existence of crises, he admits there was nothing quite like 1929 and its aftermath. "The global economy did not break down, even momentarily, although the Golden Age ended with something like a classical cyclical slump which reduced industrial production by ten per cent in the developed market economies and international trade by thirteen per cent" (Hobsbawm, 1996, pp. 403–405). He has to admit, however, that, despite these crises, by the end of the short century, "the countries of the developed capitalist world were, taken as a whole, far richer and more productive than in the early 1970s, and the global economy of which they still formed the central element was vastly more dynamic."

What replaced serious crisis was greater inequality between those who could take a significant share of the surplus and those who could not. The system of production is always restructuring in the interests of the producers so that technological changes cause stresses to the labour market: in the more extreme cases many individuals are cast out into the so-called underclass. Hobsbawm makes the point that the extremes of poverty and wealth both grew, as did the range of income distribution in between. Indeed, this seems to be the case generally, and is almost an iron law: economic growth as measured by the gini coefficient indicates that economic disparities increase during periods of growth. Policymakers had difficulty in catching up with what Hobsbawm refers to as the out-of-control nature of the capitalist system. Policy prescriptions in the period after the second world war appeared to work up to a point, not least because they were based on Keynesian policy: important, too, was the alleged associated social psychology based on public confidence and the powerful role of a managed mass of consumers through budget deficiting associated especially with the election cycles in many countries. These political contingencies exaggerated the tendency toward cyclical fluctuation in many capitalist countries. The appearance of stagflation put an end to such overt confidence in Keynesian-style consumer manipulation and its associated public expenditure on increasing the size and scope of the welfare state. Thatcher's attempted rolling back of the welfare state, Reagonomics and disenchantment generally with economic policies shifted attention back to more neoclassical approaches to the economic theory. The attack on the big state, attempts to cut large government expenditures, granting tax relief for the rich and big corporations matched the power shift occasioned by the ever-increasing concentration of capital that made possible the ever-increasing concentration of political power. Anything else would simply not be possible. Concentration of capital cannot exist with the dispersal of political power in the form of more genuine forms of democracy. And, as we shall see in more detail, the steady increase of the rate of profit, which was largely unproblematic in the period of post-war growth, became an issue and is at the root of policy responses in more recent decades. Predictably for this period was the promotion of so-called supply-side economics as if that constituted a novel analysis. In 1978, Jude Wanniski and Victor Canto, as a reaction to the disillusionment with Keynesian demand side economics, were among those who popularized and justified this seemingly new approach (Canto, 1983). In crude terms, the theoretical emphasis on supply-side was a justification to cut taxes as a way of increasing production, and therefore of employment and creating higher living standards (through trickle down). Supply-side economics was thus seen as a way out of the strange phenomenon of stagflation. Looking back it was nothing more than a normal reaction of the system to maintain the profit level and sustain the process of production. As the term supply-side refers to the process whereby levels of production (for profit) should be maintained, it is hardly surprising that a theory was developed to justify tax cuts leading to higher rates of profit. In addition, the theory also gave the US firms a greater competitive advantage in the system where they were facing threats from Asian Tiger economies and elsewhere. Again, Hobsbawm's comments are interesting: "...the central fact about the Crisis Decades is not that capitalism no longer worked as well as it had done in the Golden Age, but its operations had become uncontrollable" (Hobsbawm, 1996, p. 408). The truth of the matter is that capitalism was never as controllable as policymakers and politicians overtly believed, and still is not. Of course many economists and policymakers claim that policymakers have done reasonably well. "Over the past seventy years, we have learned a great deal ... and how to intervene actively in the economy to make it more stable. By and large the Keynesian medicine has worked: downturns are shorter and shallower, upturns are longer" (Stiglitz, 2003, p. 198). However, the truth of the matter is that capitalism has its own dynamic and interference can exist to make it more or less efficient *qua* an economic system and *qua* a political system. At certain historical moments distributing the surplus in the form of a welfare state has certain economic and political advantages. At certain moments in time the welfare state favours, say, maintaining low wages at times of growth through the provision of a social wage where state benefits and health provision and free or nearly free education is an alternative to paying the higher wages that would be necessary in the absence of such benefits. The struggle between gurus of the mixed economy and those of the "free" market systems posed as an ideological struggle by Hobsbawm, however, was not really an ideological struggle at all but a shift of convenience in the face of the successful fight for hegemony between industrial and finance capital. After all it was the Republican President of the United States, Richard Nixon, who claimed that we are all Keynesians now. Keynesianism was always an orthodoxy that was based conveniently on a reformist theorization to maintain the strength of industrial capitalism in the struggle against finance capital.[8] Hobsbawm may well believe that capitalism is out of control but what we are really seeing is the next step toward hegemony of finance capital over industrial capital. After all globalization is to a large extent the massive and qualitative expansion of finance capitalism. Thus, associated with this development economic orthodoxy has to shift its position from market interference and support, to allowing market forces to work more freely. It is free capital movement, at the end of the day, which is out of control. The other potentially mobile factor of production, labour, is far from out of control. Labour is firmly fixed in place within national economies and nation states. (The terrorist threat plays into the hands of those who wish to see international labour movements under firm control.) When Hobsbawm says (in company with many other commentators) that the "crisis decades were the era when the national state lost its economic powers," he gets reality rather skewed. The nation states released control of the movement of capital for the purposes of maintaining the level of the rate of profit, but kept the movement of labour firmly under control (The serious consequences of all this on many of the less-developed countries is outside the scope of this work). One of the consequences (for the concerns of this discussion of the absorptive class) of this tight control over movements of labour is the geographical concentration of the absorptive class. While all countries will have an absorptive class, the bulk of the class remains concentrated currently in the major OECD countries, though China and to a lesser extent India are of key importance.

Individual shock absorbers experience different degrees of security as the labour market becomes restructured to take account of restructuring of capitalism itself. The underclass and the nightmares associated with disappearing into it haunt major segments of the absorptive class. For an individual whose existence is determined by his or her capacity to absorb with all the concomitant social significance associated with absorption, failure to be able to do so is not only a personal and family disaster but is a matter of ultimate social shame. One way of identifying the effect of the absorptive class is to ask the question: can the collapse of 1929 and its aftermath, the depression that lasted for a full decade, happen again? One leading commentator, John K Galbraith, answers the question as firmly as one might expect from an economist, even of Galbraith's heterodoxy, with a reasonably confident "no." He does so in the introduction to the 1997 edition of his mini-masterpiece, *The Great Crash*. In Galbraith's *apologia* for yet another edition of the book, he says with the laid-back cynicism and confidence of a nonagenarian, that economic crises appear with such regularity that his book is always topical. He refers to the "off-shore funds insanity of the seventies, the big bust of 1987, less dramatic episodes and fears, all brought attention back to 1929 and kept the book in print. And so again now in 1997."[9] He watched as did we all who had sufficient interest, the amazing bull (and in the case of the dotcoms, stag) market; as mentioned earlier the upward movement of share values defied gravity, but anyone who was anyone knew it had to end, yet the prices of shares kept going upward and for a much longer time than many economic and financial gurus expected. As Galbraith commented at the time: "The process continues; optimism with its market effect is the order of the day. Prices will go up even more. Then, for reasons that will endlessly be debated, comes to an end. The descent is always more sudden than the increase; a balloon that has been punctured does not deflate in an orderly way" (Galbraith, 1997). The end of the bull market was predictable. But what would be the consequences? Galbraith's answer then makes the case for one of the vital functions of the absorptive class, though, while he does not fully recognize its existence, he does realize, naturally, the all-important function of shock absorption. "If we do have a downturn ... some things can, indeed, be foreseen. By some estimates a *quarter of all Americans*, directly or indirectly, are in the share market. Were there to be a bad slump, it would limit their expenditures ... and put pressure on their very large credit card debt. This *would not be as painful* as the after effects of 1929 ... " (Galbraith, 1997, xiii). This position is consistent with Galbraith's explanation of why the Crash of 1929 hit so hard and was so prolonged. Basically one of the reasons was that the absorptive class at that time was too small to absorb the worst of the crisis. Galbraith posed five reasons for the disastrous consequences of the 1929 Wall Street Crash. Overall, the economy was fundamentally unsound. But what exactly did unsound mean? The first point of the five posited by Galbraith refers to the "bad distribution" of income. He argues that the rich were indubitably rich, but there were not enough of them. The "rich" were simply not numerous enough and income and wealth was not sufficiently well spread to act as a buffer when the crash came. Of course, there are many other reasons and other emphases, the least of which was not the state of the world economy as much as the state of the US economy (which Galbraith over-focuses on). Nevertheless, this seems to be a key observation that provides a clue to the existence, importance of and key function of the absorptive class in maintaining the resilience of the capitalist system in recurrent and permanently threatening crises.

3. EAST ASIAN CRISIS OF THE NINETIES

Now, let us look at the Asian crisis as an instructive example following Galbraith's comments of 1997. Joseph Stiglitz's view of the East Asian crisis in the latter end of the 1990s serves as being a more or less conventional analysis. Stiglitz lays the blame for the crisis in East Asia at the door of the International Monetary Fund (IMF).

> "When the Thai bhat collapsed in July 2 1997 no one knew that this was the beginning of the greatest economic crisis since the Great Depression...the crisis is over now (2002)...Unfortunately the IMF policies imposed during these tumultuous times worsened the situation.... Indeed, in retrospect, it became clear that the IMF policies not only exacerbated the downturns but were partially responsible for the onset." (Stiglitz, 2002, p. 89)

How could this be? After all, the IMF had been set up at Bretton Woods precisely to prevent the international transmission of depressions or recessions? Stiglitz continues:... "excessively rapid financial and capital market liberalization was probably the single most important cause of the crisis."

Of course, this was not the view of the IMF, which blamed the Asian governments of Malaysia, Singapore, Thailand, S. Korea, Indonesia as well their form, ironically, of so-called crony capitalism. Stiglitz, rightly, was shocked by the IMF response since over the previous quarter of a century it was those very Asian governments, for good or ill, which had been central and successful in the economic advance of their national economies. Overnight, governments that had been credited with guiding economic miracles and achieving massive, unheard of economic growth rates, productivity gains and increases in per capita incomes, were suddenly pilloried by the US Treasury and the IMF. Stiglitz is clear. The IMF, led by the US government, had caused and exacerbated the massive falls in the stock market, which, in turn, had led to the fall in the value of shares, the reduction in levels of production in the real economy and massive hardship for millions as a result of a substantial rise in unemployment.

> The crisis economies of East Asia were clearly threatened with a major downturn and needed stimulation. The IMF pushed exactly in the opposite course, with consequences precisely of the kind that one would have predicted. (Stiglitz, 2002, p. 105)

Stiglitz then unwraps what should have been done by the US-led IMF. To him the answer is simple: maintain the economy as close to full employment as possible: make sure there was a steady flow of finance, restructure institutions where necessary, change bankruptcy laws, restructure debt repayment. Stiglitz seems quite flummoxed as to why this was not done. To him economics seems to be about actors and institutions. Get the actors to act correctly and fix the institutions and you can solve the problem. Of course, he is correct up to a point. But the point is that capitalist economics are holistic systems, and that they behave according to the best interests of those systems... generally speaking. We have to ask, therefore, a fairly simple question, which Stiglitz does not, nor do most economists or economic journalists. What was the economic function of the Asian crisis? The short answer is that the crises behaved in such a way as to burn off capital. Stemming from the argument that the global capitalist system suffers from a tendency toward over-production, which puts pressure on the rate of profit, the function of the East Asian crisis was to write off the capacity to accumulate capital in the East Asian economies in the interest of maintaining either mass profit, or better still the rate of profit, in the United States and elsewhere in the West. The function of the absorptive class in the United States in particular is to cushion whatever pressure might occur, while in the East Asian countries (and others that suffered the spin-off in Latin-America or Russia) the depression was deeper and has had longer term effects in that the absorptive class there, like their economies, is not as yet fully developed. We now turn to the theory that is fundamental to understanding the underlying reason for the recurrent crises in capitalism for which the system has produced the absorptive class as shock absorbers.

4. CRISIS 2007–2009

The background to the economic environment of globalization in which we can locate the 2007 crisis is well known. First of all, globalization is best described as global capitalism (Hutton & Giddens, 2000). In this way we know much more clearly what we are talking about. Second, we can indicate the main events contributing to the current conditions by identifying some simple sign posts.

- During the years 1973–1983 floating exchange rates became the norm.
- In the years 1984–1990 direct foreign investment increased fourfold.
- In the years 1980–1992 cross border flows of capital from G7 countries went up tenfold.
- In the decade 1980–1990 cross border equities went from $120 billion to $1.4 trillion.

- In the decade 1980–1990 International bank loans went from $324 billion to $7.5 trillion.
- Similarly, trading in international bonds went from $295 billion $1.6 trillion.

The huge capital movements had led over a period of 30 years to a vastly enhanced capacity for the world's forces of production to have access to finance capital; the world had developed a massive ability to produce by, among other things, moving capital to sources of labour; the gap between the finance economy and the real economy was always likely to tend toward divergence unless forced back into alignment by crisis.

Capital markets continued to expand in the first years of the twenty-first century. During the period 1993–2004 capital markets expanded at twice the rate of global GDP. *The Economist* on May 26th 2007 reported: "as stock derivatives and bond markets get bigger, investors are shifting money into a vast array of tradable financial products." By 2006 the value of shares traded worldwide was in the region of $70 trillion. In October 2007, an economic crisis was seen to be well on its way. This time the crisis demonstrated that financial institutions had become ever more heavily interdependent, and that many of the leading financial institutions had no real clue as to the overall security of their investments or their real value. It took the collapse of the sub-prime market in the United States to expose the fragility of so-called investment in financial instruments, though the truth of the degree of interdependence was relatively slow to dawn on economic observers, institutions and politicians and policymakers. Among the problems was the way in which new "tradable financial products" were packaged for short-term profit. One of these was known as the collaterized debt obligation (CDO) and another was the structured investment vehicle (SIV). As *Business Weekly* (October 29, 2007) sought to explain (believing that any credit market rescue plan would involve a mere $80 billion) that CDOs had heavily infected SIVs leaving considerable doubt as to whether any institutions might be prepared to rescue the system of credit markets. Thus, after the collapse of the sub-prime market, banking institutions worldwide began progressively to declare enormous losses with economists, governments and journalists unable to add up the losses, not knowing what institutions, who and how much were involved. Mervyn King, Director of the Bank of England, said on 5 November 2007 that it was likely to be several months before banks returned to normal after the crisis, because it could take that long for them to disclose all their losses from financial instruments linked to US sub-prime mortgages. Meanwhile one of the earlier casualties, Citigroup, reported a huge holding in the sub-prime mortgages and the chairman resigned from the group that boasted 200 million customers and 300,000 employees. Shares fall immediately by around 5%. But the exposure of Citigroup of $15 billion was not thought to be of massive importance against the $trillions of assets held by the banking corporation. A few days later the BBC reported some of the earliest casualties with estimated losses thus:

Citigroup: $11bn
Merrill Lynch: $8bn
Morgan Stanley: $3.7bn
Bear Stearns: $3.2bn
UBS: $3.4bn
Deutsche Bank: $3.2bn
Credit Suisse: $1bn
Wachovia: $1.1bn

Some estimates made by pundits gave a figure of half a $trillion losses in the sub-prime market. But what continued in the reports was the threat of a credit squeeze, termed as credit crunch for added media effect, that would result in bankruptcies, profit reduction, loss of jobs and general economic downturn affecting most economies linked to global capitalist activity. While Mervyn King, Governor of the Bank of England, could say of the Northern Rock debacle in the United Kingdom that no retail depositor had suffered, the economies worldwide were showing falls in the value of financial instruments and banks in the United States were continuing to collapse up to the end of 2008. Anyone investing in the stock markets at this time saw their paper assets melting away. Countless numbers of people who thought they would be getting their own homes through the sub-prime market were losing whatever little they had in the United States. Risk had been shifted down the line to holders of financial instruments of dubious value and to millions of poor families in the United States. The record showed a marked loss of the value of shares on all the major world stock markets from early October onward. In the briefest of terms, the surplus that the capitalist system produced was being continuously turned into a host of financial instruments by the system of financial capitalism. Wall Street, to use journalistic shorthand, wanted to get rid of this surplus by creating the sub-prime market the collapse of which ensured the burning off of excess capital. Thus, though the 2007–2009 crisis may differ in detail from other economic crises it has the same function, to burn off surplus capital, allow credit squeezes, reduce production of commodities of all kinds and create unemployment to provide a respite before the next boom. For the

very rich or the well-placed, there is some safety arising from their ability
to weather the storm of recession, but, for the most part, they see their
paper fortunes much diminished while the crisis lasts even though they are
able to move assets around or simply wait for the recession to "bottom out."
For the average man or woman on the top of the Clapham omnibus or in
the street, there is continuing uncertainty with house prices collapsing,
unemployment threatening and real wages falling. The absorptive class
rather than absorbing commodities now, by necessity, demonstrated its
capacity for absorbing the economic shock caused by the crisis. World over-
production and over-capacity had reappeared. Despite its best endeavours
the absorptive class have to turn from absorbing commodities to absorbing
the shock of the inevitable crisis. It is not that easy, however, to burn off
some of the massive surpluses. The brief dramatic rises in oil prices led to the
accumulation of enormous sums of money in the short run by a small
number of sovereign states while others were accumulating huge trade
surpluses. Subsequently, oil prices fell as the threat of falling production
became a reality. In June 2008, the OECD noted the vast accumulation
of funds by Abu Dhabi, Norway, Singapore, China and Kuwait. These
states alone accounted for over $2 trillion of currency holdings. These
states present a new issue in the structuring of the world surplus with, as yet,
unknown short- and medium-term consequences. "The rise of sovereign
wealth funds is one sign of the shift of the power in the world economy from
Western countries to the new emerging markets giants like China and the
oil-rich Middle East."[10] Burning off surpluses is no easy matter. The class of
shock absorbers respond politically in a strange way. Instead of turning on
the capitalist-run political system, they become more likely to turn to the
right rather than left. Hence, the crisis has led the UK electorate to the right
while in the United States the Democratic Party under the leadership of
Barack Obama faced much difficulty in preventing the electorate from
voting in another Republican president in the wake of the woeful Bush who
has presided over the crisis of 2007–2008. While Obama won the election of
2008, there was no landslide, and his early noises on preparing for the
presidency while hitting the ground running did not indicate a massive
restructuring of the capitalist system. Indeed, his intentions are mildly
reformist, consistent with support from the barely conscious absorptive
class. Governments in the advanced industrial countries facing recession
have to protect the scope for economic growth despite the capitalist system's
need to burn off capital. Governments must continue to boost the
absorptive class through protecting the numbers seeking house ownership

or to retain house ownership and all that follows from it; thus in the United States it was vital in 2008 to protect Fannie Mae and Freddy Mac even to the extent of quasi nationalization. The rest of the banking system also needed to be sustained with a colossal $700 billion loan to maintain the flow of credit and keep economic growth going even though rescuing banks may only sustain a ramshackle, inefficient and overblown system desperately in need of long-term regulation. In the case of the motor car industry in the United System, public funds can only be supplied for a short period before the car industry suffers the fate of car industries in some other countries such as the United Kingdom which long ago failed to compete with the restored economies of Japan and Germany. One outcome most likely will be defensive mergers or acquisitions as has already happened in the banking and insurance industries. Mergers in the car and other industries are likely in due course, though it was 2007 that saw many defensive mergers with mergers slowing up in the uncertain and credit strapped year of 2008. The 2007–2009 economic crisis has had the effect of holding up economic growth, reducing the capacity for world capitalism to produce commodities and has had the effect of some international restructuring with a serious weakening of US capitalism. Nevertheless, the United States still has a huge capacity for production and will grind back even though its economy may face some restructuring. After all, the US economy in 2007 had a measured GDP of nearly $12.4 trillion, leading Japan with a mere $4.5 trillion and Germany with $2.8 trillion (the Euro area totalling $10 trillion). China was not far behind Germany with $2.2 trillion. This makes China the absorptive hope of the rest of the world. Thus, however bad is the recession of 2007–2009 and however much economic restructuring takes place from country to country (with the United States and Japan most likely to experience such restructuring), the huge capitalist world economy will bounce back from this period of burning off of productive capacity . . . until the next time and will be protected by the shock-absorbing capacity of the absorptive class worldwide. So far the sheer capacity of the United States to absorb commodities and, more recently, to absorb the shock of the economic crisis has been massive simply at the household level. "Americans (sic) have lost one-quarter of their net worth in just a year and a half . . . Total home equity which was valued at $13 trillion in 2006 dropped to $8.8 trillion . . . Total retirement assets dropped from $10.3 trillion in 2006 to $8 trillion in 2008 . . . taken with other losses the total is around $8.3 trillion."[11] The shock absorbers are doing their job well!

5. THE THEORY OF THE TENDENCY OF THE RATE OF PROFIT TO FALL (TRPF)

At the heart of the Marxist explanation for the recurrent crises in capitalism is the theory of the tendency of the rate of profit to fall (TRPF). In the identification of the absorptive class in this book, the tendency (TRPF) is central. This theory not only provides the answer to why crisis? But also why survival? Meghnad Desai asks the following question: "But could it be that Marx provides a better argument for the long-term survival of capitalism than his detractors or followers have given him credit for?" (Desai, 2002, p. 83). He points out, correctly, that the problem of the falling rate of profit was a standard concern for all the political economists, Smith and Ricardo especially. In analysing the fall in the rate of profit under capitalism Marx was in the classical tradition, though needing to adjust his arguments to accord with his view of the eventual collapse of capitalism and its replacement with a new mode of production to which Marx had already committed himself in all his writings since the Communist Manifesto. There was, and is still, general agreement among economists and policymakers that real wages increase as production reaches full employment. Capitalists, therefore, substitute machinery (this is known as increasing the organic composition of capital) to counter this, and thus increase productivity. It may be that substituting machinery for labour does not do the trick because the surplus does not increase sufficiently. "Wages must not rise faster than growth in productivity" otherwise profit rates will then fall (Desai, 2002, p. 76). Understanding this process, which results in an inbuilt TRPF, was, for Marx, enormously important. After a couple of pages of Chapter 13 "The Law Itself" in "discovering" how the organic composition of capital may change, he wrote:

> ...this ratio between the mass surplus-value and the total capital applied in fact constitutes the rate of profit, which must therefore steadily fall. Simple as the law appears from the above arguments, not one of the previous writers on economics succeeded in discovering it...And given the great importance that this law has for capitalist production, one might well say that it forms the mystery around whose solution the whole of political economy since Adam Smith revolves.[12]

The motor force of capitalism thus becomes clear: the system is driven by the need to constantly increase productivity through the introduction of machinery, resulting in recurrent unemployment to keep real wages from impinging on the rate of profit. Increasing the mass of profit simply will not do. Marx continues: "Previous economists, not knowing how to explain the law of the falling rate of profit, invoked the rising mass of profit, the growth in its absolute amount, whether for the individual capitalists or for social capital as a whole, as a kind of consolation, but this was also based on mere commonplaces and imagined possibilities."

Modern observers persist on rediscovering this technological imperative at frequent intervals. For instance, Thomas L Friedman in the Lexus and the Olive Tree writes:

"Another reason globalization is easy to distort is that people don't understand that it is a technology driven phenomenon, not a trade one." (Friedmann, 1999, p. 357). "People" do not understand because it is not properly explained; in fact the opposite is true. Alternative theories and expressions are used in both the economic and journalistic literature to obscure the validity of the tendency for the rate of profit to decline. Such terminologies as viability, cost minimization, profitability, profit maximization and super profits are all used instead. Rarely is the term declining rate of profit used with its full implications. Whether "people" understand that technology drives global capitalism or not, the whole process of industrial capitalism has always been driven by technology, but it must be understood that this is itself a function of racing to avoid the fall in the rate of profit; globalization, which, as we have seen, is really better described as global capitalism, is subject to the same imperatives.

Laws in the social sciences and the sciences have a predictive quality given certain assumptions or conditions. That is the important feature of a law and why they are sought out. Given certain circumstances, apples will always fall toward the ground. Given certain assumptions supply and demand will be mediated by price. Many in the social sciences and those who wish for their own reasons to distort the laws of social sciences, many of which are fragile and have severe limitations anyway, wilfully ignore the conditions under which they may hold. The law of the TRPF has suffered in the literature from many distortions. Marx is clear that the law is only a tendency and he devotes two full chapters, 14 and 15, in Volume III of Capital explaining why. Indeed he begins Chapter 14, "Counteracting Forces," with a clear exposition of the tendential nature of the law.

If we consider the enormous development in the productive powers of social labour over the last thirty years (1835–65) alone, compared with earlier periods, and particularly if we consider the enormous mass of fixed capital involved in the overall process of social production quite apart from machinery proper, then instead of the problem that occupied previous economists, the problem of explaining the fall in the profit rate, we have the opposite problem of explaining why this fall is not greater or faster. Counteracting influences must be at work, checking and cancelling the effect of the

general law and giving it the character of a tendency, which is why we have described
the fall in the general rate of profit as a tendential fall. (Marx, 1972, Vol. III, p. 339)

He then indicates that one or more of six possibilities may operate: more intense exploitation of labour, reduction of wages below their value, cheapening of the elements of constant capital, relative surplus population, foreign trade and the increase of share capital.

Of all these the last one, increase of share capital, provides one of the clues for our claiming that the absorptive class rather than capitalists per se are of such great importance in contributing to the resilience of capitalism. Of all the changes that have taken place since the mid nineteenth century, one of the most important has been the development of stock markets round the world and the growth of share holding, a tendency observed by Marx in the early stages of the development of limited liability. He observed under the heading of "the increase in share capital":

> As capitalist production advances ... one portion of it is considered simply to be interest
> bearing capital and is invested as such ... these capitals, although invested in large
> productive enterprises, simply yield an interest, great or small, after all costs are
> deducted – so-called 'dividends'. This is the case with railways, for example. These do
> not therefore enter into the equalization of the general rate of profit, since they yield
> a profit rate less than the average. If they did go in, the average rate would fall much
> lower .... (Marx, 1972, p. 348)

For our purposes this is a truly astounding passage. General limited liability had been allowed by law in Britain only since 1855: Marx within a decade has already observed a crucial consequence of corporations expanding on the basis of share issues. Such companies would be able to maintain higher rates of profit for longer periods. This is precisely the general observation in the last decades of the twentieth century, and why capitalism has taken on the appearance of greater resilience than in the first half of the twentieth century. It has been the absorptive class that functions to purchase and hold financial instruments and thereby assist in maintaining the rate of profit, but also it is the absorptive class which disposes of the shares (burning off surplus capital) at the required moment and absorbing the losses (and pain). We have reached the point in the central argument of this book where we can say that the real crisis is that of over-production while the apparent crisis manifested on the stock markets around the world by a fall in share prices followed by rising unemployment in the real economy is not the crisis at all but the solution to the crisis.

6. SURPLUS AND ABSORPTION IN THE WORK OF BARAN AND SWEEZY

Baran and Sweezy's now "classic" work contains some of the clues we need in terms of surplus and of absorption. Four of the chapter headings involve the use of the word "absorption," and these follow the chapter called "The Tendency of the Surplus to Rise," which the authors offer as a Law which more or less replaces the Law of the TRPF (Baran & Sweezy, 1966, p. 72). Whatever the rights or wrongs of this approach, the authors offer a convincing argument to support their conclusion that, indeed, modern capitalist economies have an increasing capacity to muster surpluses. Moreover, these surpluses are a problem if invested because such investment produces even greater surpluses. The system requires as part of the process a limitation on the size of the surplus other than savings-investment. The solution, in their terms, is consumption or waste. Some of the surplus, they claim, is absorbed actually in the process of producing and in the operation of the corporate system. The authors quote Marx to make their point. Those who doubt the prophetic character of much of *Capital* should at least take note of the following: "It [the corporate system] reproduces a new financial aristocracy, a new variety of parasites in the shape of promoters, speculators, and merely nominal directors; a whole system of swindling and cheating by means of corporate promotion, stock issuance and stock speculation."[13] Baran and Sweezy go on to argue that the civilian government not only consumes a gigantic proportion of the surplus but also becomes increasingly irrational and destructive in the process of doing so. Of course, where military spending is concerned the actions of governments, and, most recently, the US and the UK governments providing the best examples in relation to their anti-Iraq bellicosity, are not only irrational but endanger the security of the whole planet. Marcuse writing in the same period as Baran and Sweezy reinforces this.

Does not the threat of an economic catastrophe which could wipe out the whole of the human race also serve to protect the very forces which perpetuate this danger? The efforts to prevent such a catastrophe overshadow the search for its potential causes in contemporary society. These causes remain unidentified, unexposed, unattacked by the public because they recede before the all too obvious threat from without. Equally obvious is the need for being prepared, for living on the brink, for facing the challenge. We submit to the peaceful production of the means of destruction, to the perfection of waste, to being educated for a defence, which deforms the defenders and that which they defend. (Marcuse, 1996/1991)

The potential misdirection of expenditure is due to reach an unprecedented scale. For instance, *The Washington Post* reported[14] as early as 2002
that: "The $355.4 billion defense bill, approved with overwhelming support
to provide most of what Bush requested, increases spending by more than
$34 billion over the previous year....The defense bill ...provides for $3.3
billion for 15 C-17 transport aircraft, $2.3 billion for two Aegis destroyers,
$3.2 billion for 46 Navy fighters and $3.5 to continue developing the Joint
Strike Fighter. Another $249 billion is allotted for Navy Tomahawk cruise
missiles." By April 2005, the US Senate was overwhelmingly approving such
sums as $81 billion for military spending in Iraq and Afghanistan alone,
taking the total bill well over $300 billion for those two operations. By 2008,
the simple figure for the cost of the Iraqi war had climbed to over half a
trillion US dollars. Some estimates set the figure at $700 billion.[15] At the end
of 2008, Stiglitz and his collaborator Linda J Bilmes were adding all sorts of
other weighted variables into their equation which gave a figure of $3 trillion
(Stiglitz & Bilmes, 2008). The formal cost of the Iraqi war approved to mid
2009 by the US government was $650 billion with the cost of the war in
Afghanistan standing at a little less than one third of that figure. The
National Debt of the United States, in the meantime, increased from just
under $6 trillion on the departure of President Clinton to approaching $11
trillion by the time of President Obama's inauguration in January 2009.

And this is only a tip of the iceberg of direct military expenditure but
indicates the fact, probably, that arms expenditure and expenditure as a
result of general bellicosity, threatened or actual, has declined markedly as a
percentage of gross national product. In other words the major state agency,
the government, has been slack in burning up the surplus, and this despite
the fact that the system itself has been writing off massive surpluses in the
last six years or so in the United States. What has not been fully explored in
any of the literature is the social relationship of the collective or collectives
of "ordinary" persons as a class, which consume the surplus left over by the
government, the military and the rather small capitalist class (in relation to
the size of the surplus). It is now supposed that the proportion of unskilled
labourers and blue-collar workers in the economies of the more advanced
countries has shrunk markedly, and a host of white collar and service
employees have taken their place. There has also been reference to a
diamond-shaped social structure rather than a pyramid-shaped one.
Reference is made to the middle classes or professional classes or managerial
class. If this huge and growing mass of people who are neither capitalists nor
proletarians have just one thing in common, it is that they purchase
commodities, and, in doing so, they eat up or absorb a considerable part of

the surplus. Just as Marx argued that the proletariat was brought into being in the circumstances of urban industrialization so this absorptive class has been brought into being because the capitalists themselves, the proletariat at home, and the proletariat and peasantry in lesser developed countries cannot absorb sufficient amounts of the surplus. The absorptive class has been brought into being by modern capitalism in the same way that classes have always been produced by the dominant class(es). The absorptive class would not exist under any system other than capitalism or without its particular history. It is not God-given nor normal, but distinctly a result of historical processes.

As we have seen it has several distinct functions, one of which is to be a shock absorber of the system by expanding and contracting in relation to the recurrent crises of capitalism from place to place and from time to time and acts as a shock absorber does in a car protecting the main suspension. One of the key elements in this is the commodity and the commodification of most aspects of day to day living from health to the joys of nature to pieces of paper called company stocks to works of art to the ephemera of the operatic note.[16] A second is to function largely, though not entirely, in the interests of social order rather than social change. Change is sought only through the process of minimal reformism. Essentially, however, in contradistinction to the role of the proletariat that was identified by Marx as a force for social change through revolution, this new and powerful class, embedded in the state economy system of modern capitalism functions both to keep the show on the road and also to foster change only in so far as the capitalist system remains unchallenged at its core. It is this latter point that brings us to connect loosely with Sklair who, in his fourth characteristic of the Transnational capitalist class, sees it as having a reformist function in that it apparently tries to solve the contradictions of capitalism. The third function is connected with the first, and that is to counteract the TRPF under capitalist production and distribution. And the class is unified by certain human characteristics. One of which is narcissism, which we discussed in some depth in Chapter 5.

Baran and Sweezy argue that their law of the tendency for the rate of surplus to rise is in some way in conflict with the law of the TRPF.[17] Forty years later, it would appear that the two laws are entirely compatible. The latter, indeed, has considerable explanatory potential, and the debate about the validity of the law of the TRPF is still, in certain circles, lively. Attempts to throw this baby out with the bath water have not fully succeeded.[18] Underpinning the law of the TRPF is the endemic competitive drive so that over any prolonged period the capacity for capitalist economies (whether territorially bound or not) increases. And, as a matter of empirical observation, this increase is enormous. Setbacks in growth periods, described as crises or recessions or depressions, are in fact functional to the system. As Marx himself put it, for instance: "under all circumstances the balance will be restored by capital's lying idle or even by its destruction" (Marx, 1972, Vol. III, p. 363). Inherent in the progress of capitalism, therefore, is that, as a result of the competitive drives of capital, at some point, the rate of profit will fall, the continued competitive drive will lead to pressure for increasing total profit (achieved through amalgamations and mergers or cartels or other forms of concentration of capital) and, when further thwarted, ultimately "frauds and swindles" will occur. At some point the system comes out of crisis. What causes the crisis also contains its solution. This is the reverse of what Marx had come to believe. Whereas he believed that the capitalist system contained the seeds of its decline, it actually contains the seeds of constant renewal (Desai, 2002).

A fully rounded explanatory theory identifying new class formation is dependent on recognizing the nature of this TRPF and the fact that it "explains" what is erroneously thought of as being the technological drive of modern capitalism.[19] TRPF explains unemployment and falling wages. In addition, and this becomes relevant for our analysis, the capitalist systems, especially that of the United States, demonstrate an unsuspected capacity to adapt and survive the inherent contradictions demonstrated by Marx and the Classical Economists in general. *In other words, the resilience of the system is more remarkable than its tendency to sink into crisis.* It is in this context that we claim a significant role for the absorptive class in enabling the capitalist systems to delay the onset of crises and minimize the effects of recessions.

7. SOME POLICY IMPLICATIONS: MIGRATION, PENSIONS, RISK AND THE WELFARE STATE

Despite the work done by Baran and Sweezy, identifying either a falling rate of profit or a rising one is not easy. Statistics and statistical methods will always come under fire. However, while there is much debate about causes for the decline of the rate of profit, there is very little substantiated debate to say that profit rates do not vary. The one exception is the debate around the Okishio Theorem.[20] It is not helpful to enter the interstices of this debate as there has been little success in proving this contentious theorem. More helpful has been the dispassionate work of Dumenil and Levy (1994). In the economics of the profit rate, the authors examine statistically the US economy for aggregate profit rates over 120 years and find that they can divide the period into three secular periods:

- 1869–1914: profits fell as a result in the decline of capital productivity.
- 1914–1950: profits rose as a result of increases in capital productivity.
- 1950–1990: profits fell as labour productivity involved high-cost capital productivity.

This is the generally accepted position in the literature with most interest focussed on the period after 1950.[21] What is at stake is less whether profits were squeezed and more why this should be so with Marxist, Marxian, post-Ricardian and Sraffan devotees vying for explanatory dominance.

I am not here seeking a monocausal explanation for this pressure on profits, but there is sufficient evidence to suggest that the tendency for the rate of profit to decline is real enough, and that if we trace the history of say the United Kingdom we find strong evidence, too. Indeed the politics of the post-war period is dominated by attempts by Conservative-led governments to restore industrial profitability to British industry by attempting to reduce public expenditure and, thereby cut taxes, and in Thatcher's confrontation with labour that was at the root of the all out miner's strike in the 1980s.

A major contradiction that we have noted about the progress of the capitalist system is this. The system depends on production, the output of which has to be consumed. However, consuming power runs out because the capitalists themselves cannot consume everything they produce. Consumers are required. Who are the consumers? Workers consume but at the same time their consuming power has to be limited because wages have to be constantly under pressure otherwise both mass profits and the rate of profit will decline. Capitalism must constantly find new markets: this can be done by geographical expansion, price reductions through mass production, diversification of products and so on. In the end, production will tend to overrun consumer demand. Thus while the logic of capitalist economics demands steady reductions in wage levels, at the very same time capitalist economics demands that there has to be ever-increasing aggregate consuming power. Henry Ford mass produces cars, lowers the price of the product and increases consumption: the British colonize and extend their power in India seeking out markets for industrial products and build the railways there. As time goes on mass production requires mass consumption. Logic assumes that there will be brought into being a class that does this because the proletariat, mere wage slaves subject to market forces cannot do this, and the capitalist class, try as it might, cannot possibly consume the surpluses in sufficiently considerable amounts.

What about the increase in aggregate population? Population does increase during early stages of economic growth. We see huge population explosions in Britain during industrialization. In the United States, we see massive immigration as well as a natural increase. The same has been true in Japan, China and elsewhere. However, we also observe population slowing down at a certain point. This is the position in Europe where the population is growing very slowly or not at all or even falling. Thus we can posit that these population movements are functional in economic terms even if they can be apparently explained in social terms. The young populations (e.g. Mexico, Brazil) function to stimulate mass production of cheap consumer products. As the population growth slows, the older populations consume more electrical products, motor cars, household contents and services, much purchased as a result of mortgaging property, extraction of so-called equity and credit. The consumption becomes denser and more closely supported by credit. It helps if there is some inflation to minimize the debt burden. In addition, the bad debts help to burn off some of the surplus needed to stabilize the tendency toward over-production.

Wage levels for particular occupational groups do not stay the same. The dynamic process whereby new technologies (changes in the organic composition of capital) redraw wage rates is a continuous one. New skills replace older ones with concomitant changes in the market rate accorded to labour. However, while some workers find their wage rates diminished, the overall level of actual impoverishment has to be kept under control by the system which has to fight simultaneously to keep up the level of consumption. Some of this can be done by the government (state) as a consumer that helps regulate the tendency to over-production (contrary to Keynesianism, which sees the state as intervening in the interests of consumption). If policy prescriptions could create a buffer to maintain production levels or at least to minimize the effect of falling production, they would do so. For instance, tax cuts do two things (depending on the forms of taxation): one is to increase profits and profit rates; and the other is to increase the ability of the consumer to buy more commodities. The producer benefits one way or the other. However, tax cutting reduces the ability of governments to distribute resources to civil and military contractors (unless there are allowable large-budget deficits over longish periods made partially possible through, say, the absorption of surpluses from other national economies through national indebtedness). What the system also wants is for wages to decline to maintain profit levels, but it also wants the consumer to consume more products. How can this be achieved? One way of looking at the problem is to look at the balance between labour mobility across national boundaries and how that contrasts with capital movements across national boundaries.

It has always been an essential part of both Classical and Neoclassical economics to argue that factors of production should, ideally, be mobile. The liberal economic system is dependent on continuous capital accumulation, free movement of capital and the free movement of labour. One the most well-known applications of this theory was the pressure to remove the so-called Speenhamland System in Britain through the passage of the Poor Law Amendment Act of 1834 in England, regretted by the path-breaking author Karl Polanyi as the real beginning of a new capitalist economic order (Polanyi, 1944/2001). The State in alliance with the new economic order were united by the belief that low-paid workers should be obliged to move to areas of high wages, thereby enabling the system to work equitably and eradicating recurrent slumps. Subsequently the banking system was revised to improve the flow of banking capital and control the amount of money and credit in the economy. As it happened both pieces of legislation had doubtful outcomes: financial crises continued to occur, and the Poor Law Amendment produced the Victorian workhouse, one of the most infamous social institutions of all time.

In more recent years, the issues related to movement of populations within national boundaries have given place to migration across national boundaries. This has vastly expanded the problem areas to be dealt with. While the capitalist system has achieved the free movement of capital, it has generally opposed the free movement of people. For instance, migration has become a serious topic of debate especially within a new area of study, that of human security.[22] While nation states resist free movement into their countries, the answer to problems associated with keeping wages equalized on the one hand, and ensuring that there is a relatively high-spending population (an absorptive class) on the other, is to move production lock, stock and barrel or nearly so across frontiers, leaving the populations where they are. Thus the absorptive class is maintained *en masse* in one country, while the production takes place in another. This process thus:

1. Makes a nonsense of the notion of development (moving productive capacity from a rich country to a poor country has nothing to with the *intention* to develop another economy, though it might do so unintentionally).

2. Must make nonsense of equalizing income and wealth across boundaries: the whole process is aimed at ensuring the absorptive class in the richer countries consume more while low cost relatively impoverished workers abroad stay there, providing low-wage labour power.

The obstacles and indignities faced by human beings who wish to move from one nation state to another is an example of how the sanctity of human life is converted into a major profanity. Thus, one of the outcomes of the global capitalism has been the almost complete freeing up of capital movements. This privilege is not granted to human beings (labour). While labour is not for the most free to move, the free movement of capital has increased migratory pressure across national frontiers. Nation states have strengthened their rules regarding illegal immigration. In turn this has led to illegal trafficking across borders on the one hand and strengthening of the police state inside nation states. The European Union is, in some respects, forward looking in accepting that a genuine economic union must allow free movement of labour. Now any EU citizen can live and work in any of the 25 national economies. American supposed equivalents, such as NAFTA and CAFTA are absolutely nothing like the EU in that free movement is allowed for capital but labour, in complete contrast to the text book economic orthodoxy that calls for free movement of factors of production, faces considerable obstacles to movement across national frontiers. For instance, Alan Dupont writes: "... national decisions to control entry and egress are influenced as much by political and security considerations as economic logic or humanitarian concerns."[23] And, certainly, the growth of unregulated population movements (UPMs) has surged since the 1970s coinciding with the freeing up of capital movements. Many reasons may be supposed for the surge, but the free capital movements must at least be a partial causal factor. Another reason for controlling immigration into rich countries is the perceived need to protect the so-called standard of living of the home citizens and their "way of life," (unless cheap labour is seen to be beneficial to economic growth). Some authors do accept that the core problem in understanding the policy issues associated with migration is the disjuncture between economics and politics (thus we return to the unity of state–economy thesis). For instance we read in a discussion of the concept of human security:

> We not only have to overcome the dominant discourse of realism/neo-realism but also liberal economic thought that separates economics from politics. Human security must strive to re-link what liberal economic theory has de-linked. Economic investment, the

penetration of distant locales and the trade in weaponry and other forms of technology bring with them political consequences and responsibilities for all involved.[24]

In economic terms, a case could be made for matching in some way the movement across borders of labour as freely as capital is allowed to move. A fair historical example is the way in which capital movements into the United States after the 1840s but especially after 1870 combined with free movement of immigration into the United States made a major contribution to the massive economic expansion of the US economy. At this period of US development capital and labour tended to go together so that US growth benefited both from immigration from the United Kingdom and vast capital movements from the United Kingdom to build the US infrastructure. Modern global capitalism, dominated as it is by finance capitals, is locked in a struggle with industrial capital: a key outcome impacts on labour movements; the restrictions lead to massive contempt for the sanctity of the life of those human beings trafficked, stuck in the hopelessness and squalor of refugee camps, dying on the Rio Grande, drowning in the Aegean sea and dying of thirst while trekking to Spain across the Sahara desert.

I am aware that the issues surrounding migration and cross border people movements are complex and may involve wide-ranging discussions on morality, failed states, the responsibility of nation states to provide for their own citizens, policing of illegal traffickers, control of organized crime, the rights of citizens to protect their liberties from the encroachments of others and so on. The point made here is that to the extent that capital can move freely, while labour cannot, renders human beings profane because that is what capitalism does, not only to labour but to its own creation, the absorptive class. In the process, the capitalist also degrades his own humanity and that of his class. It is ironic that this process stems from the "civilized" world, the so-called "developed" world and the most "cosmopolitan," that part of the human species that claims it knows best with its belief in so-called progress.

8. PENSIONS AND SOCIAL SECURITY

One of the recent policy measures by the Bush government in the United States that can be interpreted using the concept of the absorptive class is the debate around reform of social security. Professor Michael Hudson outlined the debate clearly and succinctly in an article in Harper's Magazine entitled "The $4.7 Trillion Pyramid: Why Social Security won't be enough to save Wall Street."[25] The issue is that employees "will be able to put some of their paycheck into the stock market" (Hudson, 2005, p. 36). "Bush himself," writes Hudson "offers two reasons for the present boldness. The first – that social security is in crisis ... Bush's second argument is if the American (sic) people will simply follow his plan ... they will become rich."

Hudson points out that, in the past, few retirement dollars found their way to Wall Street. He then explains how many large and medium firms used their pension funds to manipulate stock (share) prices and this requirement government intervention with the creation of the Pension Benefit Guarantee Corporation (PBGC) in 1974. Now, therefore, "most companies offer their employees a broad array of mutual funds instead of just their own stock. In itself this is good common-sense investing practice, and it also protects fund managers from charges of scheming. The other result of this practice is that workers' fortunes are now tied not just to their own companies but to the market as a whole." In other words, what we see here is the steady building of the capacity of the absorptive class to absorb. The pension contributions are part of the surplus that has been created. This surplus is then increasingly deposited in Wall Street where it sits as a shock absorber as the price of the financial instruments thus purchased fluctuate according to the recurrent economic fluctuations that we have discussed. Should the market fall, the existence of the additional funds acts as a buffer to maintain the level of prices, and, should there be more serious crises, the absorptive class will take the first shocks, not the real economy. Because the absorptive class is most concentrated in advanced capitalist economies, the system of global capitalism will tend to export financial crises to some of the in-waiting (developing countries) as we saw when we discussed the East Asian crisis.

Hudson examines what he calls the "problem" and the "scam." Fears of the social security becoming insolvent he regards as "unwarranted." But "many corporate pension plans – the ones that have been so important in bankrolling the stock-market rise of the past few decades – are themselves threatening to go bust, taking their parent companies down with them." He quotes airline and steel, with cars looming up in the near future. So, in this way, we see the relationship between the absorptive class, the price of financial instruments and the real economy. The absorptive class holdings need to be expanded to create the shock absorber in the face of both financial crises and de-industrialization, in the face of recurrent financial crises as well as longer term crises caused by technological change to the real economy. Hudson observes this absorptive function when he writes as follows:

> This phenomenon of risk rolling down can be seen most clearly in the move by many companies from defined-benefit programmes to "defined contribution plans, in which workers know nothing else except how much is being deducted from their paychecks. The payout rate is decided by how well the stock market performs, which shifts the risk onto employees even as it frees up more revenue for their employers and generates rich commissions for money managers. The risk flows down the economic scale even as the cash flows up. (Hudson, 2005, p. 35)

Thus we see clearly another step in the formation of the absorptive class to protect the rate of profit while potentially obviating the worst impact of crises and protecting the real economy.

Savings in the United States have plummeted. The national savings ratio is around nil because "personal discretionary income is *absorbed* in repaying debt" (Hudson, 2005, p. 39). Thus the policy can be seen clearly as a way of using the power of the absorptive class to absorb where the policymakers (representatives mainly of corporate interests) will benefit most. Can it be that the absorptive class is not being produced at a fast enough pace to deal with the tendency toward over-production? Fortunately, I do not pretend to be able to predict. As the US economy along with many other more mature ones around the world faces aging it needs to find a way in which retirees will remain firmly in the absorptive class with the economic mission of absorbing goods and absorbing economic shocks caused by financial fluctuations or technological change and structural changes in the real economy. One TV personality, Jay Leno, commented, "to-night President Bush introduced his plan for Social Security. His plan: take the security part out of it." Opposition to the plan came from a number of directions other than that TV personality's scriptwriter. It is not too difficult to see the dangers for potential retirees. *The Washington Post* headline in this issue for 28 April 2005 read: "Bush social security plan proves tough sell among working poor." Among the quotes in the article are these:

> "When you know you are entitled to Social Security, you know it is going to continue to come until you breathe your last breath"

> "People are wary about taking control of their Social Security, just as I'm wary of fixing my own car."

> "I like the check."

These are working-class responses. (See also Stiglitz, 2003, Chapter 8.) That is, they are responses from those who already live in the most insecure part of the economic system; they are those who are, when in employment, the obvious wage slaves. They are not prepared to risk the one piece of security old age may offer. The most interesting quote is from a "retired postal worker whose retirement savings are in accounts that she doesn't really understand or monitor." She says "I don't know what's going on with it. I just know I have these three accounts. Let's hope and pray it's not going into Enron. Let's hope and pray it's not going into Tyco." Then she goes on: "it's just hard to absorb all I'm supposed to absorb." Here she is referring to information regarding the proposals for the new Social Security. But, maybe stretching a point, by contrast, the absorptive class are able to absorb that part of the plan the system has equipped them to absorb: bolster the stock-markets. That's their job.

To what extent then have the absorptive class been sufficiently educated/ trained to deal with the fluctuating financial markets? The answer appears to be not as well as might be expected. Weisman quoting David Laibson, Harvard economist, as saying that 40% of those who qualify for 401(k)s do not participate. However, the whole trend of making it "attractive" to invest retirement funds in the stock markets is a combination of how the system works and how the policymakers with the power to assist the system: in this case to expand and consolidate the absorptive class which the system needs for the purposes of minimizing the instability of both the real economy and financial markets. There is persistent pressure to expand the role of the class and ensure that it plays its part in absorbing financial instruments, maintaining the price of them in the market and absorbing losses as their market value inevitably fluctuates. It certainly helps that institutional shareholders (stockholders) replace individual shareholders if this helps in the vicarious rather than direct ownership of shares. Institutional share ownership expanded massively in the 1980s and 1990s, though individual ownership remained high as a percentage of the total. Mitchell gives the following figures for the end of the 90s:

> ... the number of institutional investors compared with individual stockholders is relatively small, with the 25 largest institutional investors controlling 22.7% of total outstanding equities in 1998 ... compared with 49 million households owning 42.4% of all outstanding equities. (Mitchell, 2001, pp. 164–165)

In fact institutional ownership seems rather high, especially as much of this institutional investment in shares (stocks) one way or another is on *behalf of* the absorptive class. The significant trend is that institutional ownership has expanded. It is as if the individual member of the absorptive class cannot be trusted to enter the risk arena, so that the capitalist system pushes the absorptive class into the forefront of the risk economy in the interests of shock absorption via institutional investors. The next section deals with the issue of risk and capitalism in more detail.

9. RISK VERSUS WELFARE STATE

This brings us to the concept of risk in economics and the extent to which the absorptive class is increasingly expected to assume greater risk (Stiglitz, 2003). In the above policy measure it would seem the case, that the potential retiree be induced to assume the inevitable risks involved in stock-market fluctuations. Some commentators have argued, in respect of risk and labour, that a core feature of the current capitalism system is the shift of risk from capital to labour. In the words of former Gaitskellite and reformist, Stephen Haseler: "It is a huge irony – and a seriously bad omen – that in the new capitalism there are more risks attendant on working for a living than there are for owning capital" (Haseler, 2000). One standard approach to risk is that it justifies at least partially the taking of the surplus in the form of profit. In the orthodox Samuelson text that we have used before, the following justifications are put forward for the taking of profit by the capitalist (Samuelson, 1976). Profit is an implicit return to factors of production; profit is a monopoly return; profit is surplus value; profit is the reward to enterprise and innovation; profit is a return to risk and uncertainty; risk is a premium for risk-bearing. Risk as a justification appears in two of the categories. One case is more or less known to everyone: the riskier the investment, the higher the return. Samuelson concludes and takes sides and summarizes that profit and loss are the "unforeseeable discrepancies created by uncertainty." Risk, uncertainty, probability and rationality are key issues within the erroneous certainty of much economic "science." No one was more certain of uncertainty in economics than John Maynard Keynes himself whose work *A Treatise on Probability* provided an important underpinning for the *General Theory* as well as informing Keynes about his everyday activity of investing on the stock market for himself and his Cambridge college as well as collecting art works. Few academic economists have been so successful in the real world of investment as Keynes. Probability is not of course the same as "risk." Probability in his treatise is a Leibnitzian discussion on epistemology. How do we assess the truth as between two statements? Nevertheless we are in the area of truth, doubt and error. The whole of human existence does depend to a considerable degree on how we, as individuals, are able to deal with probabilities.

Jochen Runde investigates these connections when discussing the relationship between the two Keynesian works, the *Treatise* and *The General Theory*:

> I have argued that Keynesian uncertainty is best interpreted on Knightian lines: that decision-makers should be seen as operating under conditions of risk where their decisions are informed by numerically definite probabilities...under conditions of uncertainty when they have no such probabilities to go on....[26]

To cut a long story short the world of the entrepreneur or investor is an uncertain one in which probabilities have to be rationally assessed and risks taken or averted. In these circumstances the capitalist may be judged as deserving not only the profit or surplus he succeeds in accruing to himself, but is also to be congratulated on accumulating capital for further investment and in providing work for those without the ability to deal with such an uncertain world with the same measure of success.

Let's contrast these arguments on uncertainty, risk and profit with those concerning the welfare state. The welfare state has been concerned with the concept of "security," of rendering the world a safe place. It was with pride that Aneurin Bevan in the Labour government of 1945–1950 could announce a policy of security for all from cradle to grave, based on William Beveridge's *Full Employment in a Free Society* (1944). Full employment, unemployment and sickness benefit, free health provision, maternity care, expansion of public housing, free secondary and vocational education, pensions and much else including financial assistance with burial, was a promise held out not only for the working class but every citizen. All this was to be provided for by progressive taxation, as well as the promise of economic growth. Neither the policy nor the provision went quite as far as a full socialist society might demand but the working class had made their important gains in practice as well as principle. Their insecure world was ameliorated in such a way that the desperate experiences of unemployment, dole queues, handouts, humiliation and defeat of the 1920s and 1930s could be put aside seemingly forever. Keynes regarded this policy as having the benefit of providing a social wage, allowing employers to pay lower wages and thus maintain their rate of profit. One effect of rolling back the welfare state is to reduce certainty and increasingly re-introduce uncertainty into the lives of all citizens. The return of uncertainty thus forces individuals to assess risk. As we saw with the Bush proposals for US social security, some individuals are more attuned to risk-taking than others. At the same time some individuals will be simply luckier and better educated than others.

Benefits may accrue to some and losses affect others on an idiosyncratic rather than rational basis.

In making a distinction between the individual and class responses, we have to consider how the response from the absorptive class as a whole may differ from individual responses. As we have seen, it is much more in the interests of the working class to opt for certainty rather than uncertainty. Their gains as a result of living in a world of increased uncertainty (and there is plenty of uncertainty as it is) are not likely to be great, because they do not have capital or wealth to risk anyway. By contrast, the absorptive class is in a contradictory position. It has been created to absorb the shocks of capitalist economic crises. The capitalist system will press the class to find economic and social positions whereby they will accept their role; after all many individuals within the class may boast of gains made as a result of risk-taking. Indeed, that was very much the case during the long boom and the huge bubble of Nasdaq. Timing is everything. We come across not only personal stories of financial loss but a growing number of stories of fraud and corruption at the highest levels within, what is described at times as, crony capitalism. The absorptive class as a whole will not be induced to take risks in a post crisis moment, though a fraction might. That fraction is the fraction of absorptive class that has placed itself closest to the corridors of political and of corporate power. It is not surprising then that some researchers have discovered that if you go on winning, you will stay in the game, if you go on losing, you leave. Thus we find that William Sharpe argues that "increases of wealth give people a thicker cushion to absorb losses; losses make the cushion thinner." The consequence is that increases in wealth tend to strengthen the appetite for risk while losses tend to weaken it. Sharpe suggests that these variations in risk aversion explain why bull markets or bear markets tend to run to extremes.[27] While there is a tendency for prices to return to the mean, in the meantime there have been winners and losers. If someone else is doing your investment for you (like your pension fund managers or your stockbroker), you are absorbing the risk but playing an uninformed part in the process.

Greed is a great if perhaps somewhat unfortunate motivator. Large segments of the absorptive class, under the thrall of advertising and of sellers of financial instruments, are readily induced to risk their savings by purchasing stocks and shares and the like. The markets for these commodities are constantly expanding or attempting to do so. The eighties saw junk bonds come and (nearly) go and now the latest is private equity. High yield, high risk Junk Bonds or "below investment grade bonds" were the speciality of Drexel Burnham Lambert and were developed as a market attraction by Michael Milken, until he landed in prison in the United States. To a considerable extent these have been superseded by the private equity market. Private equity promises also the potential for high returns if the purchased unquoted companies become public whereby substantial gains can then be made from what is essentially an illiquid asset; or the private equity company can be sold to investors who can be persuaded of the potential for the company involved. Pension funds are players in this market and in 2004 it has been calculated that investment in global alternative (high-risk) prospects involved 49% going into property, 38% going into private equity and 13% into funds of hedge funds. This in money terms meant $17 billion in private equity: this represents a new baby, small but growing rapidly. The absorptive class via its pension funds are thus involved in high-risk investment, know it or not, like it or not.

NOTES

1. Brenner (2006). Brenner sets out to discover in particular the reasons for turbulence at the end of the twentieth century when crises became again to be discussed more seriously by economists after three decades of relative economic tranquillity.

2. Samuelson (1991, pp. 168–170).

3. http://www.southerndomains.com/SouthernBanks/p2.htm#10: downloaded 4 April 2005.

4. http://pubs.socialistreviewindex.orguk/isj100/cox.htm page 3 of 9, downloaded 4/18/2005.

5. Quoted by Cox p. 4 of 9.

6. Miliband (1969, p. 19). Ironically, Miliband's two sons are entrenched in the current Labour government and are the strongest proponents therefore of the third way and, in effect, spokesmen for the absorptive class if unconscious of the fact. Lawrence James in his highly acclaimed and interesting social history *The Middle Class: A History* (Abacus, James, 2006) does not help us much either in placing the middle class in full economic perspective, but, then, he talks about the rising middle class with no mention at all of the role of commercial capitalists in the English Civil Wars, for instance.

7. Cox, op. cit, p. 4 of 9.

8. Hence the uncomfortable introduction by Keynes to the German translation of his *General Theory* which says that the current regime, of National Socialism, should be especially interested in what he has to say. Nazi-ism was in economic terms "THE" struggle to re-establish the hegemony of industrial capitalism in the face of the growing dominance of finance capital.

9. Galbraith (1997, p. xii). The term depression became so terrifying that it was replaced with the term recession which became defined in terms of lagging economic

growth. The difference between a depression and a recession is unknown. The economic crisis of 2007–2009 is probably so severe that it will become known as a severe recession or maybe the Great Recession. The economist who invents a term to denote something between a depression and a recession and suggests a measurement for it may well achieve immortality.

10. Steve Schifferes, BBC News, 4 June 2008.

11. Altman (2009).

12. *Capital*, p. 319. References to Marx's are to *Capital*, Lawrence and Wishart, 1972, p. 319. There are many versions of *Capital* published over the years and also translations differ. It is possible to find versions on the Web: for instance Karl Marx, Capital, Volumes I-III, Lawrence and Wishart, 1972. See also, for instance, internet edition: www.econlib.org/library/YPDBooks?Marx/mrxCpC13.html#PartIII, chapter 13 where this same quote is to be found at Volume III, xiii, 5 but in a different translation. The advantage of these internet editions is they offer a search facility for the text.

13. Ibid p. 141 and quoted from *Das Kapital*, Volume 3, Chapter 27. The press has been full of examples in recent years. See Bogle (2005) for corruption and deception among Mutual Fund managers, for instance.

14. Loven (2002).

15. There are many respectable sources on the internet providing daily updated figures. See, for instance, http://zfacts.com or www.newsmeat.com

16. Adam Smith adapted from the Physiocrats the distinction between productive and unproductive labour. For instance, he identified the opera singer as being unproductive because the notes of an operatic aria, no matter how exquisite, died in the moment of their creation. Now, however, the late Luciano Pavarotti's exquisite notes, along with many others, are heavily commodified.

17. They were possibly misled by the long post-war boom and the success of the US corporations in maintaining their rate of profit.

18. Brenner (2006) op. cit.: Fred Moseley, The decline of the Rate of profit in the post-war US economy, Mount Holyoke College, www.mtholyoke.edu/~fmoseley/HM.html; Dumenil and Levy (1994), Foley (1997, 2006).

19. cf. Friedmann (1999): "Another reason globalisation is easy to distort is that people don't understand that it is a technologically driven phenomenon, not a trade driven one." However, much confusion and mis-analysis exists. Cf Hannah Arendt: "The enormous growth of productivity in the modern world was no means due to an increase in workers productivity, but exclusively the development of technology and this depended neither on the working class nor the bourgeoisie, but the scientists." *On Violence*, Brace, Harcourt and World, 169/70, p.72.

20. As one author has said: "... the Okishio Theorem has been a misguided and mistaken distraction that has occupied Marxian economics for too long."

21. Again we do not intend to enter the detail of the discussion because the literature is fairly clear as to the periods of high and low profits: Robert Brenner (1998/2006). Moseley (1992). Glyn and Sutcliffe (1972). Moseley (2000).

22. For a comprehensive discussion of the concept of human security see: www.humansecurity-chs.org

23. Dupont.

24. Poku, Renwick, and Glenn (2000).

25. Hudson (2005, p. 35 et seq). There have been a plethora of books of all hues about the US social security debate e.g. Diamond (2002); Diamond and Orszag (2004); Tanner (edit) (2004); Feldstein (edit.) (1998); Baker and Weisbrot (1999).

26. He refers to Knight (1921). It was Knight who began the convention in economics of defining uncertainty in opposition to risk. Jochen Runde in Runde and Mizuhara (2003); Graham et al. (2000).

27. Bernstein (1996, p. 264) taken from Sharpe (1990).

CHAPTER 7

REFORMISM, CLASS CONSCIOUSNESS AND CLASS ACTION

1. REFORMISM

The term reformism has been in frequent use by leftist critics who have seen reform as the biggest enemy of the revolution. If the capitalist system were proved to be in danger of collapsing under its own weight, then intervention by the "bourgeois" state to reform the system and to make concessions to, say, labour, then the system would continue essentially unchanged. Examples of reformism are, therefore, free elementary and secondary education for all, the welfare state generally, trade union legislation permitting collective bargaining and so on. The main philosophical ideologist of such reformist strategy was originally John Stuart Mill, simultaneously a classical economist and utilitarian and proponent of reformist tendencies and government intervention. The term reformism is also applied to the political process whereby socialism might be implemented through parliamentary means. The working-class interest could be introduced into a parliamentary system via the electoral process and lead to reform progressively that would result in steps or increments to a socialist society. This was very much the view of Sidney and Beatrice Webb and their Fabian followers in the Britain. One of the main opponents of reform or social reform, as she put it, was Rosa Luxemburg who saw such a process as leading to the death knell of the German socialism and, by extension, of socialism everywhere (Howard, 1971, p. 52).

This brings us to the question: is there a modern day reformist movement? The answer is, of course, reformists and reformism never went away. Whenever the crises of capitalism are serious enough we discover those who argue for reform of various kinds with various degrees of urgency. Reformism is, in effect, seemingly endemic to capitalism. While Mill produced the rationale for nineteenth-century reformism in both political and economic terms, John

Maynard Keynes provided the major theoretical underpinning for twentieth-century reformist orthodoxy. Recently, with a tone of mild wonderment by some onlookers, reformers have pushed their way forward on all fronts. They exist at all levels and come from all directions from Ralph Nader in the United States, to the Greens in the German Bundestag, to George Soros, the billionaire financial capitalist, Lula da Silva of Brazil and Joseph Stiglitz are among them. Some recent writers also consider that capitalism has a built-in tendency to reform. Emmanuel Todd argues that the drive toward change is predicted by increases in general literacy and the spread of lower birth rates. "Learning to read and write brings each person to a higher level of consciousness," argues Todd, and this combined with "demographic stability" leads to more established democratic regimes. While there will be many sub-species of democracy and neoliberalism, stability is the undoubted outcome, according to Todd (Todd, 2003). These reformists, however, are individuals who appear as simply actors whose motivations are entirely personal. In fact, though they do not represent any organized reformist movement, they are acting in a predictable way. But it is reasonably clear that reform is endemic to capitalism. Later I will deal with the absorptive class as a whole and its reformist nature: in other words having been produced to absorb surpluses it must also absorb political crises, too. First, let us look at some reformist tendencies that are current as expressed by individuals and by the movements known as corporate social responsibility and social entrepreneurship.

2. SENNET, BOGLE AND CAPITALISM

Judging from the concern of some recent publications, reformism is very much in the air. Richard Sennet a lifelong academic, continues with his critical deliberations, this time on *The Culture of New Capitalism* while, from inside the capitalist citadel, John Bogle (2005) is deeply concerned with *The Battle for the Soul of Capitalism*, while the economists Jeffrey Sachs (Sachs, 2005) and Joseph Stiglitz who have both moved from academic life to government and back write with some passion on reformist issues. Sennett is an advocate for the most part of the Third Way most evident in the United Kingdom, but which also spilled over to the Clinton era in US politics and seems to be infecting President Obama's strategies. Sennett argues that the UK model is a progressive model that largely goes uncredited by the very people it has benefited. Interestingly, Sennett uses the term consuming politics, and thus we see that it is possible to argue that politicians have been commodified just as every other service and profession has (If the politician has become indistinguishable from a washing machine, no wonder we would rather have the washing machine as it may appear to be "cleaner" and more efficient, longer lasting and require less servicing than the politician.) Generally speaking he argues that capitalism has promoted a culture of feebleness and shoddiness that can be saved through social capitalism and he calls for "a revolt against this enfeebled culture" that will "constitute our next fresh page."

John Bogle calls for a reform of the capital system that will release some of the surplus for solving problems of poverty though he says little about how that surplus might be distributed and managed. His main concern is the basic dishonesty of managers throughout the corporate system and within institutions of finance capitalism. He argues that institutional change supported by government intervention can improve corporate governance and hand capitalism back to its owners rather than managers. However, this approach ignores some of his own arguments. He asks the question: why did investment go wrong (1997–2000)? His answer is: "because it focused on the monetary precision of stock prices rather than the eternal importance of intrinsic corporate value, however difficult to measure. Because it forgot that long-run stock values are created by the enduring economics of investment return rather than the transitory emotions of speculative returns" (Bogle, 2005, p. 115). At one level there is nothing mysterious about this statement. Whoever were buying stocks/shares on the stock exchanges were not differentiating between investment and speculation. Equities were being held for days or weeks rather than months and years. The sensible thing (Bogle instances Buffett as a sound example) is to keep in mind the relationship between the price of equities and the real earnings of the corporation and the wider real economy. But it is not so easy, as Bogle himself says, to measure the price of equities against the real economy. The absorptive class or shock absorbers are there precisely to take the loss and thus bring capitalism back to its senses; in the case of events between 1997 and 2000 he claims that the loss to the system amounted to $2.275 trillion while insiders made considerable personal gains (Bogle, 2005, p. 10). This gives some idea of the scale of absorption required of the shock absorbers. Sennett provides an underlying reason in his discussion of the *Culture of the New Capitalism* why short-termism and therefore speculation may be a strong built-in tendency. He calls this "impatient capitalism." The essence of older bourgeois behaviour was deferred gratification. This has been replaced by something closer to a drive toward immediate gratification made possible by easy credit and the massive production of more and more diverse commodities. This line of thinking is more or less consistent with the narcissism of the shock absorbers (discussed in Chapter 3) who have been produced to take the shock caused by the wild movement of financial instruments.

We see in the work of the prolific commentator Joseph Stiglitz a strong reflection of how the absorptive class as a whole might respond to the current state of capitalist domination. Stiglitz is not a capitalist. He is an academic and winner of the 2001 Nobel Prize for Economics jointly with George Akerlof and A. Michael Spence for the "analysis of markets with asymmetric information." He has also spent time as an economic adviser to the Clinton Government and to the World Bank. This put him at the heart of the globalizing process. During his time as an economic adviser, especially with the World Bank, he saw the (not, in his terms, inevitable) devastating effects that globalization can have on developing countries despite his strong belief in the benefits of free trade. He believes in the effectiveness of the market (as might be expected he sees no distinction between the market and capitalism and by the "market" he probably means capitalism but does attack *market fundamentalism*). He blames most of the global mismanagement not on the World Bank (International Bank for Reconstruction and Development) but on the IMF along with the US Treasury and the so-called Washington Consensus. He shows how the United States is the only nation state that has a veto at the IMF but also how senior personnel are drawn from the US private financial sector. The misguided policies that have been applied have led to, according to Stiglitz, urban violence, massive unemployment and ethnic conflict. The IMF, charged with achieving global stability since Bretton Woods, has failed miserably, having seen crises in about 100 countries in the time of its existence. He claims:

> Globalization is neither good nor bad . . . . Globalization can be reshaped, and when it is, when it is properly run, with all countries having a voice in policies affecting them, there is the possibility that it will create a new global economy in which growth is not only more sustainable and less volatile but the fruits of growth are more equitably shared. (Stiglitz, 2002, pp. 20–22)

When he joined the World Bank he observed that 45% of the world's population lived on less than $2 per day. The position is now worse. He lays blame, essentially, on wrong ideas and institutional rigidities that are correctable. His final chapter, "The Way Ahead," focuses entirely on reform: the IMF, the WTO the World Bank with the *leitmotif* of the need for transparency, and he concludes that it is possible that globalization can have a human face. The point for our purposes is that, though it might seem surprising that someone of Stiglitz's training and experience and status, attacks the motor force of globalization and the liberal economic system. In fact, he is in the straight tradition stemming from the reformist works of Mill and the state interventionist policies of Keynes.

We are back with our argument that, importantly, it is the absorptive class, as it exists within national boundaries of the advanced nations, which performs the crucial functions that tend toward achieving international and global stability. It is from this class that we would expect to see reformist movements that have yet to gather pace. Thus, when we see reports of dissent at WTO and IMF meetings and so on, the hotch-potch of alliances may confuse the issue because what is really happening is class formation, in this case of the absorptive class, in a more or less straight historical line from the 1960s. It is this class that the Washington led leaders of the global institutions are likely to heed, eventually.

3. CORPORATE SOCIAL RESPONSIBILITY

Another source of reformist tendencies lies, it is claimed, with big business, though many commentators would argue that a system based on private ownership of the means of production, profit, competition and the drive to capital accumulation is unlikely to reform much. Strong arguments exist on both sides of the debate and are contained in a steady flow of publications.[1] A standard analytical beginning is provided by Marx in Chapter 10 of volume one of *Capital*. He makes the case that the Factory Acts that controlled the hours and conditions of labour in textile factories were made possible by the following combination: the intimate relation between capitalists and the state; the interest of big factory owners to limit competition from small owners attempting to enter the industry and undercut the big producers and the interest of capital to exploit labour rather than spoliate or destroy it. Doubtless some "werewolf" capitalists actually had consciences, too, but as far as Marx was concerned this did not constitute a significant drive toward reforming factory conditions and hours of work. There was pressure too from the rising proletariat and also the old aristocracy or landowning class, allied with the working class, to exercise a degree of revenge on the manufacturers as a result of the abolition of the Corn Laws, which, it had been perceived, offered protection to landowners while inflating urban wages through artificially high bread prices. The concentration of capital and the particular formation of the ruling classes and the fractionalization of classes and their alliances thus made possible reform of the capitalist system in the broader and longer term interests of capital.

Currently, in the organization of big business within national boundaries, internationally and globally the possibilities for significant reform of the way in which the private sector operates with its drive to accumulate capital appear to be limited. Despite pronouncements by huge conglomerates that they have a significant interest in implementing policies of corporate (social) responsibility, the outcomes to date are limited or, even, retrogressive. Similarly, social entrepreneurship has been an informing idea and, to some extent, has led to developments of supposedly new forms of enterprise. Social entrepreneurship is about as hard to define as corporate social responsibility, though useful definitions have been made by a number of "pioneers" in this field.[2] Two notable examples of social entrepreneurship are the Grameen Bank (began specifically to help provide small loans to women in Bangla Desh by Mohammad Yunus) and the worldwide Montessori schools movements. While individual capitalists may wish to see the capitalist system reformed through corporate responsibility or through social entrepreneurship or whatever other ideas present themselves, they remain as individual capitalists. The capitalist *class* and the capitalist *system* operate quite differently. For instance Soros who, while continuing to operate as a leading finance capitalist in the world, insists that capitalism itself is the greatest danger to democracy and warns against it (Soros, 2002, 2004). Other individual capitalist do the same. Another example is Ben and Jerry the ice cream manufacturers who genuinely desired to make a financial success of making and selling ice cream while being socially responsible and make a positive social impact. "They told their managers to choose actions that had a positive impact on both sides of the bottom line ... Ben (Cohen) and Jerry (Greenfield) absolutely insisted upon counting and measuring quality of life issues ... no matter how soft and intangible they would have seemed to most accountants" (Hollender Fenichell, 2004, p. 168). Other individual capitalists in the list would include the late Anita Roddick (Body Shop), Wayne Silby (Calvert Group of mutual funds) and Joshua Mailman. No matter how well intentioned are such businessmen, the danger to their own ideas on corporate responsibility/corporate social responsibility is contained in their very success. "In April 2000, the news that Ben and Jerry's Homemade had agreed to be acquired by Unilever for $326 million sent shudders and shivers through the socially responsible business community ... It seemed like the end of an era ... our best known example of 'caring capitalism' had been gobbled up by the enemy." Unilever is a huge multinational with an annual $50 billion operation. Much the same happened to Anita Roddick who sold out The Body Shop chain and products to L'Oreal for over a billion dollars in March 2006.

However much an individual entrepreneur may wish to buck the system (and, famously, according to Margaret Thatcher, "you can't buck the system"), in the end big, big business will force corporations on to the only road they know, that of profit, competition and capital accumulation with no real frills unless it aids profit by dressing up corporate image (Roland Marchand, 1998). In these circumstances, the pressure for reform must come from "without," that is from pressure on big business. While there is a small capitalist fraction that looks toward producing commodities at the same time as having a concern for the suitability of the product, its social benefits, compensating its workers reasonably, providing benefits to them and ensuring working conditions are healthy and safe, the history of "improved conditions" and responsible behaviour by big business is one that has involved external pressure from workers, and fractions of class as determined by historical circumstances and the state. Hope for reform tends to lie with improved regulation by government agencies. In the crisis of 2007–2009, many voices have been heard calling for better regulation of the financial sectors. We are back to the observation made by Marx about the passage and implementation of factory legislation in England in the 1840s. Individual firms cannot be expected to resist the drive for profit by any means and the capitalist state, acting in the common interests of capitalism, has to intervene therefore in the interests of the system as a whole.

Noreena Hertz believes she has identified the rise of external pressure, though she dismisses the role of government somewhat prematurely:

> ....while the power and independence of governments wither and corporations take over ever more control, *a new political movement is beginning to emerge.* Rooted in protest, its advocates are not bounded by national geography, a shared culture or history, and its members comprise a rag tag of by now millions, made up of NGOs, grassroots movements, campaigning corporations, and individuals. Their concerns, while disparate, share a common assumption: that the people's interests have been taken over by other interests viewed as more fundamental than their own – that the public interest has lost out to a corporate one. (Hertz, 2001, p. 194)

She claims that the protest movement "gives a voice to people who have been denied the right to elect their governments, as well as to people who no longer feel that their representatives are acting on their behalf." The problem here is at least twofold. National governments are much stronger than is being argued. The other is the vague term "people." It is vitally important to accept that governments are a lot more pivotal than Hertz is suggesting because, as I insist throughout this work, that state and economy are entwined and virtually indivisible. Also the direction that history takes is heavily dependent on how class forces play out so that the term "people" is not analytically helpful. The issue of consciousness (of the absorptive class in particular) and the role of dissent (or protest) with special reference to the United States is discussed in later in this section in the expectation of developing a stronger analysis.

Another possibility for organizing and developing corporate responsibility from without would be through the organized pressure of the international supra-state, if there were one. The nearest equivalent is the United Nations and Secretary-General Kofi Annan, convinced that the private sector should and can make a significant contribution to unifying big business around a range of objectives related to corporate responsibility has set up the Global Compact.[3] So far, it has brought a number of companies together from several countries, and, though the developments are still essentially embryonic, there are signs that this external persuasive pressure may focus attention on what is, and is not, possible. The global compact may help to serve as an alternative to the direct pressure as identified by Noreena Hertz, though the likelihood is that reformist movements will take both routes simultaneously. The strongest possibility for reform given the nature of the current crisis is for the creation of a new Bretton Woods but that would require a crisis deeper than exists as this article goes to press. After all, the original Bretton Woods wasborn out of the 1930s depressions, the rise of Fascism, the Second World War and the threats inherent in the existence of the Soviet Union.

4. CLASS FRACTIONS, CLASS CONSCIOUSNESS AND CLASS ACTION

My conviction has been throughout this book that class analysis should be restored to a more central position in social science debate, and I am especially convinced of the existence of the absorptive class on an *a priori* theoretical basis and on the basis of this initial discussion as developed in this volume. In essence, the producer economy has produced the class it requires for its own continuance. Had it not done so there would be no such society in existence in its current form. I am also convinced of the importance of class fractions, and I am equally convinced that the absorptive class must be fractionalized in such a way as to respond importantly to the "ruling class(es)." More work needs to be done on unravelling the nature of the capitalist class as it stands today. But it is safe to say that the dialectic relationships that exist among the fractions of the absorptive class and the fractions of the other two big classes, capitalist and proletarian, determine the general lines of future economic development and the strength and characteristics of the capitalist system.

While the economic functions discussed in the preceding chapters are common to the absorptive class and are what distinguish that class from other classes, it is (and will be, no doubt) the responses of the fractions of the absorptive class that provide an important dynamic for change and for social control simultaneously. The fractions of the working class have been identified and their role widely discussed. For instance in UK history the aristocracy of the working class, created by imperialist expansion, have been supposed to account, at least partially, for the particular form of non-revolutionary socialism in Britain, the growth of its trade unions, the formation of the Labour Party, incremental socialism and the failure to provide fertile ground for the growth of Marxist ideas (Crosland, 1956). By contrast, the *lumpenproletariat* as a class fraction has always been consigned to a historical dustbin where it has remained as underclass or mere *träger*. The fractionalization of the bourgeoisie has been more varied with such varying labels as small or petty capitalists, banking capitalists, *rentier* capitalists, finance capitalists, industrial capitalists, commercial capitalists, big capitalists, international capitalists and so on.

It is possible to speculate just how the absorptive class is fractionalized and how those fractions might interact in such a way as to affect the future of the world generally and of capitalism in particular. It is also a matter of conjecture how the alliances of fractions of different classes might develop (Aronowitz, 2003, p. 92). Coming from the tradition of class analysis without the awareness of the existence of the absorptive class, the predictive analysis is especially difficult to imagine and sounds, when it is encountered, somewhat historically hidebound. Take this view of Castells, the doyen of leftist urban sociological analysis, written some 30 years or so ago.

> If the working class is that class which is most conscious of its situation and which most supports political organizations which are alternatives to the power organized around the bourgeoisie, it is mostly because it has an experience of organization and struggle, even though these are derived from its fundamental place in the production process. Now, the working class cannot on its own...pose a socialist alternative in Western Europe. This can only be possible by the organization of popular classes *objectively interested* in going beyond capitalism.... (Castells, 1978, p. 172)

This particular view as expressed by Castells is somewhat dated, and the left have since become more sanguine. Now, however, we can argue that, once the absorptive class, has been identified, alliances are possible and likely whereby segments of the working class, absorptive class and reformist capitalist class may coalesce around issues that will produce significant change: such activity may not alter the capitalist system fundamentally but may well set it on a course that will ensure some of the aims of the constituent fractions may regard as important gains. The tendency toward social democratic forms of socialism may be very much weaker than was once thought possible by leftists in Western Europe, but substantial benefits may nevertheless accrue to the population at large.

Turning to the United States, Lasch's discussion in *The True and Only Heaven* provides some clues as to how the absorptive class is fractionalized there. His discussion of the new class as it developed from the seventies onwards is potentially revealing (Lasch, 1991, p. 509 et seq). He is right when he says the right-wing theorizing was unable to disentangle the three distinct traditions that he claims gave rise to the new class and, quoting Daniel Bell, the debate arrived at a "muddled concept." The new class was a "verbalist elite" that "comprised neither businessmen nor manufacturers, blue-collar workers or farmers." Moreover it was an elite that seemingly the right in US politics wished to control or even repress. Lasch's explanation for the origin of the *new class* lay in three more or less distinct traditions. First, he points to a Saint-Simonian progressive tradition of "technical intelligentsia." This "class" was otherwise labelled as the "knowledge class" which in the context of managing corporations had, it was claimed, a significant degree of autonomy from the capitalist system of private ownership and profit motivation. On one level, this segment could be seen as brain workers and potential agents of change that one day would help produce a socialist rather than a capitalist-based economy. Second, is the tradition emanating from the dissident movement in the Soviet tradition and associated with convergence theory which argued that a new class of managers would emerge that would drive capitalist economy not to socialism but to totalitarianism.[4] Third, Lasch points to the tradition of the adversary culture of intellectuals deriving from a long historical tradition from French Revolutionaries and Edmund Burke through to Zola and Orwell. It was this adversary culture that the neoconservatives, in the struggle for ideological hegemony that would serve the US state based on the industrial–military complex, were at pains to attack and destroy. Lasch provides, however, no economic base for his argument regarding the new class except to see some sort of relationship between technocrats and corporations and the big state. But he has no unifying economic and political theory with which to make sense of the emergence of what is in essence a burgeoning protest against the particular form that US capitalism has taken. We may also add a small number of loud voices to the so-called new class such as Nader and Chomsky.

To what extent is there a new class of any sort in the United States? The answer is, from the foregoing chapters, that what we observe is the formation of a genuine new class, *the absorptive class*, whereas Lasch's new class has to be interpreted as a fraction of the absorptive class bent on reform and is ripe for alliances to achieve them, more in the interests of the survival of capitalism rather than any of the three traditions outlined by Lasch. The reformist tendency will not achieve any form of socialism, as we have already argued, but significant reformist fractions of the absorptive class have the capacity to draw the capitalist system away, at least in part, from the overweening domination created by the concentration of economic and political power.

Another approach that might be taken is to use Habermas's conception of the bourgeois public sphere (*bürgerliche Öffentlichkeit*) and consider to what extent this sphere is, or could be, occupied by the absorptive class (Habermas, 1989; Seidman, 1989). Habermas argued that the public sphere in the eighteenth century of France and Britain (by which he means England) existed between the private realm, that of civil society and of bourgeois internal space on the one hand, and the sphere of public authority (the state and the royal and aristocratic court). The function of the public sphere was to put the state in touch with the needs of the emerging bourgeoisie. Habermas takes this long historical analysis of the public sphere and discusses the concept in relation to the "liberal model" as it emerged in nineteenth-century Europe. In the public sphere "stands the domain of private persons who have come together to form a public and who, as citizens of the state, mediate the state with the needs of the bourgeois society." He regards the model as still useful as he extends it to the "mass welfare-state democracies." He sees his model breaking down to some extent as under capitalism there is "refeudalization" of the public sphere. For instance: "Large-scale organizations strive for political compromises with the state and with one another, behind closed doors..." Habermas clearly considers that what the bourgeois class had created for themselves, a public sphere useful for rational debate with the aristocratic- and monarchical-based state, is disintegrating. However, it is fairly obvious, if one were able to make a sum of the weight and range of dissent and look at the sphere available, that this sphere still exists and that it can be occupied by significant fractions of the absorptive class. Press and public relations, important to seeing how the public sphere works as far as Habermas is concerned, is clearly important, and though sometimes dissenting opinion despairs at the way in which the space is occupied by huge media corporations and the weight of corporate public corporations and their legal backing, space is still available through radical publishers, uncensored internet sources and the snowballing effect of personal contact via the new methods of communication. However, these positions lead us to an important consideration of what might be meant by the absorptive class being "conscious" of its situation. The absorptive class to be effective has to be aware of what may well be now its historical reformist mission to replace the aristocracy of the working class or act within the "public sphere" through forms of collective class action.

The concept of class consciousness owed its origins to Hegelian philosophy, which held that history had a purpose. This view, as developed by Engels, became "nothing happens without a conscious purpose or intended aim" (Lukacs, 1971, p. 46). Lukacs, who more than any other single writer had brought the concept of class consciousness to the serious attention of leftist ideologues, came to reject much of what he had to say on history and class consciousness on the grounds of its Hegelian roots, and rejected in essence the predictive and teleological nature of the historical process. But it is possible to take away the Hegelian aspects and concentrate on the concept of consciousness alone (leaving the historical or teleological aspects aside) to see if it might inform us as to the possible parameters of class action in respect, not simply of the proletariat, but of the absorptive class wholly or fractionally in alliances. Lukacs quotes Marx at the outset of his Chapter on Class Consciousness thus:

> The question is not what goal is *envisaged* for the time being by this or that member of the proletariat, or even by the proletariat as a whole. The question is *what is the proletariat* and what course of action will it be forced to take in conformity with its own nature. (Lukacs, 1971, p. 46)

Given that we accept the existence of the absorptive class, let's rewrite these two sentences for heuristic purposes, thus:

> The question is not what goal is *envisaged* for the time being by this or that member of the absorptive class, or even by the absorptive class as a whole. The question is *what is the absorptive class* and what course of action will it be forced to take in conformity with its own nature.

I have answered the first question to some extent: the absorptive class is a product of capitalism "designed" to help prevent its collapse as a result of over-production. I do not think the second question, what course of action will it be *forced* to take, is easily answered. For one thing the class may not be forced to do anything if capitalism continues to produce it at the required rate. However, it has been claimed that the planet cannot sustain continuous over-production and that might *force* the absorptive class to prevail upon capitalism not to destroy itself and the whole planet. In any case, short of the destruction of the planet, the absorptive class may well become conscious of its role to reform capitalism, but in what ways and in what direction?

Another key question is one that obsessed the Bolsheviks. What is the process whereby the class becomes conscious of its historical role? Interestingly, for Lenin, Kautsky and others, including Marx and Engels, the revolutionary class, the proletariat, would be informed by the intelligentsia or by bourgeois intellectuals. For Lenin, in particular, the main weapon would be the "party" which would provide the consciousness of the class and take the class forward to revolution. This is the kind of position to which Antonio Gramsci adhered and was followed by several generations of Euro-Communists:

> ...it is only the proletariat which becomes revolutionary and socialist before the conquest of power and which struggles against capitalism. Furthermore, once socialist theory has emerged and been developed scientifically, the workers too assimilate it and develop it further. The Communist Party is, precisely, that part of the proletariat that has assimilated socialist theory and is continuing to propagate it. The task at the beginning of the movement was performed by intellectuals.... (Bellamy, 1994, p. 270)

Let's take our heuristic exercise one step further and substitute reform or reformist for socialist or Communist and absorptive class for proletarian. We now read:

> ...it is only the absorptive class which becomes dedicated to reform and reformism before the conquest of power and which struggles against capitalism. Furthermore, once reformist theory has emerged and been developed scientifically, the absorptive class assimilates it and develops it further. The Reform Party is, precisely, that part of the absorptive class that has assimilated reformist theory and is continuing to propagate it. The task at the beginning of the movement was performed by intellectuals...

A quasi neo-Leninist–Gramscian approach, then, to keeping capitalism within bounds involves the following:

> Step 1: Intellectuals have to expose the existence of the absorptive class, their role and the extent of their potential reformist "gains" in improving not just their own position but that of their "allies" (workers, peasants, small capitalists etc), but they have to get the analysis right or, as Gramsci, Marx and Engels would have it, be "scientific".

> Step 2: Politicize the absorptive class as widely and as deeply as possible through constant agitation.

> Step 3: Organize (the operative Leninist word is organize) the political party, though the party of the absorptive class would seek change within the system rather than overthrow the system as was Lenin's aim. This approach constitutes a new parliamentary incrementalism with the absorptive class as the starting point (maybe with significant fractions of the proletariat as allies) rather than the proletariat as the starting point.

From an *a priori* point of view it might be argued that the initiative lies with the absorptive class in the United States since the United States is not only the hegemon as far as international relations is concerned but as far as global capitalism is concerned. Thus, it is the decline in the rate of profit (see Chapter 6) in the United States that has driven other world economies in the direction of structural adjustment and rolling back welfare. Demands by the US absorptive class to use the surplus for improved welfare in the United States might reduce the tendency on other economies to reduce the scale of their welfare provision. Hence, a higher proportion of the surplus generated by the capitalist system could be used for the benefit of the whole population and replace, to a significant extent, the production and absorption of commodities. The future might unfold on the basis of the image determined loosely by an alliance between the absorptive class and reformist capitalist elements, and this image would be imposed on all the advanced economies as well as the rest of the world. It would not lead to a perfect set of solutions by any means, but a conscious absorptive class might well contain a kind of *conscience collective* that would arrest the worst excesses of capitalism and capitalist induced narcissism, protect the weak, contain overarching greed, bring peace, prolong the life of the planet, provide employment, guarantee welfare and protect liberty.

There is no shortage of intellectual leadership in the United States. Reformist questioning voices, suggestive voices, pleading voices, reasonable and reasoning voices are everywhere. They run much deeper than the few that get the headlines or are deliberately scrubbed from the headlines like the stalwarts Chomsky or Zinn. Take for example Lawrence E. Mitchell who has written a deliberately reflective book called *Corporate irresponsibility: America's New Export* (Mitchell, 2001). After running through examples of what he calls corporate misbehaviour, he summarizes his wide-ranging concern with capitalism in the United States and the big corporation in particular: "As we begin to examine liberalism and its modern manifestations, we can identify two themes . . . The first is an ethic of radical individualism which, in the limited moral universe of the corporation, results in an attitude of grab and get. The other is an impulse to care about the welfare of others" (Mitchell, 2001, p. 30). He laments that corporate capitalism has gone seriously awry and that the "fault lies with nobody in particular and everybody in general." And not only is this bad for the society, but it is bad for the corporations themselves. While in the body of the book, Mitchell is outspoken about many of the outrageous acts, including pollution of drinking water, condoning rape and allowing heartless mass redundancies that can be laid at the door of specific corporations and these acts clearly and unequivocally have been the result of profit seeking on behalf of shareholders (stock-holders), his reformist prescription is of the mildest kind: change the system at the edges with more responsible regulation. In other words, the capitalist state should intervene in the interests of the capitalist system itself. Such reform, at least, should be within the grasp of the absorptive class. Tony Blair and his immediate supporters, including his successor Gordon Brown, it would appear, captured the support of a major element of the absorptive class in their presentation of the so-called Third Way, and in their management of the political process and relevant mechanisms in the United Kingdom. Blair subsequently lost a segment with his bellicosity over Iraq, itself, no doubt, a product of the demands of BAe Systems and British Petroleum. Oddly, of course, Bush and his political backers increased the support of his segment of the absorptive class through the bellicosity of his government. The diverging outcomes lie in the differences between the structure or fractions of the absorptive class in the United States and the United Kingdom, and, in particular, the political failure of the Democratic Party in their inability to appeal to those fractions of the absorptive class that would support peace rather than war as well as the differential power of the ideological apparatuses in the two countries. British society because of its imperialistic past has a more militaristic fraction of the absorptive class than the United States but the class as a whole is less bellicose. In the United States, the absorptive class is more bellicose but is less militaristic.[5] The capitalist class, in the form of certain huge corporations and agglomerations, is bellicose. In the United Kingdom, the capitalist class is bellicose and militaristic, but the absorptive class, outside the military, is neither. The working class, who provide most of the personnel in violent conflicts, particularly the ones who die or are maimed physically and mentally, are in a contradictory position in that the military provides jobs and bonuses, and industry also provides jobs, though, as industry become more and more hi-tech, relatively fewer jobs are provided for the working class. Overall, the absorptive class in the United Kingdom is probably the most conscious. The political responses began with Gaitskill and his heirs, the so-called gang of four composed of Shirley Williams, William Rodgers, David Owen and Roy Jenkins, attempting to "break the mould" of British politics, were all precursors of Blair, all of whom, made efforts to carry with them their own special silent majority, the absorptive class, and seeking support from that class as much as from the old Labour representatives of the traditional aristocracy of the working class. This is why Tony Blair and Gordon Brown (with the kind of heavy-weight intellectual underpinning of Anthony Giddens) are able to follow the kind of reformist policies that deal, however poorly, with global warming, anti-corruption, absolute poverty, HIV/AIDS in Africa and so on.

5. DISSENT IN THE UNITED STATES: A NOTE

Much has been written about the failure of socialism to take hold in the United States.[6] Leftist dissent, however, has had a long and honourable tradition .... from the collective struggles of Industrial Workers of the World (IWW) to the single-handed intellectual efforts of Chomsky to the recent electoral intervention of Ralph Nader. Much has been written, too, about the scope for, the legitimacy of, the justification for dissent and confrontation in politics within the constraints of modern democracy.[7] Ever since the capitalism of rugged individualism began to emerge in the United States in the nineteenth century, dissent has occurred in the United States, and has been answered with tough measures by the state, the federal government and by individual capitalists. Proletarian dissent has been more marked in Europe than in the United States. There has never been a successful attempt at a general strike, for instance as has occurred in a number of other advanced industrial countries. The kind of mass street demonstrations as have occurred in, say, France do not take place in the United States, though some high turn-outs have taken place from time to time, notably in the 1930s and in the 1960s and 1970s and more recently in pro-peace demonstrations. However, the US government (at federal and state levels) when faced with serious mass demonstrations have tended to act with excessive force. Generally speaking the United States with its adherence to the death penalty and harsh prison sentencing and high prison populations demonstrates the existence of a more violent and harsher state than exists in many other advanced industrial nations.

For the individual, in practice, dissent involves overcoming a great deal of inertia; it involves, to be really effective, collective action; it involves considering the use of forms of violence, anathema to most people; it may involve considering loss of jobs, imprisonment and financial deprivation; it involves personal and collective courage and will; it involves persistence and determination; it involves belief in the cause. For the collective, action involves organization, politicization, training and education, provision of leadership, financing, creation of justificatory ideology and of a real cause; it involves the ability to make and sustain alliances; it means the creation of a culture of dissent; it means writing, publishing, broadcasting and general promulgation of the cause. In other words, effective dissent does not come easily. A tradition or, at least, examples of successful dissent are probably required, even if previous dissent has to be mythologized.[8] One problem is that dissent in the United States has either been proletarian, perceived as having failed, or black, more successful but some of its heroes in the mental hall of fame (Martin Luther King) while others have been seen as violent and thus difficult to emulate (Malcolm X, Black Panthers). The mass of the absorptive class may not wish to identify itself with either a working class or an "ethnic" movement,[9] especially one at least partially marked by violence. The absorptive class would therefore have to develop its dissent on the basis of a specific culture based on one, or at least, a limited number of pegs. It is not immediately obvious what they may be. After all, the term civil society that we saw had currency and also saw that it obscured more than it revealed; equally the term is used with the accent on civil in the derived sense of meaning non-violent, decent and largely un-protesting or, generally speaking, "civilized" and closely associated with the word reason which is also associated in the vernacular with the word reasonable.

Currently, for instance, the "protest" movements across frontiers have a proletarian, even at times, anarchist feel, that the absorptive class may be unwilling to follow. "Seize the Streets"[10] may seem too radical and personally interventionist for many. In addition, much protest follows a proletarian agenda being aimed at ending sweat shops, "watching" large corporations, pressing for equal wages for women workers, seeing capitalism as the main enemy, attacking symbols such as MacDonald's. In a recent publication *Coalitions across Borders*, we do see some growth of non-proletarian movements in relation to human rights, environment, peace, women's rights, self determination and so on (Bandy & Smith, 2005). Nevertheless, the weight is still in the direction of anti-capitalism. The authors quote Sklair as follows: "Large majorities of people will take alternatives seriously if they are persuaded that they are serious alternatives." The large majority in the advanced countries is the absorptive class and effective action will occur only if the agenda are developed by it (which is likely to be substantially in its own interest and that of its allies).

Hertz suggests an agenda which in many ways lacks practicality because it does not take account of how, in real terms, alliances are made and ends achieved. Her agenda are these:

> Disenfranchise corporations by cutting their ability to finance election; end trickle down economics; corporations should be more closely regulated at the national level; corporations should be curbed at the international level through subsidised legal intervention by workers and communities; a World Social organisation should counter the dominance of WTO without allowing the evils of protectionism to take-over and something has to be done about the billions excluded from the benefits of economic growth. (Hertz, 2001, p. 209)

This is all very well, but the historical process whereby this might come about is not well developed. If you attack the economic power base, you

attack political power too, and to do that you need massive strength.
Moreover, at the risk of being outrageous, in the context of discussing the
possibilities for and the direction of dissent on the part of the absorptive
class, can we imagine that, in its fractionalization, we might consider the
existence of a fraction labelled *lumpen* absorptive class? That is, a fraction of
a class that could never be moved to effecting change as part of a class
movement: ignorant, conservative, so dominated by capitalism that it would
not be able to consider any kind of assistance to a reformist agenda, and,
indeed, would, through its apathy and ignorance, serve only the narrowest
of conservative causes?

Before answering this question let's look at some of the reasons set
forward as the supposed causes for the failure of socialism to take root
in the United States. These are: affluence, social mobility (one might add
occupational and geographical mobility), the frontier, universal franchise
(for men), openness of the society (no residual feudal or militaristic or other
forms), continual process of immigration and assimilation. To this we might
add the rapid rate of technological change (de-skilling of labour), and the
tendency toward concentration of capital and political power (violent
responses by corporations, mine owners and other businessmen in collusion
with state and federal authorities). The physical frontier no longer exists but
other frontiers exist and while immigration is massively slowed, the United
States still has an ideology of assimilation (assimilation, albeit, into what is
still white, rich and largely Anglo-Saxon though with increasingly Judaic
overtones), the capitalism of big business continues to be strong and ruthless
and the general milieu is violent and solipsistic. Proletarian responses are
not suggested by these circumstances. One major difference does exist, at
least if we take note of the earlier suggestion by socialist revolutionaries who
were convinced that consciousness had to be introduced from "outside"
because the proletariat, as a result of their impoverishment and oppression,
required the leadership of intellectuals. Given the scope for intellectual
intervention consciousness for the absorptive class can come from within.
Thus reformists, to adjust the old Marxist expression, would be genuinely
of the reforming class rather than simply *for* it. On the other hand, observation, as opposed to close empirical research, does suggest that a large
segment of the absorptive class is *lumpen*. That is, I would bet that there
is an ineducable mass that can never see the shortcomings of the society
they live in sufficiently to be mobilized into a social movement in the
interests of significant change. However, in political terms they would not be
a danger to change but would remain as a residual rump. The lumpen shock
absorbers would create inertia and could be utilized by the system to stand

as dumb obstacles in the way of change. The term dumbing down in common usage referring to the state of mass education, media content and culture indicates the way in which more alert observers fear the ghastly inertia of this new lumpen class. Nevertheless, the absorptive class as a whole may well have the required strength to secure important change.

6. LAST WORD

The arguments in this book have been based on the acceptance of the following where the capital system is more or less dominant:

- That capitalism produces massive surpluses and that the concept of the surplus should not be confused with the concept of profit.
- That the market system and capitalism are not the same, though they occupy the same economic milieu. Therefore the big state, required by the surpluses produced by capitalism, exists in permanent contradiction with the small state, required for the more or less efficient operation of resource allocation by the market.
- That capitalism and democracy are in permanent contradiction: in that democracy in its nature seeks the dissipation of power while modern forms of capitalism tend toward the concentration of economic and political power.
- That society is largely the product of the capitalist system of production, and therefore that the consumer is not sovereign.
- That there are three big classes: the working class (including agricultural workers), the absorptive class and capitalists; thus it is no longer to necessary to be concerned whether the middle class is proletarianized labour since the "middle class" is in fact a significant segment of the absorptive class.
- That social change, a continuous though uneven process of reform, under capitalism occurs through alliances of fractions of the big three classes.
- That each individual is made up of fractions.
- That each individual and culture is becoming increasingly narcissistic and is most pronounced where capitalism is most advanced.
- That chattels should not be confused with property.

Marx argued that capitalism would fall under its own weight pushed by the proletariat. Schumpeter argued that capitalism would decompose and give way to socialism. Sidney and Beatrice Webb thought we might achieve incremental socialism. Regretfully, I (immodestly in such company as Marx and Schumpeter and the Webbs) suggest capitalism will survive for the foreseeable future, but may well be reformed (prediction is now quite rightly unfashionable) by the class capitalism has created for its own survival, the absorptive class, assuming it reaches a state of consciousness.

To turn to the science fiction mode for inspiration, we could see the absorptive class as a vast robot with no mind of its own created to obey the instructions of its capitalist maker, but, then, amazingly, it does develop a mind and will of its own and, like the gunfighter in Westworld, it turns on its maker and pursues its own agenda. The absorptive robot, however, will not shoot its maker but may hold it to ransom in order to create a better world, and, maybe, offer to swap its storage units and their contents for a more sensitive, creative and, above all, humane use of the vast surplus that is being created day by day.

NOTES

1. A few are listed here: Boman-Larsen et al. (2004); Buono et al. (1985); Harvard (2003); Hertz (2001); Hollender and Fenichell (2004); Makower (1994); Soros (1995). In addition, the former UN Secretary-General Kofi Annan established the Global Compact (www.unglobalcompact.org/portal) specifically to involve the private sector in helping deal with issues of development, poverty and violent conflict.

2. Bornstein, http://www.ashoka.org; Bornstein (2004); Hartigan & Billimori (2005); Johnson (2000). I am indebted to the research and enthusiasm for her subject of Lyndsey Spicka for these references and for discussion of the issues raised.

3. www.unglobalcompact.org/portal

4. Djilas (1957); Giddens (1973).

5. By bellicose, I refer to the apparent readiness of the state in the United States to make war. The American people generally have supported this, but they are not militaristic in the way the British are with their long-established tradition of fighting wars and their adherence to militaristic symbols such as the present Prince Harry as a trained soldier and fully entrenched member of the officer class as is Prince Andrew. In the United Kingdom, militarism stems from the persistence of an officer elite, going back in some cases to William the Conqueror. There is no real officer elite in the United States and recruitment to the military tends to decline when there is fighting to be done. See also Todd (2003), on the weakness of the US military.

6. Turner's Frontier Thesis stands as a major debate that may or may not account for the limited advance of socialism in the USA. Sombart work stands as a classic text (originally published in 1906). More recent texts include Irving Howe, Howe (1985); Stanley Aronowitz (2003), Chapter 1. Of course, socialism is not dead in the United States. There are plenty of socialists, leftist libertarians and the like in the United States and there is still a trade union movement, but there is no organized socialist movement in the United States of measurable strength. Were the absorptive class to mobilize, socialist elements might well do so, too.

7. Quite apart from Marx, Weber, Luxemburg, Bertrand Russell, Arendt, Marcuse, Chomsky and other works quoted earlier and many others, a cursory examination of library shelves reveal the following: Hanson et al. (1971); Held et al. (1972); Klein (1971); Steinberg (1978); Sunnstein (2005); Tilly (1978); Zashin (1971); Zwiebach (1975).

8. Russian nihilists romanticized Pugachev and other rebel leaders as well as the honourable tradition of Russian banditry (See: *Catechism of the Revolutionist* by Bakunin and Nechaev). When Margaret Thatcher introduced a poll tax, opponents protested, reviving memories of the rebellion of Watt Tyler against the poll tax in the reign of fifteenth century boy-king Richard II.

9. The earlier point I have made should not be lost, and that is much of the civil rights and integration gains into the mainstream culture arises from the need to expand the absorptive class through the "discovery" of the black consumer.

10. See for instance Notes from Anywhere, 2003.

ACKNOWLEDGMENTS

The author thanks Professors Paul Zarembka and Victor Kasper for their help, advice and encouragement. He was also assisted by Dr. Amr Abdalla and the UN mandated University for Peace with a small grant and paid leave of absence during which time he was able to prepare a first draft of "The Shock Absorbers." The author also thanks Manuel Cerdas for references to Frederick Pohl, and Francisco Sagasti, Julie Carlson and Neffy Carlson for their encouragement.

REFERENCES

Achbar, M., et al. (2004). *The corporation, DVD*. Toronto: Zeitgeist Films.

Altman, R. (2009). A weakening of the west. *Foreign Affairs*, 5.

Arendt, H. (1970). *On violence*. New York, NY: Harvest Book.

Aronowitz, S. (2003). *How class works*. New Haven, CT: Yale University Press.

Aronowitz, S., & Paul, B. (2002). *Paradigm lost: State theory reconsidered*. Minneapolis, MN: University of Minnesota Press.

Baker, D., & Weisbrot, M. (1999). *Social security: The phoney crisis*. Chicago, IL: University of Chicago Press.

Bandy, J., & Smith, J. (Eds). (2005). *Coalitions across borders: Transnational protest and the neo-liberal order*. New York, NY: Rowman and Littlefield.

Baran, P., & Sweezy, P. (1966). *Monopoly capital*. London: Penguin.

Barber, B. (2008). *Consumed: How markets corrupt children, infantilize adults and swallow citizens whole*. New York, NY: W.W. Norton.

Baudrillard, J. (1998). *The consumer society: Myths and structures*. London: Sage.

Bauer, R. A., et al. (1998). *The marketing dilemma of negroes*. In: G. Joyce, op. cit. p 239ff. This is a reprint of an article published in 1965.

Baumol, W. J., & Blinder, A. S. (1994). *Economics* (6th ed.). New York, NY: Harcourt Brace.
Bellamy, R. (Ed.) (1994). *Antonio Gramsci: Pre-prison writings*. Cambridge: Cambridge University Press.
Bendix, R., & Lipset, S. M. (1966). *Class status and power* (2nd ed.). The Free Press.
Berdal, M., & David, M. M. (2001). *Greed or grievance*. Boulder, CO: Lynne Rienner.
Bernanke, B. S. (2000). *Essays on the great depression*. Princeton, NJ: Princeton University Press.
Bernstein, P. L. (1996). *Against the gods: The remarkable story of risk*. New Jersey: Wiley.
Bertell, O. (1971). *Alienation: Marx's conception of man in capitalist society*. Cambridge: Cambridge University Press.
Bogle, J. (2005). *The battle for the soul of capitalism*. New Haven, CT: Yale UP.
Boman-Larsen, L., et al. (2004). *Responsibility in world business*. Tokyo: United Nations University Press.
Bornstein, D., "What is a social entrepreneur?" Ashoka International. http://www.ashoka.org
Bornstein, D. (2004). *How to change the world: Social entrepreneurs and the power of new ideas*. Oxford: Oxford University Press.
Bottomore, T. (1980). *Theories of modern capitalism*. London: George Allen and Unwin.
Boundas, C. V., & Olkowski, D. (1994). *Gilles Deleuze and the theatre of philosophy*. London: Routledge.
Braudel, F. (1977). *Afterthoughts on material civilization and capitalism*. Baltimore, MD: Johns Hopkins University Press.
Brenner, R. (2006). *The economics of global turbulence*. London: Verso.
Buono, A. F., et al. (1985). *Corporate policy, values and social responsibility*. Westport, CT: Praeger.
Canto, V. A. (1983). *The foundations of supply-side economics*. Burlington, MA: Academic Press.
Carchedi, G. (1987). *Class analysis and social research*. Oxford: Blackwell.
Castells, M. (1978). *City, class and power*. London: MacMillan.
Chandhoke, N. (2003). *Conceits of civil society*. Delhi: Oxford University Press.
Chatterjee, S. (2004). *Failsafe strategies*. Philadelphia, PA: Wharton School Publishing.
Christman, J. (1994). *The myth of property: Toward an egalitarian theory of ownership*. Oxford: Oxford University Press.
Clecak, P. (1983). *America's quest for the ideal self: Dissent and fulfillment in the 60s and 70s*. Oxford: Oxford University Press.
Cloward, R., & Piven, F. (1982). *The new class war: Reagen's attack on the welfare state and its consequences*. New York, NY: Pantheon Books.
Cloward, R., & Piven, F. (1998). *Why Americans don't vote*. New York, NY: Pantheon Books.
Cloward, R. A., & Piven, F. (1972). *The politics of turmoil*. New York, NY: Pantheon Books.
Collier, P., & Horowitz, D. (1996). *Destructive generation: New thoughts about the sixties*. Boston, MA: Free Press paperbacks.
Corlett, W. (1998). *Class action: Reading labor, theory and value*. Ithaca, NY: Cornell University Press.
Crosland, A. (1956). *The future of socialism*. London: Vintage.
Crossley, N. (2002). *Making sense of social movements*. Maidenhead: Open University Press.
Dahl, R. A. (2000). *On democracy (Yale Nota Bene)*. New Haven, CT: Yale University Press.
Dahl, R. A., & Lindblom, C. E. (1953). *Politics, economics and welfare*. New York, NY: Harper and Brothers.
Dawkins, R. (1996). *The blind watchmaker*. New York, NY: W.W. Norton.
Debord, G. (1983). *Society of the spectacle*. Paris: Black and Red.

Della Porta, D., & Diani, M. (1999). *Social movements: An introduction*. Oxford: Blackwell.
Demirovic, A. (2000). *NGOs: Social movements in global order?* p. 5.
Desai, M. (2002). *Marx's revenge: The resurgence of capitalism and the death of statist socialism*. London: Verso.
Diamond, P., & Orszag, P. R. (2004). *Saving social security: A balanced approach*. Washington, DC: Brookings.
Diamond, P. A. (2002). *Social security reform*. Oxford: Oxford University Press.
Djilas, M. (1957). *The new class*. Orlando, FL: Harcourt, Brace.
Dollar, D., & Aart, K. (2001). Growth is good for the poor. Working Paper no. 2587. World Bank Policy Research.
Dumenil, G., & Levy, D. (1994). *The economics of the rate of profit*. Camberley: Edward Elgar.
Dupont, A. Refugees and the myth of the borderless world, p. 12. http://rspas.anu.edu.au/ir/keynotes/documents/keynotes-2.pdf
Durkheim, E. (1995). *Elementary forms of religious life*. New York, NY: The Free Press.
Durning, A. T. (1992). *How much is enough?* New York, NY: W W Norton
Eade, D. (Ed.) (2000). *Development, NGOs and civil society*. Oxford: Oxfam.
Easterbrook, G. (2003). *The progress paradox*. New York, NY: Random House Trade Paperbacks.
Ehrenberg, J. (1998). *Civil society: The critical history of an idea*. New York: New York University Press.
Eliade, M. (1959). *Sacred and profane*. Orlando, FL: Harcourt Brace.
Feldstein, M. (Ed.) (1998). *Privatizing social security*. Chicago, IL: University of Chicago Press.
Fenby, J. (2008). *Modern China: The fall and rise of a great power 1850 to the present*. New York, NY: Ecco.
Florida, R. (2003). *The rise of the creative class*. New York, NY: Basic Books.
Florida, R. (2005). *Flight of the creative class*. New York, NY: Collins.
Foley, D. K. (1997). Notes on the theoretical foundations of political economy. http://cepa.newschool.edu/~foleyd/poleconprint.pdf
Foley, D. K. (2006). *Adam's fallacy: A guide to economic theology*. Cambridge, MA: The Belknap Press of Harvard University Press.
Frank, R. H. (2008). *The economic naturalist: Why economics explains almost everything*. London: Virgin.
Friedmann, T. L. (1999). *The lexus and the olive tree*. New York, NY: Farrar, Straus and Giroux.
Funk, McKenzie (2007). The cold rush. *Harper's*, September 2007.
Galbraith, J. K. (1958). *The affluent society*. London: Penguin (updated 1996).
Galbraith, J. K. (1973). *Economics and the public purpose*. Boston, MA: Houghton Mifflin Company.
Galbraith, J. K. (1997). *The great crash*. New York, NY: Mariner Books.
Galeano, E. (2001). *Upside down: A primer for the looking glass world*. New York: Picador.
Gerth, H. H., & Mills, C. W. (1958). *Weber: Essays in sociology*. Oxford: Oxford University Press.
Giddens, A. (1973). *The class structure of advanced societies*. London: Harper and Row.
Gilad, B. (2004). *Early warning: Using competitive intelligence to anticipate market shifts, control risk, and create powerful strategies*. New York, NY: Amacom.
Gini, A. (2003). *The importance of being lazy*. London: Routledge.
Glyn, A., & Sutcliffe, B. (1972). *British capitalism, workers and the profit squeeze*. London: Penguin.

Goldthorpe, J., et al. (1969). *The affluent worker in the class structure.* Cambridge: Cambridge.

Goldthorpe, J., et al. (1987). *Social mobility and class structure in modern Britain.* London: Clarendon.

Goodwin, J., & Jasper, J. M. (2003). *The social movements reader.* Oxford: Blackwell.

Graham, D. T., et al. (2000). *Migration, globalisation and human security.* London: Routledge.

Habermas, J. (1989). *The structural transformation of the public sphere: An enquiry into a category of bourgeois society* (First published in German in 1962). Cambridge, MA: MIT Press.

Hall, J. R. (1995). *Civil society, theory, history, comparison.* London: Polity.

Hanson, D. W., et al. (Ed.) (1971). *Obligation and dissent.* Little, Brown and Co.

Harding, N. (1996). *Leninism.* Durham, NC: Duke University Press.

Hardt, M., & Negri, A. (2000). *Empire.* Cambridge, MA: Harvard University Press.

Hardt, M., & Negri, A. (2004). *Multitude.* London: Penguin.

Harford, T. (2008). *The logic of life: Uncovering the new economics of everything.* London: Little Brown.

Hartigan, P., & Billimori, J. (2005). Social entrepreneurship: An overview. *Alliance, 10*(1). http://www.allavida.org/alliance/mar05f.html

Harvard. (2003). *Harvard business review on corporate responsibility.* Cambridge, MA: Harvard Business School Press.

Harvey, D. (2006). *Limits to capital* (New and Fully Updated Edition). London: Verso.

Haseler, S. (1999). *The super-rich.* London: MacMillan Press.

Haseler, S. (2000). *The super-rich: The unjust new world of global capitalism.* London: Macmillan Press.

Heath, J., & Potter, A. (2004). *Nation of rebels: Why counterculture became consumer culture.* New York, NY: Harper Business.

Held, V., et al. (Ed.) (1972). *Philosophy and political action.* London: Oxford University Press.

Hertz, N. (2001). *The silent takeover: Global capitalism and the death of democracy.* New York, NY: The Free Press.

Hewitt, D. (2008). *Getting rich first: Life in changing China.* New York, NY: Vintage.

Hobsbawm, E. (1996). *The age of extremes: A history of the world, 1914–1991.* New York, NY: Vintage.

Hollender, J., & Fenichell, S. (2004). *What matters most: How a small group of pioneers is teaching social responsibility to big business and why big business is listening.* New York, NY: Basic Books.

Homer-Dixon, T. (2000). *The ingenuity gap.* New York, NY: Alfred A Knopf.

Horowitz, D. (1985). *The morality of spending: Attitudes toward the consumer society in America, 1875–1940.* The John Hopkins University Press.

Horowitz, D. (1994). *Vance Packard and American social criticism.* University of North Carolina Press.

Horowitz, D. (2004). *Anxieties of affluence.* Amherst: University of Massachussets Press.

Howard, D. (Ed.) (1971). *Selected writings of Rosa Luxemburg.* New York, NY: Monthly Review Press.

Howe, I. (1985). *Socialism and America.* Orlando, FL: Harcourt Brace Javanovich.

Hudson, M. (2005). *Harper's.* April 2005.

Huizinga, J. (1971). *Homo ludens: A study of the play element in culture.* Boston, MA: Beacon Press.

Hutton, H. (1995). *The state we're in*. London: Jonathan Cape.

Hutton, W. (2007). *The writing on the wall: China and the west in the 21st century*. London: Abacus.

Hutton, W., & Giddens, A. (Eds). (2000). *Global capitalism*. New York, NY: New Press.

IDEA. (2004). Voter turn out in western europe. www.IDEA.int

James, L. (2006). *The middle class: A history*. London: Abacus.

James, O. (2007). *Affluenza*. London: Vermilion.

Jessop, B. (1982). *The capitalist state*. New York: New York University Press.

Johnson, S. (2000). *Literature review on social entrepreneurship*. Canadian Centre for Social Entrepreneurship.

Joyce, G. (1971). *Black consumer*. New York, NY: Random House.

Kahler, E. (1957). *The tower and the Abyss*. New York, NY: George Braziller Inc..

Kamien, M. I., & Schwartz, N. L. (1982). *Market structure and innovation*. Cambridge: Cambridge University Press.

Keane, J. (1998). *Civil society: old images, new visions*. Stanford, CA: Stanford University Press.

Kennedy, P. (1987). *The rise and fall of the great powers*. New York, NY: Random House.

Keynes, J. M. (1973). *The general theory of employment, interest and money* (first published 1936) as Volume VII of the collected works for the Royal Economic Society. London: MacMillan.

Kindleberger, C. (1976). *Manias, panics and crashes*. New York, NY: Basic Books.

Klein, A. (Ed.) (1971). *Dissent, power and confrontation*. New York, NY: McGraw Hill.

Knight, F. H. (1921). *Risk, uncertainty and profit*. Chicago, IL: Chicago University Press.

Kowinski, W. S. (1985). *Malling of America: An inside look at the great consumer paradise*. London: William Morrow and Co., Inc.

Krugman, P. (1999). *Return to depression economics*. New York, NY: W.W. Norton.

Krugman, P. (2009). *Return to depression economics* (2nd ed.). New York, NY: W.W. Norton.

Kurtz, L. (1999). *Encyclopaedia of violence, peace and conflict* (pp. 269–278). San Diego: Academic Press.

Lasch, C. (1979). *The culture of narcissism*. New York, NY: W.W. Norton.

Lasch, C. (1991). *The true and only heaven: Progress and its critics*. New York, NY: W.W. Norton.

Lee, M. J. (Ed.) (2000). *The consumer society reader*. Oxford: Blackwell.

Linn, S. (2004). *Consuming kids: The hostile takeover of childhood*. New York, NY: New Press.

Lippit, V. (1985). The concept of surplus in economic development. *Review of Radical Political Economics, 17*(1–2).

Loven, J. (2002). www.WashingtonPost.com, 23 October 2002.

Lukacs, G. (1971). *History and class consciousness*. London: The Merlin Press.

Luxemburg, R. (2003). *The accumulation of capital*. London: Routledge Classics.

Lyons, P. (1996). *New left, new right and the legacy of the sixties*. Philadelphia, PA: Temple University Press.

Macpherson, C. B. (1978). *Property: Mainstream and critical positions*. Toronto: University of Toronto Press.

Makower, J. (1994). *Beyond the bottom line*. New York, NY: Simon and Schuster.

Marchand, R. (1998). *Creating the corporate soul: The rise of public relations and corporate imagery in American big business*. Berkeley: University of California Press.

Marcuse, H. (1964/1991 edition). *One dimensional man*. Boston: Beacon Press.

Marglin, S. A. (2008). *The dismal science; how thinking like an economist undermines community.* Cambridge, MA: Harvard.

Marx, K. (1972). Capital, Volumes I–III, London: Lawrence and Wishart (see also, for instance, internet edition: www.econlib.org/library/YPDBooks?Marx/mrxCpC13.html# PartIII).

Marx, K., & Engels, F. (1848/1969). *Manifesto of the Communist Party.* International Publishers Co. Ltd.

McCarthy, M. P., & Flynn, T. (2004). *Risk from the CEO and board perspective.* McGraw-Hill.

Meade, M. (1989). *Dorothy Parker: What fresh hell is this?* New York: Penguin.

Miliband, R. (1969). *The state in capitalist society.* New York, NY: Basic Books.

Mill, J. (1963). *Elements of political economy.* Reprints of Classical Economic Classics, Augustus M Kelley.

Miller, J. (1997). *Egotopia: Narcissism and the New American landscape.* Tuscaloosa, AL: Alabama University Press.

Mitchell, L. E. (2001). *Corporate irresponsibility: America's new export.* New Haven, CT: Yale University Press.

Moseley, F. (1992). *The falling rate of profit in the post war US economy.* London: St. Martin's Press.

Moseley, F. (2000). The decline of the rate of profit in the post-war US economy: A Comment on Brenner, www.mtholyoke.edu/~fmoseley/HM.html

Nevaer, L. E. V. (2004). *The rise of the hispanic market in the US: Challenges, dilemmas, and opportunities for corporate management.* New York, NY: M.E. Sharpe.

New York Times. (2005). *Class matters.* New York: Henry Holt and Co.

Notes from Nowhere. (2003). *We are everywhere.* London: Verso.

Packard, V. (1958). *The hidden persuaders.* New York, NY: Pocket Books Inc. (Simon and Shuster).

Packard, V. (1960). *The waste makers.* New York: Pocket Books Inc. (Simon and Shuster).

Packard, V. (1961). *The status seekers.* New York, NY: Giant Cardinal.

Panagariya, A. (2008). *India: The emerging giant.* Oxford: Oxford University Press.

Perkin, H. (2002). *Origins of modern English society* (2nd ed.). London: Routledge.

Pilling, P. (1980). *Marx's capital: Philosophy and political economy.* London: Routledge & Kegan Paul.

Pohl, F. (1982). *Midas plague* (1954). New York: Bonanza Books 1982, pp. 167–231 (reprinted in the *Seven deadly sins and cardinal virtues of science fiction*).

Poku, N., Renwick, N., & Glenn, J. (2000). Human security in a globalising world, Chapter 2. In: D. T. Graham, et al. (Eds), *Migration, globalisation and human security.* London: Routledge.

Polanyi, K. (1944/2001). *The great transformation.* Boston, MA: Beacon Press.

Proudhon P. J. (1966). *What is property.* Howard Fertig, Inc. (Based First English Edition 1890).

Reynolds, D. (2001). *One world indivisible.* New York, NY: W. W. Norton.

Riesman, D. (1950/1961). *The lonely crowd.* New Haven, CT: Yale University Press.

Robert, H. S. (2005). The lurking rule against accumulations of income, http://law.bepress.com/ nwwps/lep/art, downloaded August 4, 2005.

Rosenberg, N. (1982). *Inside the black box: Technology and economics.* Cambridge: Cambridge University Press.

Rubin, I. I. *Essays on Marx's Theory of Value*, available at www.marxists.org/subject/economy/ rubin/1ind.htm

Rubinstein, W. D. (Ed.) (1980). *Wealth and the wealthy in the modern world*. London: St. Martin's Press.

Runde, J., & Mizuhara, S. (2003). *The philosophy of Keynes's economics: Probability, uncertainty and convention*. London: Routledge.

Ryan, A. (1984). *Property and political theory*. Oxford: Blackwell.

Sachs, J. D. (2005). *On poverty*. London: Penguin Press.

Samuelson, P. A. (1976). *Economics* (10th ed.). New York, NY: McGraw Hill.

Samuelson, P. A. (1991). A personal view on crises and economic cycles. In: M. Feldstein (Ed.), *The risk of economic crisis*. Chicago, IL: University of Chicago Press.

Schor, J. B. (2004). *Born to buy: The commercialized child and the new consumer culture*. New York, NY: Scribner.

Schor, J. B., et al. (2002). *The consumer society reader*. New York, NY: The New Press.

Schumpeter, J. (1939). *Business cycles: A theoretical, historical and statistical analysis of the capitalist process*. New York, NY: MacGraw Hill.

Schumpeter, J. (1950). *Capitalism, socialism and democracy* (3rd ed.). New York, NY: Harper and Bros.

Schwartz, B. (1994). *Costs of living: How market freedom erodes the best things in life*. New York, NY: W.W. Norton.

Scott, R. (1975). *The female consumer*. New Jersey: Wiley.

Seidman, S. (1989). *Jurgen habermas on society and politics: A reader*. Beacon Press.

Sennet, R. (1977). *The fall of public man*. New York: Alfred A Knopf.

Sennett, R. (2006). *The culture of the new capitalism*. New Haven, CT: Yale UP.

Sharpe, W. F. (Ed.) (1990). Investor wealth measures and expected return. In: *Quantifying the market risk premium phenomenon for investment decision making*. Institute of Chartered Financial Analysts.

Sitkoff, R. H. The lurking rule against accumulations of income. Available at http:// law.bepress.com/nwwps/lep/art. Retrieved on August 4, 2005.

Sklair, L. (2001). *The transnational capital class*. Oxford: Blackwell.

Sombart, W. (1976). In: C.T. Husbands (Ed.), *Why is there no socialism in the United States?* International Arts and Science Press (originally published in 1906).

Soros, G. (1995). *Soros on Soros*. New Jersey: Wiley.

Soros, G. (2002). *Soros on globalization*. New York, NY: Public Affairs.

Soros, G. (2004). *Bubble of American supremacy*. New York, NY: Public Affairs.

Steinberg, J. (1978). *Locke, Rousseau and the idea of consent*. Westport, CT: Greenwood Press.

Stiglitz, J. E. (2002). *Globalization and its discontents*. New York, NY: W.W. Norton.

Stiglitz, J. E. (2003). *The roaring nineties*. New York, NY: W.W. Norton.

Stiglitz, J. E., & Bilmes, L. J. (2008). *The three trillion dollar war: The true cost of the Iraq conflict*. New York, NY: W.W. Norton.

Strachey, J. (1957). *Contemporary capitalism*. London: Victor Gollancz.

Sunnstein, C. R. (2005). *Why societies need dissent*. Cambridge, MA: Harvard University Press.

Sweezy, P. (1966). *Modern capitalism*. New York, NY: Monthly Review Press.

Sweezy, P. (1972a). *Modern capitalism*. New York, NY: Monthly Review Press.

Sweezy, P. (1972b). *On the theory of monopoly capitalism and other essays*. New York, NY: Monthly Review Press.

Tanner, M. D. (Ed.) (2004). *Social security and its discontnents: Perspectives on choice.* Cato
    Institute.
Teixeira, R. A. (1992). *The disappearing American voter.* Washington: Brookings.
The Economist, Volume 375, No. 8420, "Crowned At Last" supplement, p. 12.
The Economist, Volume 375, No. 8420, p. 14.
The Economist, Volume 375, No. 8420, p. 15.
Tilly, C. (1978). *From mobilization to revolution.* New Jersey: Addison Wesley Publishing Co.
Todd, E. (2003). *After the empire.* New York, NY: Columbia University Press.
Underhill, P. (2004). *The call of the mall.* New York, NY: Simon and Schuster.
Vankovsa, B., & Wiberg, H. (2003). *Between past and future: Civil–military relations in the post
    communist balkans.* IB Taurus.
Veblen, T. (2001). *The theory of the leisure class.* New York, NY: The Modern Library Classics.
von Mises, L. (1960). *Epistemological problems of economics.* D. van Nostrand and Co.
von Mises, L. (1963). *Human action: A treatise on economics.* New Haven, CT: Yale University
    Press (New Revised Edition. First edition 1949).
Wardlow, D. L. (1996). *Gays, lesbians, and consumer behaviour: Theory practice and research
    issues in marketing.* The Haworth Press Inc.
Wiefek, N. (2003). *The impact of economic anxiety in postindustrial America.* Westport, CT:
    Praeger.
Wright, E. O. (1989). *The debate on class.* London: Verso.
Wright, E. O. (2005). *Towards a new class analysis.* Cambridge: Cambridge University Press.
Wright, E. O. (2008). *Towards a new class analysis.* Cambridge: Cambridge University Press.
Yasheng, H. (2008). *Capitalism with Chinese characteristics: Entrepreneurship and the state.*
    Cambridge: Cambridge University Press.
Zashin, E. M. (1971). *Civil disobedience.* New York, NY: The Free Press.
Zweig, M. (Ed.) (2004). *What's class got to with it?* Ithaca, NY: Cornell University Press.
Zwiebach, B. (1975). *Civility and disobedience.* Cambridge: Cambridge University Press.

PART II
VALUE THEORY AND METHODOLOGY IN POLITICAL ECONOMY

CHAPTER 8

ON THE LABOR THEORY OF VALUE: STATISTICAL ARTEFACTS OR REGULARITIES?[☆]

Lefteris Tsoulfidis and Dimitris Paitaridis

ABSTRACT

This paper subjects to empirical testing the standard (based on the notion of vertical integration) method for the estimation of labor values and prices of production against an alternative one known as the Temporary Single-System Interpretation (TSSI), an approach that finds strong support among a new generation of researchers. Our empirical findings from the Canadian economy suggest that both methods give rise to estimates of labor values and prices of production that are surprisingly close to observed prices. Further examination however reveals that the TSSI contradicts some of the basic tenets of logical consistency of the theory that indents to vindicate. These results lend support to the standard Marxian theory, and the estimating methods associated with it constitute a fertile ground for further research.

[☆]A version of this paper was presented in the Workshop on Political Economy at Panteion University, March 29, 2007.

Why Capitalism Survives Crises: The Shock Absorbers
Research in Political Economy, Volume 25, 209–232
Copyright © 2009 by Emerald Group Publishing Limited
All rights of reproduction in any form reserved
ISSN: 0161-7230/doi:10.1108/S0161-7230(2009)0000025005

1. INTRODUCTION

In recent years we are witnessing a flow of studies that measure the extent of deviations of labor values and prices of production from market prices. These studies usually report that the three types of prices are close to each other and their closeness is being measured by various measures of deviation such as the mean absolute deviation (MAD) and the mean absolute weighted deviation (MAWD), the weights being the share of each industry's output to the economy's total. Steedman and Tomkins (1998) argued that these measures of deviation depend on the adopted normalization condition and chosen numéraire, which may give rise to a certain degree of bias, and for this reason, they introduced a bias-free measure of deviation. There is another critique of traditional studies emanating from a strand of Marxian theory known as the Temporary Single-System Interpretation (TSSI) that claims an alternative way of estimating the closeness of labor values and prices of production. Freeman (1997) initially and Kliman (2002, 2004, 2007) subsequently argued that the reported high correlation coefficients between labor values and market prices are due to a certain type of bias caused by the size of industries and once we somehow get rid of the size-bias the correlation coefficient is reduced to near zero. This line of research continues by Diaz and Osuna (2005–2006, 2007) who conclude that any efforts to eliminate the size-bias are meaningless, simply because we do not really know the physical units of measurement of output and so there is no way of knowing the actual market prices.

In this paper, we take issue with these claims and show on the basis of input–output data of the economy of Canada that market prices, labor values, and prices of production are close to each other. In addition, we find that the alleged bias in the measures of deviation is relatively small and, therefore, does not affect the results in any qualitatively different way. The remainder of the paper is structured as follows: Section 2 reviews the empirical literature on the subject at hand. Section 3 discusses the methods of estimation of labor values and prices of production according to the two competing approaches. Section 4 presents the results of the analysis and shows that the extent of the suspected bias in the various measures of deviation. Section 5 contrasts the two alternative estimating methods and subjects them to empirical testing of their consistency with the requirements of the Marxian theory. Finally, Section 6 concludes and makes some remarks about future research efforts.

2. REVIEW OF EMPIRICAL STUDIES

The empirical research on the relation between labor values, prices of production, and market prices using input–output data for the economies of the United States, former Yugoslavia, Italy, England, Greece, and S. Korea has shown that the three types of prices are surprising close to each other. More specifically, Shaikh (1984) reports that the MAD of direct prices (i.e., prices proportional to labor values) or prices of production from market prices are in the order of 17–19% for the economy of Italy, while using crude input–output data for the US economy, and a circulating capital model finds that the order of price-value deviations ranges between 20 and 25%. Ochoa (1984, 1989), using the same methodology and by working with more detailed data, found that the MAD of direct prices and market prices for years spanning the period 1947–1972 is about 12%, the MAD of market prices and prices of production is about 13%, while the MAD of direct prices and prices of production is almost 17%. The research for the economies of the UK (Cockshott, Cottrell, & Michaelson, 1995; Cockshott & Cottrell, 1997), former Yugoslavia (Petrovic, 1987), Greece (Tsoulfidis & Maniatis, 2002; Tsoulfidis & Mariolis, 2007), S. Korea (Tsoulfidis & Rieu, 2006), and Japan (Tsoulfidis, 2008) gave results similar to the above. Zacharias's (2006) study presents estimates of labor values for a number of OECD countries, which are favorable to the idea of proximity of labor values to market prices.

By contrast, the study by Steedman and Tomkins (1998) for the UK, Ireland, Australia and for a sample of Australian regions gave quite large deviations. However, it is important to note that Steedman and Tomkins's (1998) results for the UK were not far from the expected bounds of deviation, whereas those derived for Ireland of the year 1985, mainly an agricultural country at that time, and various agricultural regions of Australia gave quite large deviations. These findings may be questioned for a number of reasons; for example, the issue of self-employment which is not accounted for and is certainly widespread for countries and regions with agricultural character. Furthermore, the lack of treatment of depreciation as well as the overall quality of data, especially the regional ones cast doubt to the validity of the results.

While all of the above studies are based on input–output data, this is not the case, however, with some recent papers, where there is an effort to compute direct prices and prices of production with the use of national income accounts data. For example, Kliman (2002, 2004) in his study of the

US economy for the period 1977–1997 derives estimates of labor values that are highly correlated to market prices; in fact the correlation coefficients are somewhat higher than those reported in Ochoa's (1984) study.[1] It is interesting to note that in these studies we do not exactly regress labor values against market prices proper, but rather the product of the labor values of industries times their respective outputs (total sales) that are regressed against total sales. The high correlation coefficients come as no surprise, since labor values are estimated relative to market prices which in input–output analysis are all equal to one. It is important to note that this kind of bias was already known in the first (unpublished) studies of the early 1980s. For example, Ochoa (1984, p. 124) notes: "In connection with cross-sectional series, the error of 'spurious correlation' is known to be a problem. Clearly, if we are trying to establish a relationship between a and b, and if we define $x = az$ and $y = bz$, the correlation coefficient between x and y will overestimate the correlation between a and b. It could be argued that, in comparing the market and computed prices of sectoral outputs, we are establishing such a spurious correlation"; this note is also cited in Freeman (1997). Shaikh (1998, p. 233) also refers to the possibility of bias in this kind of regressions, and for this reason, he opted for the measures of deviations instead of correlation. Kliman raises, once again, the issue of bias in the regressions by characterizing the high correlation coefficients as "artefacts" and thus one should not take them as an index of proximity of labor values to market prices. More specifically, Kliman repeats that the correlation coefficients in studies where labor values times sales are regressed against sales are artificially high (usually above 95%) and this is the result of the industry size. Large industries use large amounts of labor and so their sales are also large; therefore, a high correlation coefficient is trivially expected. For this reason Kliman proposed to scale down, or in his wording to "deflate", both variables by the total (labor and non-labor) cost of production in his effort to reduce the "size-induced bias." The regressions that he ran in the "deflated" variables gave correlation coefficients near zero.

Diaz and Osuna (2005–2006, p. 352n), using data from the national income accounts of the Spanish economy for the period 1986–1994, also found relatively small price-value deviations and extremely high correlations (an R-square in the range of 97%). Furthermore, they took issue with Kliman's claims arguing that controlling for the size of an industry by its total cost is inappropriate, since it severely reduces the variability of both the independent variable (sales evaluated in terms of labor values) and the dependent variable (sales), thereby giving correlations near zero. If the size of industries is controlled otherwise, then Diaz and Osuna conclude that any results might be possible. More specifically, when they deflated by just the non-labor cost their R-square increased from near zero to about 40%, and when finally the size of industries was deflated by the gross capital stock, the high correlations were restored, with the R-square lying in the range of 90%.[2] From these findings one would expect that Diaz and Osuna (2005–2006, 2007) would propose a more appropriate "deflation" process; nonetheless, this is not the case because they draw attention to a more fundamental problem associated with the lack of exact knowledge of the physical units of measurement that render market prices indeterminate magnitudes. As a consequence, they are led to the conclusion that no inference whatsoever can be made about the closeness of computed prices (direct prices or prices of production) and the "unknown" market prices.

In a sequel of papers, Diaz and Osuna (2005–2006, 2007) showed the ad hoc nature of Kliman's deflation process, something that has been also criticized, from a different perspective, by Cockshott and Cottrell (2005). More specifically, Cockshott and Cottrell (2005) argued that if labor values are close to market prices, as the regressions show, and if this is an "artifact," as Kliman claims, then "alternative value bases" such as the electricity or agricultural content of commodities should also give high correlations. Something that is not necessarily true, as it has been shown in the studies by Cockshott et al. (1995), Chilcote (1997), Cockshott and Cottrell (1997), and also Tsoulfidis and Maniatis (2002). However, the agnostic position of Diaz and Osuna (2005–2006, 2007) according to which since we cannot know the exact physical units of measurement the actual market prices remain unknown is questionable. We know that in the input–output analysis we need not know the exact physical units of measurement; we only need to assume that whatever the physical units of measurement they remain fixed during the analysis. Once we stipulate such an assumption then the direct prices and prices of production are derived as a proportion to market prices whatever these might be.[3] By way of an example, suppose that milk is sold for 80 cents a liter. By adopting the evaluation of the product in terms of dollars, we essentially say that 1.25 l of milk will be equal to 1 dollar. The physical unit of measurement of milk becomes 1.25 l (see also Ochoa, 1984, p. 58). Consequently, in input–output analysis market prices are set equal to one because it is impossible (and also meaningless) to collect data on the physical output produced, we only assume that whatever the units of measurement are, they remain constant. Leontief (1966), for example, notes "[a]ll figures [of an input-output table] can also be interpreted as representing physical quantities of the goods or services to which they refer. This only requires that the physical units in which one measures the entries in each row be redefined as being equal to the amount of output of the particular sector which can be purchased for $1 at prices which prevailed during the interval of time for which the table was constructed" (Leontief, 1966, p. 137).[4] Once we stipulate such an assumption then the direct prices and prices of production are derived as a proportion to market prices whatever these might be.

   This is the reason why we bring additional empirical evidence about the relationship between values, prices of production, and market prices from the Canadian economy. The reason for selecting this particular country is the availability and high quality of input–output data of a relatively recent year and also the fact that the input–output data of this country have not been used, so far, for testing the validity and the scientific status of the labor theory of value. Implicit in our selection is that as the labor theory of value is tested with data of more and more countries it is expected to reveal regularities, which will establish this theory as a realistic and, at the same time, a viable alternative to the orthodox microeconomic theory.

3. LABOR VALUES AND PRICES OF PRODUCTION IN THE TWO COMPETING APPROACHES

The so-called TSSI for the estimation of labor values and prices of production emphasizes the temporal disequilibrium and, therefore, dynamic nature of both labor values and prices of production. The latter must be estimated not simultaneously, as in the standard approach, but rather in terms of historical cost.[5] In this sense the TSSI is not dualistic since prices of production must be estimated in a way that inputs and outputs will be evaluated in two different price systems.[6] In what follows, we show how labor values and prices of production are estimated according to this novel approach. The required data include the cost of intermediate inputs plus the constituent components of value added, usually wages and gross profits, and also data on total employment in terms of the number of employees or total working hours (see Appendix for detail data of 34 industries). The TSSI proponents further claim that since we do not exactly know the actual market prices, we may approximate them for each industry by just dividing the total sales by the labor and non-labor cost of production (Kliman, 2002). Clearly, the result of this division is neither the market price of the industry nor its "proxy" as Kliman asserts, but rather the markup on cost.

This idea of the TSSI works even worse in the case of prices of production, that is, cost prices that incorporate a uniform rate of profit. More specifically, in the context of the circulating capital technology that we use, as the cost price is multiplied by a markup (i.e., one plus the uniform rate of profit) and then deflated by the labor and non-labor cost, we end up with the uniform markup. This is clearly depicted in Table 1. Naturally, dealing with the case of circulating capital alone Kliman restricted his estimations to labor values, thereby not mentioning at all the possible estimation of prices of production.[7] This is not the case, however, with Diaz and Osuna (2005–2006, 2007) who, by using more detailed data on both flow and stock variables, extended their analysis to prices of production. However, the TSSI must be convincing first within a circulating capital technology model and then to expand to include the case of capital stock, after all stock variables are formed from the accumulation of flow variables. In what follows we replicate Diaz and Osuna's (2005–2006, p. 351) estimating method by restricting to the case of circulating capital technology and also

Table 1. The TSSI Estimation of Labor Values and Prices of Production.

Variable Notation	Variable Name
1	Intermediate inputs
2	Labor costs
$3 = 1 + 2$	Total costs
4	Gross profit
$5 = 4 + 2$	Gross final income
$6 = 1 + 5$	Total production valued at market price
6/3	Proxy to market price (cost deflated)
$7 = 4/3$	Rate of profit
$8 = \Sigma 4/\Sigma 3$	Uniform rate of profit
$9 = 3 + 8 \times 3$	Total production valued at production prices
9/3	Proxy to production price (cost deflated)
9/6	Proxy to production price (output deflated)
$10 = 1/MELT(-)^a$	Non-labor costs measured in work hours (millions)
11	Millions of work hours
$12 = 10 + 11$	Labor value of the total production
$13 = \Sigma 6/\Sigma 12$	MELT
$14 = 12 \times 13$	Total production valued at direct prices
14/3	Proxy to direct price (cost deflated)
14/6	Proxy to direct price (output deflated)

[a]The minus sign refers to previous time periods.

by proposing what we think would be a more meaningful and, therefore, useful deflation, in the sense that the results in terms of labor values and prices of production are directly comparable to those derived from the notion of vertical integration and input–output analysis.

We start with the estimation of total production evaluated in market prices, whose division by the total cost gives us Kliman's proxy of "market prices" against which the labor values will be compared. The latter are estimated as the sum of non-labor cost and labor cost measured in terms of labor hours. The next step is to translate these magnitudes in monetary terms, which is done through the device of the monetary expression of labor time (MELT) defined in Diaz and Osuna (2005–2006) as the ratio of gross product (total sales) to total labor time. More specifically, Diaz and Osuna divide the sum of the intermediate inputs and the gross value added by the amount of labor that has been employed. All these data are readily available; the difficulty lies in the conversion of the intermediate inputs measured in dollars (monetary terms) to labor values. This problem is dealt with by dividing the intermediate inputs of the current period by the MELT of the previous period. The idea behind this treatment is that intermediate inputs are the output of past processes of production. By doing so, Diaz and Osuna reduce the monetary measures to labor values, which reflect past conditions of production. Consequently, we may write:

$$\text{MELT}_t = \frac{(C_t + W_t + P_t)}{[(C_t/\text{MELT}_{t-1}) + H_t]}$$

where C denotes the intermediate inputs, W the labor compensation, and P the gross profits, whereas H denotes the total hours worked in a year and t stands for time. By assuming that the current MELT depends on the MELT a year ago which in turn depends on the MELT two years ago and so forth, we end up with a recursive process of MELT estimation. Diaz and Osuna (2005–2006, 2007) deal with this problem by starting with the estimation of the time series setting the MELT for the first year as the ratio of monetary value added to newly added labor, a method used by the followers of the so-called "new solution" to the "transformation problem" (Foley, 1982; Duménil, 1983, inter alia). For the next year they use the so-derived MELT to transform the intermediate inputs into labor values. The result is added to the newly added labor in order to estimate the labor value of the gross product, which in turn is used for the estimation of the MELT. Repeating the process, any deviations are being eliminated as long as new living labor is added to the product.[8]

Similarly, Freeman (1997) sets the MELT as the ratio between the gross output measured in monetary units and the gross output measured in labor hours. For Freeman, the MELT is not a ratio between two flow quantities but rather a ratio between two stock quantities as it expresses the amount of past labor that a given amount of money can purchase. In a similar fashion, Kliman (2002) estimates the labor time equivalent of a dollar as the ratio between total labor time to total gross output.

From the above discussion, it follows that the deflation method involving total sales (production) is much more promising than that of total (or partial) cost of production and capital stock. The intuitive idea is that total sales give rise to market price of a given quantity of output equal to 1 dollar, and by doing so, the results of the TSSI are rendered comparable to those of the standard or "non-sequential" estimating method. In our view, a comparison of the two methods will reveal their advantages and disadvantages, and so a choice between them can be made on the basis of theoretical consistency and predictive content. The decisive criterion for selection, therefore, will be the relative accuracy of the predictions of market prices in conjunction with the theoretical consistency. If both approaches predict equally well and are both theoretically consistent with their fundamental premises, then naturally the simpler approach is preferred to the more complicated.

Prices of production are estimated by bringing into the analysis the economy's uniform rate of profit; the latter can be viewed as a markup which when multiplied by the cost of production gives the aggregate sectoral price of production. The trouble with this estimation is that when we apply the deflation by cost, we end up with just the markup (profit rate) which, of course, is uniform across sectors. Diaz and Osuna (2005–2006, 2007) sidestep this problem by bringing into the analysis the capital stock, whereas Kliman (2002, 2004) is silent about the desirability of estimating prices of production.[9] To our view prices of production must be estimated in a logically consistent way first in the case of a circulating capital model which in a second stage can be expanded to include the case of capital stock.[10] In fact, it is commonplace by now that in these estimations the results that one derives from circulating capital models should not be out of touch from those that are derived from models with capital stock (see for example, Ochoa, 1984, pp. 50–58). We, therefore, decided to "deflate" by total sales rather than the cost of production because of its odd results, especially with respect to prices of production. It seems that our proposed method of "deflation" generates estimates that are close to market prices, which in input-output analysis by definition are equal to one (Miller and Blair, 1985), and also makes these results directly comparable to those derived by the standard input–output methods. Such a comparison is very useful because if the so-modified TSSI gives reliable results, then it might be preferred, since its data requirements are much easier to fulfill and the national income account data are readily available.

Turning now to the standard or, according to TSSI proponents, non-sequential estimating methods making use of the input–output analysis, we begin with the labor values (λ), that is, the total (direct and indirect) labor requirements per unit of output produced. More specifically, the labor values of each of the 34 industries of the Canadian economy are derived from the solution of the following system of equations in matrix form:

$$\lambda = a_0(I - A)^{-1}$$

where, λ is the row vector of labor values or vertically integrated labor input coefficients (Pasinetti, 1977), A the square matrix of input–output coefficients, a_0 the row vector of adjusted for skills direct labor coefficients, and I the identity matrix. Furthermore, we scale the so-estimated labor values to prices proportional to values, that is, we equate the sum of labor values expressed in money terms (direct prices) to the sum of market prices according to the usual condition of the transformation problem. That is, $v = \lambda(ex)/(\lambda x)$ where v is the row vector of direct prices, e the row vector of ones identified with the market prices, and x the column vector of gross output. With this normalization, the equality between the gross output evaluated in direct prices (vx) and the gross output evaluated in market prices (ex) will always hold true. In other words, the proposed normalization condition of prices maintains the value of money constant. In effect, the ratio ex/vx represents the corresponding MELT, with the difference that now it is estimated in terms of vertical integration analysis and the same time period. The prices of production are estimated from the following equation:

$$P = (1 + r)P(ba_0 + A)$$

where P is a row vector of relative prices of production, b the column vector of the basket of goods that workers normally consume with their money wage $w = Pb$, and r a scalar representing the economy's uniform rate of profit. Prices of production are normalized such that $p = P(ex/px)$.

4. RESULTS

The estimates of both labor values (direct prices) and prices of production according to the two competing approaches are displayed in Table 2. We have also estimated the TSSI cost-deflated prices whose deviation

Table 2. Estimates of the Two Competing Methods.

S. No.	Industries	Standard		TSSI or Sequentialist	
		Prices of production	Direct prices	Prices of production	Direct prices
1	Agriculture	1.216	1.136	1.132	1.232
2	Mining	0.609	0.602	0.641	0.565
3	Food and beverage	1.112	0.937	1.015	0.934
4	Textiles	1.024	0.981	1.021	1.086
5	Wood	1.174	1.038	1.047	0.944
6	Paper	1.037	0.982	1.013	0.954
7	Petroleum	0.857	0.702	1.185	1.000
8	Chemicals	0.852	0.738	0.923	0.766
9	Rubber	0.957	0.897	1.010	0.993
10	Other non-metallic products	0.930	0.902	0.984	0.907
11	Iron and steel	0.975	0.855	1.071	0.814
12	Fabricated metallic products	1.064	1.009	1.051	0.929
13	Machinery and equipment	1.032	0.949	1.000	0.998
14	Office machinery	1.730	1.120	1.185	1.012
15	Electronic machinery	1.051	0.962	1.039	0.937
16	Radio, TV	1.064	0.933	1.009	0.934
17	Motor vehicles	1.273	0.917	1.082	0.906
18	Shipping	1.038	1.125	1.022	1.539
19	Aircraft	0.961	0.930	0.957	0.805
20	Railroad equipment	1.069	0.933	1.025	0.842
21	Manufacturing nec.	1.049	1.016	1.033	1.021
22	Utilities	0.458	0.486	0.474	0.373
23	Construction	1.129	1.122	1.121	1.037
24	Trade	1.009	1.143	1.032	1.260
25	Hotels and restaurants	1.042	1.067	1.014	1.602
26	Transportation	1.004	1.035	1.001	1.034
27	Communications	0.792	0.850	0.785	0.751
28	FIRE	0.771	0.805	0.874	0.663
29	Computer	0.979	1.089	1.067	1.382
30	Other business	0.962	1.075	1.076	1.225
31	Public Administration	1.049	1.130	1.035	0.762
32	Education	1.160	1.407	1.145	0.956
33	Health	1.023	1.212	1.017	1.320
34	Social services	1.034	1.144	1.046	1.092

from market prices were quite large as expected, and so we decided not to use them for further investigation. However, in order to make the two approaches comparable we deflate the TSSI direct prices and prices of production with total sales, a deflation process that has not been tried so far by the followers of the TSSI approach. Clearly, the deflated by total sales estimates of direct prices and prices of production, according to TSSI, become comparable to those derived from the standard estimating procedures. The first two columns of Table 2 report our estimates of prices of production and labor values according to the standard estimating method and the next two columns report the TSSI estimates of prices of production and labor values. An inspection of the results of Table 2 shows that both the TSSI and the standard approach give rise to estimated prices that are surprising close to the market prices, which by definition are equal to one.

The deviations of direct prices and prices of production are estimated through the MAD, that is, the average absolute deviations of direct prices (or prices of production) from market prices and the MAWD, that is, the absolute deviations of prices of production (or labor values) from market prices weighted by each sector's share of total output. The root mean square error (RMSE) suggested by Petrovic (1987) is another statistic of deviation defined as the square root of the average square differences of direct prices (or prices of production) from market prices. The normalized vector distance (NVD) defined as $NVD = \|e<x> - v<x>\| / \|e<x>\| = [\sum (e_j x_j - v_j x_j)^2]^{1/2} / [\sum (e_j x_j)^2]^{1/2}$ has also been used in the relevant literature. These four are the most frequently used summary statistics of deviation; it has been argued by Steedman and Tomkins (1998) that they suffer from a certain degree of bias stemming from the applied normalization condition. The size of the bias, theoretically speaking, might be serious. This is the reason that Steedman and Tomkins (1998) proposed a measure of deviation independent of the normalization condition: the d statistic defined as: $d = [2(1 - \cos \theta)]^{1/2}$, where θ is the angle between the two vectors in comparison. Thus, it is interesting to compare the proximity of values and prices of production with respect to market prices taking data from a real economy, thereby obtaining a more precise idea of the extent of the suspected bias (see Table 3).

Clearly, the five measures of deviation convey approximately the same picture with respect to the degree of proximity of the estimated prices of the two competing approaches. Starting with the standard approach, we observe that the summary statistics of deviation for the Canadian economy are in line with those estimated, for example, for the US economy (see Ochoa, 1989; Shaikh, 1998). Turning now to the TSSI estimates, we observe that both types of computed prices are also pretty close to actual prices.

Table 3. Measures of Deviation[a].

Measures of Deviation	Standard or Non-Sequential Approach		TSSI or Sequential approach	
	Direct prices	Prices of production	Direct prices	Prices of production
MAD	0.133	0.126	0.180	0.084
MAWD	0.149	0.125	0.195	0.089
NVD	0.175	0.165	0.250	0.116
RMSE	0.177	0.200	0.248	0.136
d	0.180	0.197	0.249	0.137

[a]There are some other statistics such as for example the coefficient of variation or the tangent of angle theta between the two vectors because they can be easily calculated from the d statistic, from the d statistic also one can calculate the correlation coefficient (Steedman & Tomkins, 1998; Diaz & Osuna, 2009).

It is interesting to note that the direct prices of the TSSI are definitely more distant than the corresponding direct prices estimated from the standard method. Furthermore, it is ironic that the prices of production estimated according to the TSSI are closer than any other kind of estimated prices to market prices. Finally, from the data of Table 3 one cannot ignore the fact that the usual measures of deviation (MAD, MAWD, NVD, and RMSE) are not out of touch from the alternative and bias-free d statistic, although they suffer from a certain (to our view negligible) degree of bias. This is not to say that one should not prefer the bias-free measures of deviation, but rather to stress the fact that the extent of bias (in actual data) is not that large and, for all practical purposes, the first four statistics convey approximately the same picture with the bias-free d statistic despite of their alleged bias.

It is important to note that while Steedman and Tomkins (1998) opted for the d statistic as perhaps the only measure suitable for the proximity of computed prices (direct or production) to market prices, Diaz and Osuna (2009) argued that even the d statistic is bias-laden and that one should dispense with the measures of deviation all together, simply because all of them depend on the choice of physical units of measurement, which affects market prices whenever these units change. Although we do not take issue with the mathematical logic of the two authors, their conclusions are derived because they violate the assumption of input–output tables, that is, the physical units of measurement are fixed and so it is not possible to experiment freely with different physical units of measurement.

5. EVALUATION OF THE TWO APPROACHES

Since both approaches give quite similar results in terms of their proximity to market prices, one wonders whether the new approach is better than the traditional, and already tested many times, approach. In our view, the litmus test for both approaches is their consistency with the basic requirements of the theory according to which labor values (and their monetary expression direct prices) must be shown to be compatible with the principle of equal profitability and prices of production. As a consequence, prices of production will be higher than direct prices in the industries whose capital intensity (organic composition of capital) is higher than the economy's average and the prices of production will be lower than their respective direct prices in those industries whose capital intensity is lower than the average. It goes without saying, that in those industries whose capital intensity coincides with the average the deviation between direct price and price of production will be nil.

Table 4, which displays the price of production labor values deviations of both approaches as well as the deviations of the various compositions of capital from the average. More specifically, for the first three columns of Table 4 the notation is as follows: $p-v$ the deviations between prices of production and values according to the standard approach; SCC the difference of simple composition of capital (evaluated in terms of prices of production) from the average composition of capital, indicated in the last row of the table; VICC the difference of vertically integrated composition of capital (evaluated again in terms of prices of production of the standard approach) from the average composition of capital. The next columns (4–8) refer to the TSSI approach, in particular, column 4 refers to the price value deviations of the TSSI and columns 5 and 6 refer to the deviations of simple and vertically integrated compositions of capital from their respective averages both evaluated in terms of TSSI prices of production, whereas columns 7 and 8 refer to the same compositions of capital evaluated in terms of market prices.

From the results displayed in Table 2 we derive that the standard estimating method, based on the notion of vertical integration not only gives extremely good approximations of market prices but moreover the differences between prices of production and labor values, shows the degree of transfer of surplus value in the form of profit across industries. The signs of these differences are absolutely consistent with the requirements of the theory. More specifically, we observe that in all of our 34 industries the signs of transfers, positive or negative, are consistent with the signs of differences

Table 4. Price-Value Deviations and Compositions of Capital.

Standard				TSSI				
	p-v	SCC POP	VICC POP	*p-v* TSSI	SCC POP TSSI	VICC POP TSSI	SCC MP	VICC MP
	1	2	3	4	5	6	7	8
1	0.08	11.45	7.01	−0.10	10.85	6.11	9.38	6.80
2	0.01	5.01	1.26	0.08	5.85	2.97	7.73	1.86
3	0.18	57.61	18.82	0.08	54.01	16.41	50.13	17.78
4	0.04	9.28	4.47	−0.07	9.44	4.69	9.25	4.75
5	0.14	31.63	13.12	0.10	28.92	10.62	25.52	12.12
6	0.06	11.05	5.67	0.06	10.67	5.89	11.30	5.56
7	0.16	188.02	22.22	0.19	205.19	34.98	285.00	24.77
8	0.11	38.90	15.53	0.16	43.09	19.91	47.15	17.60
9	0.06	10.49	6.73	0.02	11.89	9.09	13.33	7.91
10	0.03	8.52	3.10	0.08	9.52	5.39	12.07	3.84
11	0.12	34.13	14.07	0.26	37.24	18.52	43.03	15.68
12	0.06	6.74	5.50	0.12	7.94	6.70	6.95	6.57
13	0.08	14.46	8.77	0.00	14.57	8.86	13.59	9.08
14	0.61	123.33	54.60	0.17	88.06	33.50	75.84	38.99
15	0.09	16.43	9.27	0.10	17.62	10.36	16.62	10.27
16	0.13	31.82	14.17	0.08	31.25	13.64	29.57	14.27
17	0.36	94.98	38.90	0.18	84.37	32.86	78.35	34.99
18	−0.09	−10.25	−7.73	−0.52	−10.24	−7.87	−10.80	−7.56
19	0.03	6.82	3.38	0.15	7.07	3.92	7.19	3.74
20	0.14	36.18	14.66	0.18	36.22	14.79	34.75	15.08
21	0.03	5.81	3.22	0.01	5.97	3.61	5.87	3.53
22	−0.03	−6.74	−5.82	0.10	−6.41	−4.93	−5.73	−5.48
23	0.01	2.58	0.56	0.08	3.02	1.02	2.85	1.00
24	−0.13	−12.25	−11.79	−0.23	−11.86	−11.3	−11.68	−11.41
25	−0.03	−4.81	−2.39	−0.59	−5.37	−3.13	−5.43	−2.84
26	−0.03	−2.60	−3.02	−0.03	−1.9	−2.42	−2.44	−2.43
27	−0.06	−6.92	−6.83	0.03	−6.79	−6.86	−7.01	−6.66
28	−0.03	−1.34	−4.17	0.21	−0.16	−2.78	0.86	−3.36
29	−0.11	−10.24	−10.20	−0.31	−9.86	−10.2	−10.14	−9.88
30	−0.11	−10.69	−10.51	−0.15	−10.35	−10.5	−10.60	−10.22
31	−0.08	−4.69	−7.21	0.27	−4.55	−7.31	−4.82	−7.08
32	−0.25	−17.53	−17.65	0.19	−17.66	−18.1	−17.93	−17.76
33	−0.19	−16.01	−15.64	−0.30	−16.08	−15.9	−16.29	−15.66
34	−0.11	−10.10	−9.70	−0.05	−9.86	−9.4	−9.79	−9.46
Average		20.28	10.40		19.63	10.17	20.54	10.10

in the capital intensities. Starting with the differences of the simple composition of capital (i.e., $\mathbf{pA}./\mathbf{a_o}$, where the symbol "./" denotes an element-by-element division and the other notation is as above) from the weighted average capital-intensity (estimated by $\mathbf{pAx}/\mathbf{a_ox}$), we observe that are always of the same sign (see column 2) with the differences of direct prices from the prices of production (column 1). Similarly, with the differences of the vertically integrated composition of capital (a more accurate indicator of the capital-intensity defined as $\mathbf{pA(I-A)^{-1}}./\mathbf{a_o(I-A)^{-1}}$ from the weighted average vertically integrated capital-intensity, estimated by $\mathbf{pA(I-A)^{-1}x}/\mathbf{a_o(I-A)^{-1}x}$, (see column 3). In all cases the differences in price-value deviations are of the same sign with the differences in capital intensities, regardless of the way these intensities are being measured.

Turning now to deviations between prices of production and direct prices (values) the estimates according to the TSSI are displayed in column 4 (Table 2). We observe that the signs of deviations are not fully consistent with the respective signs of deviations of the two expressions of capital intensity. In fact, we observe that in 7 out of 34 industries the signs are opposite of the theoretically expected indicating that it is possible for these industries, although their capital intensity is higher than the average, nevertheless they transfer (surplus) value in the form of profits to the industries with capital intensity lower than the economy's average. The signs do not change in the different evaluations of capital intensities, that is, simple or vertically integrated and the different evaluations of the composition of capital.

The next step is to test whether or not the size differences in price-value deviations are proportional to the size differences between capital intensities from the average. To facilitate the exposition, Fig. 1 portrays the price-value deviations (of both approaches), where on the vertical axis of each of the four graphs, we place the price-value differences and on the horizontal axis the respective capital intensities (simple and vertically integrated composition of capital) differences from the economy's weighted average. In each graph, we also report the results of our indicative simple regression along with the R-square. The top pair of graphs refers to the standard approach, and the top left graph compares the price-value deviations of the standard approach with the simple composition of capital showing a positive slope and an R-square of 59.2% The top right-hand graph displays the price-value deviations against the deviations of the vertically integrated composition of capital from the weighted average. We observe a positive relationship and the R-square increases to 97.8% indicating that the price-value deviations follow strictly the behavior anticipated by economic theory. That is, the signs of the price value deviations are those expected from the

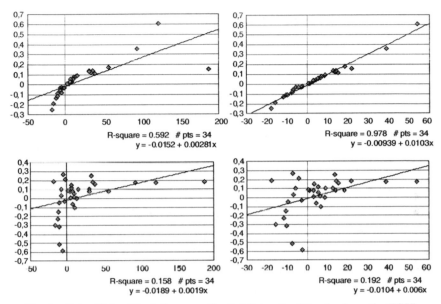

Fig. 1.   Price-Value Deviations vs. Capital Intensity (Standard vs. the TSSI).

Marxian theory but also the size of these deviations is proportional to the size of deviations of the respective capital intensities.

The results with respect to the TSSI approach are displayed in the bottom two graphs. We observe that the price-value deviations of TSSI, when plotted against the simple composition of capital evaluated in terms of prices of production of the standard approach (left-hand side bottom graph of Fig. 1), shows a very poor fit; the R-square is less than 16%. The adjacent graph that compares the TSSI price-value deviations with the deviations of vertically integrated composition of capital from the average is far from being satisfactory, inasmuch the R-square is only 19.2%.

The above-mentioned results lend support to the standard estimating method and cast doubt to the TSSI and this despite the fact that the TSSI gives estimates of both direct prices and especially prices of production, which are extremely close to market prices. The proponents of the TSSI could counter argue that the way that the capital intensities are being measured, that is, in terms of prices of production is consistent with the standard estimating methods and are not consistent with the TSSI. Naturally, the next step would be to test the TSSI price-value deviations against the deviations of capital intensity evaluated in terms of TSSI prices

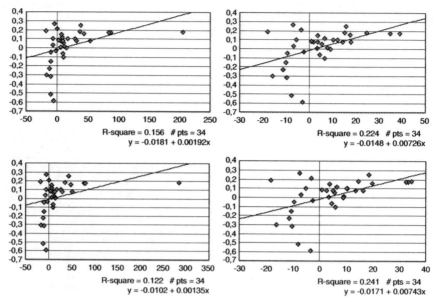

Fig. 2.   Price-Value Deviations vs. Capital Intensity (TSSI).

of production and also market prices. The top left-hand side graph of
Fig. 2 above refers to price-value deviations against the deviations in
capital intensities as measured by the simple composition of capital.
We observe that still the R-square of 15.6% is too low to claim a strong
positive relationship between the two types of deviation as the TSSI would
require. Similarly, the comparison between price-value deviations and the
vertically integrated capital composition deviations from the average
portrayed in the right-hand side graph of Fig. 2 did not give any better
results, the R-square increased to only 22.4%. The results with respect to
the evaluation of capital intensity in terms of market prices were not
better. The respective graphs are displayed side by side in the bottom
of Fig. 2.

6. CONCLUSIONS

This paper has investigated price-value deviations using the input–output
data of Canada (1997), an economy whose data have not been subjected
so far to empirical testing for the validity and scientific status of the labor

theory of value. Two types of methods have been used to address the proximity of direct prices and prices of production to market prices: the standard methodology and the rather recently developed TSSI methodology. Our analysis showed that for the Canadian economy the results are consistent with the standard approach and are therefore in line with those reported for a number of other countries. The same kind of estimations and the same database were used to test the TSSI. The results showed that overall, the estimated direct prices and prices of production are extremely close to market prices. Further investigation however revealed that the estimates of direct prices and prices of production of the TSSI display inconsistencies, at the industry level which render the approach unreliable and certainly not a convincing alternative to the standard one.

A crucial issue in these studies, which however has not been discussed so far, is that both direct prices and prices of production are (weighted) average magnitudes and not necessarily those that regulate the market prices. This does not mean that the average magnitudes are not good approximations to market prices, but rather indicates that there are even more concrete centers of gravitation that we need to estimate. For example, we already know from the classical economists that in agriculture and mining the regulating values and prices of production are those that are formed on the marginal lands and so one cannot just use the average direct price in agriculture or mining as the best centers of gravitation of market prices. The idea of marginal conditions are generalized in Marx (1982) by discussing, for example, the case of manufacturing, where the regulating direct price and price of production will be, in general, different from the average. In fact, the regulating conditions, corresponding to these direct prices and prices of production, are identified with those firms or capitals of an industry where there is acceleration or deceleration of capital accumulation. This crucial aspect of Marx's work has received very little attention so far, precisely because the concept of regulating capital and the associated notions of regulating value and price of production are extremely difficult to operationalize. As a consequence, the empirical analysis until today has been restricted exclusively to average direct prices and average prices of production, and although these are very good approximations to market prices, they are not the most appropriate ones. Future research efforts, besides further investigation and operationalization of the concept of regulating conditions of production and estimation extend the analysis to other countries and also include in the pricing model taxes and subsidies, turnover times, fixed capital, depreciation, and the industry rates of capacity utilization.

NOTES

1. Similarly with the deviation statistics where in Kliman's study the MAD between labor values and market prices was found even smaller than those in Ochoa's (1989) study.

2. As expected, their results with respect to the US economy (Diaz & Osuna, 2007) were similar.

3. If for example the direct price of an industry is 1.05 and the price of production is 0.97, this means that the deviation of the direct price from the market price is 5% and the deviation of the price of production from the market price is −3%, regardless of whether the actual market price equals to say 1 or 60 dollars.

4. For a comprehensive discussion of the same issue and an appropriate numerical example (Ochoa, 1984, pp. 58–70) and for a discussion within the context of Leontief's price model (Miller & Blair, 1985, pp. 351–7).

5. That is to say, the price of inputs and outputs will be different because they are evaluated at two different time periods.

6. For a summary and critical evaluation of the TSSI approach see Mohun (2004) and Veneziani (2004).

7. Another reason might be that the TSSI approach questions the notion of prices of production as an equilibrium and, therefore, is an unrealistic assumption.

8. In a private communication with Osuna we were informed that the estimation of MELT in the case of Spanish data began in the year 1980. As a consequence, by the year 1986 which was the first year in the study by Diaz and Osuna (2005–2006), any possible error in the estimation of the MELT was expected to be eliminated.

9. It is important to point out that the TSSI, as it is oriented toward disequilibrium, would rather be critical to all efforts to estimate prices of production. The idea is that equilibrium and, therefore, equilibrium prices do not exist in capitalist economies.

10. After all the "transformation problem", which is in the background of this discussion for reasons of simplicity, is cast in terms of circulating capital.

ACKNOWLEDGMENT

We are indebted to Theodore Mariolis and Hindenori Oda for their helpful and constructive comments. We also thank an anonymous referee of this journal for a number of critical but helpful remarks. The usual caveat applies.

REFERENCES

Chilcote, E. (1997). *Inter industry structure, relative prices, and productivity: An input-output study of the US and OECD countries.* Ph.D. Dissertation, New School for Social Research, New York.

Cockshott, P., & Cottrell, A. (1997). Labour time versus alternative value bases: A research note. *Cambridge Journal of Economics, 21*, 545–549.

Cockshott, P., & Cottrell, A. (2005). Robust correlations between sectoral prices and labour values: A comment. *Cambridge Journal of Economics, 29*, 309–316.

Cockshott, P., Cottrell, A., & Michaelson, G. (1995). Testing Marx: Some new results from UK data. *Capital and Class, 55*, 103–129.

Diaz, E., & Osuna, R. (2005–2006). Can we trust cross-sectional price-value correlation measures? Some evidence from the case of Spain. *Journal of Post Keynesian Economics, 28*, 345–363.

Diaz, E., & Osuna, R. (2007). Indeterminacy in price-value correlation measures. *Empirical Economics, 33*, 389–399.

Diaz, E., & Osuna, R. (2009). From correlation to dispersion: Geometry of the price-value deviation. *Empirical Economics, 36*, 427–440.

Duménil, G. (1983). Beyond the transformation riddle: A labor theory of value. *Science and Society, 47*(4), 427–450.

Foley, D. (1982). The value of money, the value of labor power and the transformation problem. *Review of Radical Political Economics, 14*(2), 37–47.

Freeman, A. (1997). Time, the value of money and the quantification of value. *Unpublished paper.*

Kliman, A. (2002). The law of value and laws of statistics: Sectoral values and prices in the US economy, 1977–1997. *Cambridge Journal of Economics, 26*, 299–311.

Kliman, A. (2004). Spurious value-price correlations: Some additional evidence and arguments. *Research in Political Economy, 21*, 223–239.

Kliman, A. (2007). *Reclaiming Marx's capital: A refutation of the myth of inconsistency*. Lanham MD: Lexington Books.

Leontief, W. (1966). *Input-output economics*. New York: Oxford University Press.

Marx, K. (1982). *Capital* (Vol. 3). New York: Random House.

Miller, R., & Blair, P. (1985). *Input-output analysis: Foundations and extensions*. New Jersey: Prentice Hall.

Mohun, S. (2004). The labour theory of value as foundation for empirical investigations. *Metroeconomica, 55*, 65–95.

Ochoa, E. (1984). *Labor values and prices of production: An inderindustry study of the U.S. economy, 1947–1972*. Ph.D. Dissertation, New School for Social Research, New York.

Ochoa, E. (1989). Values, prices and wage-profit curves in the US economy. *Cambridge Journal of Economics, 13*, 413–430.

Pasinetti, L. (1977). *Lectures on the theory of production*. New York: Columbia University Press.

Petrovic, P. (1987). The deviation of production prices from labour values: Some methodological and empirical evidence. *Cambridge Journal of Economics, 11*, 197–210.

Shaikh, A. (1984). The transformation from Marx to Sraffa. In: A. Freeman & E. Mandel (Eds), *Ricardo, Marx and Sraffa* (pp. 43–84). London: Verso.

Shaikh, A. (1998). The empirical strength of the labour theory of value. In: R. Bellofiore (Ed.), *Marxian economics: A reappraisal* (Vol. 2, pp. 225–251). New York: St. Martin's Press.

Steedman, I., & Tomkins, J. (1998). On measuring the deviation of prices from values. *Cambridge Journal of Economics, 22*, 379–385.

Tsoulfidis, L. (2008). Price-value deviations: Further evidence from input-output data of Japan. *International Review of Applied Economics, 22*, 707–724.

Tsoulfidis, L., & Maniatis, Th. (2002). Values, prices of production and market prices: Some more evidence from the Greek economy. *Cambridge Journal of Economics, 26*, 359–369.

Tsoulfidis, L., & Mariolis, Th. (2007). Labour values, prices of production and the effects of income distribution: Evidence from the Greek economy. *Economic Systems Research, 19*, 425–437.

Tsoulfidis, L., & Rieu, D.-M. (2006). Labor values, prices of production, and wage-profit rate frontiers of the Korean economy. *Seoul Journal of Economics*, *19*, 275–295.

Veneziani, R. (2004). The temporal single-system interpretation of Marx's economics: A critical evaluation. *Metroeconomica*, *55*, 96–114.

Zacharias, D. (2006). Labour value and equalisation of profit rates: A multicountry study. *Indian Development Review*, *4*, 1–21.

APPENDIX: A NOTE ON THE DATA

The input–output tables of Canada are available from the OECD STAN database at the 34 sectors level of detail. The matrix of input–output coefficients, **A**, is obtained by dividing element by element the inputs of each industry by its gross output. The vector of direct labor coefficients a_0 is estimated using the wage bill of each sector (the product of annual wage times the number of employees) from the input–output table for each year of our analysis. The problem with this estimation is that the self-employed population is not accounted for. For this purpose, we created an index of self-employment calculated by the ratio of the total employed population (the number of employees plus the self-employed) to the number of employees. The information on employment in thousands is available in the OECD STAN database (www.sourceoecd.org) and the hours of work in millions from the Groningen Growth Development Center database (www.ggdc.net). In order to account for the differences in skills across sectors, we divided the annual wage of each sector by the economy's minimum wage, the so-derived ratio is in turn multiplied by the employment and so we derive the homogenized sectoral employment. This reduction, of course, is only meaningful when the relative wages express with precision the differences in skills and intensity of labor that is employed in each sector of the economy. The division of the adjusted for skills total employment (employees plus self-employed) by the industry total output gave the homogenized employment coefficients, that is, the vector a_0. The basket of wage goods normally consumed by workers (vector **b**) was formed by taking weights of the personal consumption expenditures, which were multiplied by the minimum wage (Ochoa, 1989). In Table A.1 that follows, we present the industry names and the correspondence of input–output industries with those of NACE as well as some of the aggregated data used in our estimations. It is important to note that some sectors such as public administration or finance and insurance could be excluded since the notion of interindustry equalization of profit rates is meaningless; however, we opted to include them because on the one hand they do not affect the results and on the other hand their exclusion might complicate the calculations.

Table A.1. Monetary Measures in Millions, Employment in Thousands, Hours Worked in Millions.

S. No.	Industries	NACE	Intermediate Inputs	Value Added	Wages	Employment	Employees	Ratio	Wages Including S.E.	Hours
			1	2	3	4	5	$6 = 4/5$	$7 = 6 \times 3$	8
1	Agriculture	01–05	33,444	18,964	6,781	538	231	2.33	15,812	1,075
2	Mining	10–14	19,203	35,655	9,570	149	143	1.04	9,997	400
3	Food	15–16	43,637	18,962	8,932	241	236	1.02	9,122	486
4	Textiles	17–19	8,827	6,677	4,061	137	129	1.06	4,308	276
5	Wood	20	17,906	9,403	5,589	125	120	1.04	5,827	262
6	Paper	21–22	28,014	20,050	11,916	222	214	1.04	12,393	608
7	Petroleum	23	20,782	1,418	1,039	15	15	1.01	1,049	31
8	Chemicals	24ex2423	20,533	12,332	4,577	71	70	1.01	4,643	146
9	Rubber	25	8,982	6,275	3,780	99	98	1.01	3,813	211
10	Other non-metals	26	4,912	3,810	2,123	48	46	1.04	2,213	102
11	Iron and steel	271 2731	24,426	9,597	5,784	45	45	1.01	5,813	93
12	Fabricated	28	14,087	10,596	7,230	140	136	1.03	7,452	301
13	Machinery and Equipment	29	11,644	8,537	5,021	134	131	1.02	5,117	291
14	Office machinery	30	4,737	853	748	14	13	1.02	762	28
15	Electronic machinery	31	4,386	2,760	1,744	37	37	1.02	1,777	78
16	Radio, TV	32	10,614	5,908	3,169	40	40	1.02	3,229	161
17	Motor vehicles	34	66,379	19,044	10,219	154	152	1.01	10,344	330
18	Shipping	351	186	329	248	10	10	1.01	251	21
19	Aircraft	353	4,979	4,611	2,609	43	43	1.01	2,641	93
20	Railroad equipment	352, 359	3,004	1,494	815	12	12	1.01	825	25

Table A.1. (*Continued*)

S. No.	Industries	NACE	Intermediate Inputs	Value Added	Wages	Employment	Employees	Ratio	Wages Including S.E.	Hours
21	Manufacturing nec.	36–37	9,090	7,331	4,469	111	100	1.12	4,991	264
22	Utilities	40–41	6,795	26,865	6,302	81	79	1.02	6,439	198
23	Construction	45	61,045	45,082	31,233	838	694	1.21	37,692	1,684
24	Trade	50–52	48,987	91,363	63,675	2,515	2,245	1.12	71,307	4,493
25	Hotels and restaurants	55	16,730	21,231	14,532	1,025	978	1.05	15,229	1,550
26	Transportation	60–63	27,992	32,114	19,216	545	477	1.14	21,959	1,187
27	Communications	64	11,125	23,218	10,661	271	256	1.06	11,255	511
28	FIRE	65–67	56,520	84,037	37,698	852	706	1.21	45,496	1,249
29	Computer	72	4,277	7,638	5,407	255	220	1.16	6,279	429
30	Other business	74	18,540	35,094	24,337	986	817	1.21	29,371	1,658
31	Public administration	75	52,857	63,014	46,659	763	763	1.00	46,659	1,208
32	Education	80	11,581	43,041	38,782	977	940	1.04	40,333	1,432
33	Health	85	13,672	43,802	30,582	1,370	1,202	1.14	34,867	2,196
34	Social services	90–93	22,106	34,903	23,613	953	822	1.16	27,398	1,405

The MELT for the year 1997 was estimated at 28.16 Canadian dollars per labor hour.

CHAPTER 9

LIMITS AND CHALLENGES OF THE CONSISTENCY DEBATE IN MARXIAN VALUE THEORY

G. Carchedi

ABSTRACT

While many inconsistencies can be found in Marx's theory if one chooses a view of reality in which time is absent, these inconsistencies disappear if the view is taken that time is an essential component of that theory. The debate is thus between the simultaneist and the temporalist camp. This article sides with the temporalist approach but at the same time it argues that both sides have focused mainly on quantitative and formal logic aspects. This is the limit of the debate. The debate should move on from being only a critique and counter-critique of each other applying only formal logic to the issue of consistency to showing how and whether the different postulates (a time-less versus a time-full reality) and the interpretations deriving from them are an instance of a wider theory of radical social change. From this angle, simultaneism implies equilibrium and thus a view of the economy tending toward its equilibrated reproduction. Capitalism is thus theorized as an inherently rational system and any attempt to supersede it is irrational. This is simultaneism's social content. Temporalism, if immersed in a dialectical context, reaches the opposite conclusions: the economy is in a constant state of nonequilibrium and tends cyclically toward its own supersession. Capitalism is inherently

Why Capitalism Survives Crises: The Shock Absorbers
Research in Political Economy, Volume 25, 233–275
Copyright © 2009 by Emerald Group Publishing Limited
All rights of reproduction in any form reserved
ISSN: 0161-7230/doi:10.1108/S0161-7230(2009)0000025006

irrational and any attempt to supersede it is rational. Simultaneist authors should now show how their approach to the issue of consistency fits into a broader theory furthering the liberation of Labor.

To choose a dialectical view of temporalism is thus to take sides for Labor.

1. INTRODUCTION

Since its appearance (and especially after the appearance of the third volume of *Capital*), Marx's theory has been the object of sustained attacks aiming at showing its logical inconsistency. The attacks have centered upon four issues: the indeterminacy of the law of the profit rate to fall, abstract labor as the only source of value, the materiality of abstract labor, and the so-called "transformation problem." These are crucial areas of Marxist theory. If the critiques were proven to be correct, there would be no sound platform on which to build a really radically alternative view of capitalism. This is the vital question behind the issues of consistency.

The debate has focused mainly on the *quantitative* and *formal logic* aspect of the four issues. But formal logic cannot explain *qualitative*, and *radical* change. And this is the limit of the debate. Looking back, this limit has been a necessary evil. Marx's critics have used the rules of formal logic and mathematical tools to support their arguments. It has then been necessary to use the same rules and tools to rebut the critique. But this is insufficient. This article will argue that both the critiques and the defenses of Marx's internal consistency suffer from a common constraint, the exclusive reliance on formal logic. To provide a complete proof of Marx's internal consistency, one has to use Marx's own method, the dialectical method as briefly highlighted below. By "Marx's own method" I do not mean that what follows is necessarily what Marx had in mind. What I mean is that the method to be set forth below is extracted from his own writing, provides a key that reveals his theory's internal consistency, and contains potentially within it the possibility to be developed in order to account for both those aspects of reality he did not develop and the new aspects he could not have foreseen. Even though evidence will be submitted that the present approach is supported by Marx's quotations, the question is not faithfulness to quotations but consistency and explanatory power.[1] It is in *this* sense that the notion of dialectics to be submitted below is argued to be Marx's own.

While there is general agreement that an interpretation that is logically consistent in its own terms (logically valid, for short) should be preferred to one that is not so, the debate, while showing that neither approach can be used as a tool of an internal critique of the other, has not produced a selection criterion commonly accepted in case two or more interpretations derive from opposite postulates and are equally logically valid. To accept or reject an interpretation, quantitative and formal logic consistency with Marx is undoubtedly a prerequisite but other criteria cannot be excluded a priori, as for example, textual evidence. But textual evidence alone, while being certainly important, leads only to a useless battle of quotations. It lacks the objectivity inherent in the consistency criterion. The point is that, purely in terms of formal logic, there is no reason why one criterion should be chosen rather than another. The cause of this indeterminacy is that formal logic is implicitly based on methodological individualism (which implies that everybody is free to choose whatever theory she likes) rather than on a dialectical and thus a class and objectively determined logic.

This article argues that, *if* (and this is the essential condition) participation in the debates is meant to be an aspect of the development of a theory representing and defending the cause of Labor, the selection criterion should be whether the different postulates and the interpretations deriving from them are *an instance of a wider theory of radical social change*. In short, the criterion should be an interpretation's *class content*. If the final aim of the debate is to contribute to Labor's liberation from Capital, this challenge cannot be avoided. If that is not the aim, the debate is not worth being pursued. The debate, then, should change focus, from exclusive reliance on formal logic to reliance on dialectical logic (of which the *tools* of formal logic are an aspect). We have to shift grounds, from a restricted focus to a wider picture, from formal logic to dialectical logic, from disregard of, to emphasis on, the different interpretations' class content. First of all, the notion of dialectics as a method of social research and its relation to formal logic have to be highlighted.

2. DIALECTICS AS A METHOD OF SOCIAL RESEARCH[2]

As well known, Marx did not explicitly write a work on dialectics. Nevertheless, he thought it would be possible to make intelligible to people with ordinary intelligence in a few pages what is *rational* in the method "which Hegel discovered and at the same time mystified." In spite of Marx's warning that Hegel mystified dialectics, traditionally commentators have tried to force Marx into conformity with Hegel. I will depart from this tradition and will submit a notion of dialectics as a method of social research, a method focused exclusively on social reality. This method is extracted basically from Marx's own work (but also from that of other Marxists) rather than from Hegel.

The starting point is a class-determined analysis of *phenomena* as the unity in contradiction of relations and process. Relations are interactions between people. Every time an enterprise is started (or goes bankrupt), a family is formed (or breaks up), a political party is founded (or is dissolved), i.e., every time a relation arises, or changes into a different type, or ends, there is a change in the social fabric (whether it is perceptible or not). *Processes* are transformations people carry out in the context of those relations. The reason why the unity of relations and processes is contradictory will be explained later. The analogy with Marx's method in Capital I is clear. Marx starts the inquiry into economic life with a class-determined analysis of commodities conceived as the unity in contradiction of use value and exchange value. The present approach starts the inquiry into social life with a class-determined analysis of phenomena as the unity in contradiction of relations and process. This method is based upon three principles.

2.1. First Principle: Phenomena are Always Both Realized and Potential

This principle rests on the empirical observation that everything is what it is and at the same time is (can be) something different. This applies to ourselves since we are actualized being and at the same time potentially different; or to an institution, like the state that is both the actualized state and a potentially different state that can evolve in many different directions and take many different shapes; to knowledge, which is subjected to a constant process of change (realization of its potentiality), etc. Thus, reality has a double dimension; it is both actual existence and potential existence. Marx makes extensive use of the difference within the same entity between its actualized and its potential existence. Suffice it to mention the distinction, fundamental for his value theory, between realized and potential value. A commodity can realize, upon its sale, more or less than the value contained in it or even nothing at all, if it is not sold. The *individual* value is then a *potential realized* value (Marx, 1976, p. 434). A particularly important example of a potential phenomenon is a type of tendency that realizes itself cyclically (as the fall in the average rate of profit, ARP): the rise (countertendency) is potentially present in the fall (the tendency) when the latter becomes realized and the fall (the tendency) is potentially present in the rise (the countertendency) when the latter becomes realized.

More generally, as Marx puts it, the "properties of a thing do not arise from its relation to other things, they are, on the contrary, merely activated by such relations." Now, *what is activated can only be what is already potentially present* even though, as we will see, *its realization is modified by its relation with other phenomena.* In short, each realized phenomenon (a person, the state, a form of knowledge, etc.) contains within itself a realm of potentialities. In symbols, given two phenomena A and B, this principle can be symbolized as in relation (α)

$$(\alpha)\ A = \{A^r, A^p\} \text{ and } B = \{B^r, B^p\}$$

where the curly brackets indicate a phenomenon's unity of its realized and potential nature and the superscripts *r* and *p* refer to the realized and the potential state, respectively. Notice that potentials are (a) *real* possibilities because they are contained in realized phenomena but (b) *formless* possibilities because they take a definite form only at the moment of their realization due to the interrelation among all phenomena. Three points follow.

First, since a phenomenon is potentially different from what it is as a realized phenomenon, $\{A^r, A^p\}$ indicates the *unity of identity and difference.* A^r is identical to itself but also different from itself, as A^p. $\{A^r, A^p\}$ is the synthetic rendition of the "affirmative recognition of the existing state of things [and] at the same time, also the recognition of the negation of that state" (Capital I, quoted in Zelený, 1980, p. 87). It is only by considering the realm of potentialities that the otherwise mysterious unity of identity and difference makes sense. Second, $\{A^r, A^p\}$ indicates also the *unity of opposites,* inasmuch as the potential features of a phenomenon are opposite (contradictory) to its realized aspects.[3] Finally, $\{A^r, A^p\}$ indicates the *unity of essence and* the form of manifestation of the essence, *appearance*: A^p is the essence of A, that which can manifest itself in a number of different realizations, while A^r is its (temporary and contingent) appearance, the form taken by one of the possibilities inherent in A's potential nature. Notice however that the essence, just like its appearance, is not immutable but subject to continuous change.

2.2. Second Principle: Phenomena are Always Both Determinant and Determined

Here too the starting point is empirical observation. We can observe that all elements of social reality are interconnected (people can live and reproduce themselves only through reciprocal interaction) into a whole (society), that this whole changes continuously (even though some changes might be minimal), that this change can be continuous or discontinuous, and that the whole interconnected parts can be contradictory (i.e., the reproduction of some phenomena might imply the supersession of some other phenomena). This apparently chaotic movement is given a conceptual structure by the notion of dialectical determination.

Consider again two phenomena, A and B. Phenomenon A is said to be determinant if it calls into realized existence the determined one, B, from the realm of its potentialities as a condition of its own reproduction or supersession. The determined phenomenon, B, was already contained in the determinant phenomenon, A, as one of its potentialities (A^p) and thus into A^r. This is how A determines B. In relation (β) below, this is indicated as $A \Rightarrow B$. Phenomenon B, after having been actualized as the condition of reproduction or supersession of A, reacts upon A and either reproduces it (in a changed form) or supersedes it. This is how B determines A. In relation (β) this is indicated as $A \Leftarrow B$. The typical example is the capitalist class that calls into existence the laboring class (Labor is potentially present within Capital). Labor is the condition of reproduction of Capital. But it can also become its condition of supersession.

If we combine the determination of A by B and of B by A we obtain $A \Leftrightarrow B$. Between $A \Rightarrow B$ and $A \Leftarrow B$ there is a temporal difference. If we take time into account, mutual determination becomes

$$(\beta) \quad A^{t1} \Leftrightarrow B^{t2}$$

where the superscripts $t1$ and $t2$ indicate two points in time. *At $t1$, A determines B. At $t2$, B determines A.* Dialectical determination takes place within a temporal setting: reality is a temporal process of determinations in which some phenomena, the determinant ones, become actualized prior to other phenomena, the determined ones. It follows that only previously existing phenomena can determine the actualization of other phenomena because the latter are initially only potentially present in the former.

If we substitute (α) into (β) we get the *relation of mutual or dialectical determination*

$$(\gamma) \quad \{A^r, A^p\}^{t1} \Leftrightarrow \{B^r, B^p\}^{t2}$$

Two points should be stressed. First, due to the action of B on A, A can reproduce itself but it does that *in a changed form* and not at $t2$ (even less at $t1$) but at a subsequent point in time, $t3$. Thus, if A reproduces itself, $\{A^r, A^p\}^{t1} \neq \{A^r, A^p\}^{t3}$. After the mutual determination has taken place, the process starts again with $\{A^r, A^p\}^{t3} \Leftrightarrow \{B^r, B^p\}^{t4}$. Second, at $t1$, before its realization at $t2$, B^r is contained in A^r as one of the many possible A^p. At $t2$, one of the many possible A^p becomes realized as B^r and this B^r contains within itself a range of B^p. The new B^r and the new B^p form a new unity, $\{B^r, B^p\}^{t2}$. It is this new unity, $\{B^r, B^p\}^{t2}$, that is a condition of reproduction or supersession of $\{A^r, A^p\}^{t3}$. Relation (γ) represents the *most concise* way to express the notion of dialectics in social reality.

The dialectical relation between phenomena can now be applied to phenomena's inner structure, i.e., to relations and processes. As just mentioned, only what has realized itself can be the condition of existence of what exists only potentially. Since relations are temporally prior to processes, they are determinant and processes must be determined. For example, under capitalism, the owners of the means of production (MP) must hire (engage in a relation with) the laborers before the production process can begin. This is why phenomena are *units in determination*. Given that a unit in determination can supersede itself by calling into existence its own condition of supersession, a unit in determination is also a *contradictory* unity in determination: a process can be a condition of supersession of the relation within which it is carried out. Two points follow: First, given that relations determine processes and given that processes are transformations, i.e. movement, relations *determine their own movement by determining their own processes*. Second, given that we can observe a relation only by observing what people do when they engage in a process, *processes* are also the specific, *empirically observable form taken by relations*.

The question now arises as to why and how the determined phenomenon can become a condition of supersession of the determinant one. This can be explained by choosing the ownership relation as the ultimately determinant phenomenon. *Given a certain time period*, production is prior to distribution and consumption (only what has been produced can be consumed). The former contains potentially the latter within itself. Therefore, only the former can be determinant of the latter. Distribution and consumption can precede temporally production but this is the production of the *following* period. This holds for all societies. But each society has its own specificity. There is thus a specific sense in which production predominates under capitalism. What is specific to this system is that the producers have been expropriated of the MP and must sell their labor power to the owners of the MP. The specificity of the production relation under capitalism (the production of surplus value) is thus the consequence of the owner-ship relation. It should be clear that by ownership relations it is meant the real relation and not the juridical one, meaning that the ultimately determinant relation is the relation between those who do not own the MP because they cannot decide what to produce, how to produce it, and for whom to produce it and those who own those MP in the sense that they can take those decisions and impose them on the nonowners. If the ownership relation is capitalism's specific element, it is also that which informs the rest of society (phenomena), the determining element in the last instance.

This feature affects the rest of the society. According to Marx our species has potentialities that set it apart from other living creatures, as for example, the capacity to create our own MP (Marx & Engels, 1970, p. 42). Other authors point out other specifically human features as for example, the capacity of creating languages and communicating through them (Geras, 1983, p. 48). These potentialities and features are not unchangeable. Society moulds them; it not only gives them an historically specific form but penetrates them and adapts them to itself. A dramatic example of society changing those potentialities is the possibility created by biotechnology to shape human life in ways functional for profit making (human cloning). It is within these socially given boundaries that humans try to develop those potentialities to the utmost.

Due to the ownership relation, under capitalism the development of the capitalists' potentialities is informed by their need to deal with the laborers as the source of the maximum feasible quantity of unpaid labor. On the other hand, the development of the laborer's potentialities is informed by their need to resist and abolish their alienation not only from their own products (which they must alienate to the owners of the MP) but also from themselves (because they are not free to fully develop their potentialities). Capital has the objective need to exploit Labor and Labor has the objective need to resist and abolish that exploitation. One class needs to hold back human development, to shape it in accordance with its own needs, the other class needs to expand it to the maximum and to break the constraint imposed by the former class. The former class needs an egoistic and exploitative behavior, the latter an altruistic and solidaristic behavior. For the former, one's well being must be based upon the others' misery, for the latter one's well being must be both the condition for, and the result of, the others' well being. The satisfaction of the former need is functional for the reproduction of the capitalist system; the satisfaction of the latter need is functional for the supersession of that system.

There is thus not only one rationality under capitalism (Capital's rationality, for example, the extraction of the maximum surplus value, profit maximization, etc.), but also there is a *double and contradictory rationality* emanating from the capitalist ownership relation: Capital's rationality and Labor's rationality. This double rationality constitutes the *ownership relation's contradictory social content*. Since the ownership relation contains potentially within itself all other phenomena, it *transfers* this double rationality to all other relations and processes. It is in *this* sense that this relation is *ultimately determinant*. Of course, there are more than the two fundamental classes, there are also the old and the new middle class, as well as fractions of classes (Carchedi, 1977) but the focus on these two classes is sufficient for the present purposes.

The above would seem to imply a contradiction. If relation (γ) is expanded to more than two phenomena, each phenomenon is determined by and determinant of all other phenomena. However, they are all determined in the last instance by the ownership relation. The contradiction is only apparent. Phenomena are not simple copies, reflections, of the ownership relation. Phenomena receive the ownership's relation social content but only indirectly because of their mutual determination. There is thus both a direct and an indirect determination of all phenomena by the ownership relation. It is because of this that each phenomenon has a social content that is a *specific* manifestation of the ownership relation's contradictory social content and it is because of this that each phenomenon is *relatively autonomous* from the ownership relation. Since phenomena are determinant of, and determined by, each other and since they are all determined in the last instance by the ownership relation, they are all condition of existence and/or reproduction and/or supersession of each other and of the ownership relation and thus ultimately of society. This is *phenomena's contradictory social content*. Society is thus *causa sui*, i.e., it both determines itself and is determined by itself. If by A we indicate the ownership relation and by B any other phenomenon, relation (γ) indicates the determination in the last instance of B (which here stands for all other phenomena) by the ownership relation. If A and B are any two phenomena determined by the ownership relation, (γ) indicates the *specific* manifestation of the determination in the last instance of B and C through their mutual determination.

We can now understand why and how the determined phenomenon can become the condition of reproduction or of supersession of the determinant one. We know that phenomena have a contradictory social content. We also know that the determinant phenomenon calls into existence the determined one from within the realm of its own potentialities. It follows that if the determinant phenomenon calls into existence the determined one from among the realm of its inner possibilities, it *transfers* to it its own contradictory social content. Upon its realization, and due to this contradictory nature, the social content of the determined phenomenon reacts upon and modifies the social content of the determinant phenomenon and in this way it reproduces or supersedes the determinant phenomenon. Thus, relation (γ) concerns the transfer of A's social content to B and the (formal or radical) modification of A's social content by B's social content. *In the last analysis, movement is powered by phenomena's contradictory social content.*

A particularly important example of dialectical determination is the determination of knowledge by the ownership relation, through the reciprocal interaction (determination) of all phenomena as in relation (γ). This means that all elements of knowledge have a social content, i.e., they represent the interest of social classes and ultimately one of the two rationalities (or, more usually, a mix of both rationalities in which either one or the other is dominant). It follows that the verification of an element of knowledge is both in terms of formal logic and in terms of dialectical logic, in terms of that element's social content. Neither formal logic verification nor dialectical verification is both necessary and sufficient. Labor's knowledge needs both of them. From the point of view of Labor, given two equally logically correct interpretations starting from two different sets of assumptions, *it is the logically consistent interpretation (and thus its initial set of assumptions) that is functional for Labor's interests that should be chosen.* This is the principle of verification that will be applied in this article. There is no class neutral knowledge.[4] For Marx, dialectical logic is class logic.

2.3. Third Principle: Phenomena are Subject to Constant Movement and Change

This principle follows from the first two. A realized phenomenon can change only because this is potentially possible, because of its potential contradictory nature that is a specific manifestation of the ownership relation's contradictory nature. Without this potential reality, realized phenomena are static, they are what they are and not also what they could be. Their potential nature makes possible not only their change but also delimits the quantitative and qualitative boundaries of that change. But phenomena do not change in isolation; they do not change only because of their own potential nature. They change through the relation of mutual determination ultimately determined by the ownership relation. Thus, *movement* is the change undergone by phenomena from being realized to being potential and vice versa; and from being a condition of existence to being a condition of reproduction and/or of supersession (and vice versa) of each other and thus of society.

Phenomena's movement exhibits different features. Here, only two will be considered, its being cyclical and tendential. A determinant phenomenon can call into existence more than one phenomenon. Phenomenon A can determine phenomena B, C, etc. Given A's contradictory nature, B can be a contradictory condition or reproduction and C a contradictory condition of supersession of A. If B is dominant, A reproduces itself in spite of the conditions of supersession. In the opposite case, it supersedes itself in spite of the conditions of reproduction. However, the contradictory reproduction is only temporary because the superseding force gains eventually the upper hand and the same for the contradictory supersession. Thus, the contradictory movement toward reproduction or supersession is cyclical. Second, this cyclical movement is *tendential* in the sense that one of the two forces, either the reproductive or the superseding, is the tendency and the other the countertendency. The principle for discerning the tendency from the countertendency will be submitted shortly.

We can now return to relation (γ). Continuity in social life requires a type of relations and processes which are independent of, and thus both preexist and survive, specific individuals, i.e., *social phenomena* (Carchedi, 2008a, 2008b). Without them, society would collapse and disintegrate. If applied to social phenomena, relation (γ) shows how all social phenomena are bound by the relation of mutual determination (in which the ownership relation is ultimately determinant). This is the *social structure* that by being independent of which specific individuals become carriers of those relations and agents of those processes keeps society together. Also, given that $\{B^r, B^p\}$ can either reproduce or supersede $\{A^r, A^p\}$, relation (γ) shows also *society's movement*, the change undergone by realized social phenomena due to the realization of their potentialities and thus both the reproduction and the supersession of society as a whole. Any contraposition between structure and movement is thus artificial. It follows that this relation represents from a class perspective the *ever changing building block of society*, the cell out of which the constantly changing social structure is made up.

There is thus no need, as in the neo-liberalist view, to ascribe this cohesive factor to the self-regulating and equilibrating function of the market, i.e., to the fact that the market, if not tempered with, tends toward equilibrium. The economy is in a permanent state of nonequilibrium, it is a cyclical movement from periods of growth to periods of crisis and vice versa.

Thus, reproduction is not equilibrium, neither static nor dynamic. Reproduction in a dialectical sense is not only a situation in which the reproductive forces dominate the superseding ones, but also a cyclical process, it is a process that tends toward supersession, it is the repression of the superseding forces. Supersession is the tendency and reproduction the countertendency (see Sections 3 and 4 below). The notion of equilibrium in economic theory can only explain reproduction (from Capital's point of view). This is its social content, it's being constitutionally blind to the possibility of capitalism's supersession.

The picture of capitalist reality inherent in this notion of dialectical determination is that of a temporal flow of determining and determined contradictory phenomena continuously emerging from a potential state to become realized and going back to a potential state in a cyclical and tendential movement toward capitalism's supersession. This is the notion of reality summed up in relation (γ). It follows that the dialectical research method (a) inquires into a phenomenon's origin, present state and further development within this view of reality and (b) tests the results of this inquiry in terms both of formal logic and of their class content. Relation (γ) thus represents not only the *most concise* way to express the notion of dialectics in social reality and the *basic unit* of social life; it is also both the *basic tool* of the dialectical method of social research.

Conclusions in many ways similar to those submitted here are reached by Resnick and Wolff (2006). Their work builds upon Lukacs, Gramsci, and especially Althusser. Its specificity is its focus on contradiction, class, and overdetermination as the three basic coordinates of analysis. *Overdetermination* holds that each process is the cause and at the same time the effect of all other processes and that processes are constituted through this interconnection (p. 36). This is society's dialectical movement. No process exercises "any more determinant influence on the others than any of those others do on it" (p. 30). This is contrary to essentialism, the view that "one aspect of capitalist society ... functions ... as an essence, that is, the determinant of the other social aspects" (p. 106). *Class* is defined in terms of production and appropriation of surplus labor (p. 21). The fundamental class process is based on the production of surplus labor and the subsumed class processes are "based on the distribution of the already appropriated surplus" (p. 77). Finally, *contradiction* arises from overdetermination, from the fact that each process is pulled and pushed "in all directions with varying force" (p. 71).

There are differences with the present approach. First, as in Althusser, overdetermination focuses on social processes as each other's condition of existence but undertheorizes their being also each other's condition of supersession. Second, if each process is constituted by an infinity of other processes with no ultimately determining factor, one falls into infinite regression. The authors answer that indeed all explanations are necessarily and inherently partial and subject to infinite regression. However, they hold that their theory is not an explanation but rather an "intervention," or "position," or "story" (p. 86). But the infinite regression implied in overdeterminism applies no matter how an explanation is called. Third, since no factor is ultimately determining, any social process or notion of it can be the "entry point" into analysis. "No reductionism is possible here, no ranking of the relative effectivity of one vs. another process" (p. 132). The authors' preferred entry point is class as the production and appropriation of surplus labor. However, if each theory has its own entry point and if each entry point is the "conceptual tool to make sense of this infinity of social processes" (p. 49), "the concept that will distinctively shape the asking of all questions" (p. 265), then each entry point is the concept of what each theorist believes is specific to social reality. This applies also to class. But the process that is specific to social reality and from which the theorist must begin her analysis is actually the ultimately determinant process if not in reality at least in theory. The authors are aware of this objection: if the theorist must "focus on but some aspects pertinent to the explanation of any event ... will not that focus amount ... to a kind of explanatory essentializing of those aspects?" (p. 82). Their negative answer is that this is only "a momentary" essentialist moment and that each subsequent essentialist moment *"changes the relation posed in the initial essentialism"* (p. 83, emphasis in the original). But this is open to the objection that the essentialism inherent in the first moment (stage of the analysis) disappears only to reappear enlarged in the next moment. A finite sequence of essentialist moments is simply an enlarged essentialist moment. In short, Resnick and Wolff are correct in stressing that social phenomena constitute themselves in their mutual interaction. But this can be combined with the determination in the last instance. Without determination in the last instance not only infinite regression cannot be avoided, but also the inherently contradictory nature of social phenomena remains unexplained.

   In spite of these differences, the authors' work is to be recommended because of a number of real achievements. Among these, one should mention the rejection of empiricism, i.e., the view that considers facts as "conceptually neutral" (p. 16); the stress on dialectics (even though this is synonymous with overdetermination) as the foundation of social analysis; the dynamic approach to social reality which is seen as a complex of continuously changing processes (p. 24); the stress on contradiction as the characteristic of social processes; and the concept of class as a process (p. 78) Moreover, there are two points of fundamental importance shared by the authors and the present approach. First, a nonequilibrium theory of capitalism deriving from the point that "Overdetermination entails rejecting...order for disorder" (p. 51) and that a deep instability describes capitalism's functioning (p. 239) Second, the *scientificity* of a "partisan reading" of reality due to an opposition to capital and a preference for communism (2008, p. 62). Even though the authors do not connect this latter fundamental insight to the presently ongoing discussion between equilibrium and nonequilibrium Marxism, there work is a welcome departure from a formal logic reading of a theory whose vital lymph cannot but be dialectics.

3. ABSTRACT LABOR AS THE (ONLY) SOURCE OF (SURPLUS) VALUE

This is *the* fundamental assumption of Marx's economic theory. First, why should laborers create (surplus) value? If this were not the case, they would not be necessary and would gladly be dispensed with by the capitalists. Attempts such as Arthur's to show that laborers, even if necessary (because exploited), create neither use value nor value (Arthur, 2004; Kicillof and Guido, 2007) are undermined by deep logical contradictions and lead to absurd conclusions (see Carchedi, forthcoming b). But the real question is: Why should the laborers' abstract labor be the *sole* source of value? The objection most often heard is that there is no reason to exclude the MP and the capitalists from being the producers of (surplus) value.

Concerning the MP, the argument can be split into two variants. The more extravagant one holds that the MP can produce (surplus) value in the absence of laborers. For example, in a fully automated system a certain input of machines can create a greater output of machines. In this case, profit and the rate of profit would be determined exclusively by the technology used (productivity) and not by (abstract) labor. If 10 machines produce 12 machines, the profit is 2 machines and the rate of profit is $2/10 = 20\%$. But, first there is a logical inconsistency deriving from the impossibility to aggregate different use values into a homogeneous quantity. Second, value here stands for the monetary expression of (quantities of) use values produced by machines. This has nothing to do with Marx's notion of value, which the monetary expression of abstract labor expended by people. This view is logically inconsistent both in its own terms and in terms of Marx's labor theory of value. However, for Marx the MP (and the same holds for nature) affect human productivity (and thus the output per unit of capital invested) as well as the quantity of labor, inasmuch as they change the quantity of labor needed for the production of a certain output.

An apparently more plausible argument could be that, given that both labor and machines are needed to produce machines, it seems reasonable to postulate that value is created by both labor and machines. But, first, one would have to explain why, if machines without labor cannot produce value, they can produce value in combination with labor. It is more logical to assume that machines increase the physical productivity of labor, the production of use values (and not of value), and thus of machines as use values. This is Marx's position. Second, since value in this approach would be produced by both machines and labor, the same quantity of value is produced by a unit of capital invested, irrespective of the relative weight of machines and labor, for example, irrespective of whether 10% of that unit of capital is machines and 90% labor or vice versa. In Marx's theory 90% machines and 10% labor create much less new value than in the opposite case. In the former approach, labor saving and productivity increasing technological innovations lead tendentially to economic growth because a percentage increase of constant capital (machines) results into a greater production of value. In the latter (Marx's) approach they lead tendentially to economic crises because a percentage increase in constant capital decreases the quantity of new value produced and thus decrease the ARP. Given that labor saving and productivity increasing technological innovations are the motor of capitalism's dynamics, for the former approach capitalism tends toward growth and reproduction while for the latter (Marx) it tends toward crises and its own supersession. In terms of formal logic both approaches are internally consistent. Two opposite initial assumptions lead to two opposite conclusions. How, then, do we verify them? According to the principle sketched above, i.e., according to their class content.

If one holds that the economy tends toward growth and thus toward its own reproduction and that crises are only temporary interruptions of this growth (the countertendencies), one deprives the working class of the objective basis of its struggle. This stand makes the struggle of the working class not only a pure act of volunteerism because contrary to the objective movement of the economy but also irrational because aiming at doing away with a rational system, a system that tends toward growth and equilibrium. This is Capital's view. On the other hand, the thesis that the system tends toward crises and thus eventually its own supersession not only grounds

Labor's struggle on sound, objective foundations because this struggle is in accordance with the real, objective tendential movement (growth is then seen as the countertendency) but also rational because it wants to do away with an irrational, exploitative, and destructive system. *Only a view stressing the capitalist economy's objective tendency toward its own supersession can provide an adequate basis for Labor's cause.* Admittedly, this is a class-determined stance. But a view of society tending toward equilibrated growth and reproduction or a view incapable to discern the tendency from its countertendency (as in many Marxists), is equally class determined and thus carries a definite class content, whether the individual theorists are aware of it or not.

Alternatively, it could be postulated that the capitalists are the producers (with the laborers) of (surplus) value. Here the capitalists would pay to themselves the value of their labor power and produce more value than that value. Income differentials between Capital and Labor would be explained in terms of the "captains of industry's higher skills," "greater responsibility" "reward for risk taking," etc. Again, this approach would be internally consistent. However, its social content would be contrary to Labor's interests because it hides exploitation. As such it would have to be rejected by Labor. Managerial theories do hold that value (understood as the monetary expression of use value) is produced by both the capitalists as the organizers of the production process and by the laborers. Marx agrees with this but adds that the organization of the labor process is one of the two functions performed by the capitalists, the function of labor. When performing this function, the capitalist is part of the collective laborer. But the capitalists perform also another function, the function of capital, the extraction and appropriation of surplus value. When performing this function, they do not produce but expropriate and appropriate surplus value (Carchedi, 1977).

4. THE MATERIALITY OF ABSTRACT LABOR

For Marx abstract labor is the substance of value and is the expenditure of human energy irrespective of, abstracting from, the concrete, specific forms it takes (concrete labors). Value is thus contained in the commodity before it realizes itself as exchange value, i.e., before the commodity is sold. At present, the protagonist of the opposite view is C. Arthur. Arthur rejects this approach and thus Marx's labor theory of value. "My position is quite different from that of the orthodox tradition, which sees labor creating something positive, namely value, then expropriated" (Arthur, 2004, p. 45). And further: "the natural body of the commodity under this description [i.e., as a use value, G.C.] is clearly a substance present to inspection. To speak of 'value' as a substance, by contrast, could be taken as highly objectionable" (op. cit., pp. 154–156). However, it can be shown that *abstract labor* and thus the substance value, *can be observed to be a material substance expended during production and thus existing materially before exchange.*[5] If this is the case, what can be observed at the moment of exchange is the social form of existence of that material substance, money.

The following proof cannot be explicitly found in Marx (it draws upon medical knowledge not available to him). However, it is inherent in and consistent with his work. The process essential for our purposes is human metabolism. The analysis of human metabolism shows that people, irrespective of their differences, produce the *same* type of energy and thus consume the *same* type of energy, no matter which specific activities they engage into.[6] This is consonant with Marx's "physiological," "material" expenditure of undifferentiated human energy. As Marx says: "all labour is an expenditure of human labour-power, in the physiological sense, and it is in this quality of being equal, or abstract, human labour that it forms the value of commodities" (Marx, 1976, p. 137). Abstract labour is a *"purely abstract activity*, a purely mechanical activity ... a merely *formal* activity, or, what is the same, a merely *material* [stofflich] activity, activity pure and simple" (Marx, 1973 [1939], p. 297, emphasis in the original). This is exactly what human metabolism is.[7] The observation of the expenditure of calories during production is the observation of abstract labor. If one wanted to, one could measure a laborer's physical fatigue or the consumption of calories while at the same time observing her producing a specific use value, i.e., engaging in concrete labor. Denial of the existence of the material substance of value is simply incompatible with modern medical science. Therefore, it lacks the scientificity needed by Labor for its struggle against Capital. Some might agree, but object that what we see is abstract human labor, the substance of value, and not value itself. However, if the substance of value can be observed to exist materially before exchange, the same must hold for value, whether it is observable or not.[8]

This would seem to be contradicted by Marx's text: "If, however, we bear in mind that the value of the commodities has a *purely social reality*, and that they acquire this reality only insofar as they are expressions or embodiments of one identical social substance, viz., human labor, it follows as a matter of course, that value can only manifest itself in the social relation of commodity to commodity" (Marx, 1967, p. 47, emphasis added, G.C.).

This passage has been read as if Marx, by stressing the purely social character of value, denied the materiality of abstract labor and thus of value. The critics think they have found yet another logical inconsistency in Marx. In reality what Marx means and cannot but mean is that the materiality of abstract labor is purely social because it acquires social significance only under capitalism. Value's reality is purely social because abstract labor could not be value without that social dimension. Value is the specific social dimension of a material reality. It is neither only physical nor only social, it is *both*.

The thesis of the immateriality of abstract labor leads Arthur to the conclusion that value and surplus value are created neither by labor, since it would be wrong to see "labour [as. G.C.] creating something positive, namely value" nor by Capital given that Capital's work of exploitation cannot be abstract: "I never argued it is abstract" (Arthur, 2004, p. 18).[9] Rather, capital *posits* value in production because concrete labor "becomes socially posited as abstract in virtue of its participation in the capitalist process of valorisation" (2004, p. 45), i.e., because it is exploited by capital. For Marx the laborers are the protagonists because their labor, under coercion, produces both the use value of the commodities and the (surplus) value contained in them. In Arthur's approach, on the other hand, the laborers have become the "servants of a production process originated and directed by capital" (Arthur, 2004, p. 47) so that labor is "reduced to a resource for capital accumulation" (op. cit., p. 51). Capital is the subject of valorisation even if valorisation depends on labor being exploited. In short, labor is the "servant" who can only be given what has been extracted by capital, the master. This view, then, gives away Marx's most precious legacy, the ability to see reality from the perspective of Labor as the protagonist, as the producer of wealth and value, a perspective which is grounded in a logically coherent, and as yet unsurpassed, economic theory of capitalism.[10]

5. THE LAW OF THE TENDENTIAL FALL IN THE AVERAGE RATE OF PROFIT (ARP)

For Marx, technological innovations tend to decrease the ARP because they tend to replace people with machines. Since only labor creates values, the output per unit of capital increases while the value incorporated in it decreases. As Marx says, "The value of a commodity is determined by the total labor–time of past and living labor incorporated in it. The increase in labor productivity consists precisely in that the share of living labor is reduced while that of past labor is increased, but in such a way that the total quantity of labor incorporated in that commodity declines"(1967, pp. 260–261). It follows that "The rate of profit does not fall because labor becomes less productive, but because it becomes more productive" (1967, p. 240).

It is this contradictory outcome, an increasing output of use values incorporating a decreasing quantity of (surplus) value, that is the ultimate cause of crises: "periodical crises ... arise from the circumstance that now this and now that portion of the laboring population becomes redundant under its old mode of employment" (Marx, 1967, p. 264). In other words, ultimately crises are the consequence of labor reducing but productivity increasing technological innovations. Therefore, "the ultimate reason for all real crises [as opposed to financial and speculative crises, G.C.] always remains the poverty and restricted consumption of the masses [due to the expulsion of labor as a consequence of labor decreasing and productivity increasing technologies, G.C.] as opposed to the drive of capitalist production to develop the productive forces [the productivity of labor through those technologies, G.C.] as though the absolute consuming power of society [rather than the poverty and restricted consumption of the masses, G.C.] constituted their limit" (Marx, 1967, p. 484). This is why new technologies decrease the ARP.

5.1. The Logical Inconsistency Critique

This stance has been criticized on two accounts. The first one has focused on the Okishio theorem (Okishio, 1961).[11] Okishio argues that capitalists introduce new techniques not when they raise the productivity of labor but when they decrease the costs of production (op. cit., p. 86). If real wages are held constant, the ARP must necessarily rise, contrary to Marx.[12] The Okishio theorem has been subjected to a number of critiques (Laibman, 1982, p. 100; Foley, 1986, p. 139; Alberro & Persky, 1981; Shaikh, 1978) whose common feature, as Kliman remarks, is that of being based on a modification of Okishio's initial assumptions. On the other hand, Marx would not object to the thesis that lower costs as a result of higher productivity increase profits.[13] Let us then consider Okishio's "cost criterion"

$$\sum a_{kj}q_j + \tau_k \tag{1}$$

where a_{kj} denotes the amount of the jth commodity directly necessary to produce a unit of the kth commodity, q_j denotes the ratio of the price of the jth commodity (p_j) to the wage rate (w), and τ_k denotes the amount of labor directly necessary to produce a unit of the kth commodity.

Formula (1) above says that, if the *physical* inputs are multiplied by their monetary prices, holding wages constant, lower costs due to increased productivity *must* increase *monetary* profits. This is contrary to Marx because the rate of profit is here *physically* determined and value in Marx's sense plays no role. But it also implies tacitly as a-temporal perspective, again contrary to Marx. The reason is that within a temporal perspective Okishio is internally inconsistent. The reason is that an increase in productivity increases the output per unit of capital invested and thus the physical rate of profit. However, the money rate of profit depends upon the quantity of money at the beginning and at the end of the period. If the quantity of money decreases sufficiently while physical productivity increases, the money profit rate falls while the physical profit rate rises. This is squarely contrary to Okishio's claim that a price fall (cost reduction) leads necessarily to an increase in profits (wages being constant). In its original formulation, which is the one invoked by Marx's critics, the theorem is invalid. Notice that these results depend crucially on a distinction between the initial and the final moment of the production period, i.e., on a temporal perspective.

Nevertheless, Okishio's theorem can be rescued if two additional assumptions are added. One is to let the quantity of money vary with the variations in the physical output. This option has been considered above. The price paid for internal consistency is the extremely limited application that makes the theorem practically useless. The other is to value the inputs at the price they would have when the output is sold rather than at the price actually paid for them when they are bought (Kliman, 1996, p. 212; Carchedi, forthcoming a). The prices of the inputs and of the outputs are made to coincide because they are computed *simultaneously* at the end of the period. Given that at the end of the period the price has fallen (as a consequence of the increased productivity), the inputs are devalued retroactively not as a consequence of a real process but simply to make accounts square. But accounts square simply because time has been cancelled. Moreover, due to simultaneous valuation, the money rate of profit is unaffected by the level of prices (as long as prices are determined simultaneously) so that only physical quantities determine the profit rate. This is the physicalist approach. It follows that, to obtain the desired result, Okishio would have to explicitly pose as its premise the simultaneous valuation of inputs and outputs. But this premise is posed neither by Okishio nor by those who defend its validity[14]. But assume this assumption is made. Then, Okishio is internally consistent. It can hardly be seriously held that an approach that jettisons value and time, even if internally consistent, can be seen as an internal critique, a refutation, of Marx's law. Yet this is what the critique boils down to.[15] Okishio's is then a theory alternative to Marx's. But, is it a *valid* alternative, a theory functional for the liberation of Labor?

First of all, it has been submitted above that a theory focusing on use values rather than on value implies a notion of capitalism tending toward growth rather than crises. This is contrary to Labor's struggle. Second, in formula (1) mentioned above, the quantities of the inputs multiplied by their prices are a cost and the labor necessary to produce the kth commodity (τ_k) is also a cost. What has escaped the commentators is that *Okishio's perspective is that of the capitalists for whom both the labor contained in the commodities' inputs and the new labor added are exclusively a cost.* Clearly, if costs are reduced and wages are unchanged, profits must rise. Okishio's critique, by seeing labor as a cost (the capitalists' point of view), disregards Marx's absolutely essential assumption that labor is the creator of value (the laborers' point of view). To show that Marx's law is logically inconsistent, Okishio would have had to use Marx's own assumption. Since he does not do this, he cannot argue that the law is internally inconsistent. Okishio could assume explicitly labor as a cost and not as the value-creating factor. But then Okishio would become explicitly irrelevant for a critique of the law.[16] The social, class, content of the Okishio theorem is incompatible with the interests of Labor. It is because of *this* inconsistency that it should be discarded.

But labor *is* a cost. Don't we have a contradiction here? No. Labor is a cost for the *individual* capitalists (when they purchase it as labor power) but is also and above all (as abstract labor) the sole value-creating factor (see Section 3 above). Less living labor might mean lower costs and thus higher profits for the capitalists introducing labor decreasing and productivity increasing technologies but it means also less new value and surplus value produced by them and thus, exclusively on this account, a lower ARP. The technological innovators do indeed realize a higher rate of profit but if they have produced less (surplus) value *ceteris paribus* their higher profit rate can be realized only at the expense of, i.e., by appropriating the surplus value produced by, the other producers who have not yet introduced those labor decreasing and productivity increasing technologies. This happens through the price mechanism. Assuming an unchanged total purchasing power, the greater combined output must be sold for a lower unit price. The innovators, by selling their greater output for the same unit price as that of the techno- logical laggards (whose output per unit of capital invested is lower), realize a greater surplus value per unit of capital invested (a greater rate of profit) at the cost of the laggards.[17]

5.2. The Indeterminateness Critique

The second line of critique focuses on the tendential nature of the law. Marx qualifies the law by ascribing to it a tendential nature, i.e., by considering factors that temporarily hamper the fall in the ARP (the countertendencies). The three countertendencies most often mentioned are the production of cheaper MP due to technological innovations, the increase in the rate of exploitation due to the production of cheaper means of consumption (MC) also as a consequence of technological innovations, and the increase in the rate of exploitation due to an increase in the length of the working day. These three factors increase the (surplus) value created and counter the fall in the ARP which is caused by the percentage decrease of variable capital, and thus of labor power, per unit of capital invested as a consequence of technological innovations. However, the tendency is only "delayed," "checked," "partly paralyzed," "retarded," "not [done] away with . . . but [simply] impair[ed] [in] its effect" by the countertendencies (Marx, op. cit., pp. 226, 232–237) and "Under all circumstances . . . the balance will be restored by the *destruction of capital* to a greater or lesser extent" (1992, p. 328, emphasis in the original).[18]

It is because of these countertendencies that the law is argued by the critics to be indeterminate (the ARP can fall or rise) and that there is no reason to assign the role of the tendency to the fall and thus the role of the countertendency to the rise in the ARP. For example, Fine and Harris (1976, p. 160) hold that the law cannot predict "actual falls in the rate of profit." Of the same opinion is Steedman (1977, p. 132). For Cullenberg, "there is no unidirectional, or teleological direction, whether up or down" in the rate of profit's movement (Cullenberg, 1994, p. 86). Of the same opinion is Reuten (2004).

After what has been said above, it is easy to see why the indeterminateness critique should be rejected. As we have seen above, whenever alternative interpretations are equally possible in terms of formal logic (the tendency is the fall versus the rise in the ARP), it is dialectical, class verification that decides. If the downward movement is the tendency, capital tends toward its cyclical self-destruction, it tends toward crises, not equilibrium, and the ARP tends toward its lowest point (the trough) as a precondition for its further ascending movement. After this destruction has taken place, growth can resume.[19] The contrary thesis or the agnostic position held by many Marxists carry a class content functional for the reproduction of capitalism because it deprives Labor of the view that the objective movement of the system tends toward its own collapse.

Notice that if the system tends toward its supersession it cannot tend toward its reproduction and vice versa. This is quite different from arguing that, given that only abstract labor creates (surplus) value, the tendency is toward crises and supersession (if less labor is employed) and the countertendency is toward growth and reproduction (if more labor is employed). There is no contradiction here because when abstract labor increases (the upward phase of the cycle) its reduction is present in a latent, potential state and when value decreases (the downward phase of the cycle) its growth is present even if only potentially.

6. THE TRANSFORMATION "PROBLEM"

The debate around Marx's transformation procedure has become one of the most obscure in the literature. The transformation of values into prices is simply the redistribution of the value contained in commodities at the moment of and through exchange under the assumption that each modal capital realizes tendentially the ARP. The supposed difficulty concerns the value of the inputs, given that the individual value of the commodity is given by the individual value of the inputs plus the new value created. Since the critique concerns the difference between values and prices, let us first set out clearly what they are and how they differ. The *individual value* is "the labour-time that the article costs the producer in each individual case" (Marx, 1976, p. 434). It should be distinguished from the *market value*, the individual value of the commodities produced under average conditions of production (average efficiency) in each sector. Both the individual and the market value are *values contained* or *embodied* in the commodity before realization. The *value realized* by a commodity upon its sale is called its *price*. The *production prices* are the value *tendentially* realized when the rates of profit are equalized among branches. The *market prices* are the value *actually* realized by those commodities when the rates of profit in the different branches differ according to the profit actually realized.

Value here is equivalent to abstract labor (under capitalist production relations) (see Table 1 below).

On the basis of these notions, let us first review Marx's transformation procedure.

6.1. The Transformation Procedure

In Table 2 below both sector 1 (the producer of MP) and sector 2 (the producer of MC) are represented by a modal producer.[20] Let i and o indicate inputs and outputs, respectively so that, for example, MPi stands for the MP as inputs. We consider first the use value aspect and focus initially on columns 2, 4, and 7. To address the critique, we assume simple reproduction, i.e., all the surplus product is consumed by the capitalists, no surplus product is reinvested.

At $t1$, sector 1 starts the production process with 60 MP$i + 40$ MCi and at $t2$ it has produced 140 MPo (column 4). Similarly, sector 2 starts its production process at $t1$ with 80 MP$i + 20$ MCi and at $t2$ it has produced 120 MCo. The 140 MPo are purchased only by the capitalists while the 120 MCo are purchased both by the capitalists and by the laborers.

Point $t2$ is the end point of period $t1$–$t2$. As an initial assumption (to be relaxed shortly), $t2$ is also considered to be the starting point of $t2$–$t3$ (column 7), i.e., there is no time lag between the end of one process and the

Table 1.   Value Contained and Value Realized (Prices) in Marx.

Value before Realization, i.e., Value Contained	Value after Realization, i.e., Prices
Individual value	Production price (tendentially realized)
Market value	Market price (actually realized)

Table 2.   The Computation of Production Prices in Marx.

	$t1$	$t1$–$t2$	$t2$	$t2$	$t2$	$t2$–$t3$
(1) Sector	(2) Inputs	(3) Value produced	(4) Outputs	(5) Market price	(6) Production price	(7) Inputs
1 MP	60 MP$i +$ 40 MCi	$60\,c1 + 40\,v1 +$ $40\,s1 = 140\,V1$	140 MPo	$150\,V1$	$130\,V1$	60 MP$i +$ 40 MCi
2 MC	80 MP$i +$ 20 MCi	$80\,c2 + 20\,v2 + 20\,s2$ $= 120\,V2$	120 MCo	$110\,V2$	$130\,V2$	80 MP$i +$ 20 MCi

beginning of the next one so that the outputs of $t1$–$t2$ become immediately the inputs of $t2$–$t3$. The 140 MPo are purchased as inputs at $t2$ by sector 1 (60 MPi) and sector 2 (80 MPi). Thus, all MP are purchased in the same proportions as at $t1$, the beginning of $t1$–$t2$. The 120 MCo are purchased by the laborers of both sectors (40 MCi in sector 1 and 20 MCi for sector 2) and by the capitalist (40 MCi in sector 1 and 20 MCi for sector 2). All the MC are again used by the laborers in both sectors as at $t1$ and the rest is consumed unproductively by the capitalists.

Let us now consider the value aspect. We assume that one unit of abstract labor (value) is represented by one unit of money (so that the following figures can be read, as in Marx, both as money and as labor, or value, quantities).[21] Each sector invests a certain quantity of money as constant capital (c) to buy MP and as variable capital (v) to buy the laborers' labor power and forces the laborers to produce surplus value (s) so that the total value produced by each sector is $c + v + s = V$. Then, column (3) gives the value invested at $t1$ as well as the value produced during $t1$–$t2$ by both sectors (140 $V1$ and 120 $V2$). At $t2$, the producers of MPo and MCo sell their products at their market price. These commodities are bought by other producers as MPi and MCi of the next production period at the same prices (if the same commodity is bought and sold at the same time it must be bought and sold for the same price). The transformation is thus, first of all, the redistribution of the value contained in the outputs if the value represented by their market price does not coincide with their value contained. This is column 5 where, for example, sector 1 sells its MPo at 150 $V1$. Given that the total value realized cannot exceed the total value contained, sector 2 must sell its MCo at 110 $V2$. There is thus a transfer of value equal to 10 V from sector 2 to sector 1, i.e., sector 1 realizes 10 V more than the value it produces at the expense of sector 2. The new production period begins with MP and of consumption whose value is not any more 140 MPi and 120 VMCi, respectively (as in column 3) but 150 MPi and 110 MCi.

Under the assumption stated above, it is a matter of empirical observation that the output of a production process is the input of the next production process so that the value of an output of a process is also the value of the same commodity as an input f the next production process. But an empirical observation is not yet a theory. The transformation implies the first principle of dialectics set out in Section 2 above, namely that phenomena are always both realized and potential. If the value contained in the outputs (140 $V1$ and 120 $V2$) is realized as 150 $V1$ and 110 $V2$, the former set of values realizes itself as the latter set of values. *The value contained in the output*

(*140 V1 and 120 V2*) *is potential value and the price realized by them is the value realized.* The quantitative transformation rests on a qualitative, dialectical, transformation from potential to realized quantities. But also the other way around. If those outputs enter as inputs the next production process, *the value realized by them as outputs* of $t1-t2$ (150 $V1$ and 110 $V2$) *becomes again the potential value of those same commodities as inputs* of $t2-t3$. This means that the initial assumption in Table 2 that the values contained in the MPi and MCi at $t1$ are $(60+80)c$ and $(40+20)v$ implies a previous production period, $t0-t1$ not shown in Table 2, whose MPo had been sold at 140 $V1$ and whose MCo had been sold at 60 $V2$. Thus, *not only the values realized by the commodities as outputs of one period but also the value of the same commodities as inputs of the following period can be expressed in money terms.* It is simply mistaken to think that the inputs can be expressed only in labor terms and the outputs in money terms. *This is why Marx can refer interchangeably to value as abstract labor as well as money.* It is thus mistaken to consider value as labor before taking, and price as labor after having taken, its money form.[22] This is the first point at which dialectics comes in, the transformation of potential into realized and back to potential values.

Up to here we have considered the transformation of the potential value of the output into its actually realized price and of this latter into the potential value of the same commodity as an input of the next process. But the transformation does not stop here. Consider two production processes, $t0-t1$ during which commodity A is produced and sold as an output at $t1$, and $t1-t2$ during which A is bought by the producer of B and becomes the input of B. At $t1$, A is bought as an input of B. At $t2$ it exits that period *not as outputs in itself but as part of* (*the value of*) *B.* Suppose now that between $t1$ and $t2$ new commodities A (call them A*) might be produced whose average value is different from the value of A. They are used by other producers of B to produce other B (call them B*). Then, at $t2$, the value that can be realized by the producer of B is that charged by the producers of B* using A*.[23] Thus, at $t2$, A might realize a different value (a value equal to that of A*) than what it had at $t1$ (its value contained). The value contained in A is the value it had at $t1$ and this is the value it transfers to B; but the value realized by B at $t2$ is the value of B* because the value of A at $t2$ (when A is sold as part of B) is the value of A*: "Although [the inputs, G.C.] entered the labour process with a definite value, they may come out of it with a value that is larger or smaller, because the labour time society needs for their production has undergone a general change" (Marx, 1988, p. 79).[24] Here too the theoretical foundation is provided by dialectics. The value of A at *t*1 is only potential because A realizes its value (in a possibly modified quantity) at *t*2 when B is sold. At *t*2, the producer of B suffers a loss to the purchasers of her B if A has a higher value than A* and vice versa in the opposite case.

The assumption that the end of a period is also immediately the beginning of the next one can now be relaxed. The above holds also if the outputs of the previous period (A) are not sold immediately upon being completed or if, even if immediately sold, they lay unused for some time before entering the production of B. The value of A might change (from A to A*) during the period they are not sold or not used. The value A transfers to B is the value it realizes when it is sold as outputs of the previous period. The value realized by B on account of A can be different. The loss or gain of the producer of the output (B) using those inputs (A) is then given by the difference between the value realized at the sale of A as an output of the previous period and first the value it has when it enters the production of B and second, as seen above, between this value and the value A realizes when B is sold.

It follows that the complete transformation must take into account not only the redistribution of surplus value but also that of the value of the inputs. It also follows that, if capitalists who are more productive than the average in their sector realize more than the ARP and vice versa for less than average productivity capitalists, the surplus value produced is redistributed among all producers but in such a way that only the producers who adopt the average technique at the moment of their products' realization receive the ARP.[25] Marx provides the example of a capitalist using a gold instead of a steel spindle. Only the capitalists using a steel spindle (the average technique) realize the ARP. The capitalist using a gold spindle realizes less than the value of the spindle transferred to the product. The difference is appropriated by the producers using the average technique (steel spindle). While the ARP is computed by dividing at *t*2 the total surplus value produced during *t*1–*t*2 by the total capital invested at *t*1 (i.e., invested both by average and non average producers), the production prices are computed by adding this average profit rate to the *average* value of the inputs at *t*1 (which is why the ARP is tendentially realized only by the average producer).

The above has dealt with the transformation of the individual values into market prices. However, market prices tend toward production prices, i.e., those prices at which all modal capitals realize the ARP. These are tendential prices. There are two reasons for conceptualizing the ARP and thus the production prices. We have seen that technological innovations, inasmuch as they replace people with MP, decrease the surplus value produced and cause a tendential fall in the ARP. The technological leaders realize a higher profit rate, the laggards a lower profit rate, and the ARP falls. After the crisis, the ARP rises again. The ARP is thus the thermometer of the economy. Second, due to capital movements from low to high profitability sectors, the ARP is the average toward which the actual profit rates tend. This tendency cannot become realized because every time a capital moves to a different sector it changes its organic composition and thus it changes the average profitability. Nevertheless, this tendency is a real, even though only tendentially so, phenomenon. Since it is a real phenomenon, the ARP is the center of gravity around which the market prices fluctuate. It is this center of gravity that reveals the inner structure of a movement (the movement of the market prices) that otherwise would seem chaotic and indeterminate. The transformation procedure applies also, *mutatis mutandi*, to the tendentially realized prices, the production prices. This procedure has been criticized on two accounts. They are the backward ad infinitum critique and the price inconsistency critique.

6.2. The Backward Ad Infinitum Critique

We have seen that, in order to compute the production price of this period's outputs, we must know the individual value of this period's inputs. But they are the production price of the previous period's outputs that, in their turn, depend upon the individual value of their inputs, Supposedly we are trapped in infinite regression. This is the backwards ad infinitum critique (Robinson, 1972, p. 202). This approach, the quest for the origin, is absurd because it would make any science impossible. However, to posit the value of the inputs at the beginning of the period as a given is a weak defense against the critique. While prices are empirically visible and thus amenable to being posited, values are not. The value of the inputs should be computed without falling in the backward ad infinitum critique. The solution hinges on the principle that abstract labor is not simply the expenditure of physical human energy in the abstract. It is its *social evaluation when the output of this real expenditure is sold* (see Carchedi, forthcoming b, *Historical Materialism*). Seen from this perspective, there is no need to regress infinitely in time. As shown in Carchedi (1996) and Carchedi and de Werner (1996), one step backward in time is sufficient.

Suppose we want to calculate the abstract labor (value) contained in the MP, for example, a machine, entering a certain period, say the $t1$–$t2$ period at $t1$. We can do that only if we start our computation in the preceding period, $t0–t1$. We can count the hours of *new* labor needed to produce that machine during $t0–t1$. This is necessary labor plus surplus labor. To it, there corresponds the quantity of money paid as wages and profits after the sale of that machine. Suppose wages and profits amount to Euro 40,000 and that the hours of new labor are 200. The ratio $200/40,000 = 0.005$ indicates that one Euro represents 0.005 of one hour of new labor. Given the *inherent homogeneity of both money and value as abstract labor* the same ratio applying to new labor can be applied to all labor realized by the sale of that machine. If the machine costs Euro 60,000, by applying that ratio we obtain the *social valuation* (300 hours) of the abstract labor (value) realized by that machine at the moment it is sold as an output, at $t1$. This is also the labor contained in that machine when it enters as an input the next production period $t1–t2$. The individual value of the inputs of $t1–t2$ is thus obtained not by endlessly counting the hours of past labor but through a *social valuation* of past labor at the end of the previous process ($t0–t1$). Starting from $t1–t2$, the labor value of the output of $t1–t2$ is also the labor value of the input of $t2–t3$ and no step back in time is needed any more. Notice that the 300 hours of labor constituting the individual value of that machine as an input of $t1–t2$ are hours of average intensity and average skilled labor. To this value, one can add new labor and thus value according to the level of intensity and skills.

6.3. The Price Inconsistency (Circularity) Critique

Even though a first critique was put forward by Von Böhm-Bawerk (1973 [1896])[26] shortly after the appearance of Capital III, by far the most influential attack on Marx's transformation procedure has been mounted by von Bortkiewicz (1971, p. 30) and has been brought to modern readership's attention by Sweezy (1973). To exemplify, in Table 2 the value of the MPo is 140 but their production price is 130. Similarly, the value of the MCo is 120 but their production price is 130. The capitalists sell their MPo at 130 but need (must buy) MPi for a value of 140 to start the new production process on the same scale. The MPo are insufficient to start a new process. Similarly, the capitalists sell the MCo at 130 but both capitalists and laborers need (buy) MCi for a value of 120. Some MCo are unsold and cannot enter the new process. *Simple reproduction fails.* The reason is that (supposedly) in Table 2 the inputs are bought at their value contained but sold at their production price. If this were the case, it would be a glaring contradiction because, if the inputs of a process are also the outputs of another process, the same commodity must be bought by the purchaser and sold by the seller at the same price (value). This is the price inconsistency critique.

It follows that if prices cannot be derived from values, there are supposedly in Marx a value system in which the value of the outputs is determined by the value of the inputs (column 4 in Table 2) and a price system in which the (production) prices of the outputs are determined by the (production) prices of the inputs. There would thus be in Marx a dual system. It also follows that there would be two rates of profit. In the words of Steedman, Marx "assumes that $S/(C + V)$ is the rate of profit but then derives the result that prices diverge from values, which means precisely, in general, that $S/(C + V)$ is *not* the rate of profit" (1977, p. 31). In Table 2, the value system gives an ARP of 30% (inputs and outputs are valued at their value). But if the inputs are valued at the production prices, the MPi are devalued to $130/140 = 0.9285$ so that sector 1 invests $60 \times 0.9285 = 57.72$ and sector 2 invests $80 \times 0.9285 = 74.28$ in MP. Similarly, the MC are revalued to $130/120 = 1.0833$ so that sector 1 invests 43.33 and sector 21.67 in MC. These would be the production prices of the inputs and thus, included in the price system (Table 3 below).

Now the ARP is not 30% (as in the value system) any more but $65/195 = 33.33\%$. The inputs are bought and sold either at their value or at their production price, but not at both.

The critique is based on confusion that, even though elementary, has held sway also among Marxists authors. The inputs MPi are bought and sold at $t1$ for 140 and the outputs MPo are bought and sold at $t2$ at 130. The inputs and outputs of a production period are *two different commodities* bought and sold at *two different moments at two different prices* (temporalism). The same for MCi and MCo. By holding that the MPi are bought at 140 (their value) and *at the same time* sold as MPo at 130 (their price of production) the critics discover a "contradiction." To escape this "contradiction," the prices of the inputs and of the outputs should be determined simultaneously through a system of simultaneous equations (von Bortkiewicz, 1973 [1907],

Table 3. The Retroactive Valuation of the Inputs.

c	v	s	V
55.72	43.33	43.33	142.38
74.28	21.67	21.67	117.62
130.00	65.00	65.00	260.00

pp. 199–221). In so doing, time is wiped out. But then, if realization is instantaneous, if time does not exist, production too must be a-temporal, i.e., the inputs must be the *same commodities* as the outputs. The inputs of one period become the outputs of *the same period.*

The postulate on which the critique rests and builds its simultaneous price determination is a reality without time. *This implies equilibrium and this is the class content of the circularity critique.*[27] This is inconsistent with the class content of Marx's theory as well as logically inconsistent with that theory. Clearly, Marx's supposed inconsistency is surreptitiously created by injecting the a-temporal assumption into an approach that, like reality, oozes with time. This inconsistency disappears if time is reintroduced in the analysis. In Table 2, MPi are bought and sold at $80 + 60 = 140$ at time $t1$ and MPo (different commodities even if they were perfect copies of the MPi) are bought and sold at 130 at time $t2$.[28] Such a simple consideration is sufficient to make the critique fail. Moreover, within a temporal dimension, reality is a succession of production and realization periods. As seen above, the price of the MPo of one period become the value contained in the same commodity as the MPi of the following period. If the end of one period coincides with the start of the following period, that commodity has at the same time both a price (a value actually or tendentially realized as the MPo of a period) and a value contained (a value not yet realized) as the MPi of the following period. While simultaneism and formal logic see the temporal coincidence of prices and values as a contradiction, temporal dialectics accounts for this coincidence.

Marx is said to have been conscious to have made a mistake and that he did not correct it: "We had originally assumed that the cost-price of a commodity equalled the *value* of the commodities consumed in its production. But for the buyer the price of production of a specific commodity is its cost-price... There is always the possibility of an error if the cost-price of a commodity in any particular sphere is identified with the value of the means of production consumed by it. Our present analysis does not necessitate a closer examination of this point" (1967, pp. 164–165, emphasis in the original). Actually Marx says is that if the output A is valued at its production price, it enters the production of B as an input at that modified value, so that it would be an error to compute the cost price of B on the basis of the individual value (rather than the production price) of A. This does not concern Marx here because he is interested in the production price of B so that the production price of A can be taken as given. In any case, we have seen (in dealing with the backward ad infinitum critique) that both the market price and the production price of A can be computed when A is sold and enters the production of B. Thus, if one wanted to, one could compute the inputs at their production price (as outputs of the previous period).[29]

Finally, it could be held that the analysis of a static, a-temporal situation can be used as a starting point for a more realistic analysis. But this is inadmissible in this case. One can start from a simplified depiction of reality in order to proceed to a more and more complex and realistic one, but on condition that each further step should retain the basic, fundamental assumptions upon which the previous stage of research rested, rather than on their rejection, i.e. on condition that the further assumptions do not conflict with the initial ones. If, at a later stage of the analysis, one rejects those initial assumptions and replaces them with other, incompatible ones, one rejects the previous analysis (the more simplified one) and creates a disjuncture rather than a bridge between the different stages of the analysis. If one starts from a static analysis based on simultaneism, one should proceed to a dynamic analysis also based on simultaneism. If this cannot be done, the analysis of a static situation is severed from, and becomes useless for, further analyses of real, dynamic situations because the initial postulate of a lack of time conflicts with the further postulate of the existence of time. Either one postulates time or one does not. In other words, a timeless dimension cannot be the starting point of an analysis of reality because it denies reality (time) rather than distilling from it its most pregnant aspects and using them as the starting point of the inquiry. This is why it is admissible for Marx to post-ulate first that the cost price is the value of the inputs and then to postulate that the inputs are valued at their production price because production prices are a modification of values and compatible with them.

6.4. Reproduction Prices and Simple Reproduction

Let us now see how the production prices of the outputs are consistent with the requirements of simple reproduction.[30]

In Table 2, at $t2$, the unit production price of the MPo is $130/140 = 0.9286$. 80 MPo are bought as MPi by the capitalists of sector 2 at the unit production price of 0.9286 and 60 MPo are bought as MPi by the capitalists of sector 1 at the same price. All MPo are sold at the unit production price. Similarly, the unit production price of the MCo is $130/120 = 1.0833$. 40 MCo are bought by the laborers of sector 1 and 20 MCo are bought by the laborers of sector 2 at the unit price of 1.0833. The values spent for the

MP*o* and MC*o* needed to start a new cycle at *t*2 are

Sector 1 : $(60 \times 0.9286 = 55.714) + (40 \times 1.0833 = 43.333) = 99.05$

Sector 2 : $(80 \times 0.9286 = 74.286) + (20 \times 1.0833 = 21.667) = 95.95$

Given that both sectors must realize 130 *V*, the profit the capitalists have to purchase the remaining 60 MC*o* is

$$\text{Sector 1} : 130 - 99.05 = 30.95 \ V$$
$$\text{Sector 2} : 130 - 95.95 = 34.05 \ V$$

With this $34.05 + 30.95 = 65 \ V$, the capitalists of the two sectors can purchase $65/1.0833 = 60$ MC*o*. Thus, 140 MP*o* are supplied and demanded at their production price and the same holds for the 120 MC*o*. All output is sold at its production prices and simple reproduction is ensured. Notice that the capitalists of sector 1 receive $30.95/1.0833 = 28.6$ MC instead of 30 and that those of sector 2 receive $34.05/1.0833 = 31.4$ MC instead of 30. The difference with the simultaneist approach is that these production prices apply to the MC and MP as inputs of the following period rather than being applied to their own inputs.[31]

6.5. Simple Reproduction with Production Prices and Parity of Purchasing Power

There is one aspect not explicitly considered by Marx that is worthwhile being considered. In Table 2, there are two sectors, one producing MP and the other producing MC. In it, all MP are exchanged for MC and vice versa. But at a lower level of aggregation, some MP will be exchanged with MP and some MC will be exchanged with MC. Sector 1 exchanges internally 60 MP for a value of 60*c*1 and buys 80 MC from sector 2 by selling 80 MP for a value of 40*v*1 and 40*s*1 (for a total value of 80). Sector 2 exchanges internally MC for a value of 20*v*2 and 20*s*2 and buys MP from sector 1 by selling 80 MC for a value of 80*c*2. As Marx finds out in Capital II, the condition for simple reproduction is then $c2 = v1 + s1$. If products are exchanged at their values, a value of 80 is exchanged for a value of 80. This concerns intersector exchange. However, if 80 MP are exchanged for 80 MC at their production prices,

$$\text{Sector 1 sells 80 MP at } 80 \times 0.9286 = 74.288 \text{ while}$$
$$\text{Sector 2 sell 80 MC at } 80 \times 1.0833 = 86.664$$

By selling its 80 MP, sector 1 receives 74.288 from sector 2 but needs 86.664 to buy 80 MC. It lacks a value of 12.376. Conversely, sector 2 has a value of 12.376 in excess. The purchasing powers of the two sectors (the value obtained by each sector through the sale of its commodities and available for the purchase of the other sector's commodities) do not coincide. Simple reproduction with prices of production would seem to be inconsistent with the purchasing power needed for intersector exchange. But this is not the case.

If the problem changes, the conditions must change too. *First*, for the purchasing powers to be equal, the capital invested to produce MP and MC for intersector exchange must be *equal*. Then, the same profit rate on the same capital gives the same value realized and thus the same purchasing power. This is the case in Table 2 if all commodities are exchanged intersectorally (in that case both the 140 MP and the 120 MC exchanged intersectorally are produced with a capital of 100) but not if we assume that only 80 MP are exchanged for 80 MC (because those 80 MP and 80 MC require different quantities of capital for their production). Thus, Table 2 is unsuited to exemplify the case at hand. *Second*, each sector is now subdivided into two subsectors. Sector 1 is subdivided in the subsector producing MP for exchange with MC (i.e., for intersectoral exchange) and the subsector producing MP for exchange with other MP (i.e., for intrasectoral exchange). Similarly, sector 2 is subdivided into the subsector producing MC for intersectoral exchange and the subsector producing MC for intrasectoral exchange. The capitals producing MP must be free to produce either for intrasectoral or for intersectoral exchange and to move to the sector producing MC. The same applies to the capitals producing MC. All capitals participate in the process of equalization of the profit rates. Under these conditions all capitals realize tendentially the same profit rate and the capitals selling intersectorally generate sufficient purchasing power for this intersector exchange to take place.

6.6. Negative Values

Consider the case of an economy in which ten bushels of seed corn (input) are planted by farmers who perform a certain quantity of labor. However, owing to a drought, only nine bushels of corn (output) are harvested. For simultaneism, given that the price (value) at the beginning of the period is equal to the price (value) at the end of it, the output is worth less than the input. In this case, "labor subtracts value instead of adding it." Kliman objects to this conclusion because in terms of Marx's value theory, (abstract) labor added must increase the value produced. The output (nine bushels) is worth more than the input (ten bushels) (2007, pp. 81–82). Actually, both positions are erroneous. In Marx's theory, abstract labor creates value *if as concrete labor it transforms use values into new use values*. If concrete labor *destroys* use values, abstract labor cannot create new value; it destroys the value contained in the seed corn. This would be the case mentioned by Baran (1968, p. xx) of a bakery paying a worker to add chemicals to the dough in order to increase the bread's perishability, thus destroying a part of the bread's use value. This is what I have called value destroying labor (see Carchedi, 1987, p. 228 and 1991, pp. 138–139 for details). The case mentioned above is similar, only the destruction of value is operated by nature rather than by laborers. The abstract labor gone in the corn destroyed by the drought has been destroyed and cannot create value, which is why if nature destroyed all corn one would be left without value no matter how much labor that corn has cost.

6.7. The Hidden Dimension

Dialectics is the hidden dimension that both makes Marx's transformation procedure intelligible and constitutes it as an element of a theory of radical social change. Consider first the dialectics of the relation between abstract labor and value.

1. If the capitalist production process has been started but is not yet finished, the laborers are performing abstract labor are thus creating the commodity's value embodied. However, that abstract labor is not yet value; more precisely it is value in forming, it is *potential* embodied value because the commodity itself, not being finished, is being created and thus it exists only potentially.
2. If the production process is completed and thus the commodity is finished (but not yet sold), the abstract labor that has gone into it becomes the value *contained* or *embodied* in it, whose material substance is abstract labor. Since a commodity must be sold in order to realize its value, its value contained is also its potential realized value.
3. The moment the commodity is sold, the value embodied in it becomes *realized* value (either tendentially or actually realized value) whose substance is the value contained.[32] The labor embodied determines the value realized because the former calls into existence the latter from the

realm of its potentialities and because the latter reacts upon the former but in the following period.

4. Since commodities are produced in order to be sold for money, the labor value realized (labor price) becomes itself a substance that takes necessarily the *monetary form* of value. Money is the form of existence of, and thus represents, value but is not value.

5. The realized value (price) of the output becomes the nonrealized value, or value contained, or potential realized value of the same commodity as an input of the following period. Here too the former determines the latter for similar reasons.

6. Finally, this potential value becomes again realized when the following period's output containing that input is sold. Here too the same reasons hold. From here the cycle of determination starts again.

The transformation seen as a dialectical process is a temporal succession of transformations, from potential to realized values and vice versa and from determinant to determined values and vice versa. Dialectics is the *necessary qualitative* dimension that accounts theoretically for the quantitative transformation. The transformation seen as a dialectical process is thus an instance of the dialectical view of social reality as a temporal flow of determining and determined contradictory phenomena continuously emerging from a potential state to become realized and going back to a potential state in a cyclical and tendential movement toward capitalism's supersession. It is a manifestation of the class-determined view of social reality. It is thus perfectly consistent with Labor's world-view.

Dialectics does not reject but makes use of the tools of formal logic. From the perspective of temporalism immersed in formal logic Marx's theory is perfectly consistent. This shows that temporalism is the principle upon which the theory rests and that simultaneism, even though internally consistent, is foreign to it. A simultaneist critique is an internal critique neither of temporalism nor of Marx. Simultaneist theories are not an "improvement" of Marxism; they are different theories with their own class content. As argued above, simultaneism implies equilibrium and thus a view of the economy tending toward its equilibrated reproduction. From this angle, this is an inherently rational system and any attempt to supersede it is irrational. This is simultaneism's social content. Temporalism, if immersed in a dialectical context, reaches the exactly opposite conclusions: the economy is in a constant state of nonequilibrium and tends toward its supersession. From this perspective, capitalism is inherently irrational and any attempt to supersede it is rational. It is from this perspective that the three above issues have been analyzed. From his perspective, the choice between temporalism and simultaneism turns out to be a choice between formal logic and simultaneism on the one hand and dialectical logic and thus temporalism on the other. This is much more than a personal preference; it is a class-determined choice based on a class-determined principle. If one is interested in radical change, one should face squarely these issues. This is the *real significance* of the dialectical (and thus temporalist) approach to the issue of consistency.[33]

Both temporalism and simultaneism should move on from being only a critique and counter-critique of each other applying only formal logic to the issue of consistency to showing how their view of consistency fits into a wider theory of radical social change, thus grounding the choice of their initial postulate into Labor's perspective. Neither of the two camps has done this and this has been the limit of the debate, on both sides. The time has come to change course and the challenge is to overcome this limit. This work has attempted to do that on the basis of a dialectical method of which temporalism is an integral part. It is only a beginning.[34] Hopefully, simultaneist authors will accept the challenge and show how their approach to the issue of consistency based on simultaneism and equilibrium is a piece of a broader theory furthering the liberation of Labor. For both approaches holds what Marx once said: Hic Rhodus, hic salta!

NOTES

1. Earlier versions of the method to be submitted below have proven their fruitfulness in dealing with the transformation of values into prices (Carchedi, 1984; Freeman & Carchedi, 1996), with the law of the tendential fall of the profit rate (Carchedi, forthcoming a, Capital and Class), with a theory of knowledge (Carchedi, 2005), with a class analysis of the European Union (Carchedi, 2001) and with a theory of social classes (Carchedi, 1977, 1991, 1983, 1987). This chapter sets out that method in more details thus providing a fuller picture of dialectical logic as a method of social research.

2. This section is a concise version of Carchedi (2008a, 2008b), to which the interested reader is referred.

3. Disregard of the potential leads to absurd conclusions. For example, Lefebvre asserts that life and death are "identical" because the process of aging starts when a living organism is born (1982, p. 164). But life and death are opposites and not identical. Life is a realized phenomenon and death is a potential within life itself that will realize itself necessarily. Contrary to Lefebvre (op. cit. p. 172) the unity of contradictions is not identity. Notice the implicit simultaneism. If life and death are identical, they are collapsed into each other and the time difference between them disappears.

4. This does not contradict the trans-epochal and trans-class elements of knowledge. See Carchedi (2005).

5. There are many similarities between Arthur and the precursor of the value form approach. For example "Rubin's approach shows a certain 'discomfort' with the materiality of the production process of human life." This leads him "to an inverted conception of the relationship between production and exchange" (Kicillof & Guido, 2007, p. 16). This inverted relation is a feature in Arthur's approach, and more generally of many value form theorists, to be discussed further down.

6. Human metabolism is a two-stage process. In the anabolic phase, human energy is produced in the form of calories and ATP (adenosine 5'-triphosphate) and stored. There are of course differences between the organs and functions of different individuals but these differences do not affect the *general, common* way in which we all produce energy in the above-mentioned form. This is followed by the catabolic phase, the use of the stored energy. This use or expenditure cannot but be the *consumption of the same type of energy* (calories and ATP).

7. The expenditure of human energy is observed and measured by referring to the basic metabolic rate, i.e., the amount of energy or calories the body of an average individual sitting and at rest burns to maintain itself in its resting state.

8. Whether value form theorists are aware of it or not, the denial of the material existence of abstract labor, or more precisely of the material existence of the abstract labor embodied in a commodity before that commodity's exchange and therefore also after exchange, clashes with the reality of human metabolism. If the original aim of the value form approach was to avoid the transformation "problem" by denying the existence of value before its exchange, the strategy has misfired. The value form approach, to be credible, must show that human metabolism does not exist or that it can be justifiably assumed not to exist.

9. In a previous critique (Carchedi, 2003), I wrongly stated that for Arthur's capital produces value. It should be said, however, that my mistake is not without justification. As Arthur concedes, "It seems that the point causing difficulty here is that I have not sufficiently made clear [that] I attribute to capital as a social form the positing of the product of labor as value. A related point is that although I slip into the standard terminology by speaking of the 'creation' and 'production' of value, I reject any analogy here with material production." However, in his new book, Arthur repeats, quite confusingly, that "to be the source of new value is to be that out of which capital *creates* value" (Arthur, 2004, p. 211, emphasis in the original).

10. For a more detailed critique, see Carchedi (forthcoming b).

11. See Cullenberg (1994), Fine and Harris (1976), Foley (1999, 2000), Freeman (1999), Kliman (1996, 1999, 2007), Kliman and Freeman (2000), Laibman (1999b, 2000a, 2000b, 2001), Shaikh (1978).

12. For some, like Brenner (2002, p. 12), this is self-evident.

13. The qualification "as a result of higher productivity" is necessary because it makes Okishio's initial assumption consistent with Marx's own. If by lower costs it is meant cheaper constant and variable capital, then Okishio becomes inconsistent with Marx. For Marx, cheaper means of production and of consumption do increase the surplus value produced but lower costs due to less labor power have the opposite effect. For Okishio, any cost reduction increases productivity. See below.

14. But see Laibman (2000a).

15. See Kliman (1996, 1999), Laibman (1999a, 1999b), Freeman (1999), Foley (1999, 2000), Kliman and Freeman (2000, 2006), Laibman (2000b, 2001), Kliman (2001), Mohun (2003), Mohun and Veneziani (2007), Freeman and Kliman (2008). The last five entries are only indirectly related to the debate around the law. For a comprehensive review of the debates, see Kliman (2007).

16. Kliman mounts a sustained defense of Marx's law in Chapter 7 of 2007 edition. However, Kliman does not explicitly criticize Okishio for having substituted labor as value creator with labor as a cost. Moreover, his defense of Marx's law is incomplete because while the mention is made of the tendential nature of the law, no argument is submitted to support Marx's thesis that the fall rather than the rise is the tendency.

17. For Kliman (2007, pp. 21–23), a less than average productivity firm (a firm employing more labor than that socially necessary) does not create more value while a firm that increases its productivity with the same amount of abstract labor produces not only more use values but also more value. The former proposition makes value vanish into nothing; the latter makes it appear out of nothing. In reality the extra value produced by the former is appropriated by the latter through the price system.

18. This is the correct translation of the MEGA text which reads: "Unter allen Umständen ... würde sich das Gleichgewicht herstellen durch *vernichtung von Kapital* in grösserem oder geringerem Umfang" (Marx, 1992, p. 328). Compare this with the English translation: "But the equilibrium would be restored through the withdrawal or even the destruction of more or less capital" (1967, p. 253). "Gleichgewicht" is translated as "equilibrium" rather than "balance" and "through the withdrawal or even" is arbitrarily added.

19. The destruction of capital that makes recovery possible is not so much that caused by technical obsolescence as the destruction of capital as social relations. See Carchedi (1991).

20. We are dealing thus with market values. For a more detailed analysis in which each sector is composed of modal and non-modal producers see Carchedi (1991, Chapter 3). To simplify matters, in what follows by individual value, it will be meant the individual value of the modal producers, i.e., the market value, unless otherwise specified.

21. To further simplify matters, there is no fixed capital here, i.e., all the MP are consumed in one period.

22. There is nothing unclear about "the value of a commodity [being, G.C.] expressed in its price before it enters into circulation" (Marx, 1976, p. 260). The value of the output before realization (its value contained) is the price paid for the inputs, plus the surplus value.

23. Of course, more (less) than average producers of B's realize more (less) than average value.

24. The inputs "add to the labour time contained in the products only as much labour time as they themselves contained *before* the production process" (Marx, 1988, p. 177). However, the value realized by the producer of B on an account of A is the value of A*.

25. This is not shown in Table 2 because each sector is represented by one producer who is thus the average producer by definition. For numerical examples, see Carchedi (1991, Chapter 3).

26. Böhm-Bawerk argued that there is a contradiction between the first and the third volume of Capital. For a refutation of this critique, see Ernst (1982), Carchedi (1984), Freeman and Carchedi (1996), and Kliman (2007).

27. Some simultaneist authors hold that the inputs are valued at their replacement cost at the end of the period. If an input A costs 100 at $t1$ but at $t2$ it would cost 80 to replace it, its value is said to be 80 at $t2$. A value of 20 is made to vanish. In reality, A has cost 100 at $t1$ and the producer of B (the output of which A is an input) realizes only 80 for A, i.e., loses 20 to the purchasers of her B because by $t2$ the average price of A has dropped by approximately 20. However, in the replacement cost approach inputs and outputs have the same prices but are not the same commodities. The replacement cost of A is the value of another, even though physically identical, A.

28. The first critique of the simultaneist approach inherent in neo-Ricardianism is Perez (1980). Carchedi (1984, reprinted in Fine, 1986, pp. 215–239) reaches independently similar results and provides the first temporalist counter-critique in English. Differently from Perez, Carchedi stresses the need for a dialectical approach, an element that has been disregarded by all other temporalist authors. This work returns to the dialectical origin of the temporalist approach.

29. Another way to look at this point is by focusing on the cost price of the inputs. As Ramos (1998–1999) correctly stresses, in Marx the cost price is the same quantity whether one computes the value or the production price of a commodity. The charge leveled against Marx has been that Marx failed to transform the value of the inputs into their production price. But, as Ramos stresses, this supposed mistake is based on a simultaneist view. In terms of this work, a commodity, e.g., a machine, is sold as an output at $t1$, the end of the $t0$–$t1$ period, at its production price. This is also what is paid for the same machine as an input at $t1$ as the beginning of $t1$–$t2$, the next period. This is therefore the value of that commodity at the beginning of $t1$–$t2$ and this is also the value transferred by that machine to the output of the new production period, $t1$–$t2$. Ramos' distinctive feature is his argument that Engels omitted a relevant passage and included a numerical example that did not appear in the original and that this omission reduced the strength of Marx's presentation, contributing to the consolidation of Bortkiewicz's interpretation.

30. The following example is taken from Carchedi (2005, p. 132).

31. Screpanti "proof" that the temporal approach is mistaken is based upon a computational mistake that, if correct, proves that the temporal approach is indeed correct. See Screpanti (2005). For the rebuttal of Screpanti's proof see Carchedi (2005).

32. Realized value is usually referred to as social value (also by Marx), as opposed to individual value. Since value has always a social content, *individual* value is here set against *realized* value.

33. Kliman holds that the TSSI (and within it temporalism) cannot prove that "Marx's theory is true" and that all it can prove is that it is logically consistent (Kliman, 2007, p. 168). This is correct if temporalism is immersed in formal logic. Kliman does an excellent job within this framework. But this is also the limit of present TSSI as it has evolved over the years. Temporalism immersed dialectical logic can indeed prove Marx's theory "true," i.e., correct from the perspective of Labor.

34. In discussing replication as a principle of verification, Mohun holds that, "What is required is not an assessment of rival interpretations, but a theory for today's world and its use in empirical analysis" (2003, p. 100). Actually, this article has argued that what is required is an assessment of rival interpretations' consistency in terms of both formal logic and class content. Dialectical verification is at the same time an element of "a theory for today's world." The ball is now in Mohun's court and in that of the Marx's critics.

REFERENCES

Alberro, J., & Persky, J. (1981). The dynamics of fixed capital revaluation and scrapping. *Review of Radical Political Economics, 13*(2), 21–37.

Arthur, C. (2004). *The new dialectics*. Leiden: Brill.

Baran, P. (1968). *The political economy of growth*. New York: Monthly Review Press.

Brenner, R. (2002). *The economics of global turbulence*. London: Verso.

Carchedi, G. (1977). *On the economic identification of social classes*. London: Routledge and Keagan Paul.

Carchedi, G. (1983). *Problems in class analysis*. London: Routledge and Kegan Paul.

Carchedi, G. (1984). The logic of prices as values. *Economy and Society, 13*(4), 431–455.

Carchedi, G. (1987). *Class analysis and social research*. Oxford: Basil Blackwell.

Carchedi, G. (1991). *Frontiers of political economy*. London: Verso.

Carchedi, G. (1996). Non-equilibrium market prices. In: A. Freeman & C. Guglielmo (Eds), *Marx and non-equilibrium economics* (pp. 164–183). Cheltenham, UK: Edward Elgar.

Carchedi, G. (2001). *For another Europe, a class analysis of European economic integration*. London: Verso.

Carchedi, G. (2003). A note on Chris Arthur's 'dialectics of negativity'. *Capital and Class, 81*, 25–31.

Carchedi, G. (2005). Sapiens nihil affirmat quod non probat. *Review of Political Economy, 17*(1), 127–139.

Carchedi, G. (2008a). Logic and dialectics in social science, Part I. *Critical Sociology, 34*(4), 495–523.

Carchedi, G. (2008b). Logic and dialectics in social science, Part II. *Critical Sociology, 34*(5), 631–656.

Carchedi, G. (forthcoming a). The falling profit rate: From Okishio to Marx. *Capital and Class*.

Carchedi, G. (forthcoming b). On Chris Arthur's "New Dialectics" and Value Form Theory. *Historical Materialism, 17*(1).

Carchedi, G. & de Werner, H. (1996). The transformation procedure: A non-equilibrium approach. In: A. Freeman & C. Guglielmo (Eds), *Marx and non-equilibrium economics* (pp. 136–163). Cheltenham: Edward Elgar.

Cullenberg, S. (1994). *The falling rate of profit*. London: Pluto.

Ernst, J. R. (1982). Simultaneous valuation extirpated: A contribution of the critique of the neo-Ricardian concept of value. *Review of Radical Political Economics, 14*(2).

Fine, B. (Ed.) (1986). *The value dimension*. London: Routledge and Kegan Paul.

Fine, B., & Harris, L. (1976). Controversial issues in Marxist economic theory. *The Socialist Register*. (pp. 141–178), London: Merlin Press.

Foley, D. (1986). *Understanding capital: Marx's economic theory*. Cambridge: Harvard University Press.

Foley, D. (2000). Response to Freeman and Kliman. *Research in Political Economy, 18*, 278–284.

Foley, D. K. (1999). Response to David Laibman. *Research in Political Economy, 17*, 229–233.

Freeman, A. (1999). Between two world systems: A response to David Laibman. *Research in Political Economy, 17*, 241–248.

Freeman, A., & Carchedi, G. (Eds). (1996). *Marx and non-equilibrium economics*. Cheltenham, UK: Edward Elgar.

Freeman, A., & Kliman, A. (2008). Simultaneous valuation vs. the exploitation theory of profit: A summing up. *Capital and Class, 94*(Spring), 107–117.

Geras, N. (1983). *Marx and human nature: Refutation of a legend*. London: Verso.

Kicillof, A., & Guido, S. (2007). On materiality and social forms: A political critique of Rubin's value-form theory. *Historical Materialism, 15*(3), 9–43.

Kliman, A. (1996). A value-theoretic critique of the Okishio theorem. In: A. Freeman, & Carchedi, G. (Eds).

Kliman, A. (1999). Sell dear, buy cheap? A reply to Laibman. *Research in Political Economy, 17*, 235–240.

Kliman, A. (2001). Simultaneous valuation vs. the exploitation theory of profit. *Capital and Class, 73*, 97–112.

Kliman, A. (2007). *Reclaiming Marx's "Capital": A refutation of the myth of inconsistency*. Lanham, MD: Lexington Books.

Kliman, A., & Freeman, A. (2000). Rejoinder to Duncan Foley and David Laibman. *Research in Political Economy, 18*, 285–294.

Kliman, A., & Freeman, A. (2006). Replicating Marx: A reply to Mohun. *Capital and Class, 88*(Spring), 117–126.

Laibman, D. (1982). Technical change, the real wage and the rate of exploitation: The falling rate of profit reconsidered. *Review of Radical Political Economics, 14*(2), 95–105.

Laibman, D. (1999a). Okishio and his critics: Historical costs versus replacement costs. *Research in Political Economy, 17*, 207–227.

Laibman, D. (1999b). The profit rate and reproduction of capital: A rejoinder. *Research in Political Economy, 17*, 249–254.

Laibman, D. (2000a). Two of everything: A response. *Research in Political Economy, 18*, 269–278.

Laibman, D. (2000b). Numerology, temporalism, and profit rate trends. *Research in Political Economy, 18*, 295–306.

Laibman, D. (2001). Rising 'material' vs. falling 'value' rates of profit: Trial by simulation. *Capital and Class, 79*, 79–96.

Lefebvre, H. (1982). *Logique formelle en logique dialectique* (3rd ed.). Paris: Terrains/Editions Sociales.

Marx, K. (1967). *Capital* (Vol. 3). New York: International Publishers.

Marx, K. (1973 [1939]). *Grundrisse*. Hardmondsworth: Penguin Books.

Marx, K. (1976). *Capital* (Vol. 1). London: Penguin Books.

Marx, K. (1988). Economic manuscript of 1861–1863. In: K. Marx & F. Engels (Eds), *Collected works* (Vol. 30). Moscow: Progress Publishers.

Marx, K. (1992). Ökonomische manuskripte, 1863–1867, MEGA, Internationales Institut für Sozialgeschichte, Amsterdam.

Marx, K., & Engels, F. (1970). *Selected works* (Vol. 3). Moscow: Progress Publishers.

Mohun, S. (2003). On the TSSI and the exploitation theory of profit. *Capital and Class*, *81*(Autumn), 85–102.

Mohun, S., & Veneziani, R. (2007). The incoherence of the TSSI. *Capital and Class*, *92*(Summer), 139–145.

Okishio, N. (1961). Technical changes and the rate of profit. *Kobe University Economic Review*, 7, 86.

Perez, M. (1980). Valeur et Prix: Un essai de critique des propositions néo-Ricardiannes, *Critiques de l'Economie Politique*, Nouvelle Série, No. 10, Janvie–Mars, pp. 122–149.

Ramos, A. (1998–1999). Value and price of production: New evidence on Marx's transformation procedure. *International Journal of Political Economy*, *28*(4), 55–81.

Resnick, S. A., & Wolff, R. D. (2006). *New departures in Marxian theory*. London: Routledge.

Reuten, G. (2004). Zirkel vicieux or trend fall? The course of the profit rate in Marx's *Capital III*. *History of Political Economy*, *36*(1), 163–186.

Robinson, J. (1972). Ideology and analysis. In: J. Schwartz (Ed.), *A critique of economic theory*. Harmondsworth, UK: Penguin Books.

Screpanti, E. (2005). Guglielmo Carchedi's the art of fudging' explained to the people. *Review of Political Economy*, *17*(1).

Shaikh, A. (1978). Political economy and capitalism: Notes on Dobb's theory of crisis. *Cambridge Journal of Economics*, *2*(2), 233–251.

Steedman, I. (1977). *Marx after Sraffa*. London: Verso.

Von Böhm-Bawerk, E. (1973 [1896]). Karl Marx and the close of his system. In: P. Sweezy (Ed.), *Karl Marx and the close of his system* (pp. 3–101). Clifton, USA: Kelley Publishers.

von Bortkiewicz, L. (1971). Calcolo del valore e calcolo del prezzo nel sistema Marxiano. In: *Ladislaus von Bortkiewicz, La Teoria Economica di Marx*. Torino: Einaudi.

von Bortkiewicz, L. (1973 [1907]). On the correction of Marx's theoretical construction in the third volume of capital. In: P. Sweezy (Ed.), *Karl Marx and the close of his system* (pp. 199–221). Clifton, USA: Kelley Publishers.

Zelený, J. (1980). *The logic of Marx*. Oxford: Basil Blackwell.

CHAPTER 10

METHODOLOGICAL DIFFERENCES BETWEEN TWO MARXIAN ECONOMISTS IN JAPAN: KŌZŌ UNO AND SEKISUKE MITA

Shūichi Kakuta

ABSTRACT

Kōzō Uno (1897 1977) was a unique Marxist economist in Japan. The Uno's three-stage theory of the capitalist economy, in a certain sense, was a typical framework in the system of Marxist economic theory. But the method in Uno's Principles of Political Economy ("Principles") is different from Marx's method in "Capital" and systematic critique of political economy. Since Uno rejected a methodological character of "capital in general" in Marx, Uno's "Principles" was a closed system in a circle. The stage theory of capitalistic development, therefore, had no connection with his general theory ("Principles"). Sekisuke Mita (1906–1975) was a severe critic of Uno's methodology. Mita, a Hegelian philosopher, criticized Uno that the methodology of his "Principles" was Hegelism, and pointed out that the method of Uno's stage theory was positivism. Mita not only criticized Uno, but also criticized orthodox views of Marxian economists who had been influenced by Stalinist views. Mita asserted that the rational dialectic in the logic of "Capital" was founded on the analytical method. The central problem is a

Why Capitalism Survives Crises: The Shock Absorbers
Research in Political Economy, Volume 25, 277–299
Copyright © 2009 by Emerald Group Publishing Limited
All rights of reproduction in any form reserved
ISSN: 0161-7230/doi:10.1108/S0161-7230(2009)0000025007

methodological meaning of the relationship between the universal and the particular. This article describes the points of rational dialectic in the methodology of Marxian political economy, overcoming Hegelism and positivism.

1. INTRODUCTION

Kōzō Uno (1897–1977) was, in a certain sense, both a unique and a typical Marxian economist in Japan. His name is well known not only at home but also, to some extent, abroad because his important book *Keizai Genron* (*Principles of Political Economy*) (originally published in Japanese in 1950–1952, revised in 1964) was translated into English by Thomas Sekine in 1980. After World War, Uno became a professor of political economy at the University of Tōkyo and trained many researchers who came to be known as the Uno school.

Andrew Barshay, an American researcher who published a book on the social sciences in modern Japan, wrote, "Uno had pursued a logical – Hegelian – reconstruction of *Capital*, developing an original framework of 'basic principles' of political economy, along with a three-stage historical model of capitalist development that culminated in 'analysis of current conditions.' Marked by its rigorous separation of economic science from ideological activity and portrayal of capital as a 'structure' of all-generative power, the Uno school represented the apotheosis of Marxism as an 'objective' science of political economy" (Barshay, 2004, p. 69. Japanese version, p. 85). I agree with Barshay on this comment, except for one thing; it was not capital that had all-generative power but commodity economy for Uno.

Uno's motivation in separating science from ideology stemmed from his revulsion against the orthodox or Stalinist view of political economy and its politicization. He was a professor of economic policy at Tōhoku Imperial University (now the Tōhoku University) in the prewar period. At that time he studied Hegel's philosophy and worked out a detailed plan for his *Principles*. Uno was arrested in 1938, with an unverified accusation that he had violated the notorious Peace Preservation Law, and spent about 15 months in prison.

Another Marxian economist, Sekisuke Mita (1906–1975), who was also arrested in the prewar period, graduated from the Philosophy Department of Kyōto University and worked for the Society for the Study of

Materialism. When he published his book, *Hegel Tetsugaku e no Michi* (*The Path to Hegel's Philosophy*) in 1934, he was only 28 years old. This book was highly praised by Jun Tosaka (1900–1945) who was a famous Marxist philosopher in prewar Japan. After the War, Mita had worked for the Philosophy Section of The Association of Democratic Scientists (*Minka*). He moved to Osaka City University in 1952 and lectured on the methodology of political economy until 1970. Mita lectured on Hegel's *Logic* from 1970 through 1975 at Osaka to many people.[1]

The most important work of Mita, *Shihonron no Hōhō* (*The Method in Capital*), was published in 1963. For about 10 years after publishing this book, he eagerly criticized the orthodox or Stalinist views of political economy as well as the methodology of Kōzō Uno. At first, he called their approaches the logical/historicist method, but later he named them Hegelism. He advanced the dialectic method founded on the analytical method. I would term it the rational method of dialectic, simply rational dialectic. We can find the most suitable model for the dialectic/analytical method in Marx's *Capital*.

In this short essay, I will compare two Japanese Marxist economists, Uno and Mita, especially the difference between their methodologies. This paper focuses on three themes. The first theme is the principles of political economy that address the relation between reality (history) and theory (logic) in *Capital*. The second is the developmental stages of capitalist economy that refers to the relation between the universal and the particular. The third is the rational method of dialectic to be used in political economy as an empirical science.

2. CLOSED SYSTEM OR OPEN SYSTEM: METHOD IN THE PRINCIPLES OF POLITICAL ECONOMY

As is widely known, Uno's *Principles of Political Economy* (hereafter *Principles*) is a revision of Marx's *Capital*. We can find Marx's *Capital* behind Uno's book very clearly. But it is not a summary, or commentary on *Capital*. Why did *Capital* need to be rewritten by Uno? The theory of capitalist economy had to be rewritten for him as if it were pure. But what does he mean by the word "pure"? For Uno, a capitalist economy exists by itself and by removing all impure things. Uno, therefore, wanted a theory that would explain the object as it is.

In the world of Uno's *Principles*, capitalist economy does "not" have its own history. It must be explained as if it would remain unchanged forever and there is a perpetual motion of capitalist economy in Uno's *Principles*.

Uno wrote in his *Principles* that capitalist economy begins with the commodity and ends with the commodity. To be precise, his book ends with the commodification of capital. The first part of *Principles* is the doctrine of circulation in the forms of commodity, money, and capital; the second part of the book is the doctrine of production; and the third and final part is the doctrine of distribution. This composition of circulation, production, and distribution, although it was seemingly very commonplace, was most clearly represented in Uno's reinterpretation of the theory of rent. The position of the theory of rent in Uno's *Principles* is different from Marx's *Capital*. *Capital* starts with an analysis of the commodity, and the first part is about the production process of capital, the second part is about the circulation process of capital, and the third and final part is about the forms of the whole process, i.e., the synthesis of the two processes of capitalistic production and circulation. The third part ends with the critique of the trinity formula in the incomes of social classes. So where does the difference lie between Uno and Marx?

Uno thought that the methodology of *Principles* must imitate its object, capitalism, and its method of abstraction and synthesis. This method is referred to as the dialectic method of total comprehension that Hegel had applied to the self-developing world of thought. According to a photocopy in *Shihonron to Watakushi* (*Capital* and Me, 2008, this book is the collection of articles written by Uno, not collected in his *Chosaku-shū* published by Iwanami Shoten, Tokyo), Uno obviously modeled his composition of *Principles* on the composition of Hegel's *Logic*. That is to say, Uno thought that the first part of Hegel's *Logic*, "Being" (das Sein) corresponds to the circulation theory of commodity and money in his *Principles*, the second part of it, "Essence" (das Wesen) corresponds to the production theory, and the last part of it, "Concept" (der Begriff) corresponds to the distribution theory.

Surprisingly, Uno said that there was a logical inconsistency in Marx's *Capital*. So when Uno started from the commodity as a product of capital, the commodity exchange only referred to the forms of circulation (not being produced by labor) which was external to the production, and then the commodity-form had to grasp the process of production through an internal dialectic logic. He asserted that it was "not" in the commodity that the labor theory of value has to be proved. The only one thing that the commodity could not govern in itself is the labor power. The notion of "commodification of labor power" therefore was the essence of Marx's *Capital* in Uno's interpretation. Capital in itself was unable to produce the labor power directly, and this was the fundamental contradiction of capitalism for Uno. But, for Uno's *Principles*, the process of commodity exchange becoming capitalism has to be developed as if the contradiction were resolved in itself, because capitalism is an independent, self-regulating, and self-perpetuating system. The logic of Uno had to be a result of applying Hegel's dialectic method characterized by self-developing concepts.

As a result, Uno's system of *Principles* is closed at the commodification of capital, interest-bearing capital: M ... M'. The theory of "pure" capitalist society could not be developed to the nation state and the international relation of production. It presupposes the abstract context of a purely capitalist society made up of the three major classes: capitalists, workers, and landowners. It is not only unwavering but also complete. *Principles*, therefore, is like the Bible on the altar. Uno's concept of "pure capitalism" does not mean a logical community, and does not really exist anywhere or at any time. In this sense, "pure capitalism" is an ideal type, and it is a speculative composition.

Because of the closed system of *Principles*, Uno rejected Marx's systematic critique of political economy that was composed of six parts: (1) capital, (2) land property, (3) wage labor, (4) concentration of bourgeois society in the form of the state, (5) international relation of production, and (6) world market and the crisis. Uno's system of three levels of political economy, *Principles*, three-stage model theory and analysis of current conditions, was quite different from Marx's system and his methodology.

The contradiction of commodification of labor power is unreasonable or unnatural for Uno. In Uno's *Principles*, the fundamental contradiction of capitalist economy, i.e., the contradiction between forces of production and relations of production in the capitalist system was neglected. It could not be explained in his *Principles*.

Then, where did Mita find the common feature between the orthodox or Stalinist approach and Uno's theory? Mita's answer was surprising. The mainstream in the Japanese Marxist tradition was strongly influenced by Stalinist view, and Uno rejected that approach. That is why he had been criticized by the orthodox or Stalinist view. There are many issues. The traditional approach by Japanese Marxists considered that the logical process of political economy was harmonious with the historical process of capitalist economy. Hajime Kawakami (1879–1946) was a representative of that approach in prewar Japan, and Minoru Miyakawa (1896–1985), Kawakami's student, was one in the postwar period. Mita criticized both

Uno and Miyakawa. This was an enigmatic argument in the sense of tradition of social science in Japan.

Mita argued that the fundamental perspective of Uno was metaphysical, because, for Uno, economic laws are not real, and they cannot be demonstrated by human experiences, practices, and facts. Mita said that Uno's word "pure" means a mere standard for understanding impurities. Uno's *Principles*, therefore, was just a subjective composition, a model (not historical) and an ideal type. The *Principles* could not grasp the contradiction between productive forces (the socialized character of production under mechanized industries) and production relationships (the capitalistic acquisition) under the capitalist system. Uno did not explain the capitalist development and the stages by his *Principles*. He rejected the law of surplus value, too; for him, the law of value only exists because he reduced capitalist economy to commodity economy.

Mita argued that there are several misunderstandings in Uno's notion of *commodification of labor power*. First, the commodification of labor power is not the essence of capital, but the basis and a precondition of capitalist society. The essence of capital refers to the production, acquisition of surplus value, and increase of capital in itself. Second, statement that the commodification of labor power is unreasonable and unnatural means that there is a contradiction between the natural and the unnatural. From a methodological standpoint, the basis of this argument means the mechanical logic. If capitalism is an unnatural system, how has it continued to exist for several centuries? If Uno's argument is true, that capitalism is unreasonable, the de-commodification of labor power is only an ideal. He could not explain the persistence of capitalist economy, or the conditions for its extinction. The capitalist economy and the commodification of labor power as a condition of the former's existence are necessary and rational processes in human history. In general, the great historical significance of productive forces under the capitalist economy has not been proved in Uno's *Principles*. Thus, the necessity of conversion of capitalist economy to socialist economy could not be proved, either. Therefore, a number of adventurous people and political groups in Japan leaped at Uno's theory. In this way, a connection between theory without practice (Uno) and practice without theory (a sort of radicalism and anti-Stalinist movement) was formed in Japan.

In short, Uno's *Principles* mistook the subject of capitalist economy, i.e., capital in general, for commodity economy. And it was a book based on a misunderstood application of Hegel's logic. That is to say, *Principles* is written as a process in which a concept of commodity economy is developing in itself and by itself. This is a Hegelian method of self-development concept without any analysis of presentation (die Vorstellung) that Marx criticized.

3. UNIVERSAL AND PARTICULAR: THE STAGE THEORY OF CAPITALIST DEVELOPMENT

Uno's second work was a three-stage historical model of capitalist development. This work of stage theory was mainly presented in *Keizai Seisaku-ron* (*The Study of Economic Policies*). The first edition of the book was published in 1936, revised edition in 1954, and final version in 1971. Why was the study of economic policies a part of the stage theory? And why was the stage theory separated from his *Principles*? The following is how Uno answered the questions.

> The three types of economic policies, mercantilism, liberalism and imperialism, give us the standard of a historical stage theory of capitalist development. But then it is not enough to define the economic policies for a historical model of capitalist development. It needs more fine descriptions of agriculture, industry, commerce, finance, transport, colonization, etc. Furthermore, the interpretation of public finance is important (Uno, 1974, Vol. 7, p. 241).

Thus, Uno thought that the study of the (capitalist) state could only be made possible in the stage theory. Marx's plan of political economy, especially the state on which a capitalist society is concentrated, was rejected by Uno in this sense.

Furthermore, Uno argued, the theory of a three stage of capitalist development is "not" universal. It only applies to a typical capitalist country and a typical industry in a typical period. For example, mercantilism of the seventeenth and eighteenth century appeared in woolen industry of England, liberalism of the nineteenth century appeared in cotton industry of England, and imperialism of the twentieth century appeared in heavy industries of Germany.[2]

In Uno's *Principles*, therefore, the universal theory of capitalist economy, "the pure theory of capitalism ... seems to me [Uno] quite impossible for economic theory to demonstrate at the same time a transformation which involves the denial of these economic laws" (Uno, 1974, Vol. 2, pp. 163–164).

In Uno's stage theory there is nothing but the particular. Between the universal and the particular lies a crucial disjunction. The universal theory lies quietly and does not move. Although Uno said that the stage theory forms the medium, the medium is not related to the universal theory.

There is no dialectic relationship between the universal and the particular. Uno limited the scope of dialectical logic to the movement and laws of commodity economy itself; commodity becomes capital, and capital becomes commodity, the conversion of capital into a commodity. The logic is closed in a circle.

Thus, his analysis of contemporary capitalism must be done by a positivist and empiricist method, because the universal does not move in itself and the particular indicates only typical phenomena. There is no other choice but a comparative method based on commonality, or by utilizing a certain standard. This type of research would require collaboration among economists who belong to Uno school.

Uno wrote that "the method of the stage-theory is therefore clearly different from the pure theory" (Uno, 1974, Vol. 2, p. 12).

Uno's "three-level analysis of political economy" instead of Marx's systematic critique of political economy was surely unique. But from the methodological standpoint the universal theory formed an ideal type, and the particular theory studied a typical phenomenon and formed the types of capitalist development.[3]

In Uno's stage theory, an actual capitalistic economy is always impure and a mixture of precapitalistic and capitalistic elements. That is why he asserts that his *Principles* is only a standard for understanding. But the scientific theory and laws are always abstract, Mita said, and, to some extent, they could grasp one side of matters. The method of science must consider things in the abstract. When this simple thing is not remembered, there is a tendency to think that the abstract theory could not be appropriate for the real world. Uno said that the method must copy its object. For Mita, however, this is a mistaken thought. Since the scientific method assumes its own epistemology, the human brain would analyze its object freely. In this sense, there is no difference in method between social science and natural science.

Although Uno thought that a real capitalist economy tended to become impure, especially in the last stage of capitalist era, the capitalist economy has developed and expelled precapitalist economic systems. After all, we could say the principles of capitalist economy that would go through all stages of capitalist economy were negated in Uno's theory.

As mentioned above, Uno denied Marx's systematic critique of political economy, especially "Concentration of bourgeois society in the form of the state," "International relation of production," and "World market." These are factors, for Uno, as to how we understand what "impure" means. The first reason why he used the word "pure" was because it was the standard for judging impurity. The second reason for it was because the word "pure" means an economy without a state. It is "pure capitalism" that is not unified into a state and is independent from a state. And the forms of state interference make the stages of capitalist development. That is the reason why he propounded the stage theory as the study of economic policies.

In this way, though Uno used the words "basis" and "superstructure" from the perspective of historical materialism, in fact, for Uno the state as a superstructure is not determined by the economic basis. Uno did not consider that an economic basis was abstracted from a real society, and he proceeded as if the principles of political economy were independent and got ahead of us. This is a classic example of "faith in theory" that Masao Maruyama, a Japanese political scientist, had put forth.[4]

Marx considered that his *Capital* fulfilled the concept of "capital in general," in the first section of "*Capital*" which was the first part of his systematic critique of political economy. Therefore, he thought that *capital in general* must be developed and embodied further. The systematic general theory of capitalist economy, for Marx, includes the state on which a bourgeois society is concentrated. A concentration of bourgeois society in the form of the state is necessary always and everywhere. But Uno rejected this view of Marx in his own way. For Uno the principles must be complete in itself. So his *Principles* did not develop in itself, and it remained a closed system in the logical sense.

One ought not to think that it was a mistake that Marx's *Capital* did not include the analysis of modern state. Marx never changed his original plan. *Capital* was a first step in his plan that showed a rise or advance of several categories from an abstract one to a concrete one. Being concentrated in the form of the state was a precondition for a capitalistic economy. A theory of capitalist economy without the state implies incompleteness, so the logic must advance toward a more concrete explanation. In this sense, Marx used the word "advance" to indicate that it was a rational and common procedure. This means an order of understanding and explanation of the things. The general theory of capitalist economy, a systematic critique of political economy in Marx, naturally includes the theory of state as a subject which concentrates a modern civil society in itself and other preconditions which must be understood after the theory of *capital in general*. Through such concreteness, the general theory becomes more complete.

Uno rejected and neglected a way of rational procedure of science, and asserted that the method of *Capital* was something specific. For Mita, if Uno thought that a method of political economy was characterized by the self-development of the concept, i.e., making a concrete category dependent on an analysis of simple category, his thought has to be called a form of Hegelism. To be precise, it follows the principle of Hegel's logic. Uno accepted a superficial principle of Hegel's logic and reconstructed Marx's *Capital* in a Hegelian way. Mita argued that if Uno thought that Marx's *Capital* must be complete as the theory of capital, Uno was very much mistaken.

In Uno's theory, Mita continued to argue, because the economic policies are separated from the economic basis, the policies of state and its order have an accidental nature, and they could not be explained by economic laws. The three stages of economic policies, mercantilism, liberalism, and imperialism, therefore, must be a mere accumulation of accidents. In Uno's stage theory, there are no relationships and struggles between social classes that arise from the economic basis. The stage theory falls into a sort of idealism because liberalism creates the stage of liberalism and imperialism makes the stage of imperialism. In Uno's idea, the economic laws have to be determined as they appear to repeat themselves. As a result, for Uno, there is no change or development in the economy in accordance with the economic laws. Mita pointed out, in short, that in Uno's theory, if we can call it a theory, the economic process is not an objective but a subjective process, because Uno thought that the economic laws are different from the laws of nature and the history of nature.

We could point out the same problem of the state, the economic policies and stage theory in political economy, and of "international relations of production" that is the fifth part of the systematic critique of political economy, but I will not go into it in detail here.

But there remains one question. Uno strongly affirmed the dialectic method. Isn't there a dialectic relationship between the universal and the particular for Uno? Marx did call his *Capital* "capital in general." Is there a difference between capital in general and the general theory of capital? Thus, I must explain the meaning of the universal in the logic.

For Marx and Mita, the theory of capital in general is a first step in the general theory of capitalist economy, a systematic critique of political economy. Capital in general, from the standpoint of methodology, means the dialectic universal.

Although capital in general as a first step has many premises which have to be explicated, the theory of capital in general still has much potential for developing into a more concrete theory; for example, competition among individual capitals, credit and stock capital, as well as, land ownership, wage labor, state, international exchange or international relation of production, and world market. Since the first step has many premises and it is an abstract theory, it must be developed further. As capital in general has potential to develop into other particular theories, it has to be called the universal ("in general"). This is the dialectic universality. This idea of method was presented by Hegel's *Logic* and that point was made clear in Marx.[5]

Well then, what is the difference between the universal in the dialectic meaning and the universality as community?

The universality as community stands up by an abstraction of several particularities. This is a common way of our thinking and science. To give an example, fruit in general subsumes all sorts of fruits, but an abstraction of particularity of all of fruits. While this concept is a genus or generality (die Gattung) – for example, fruit in general does not exist in itself – other concepts of particularity – for example, apple, banana, etc. – is a kind or sort (die Art) that really exists alone and does not relate to any other. Naturally, the distinction between genus and kind is a relative concept. On the other hand, in a dialectic method, the universal is one of the particulars. It is not an abstraction, but concrete. The particulars relate to each other and they form a whole or totality, and the one of particulars as the universal generates all things and produces all other particulars. It refers to a logic of organization, like human body. To give an example, a knife is composed of edge, handle, and so on. Although the edge is only a particular part of a knife, it is the main component of a knife, and we consider it as the knife as a whole. In the case of a knife, the edge is one of particulars, and at the same time it has universality.

The method of political economy needs both meanings of universal, the universality as an abstract community and the universal as dialectic and concrete one. The concept of capital in general is a common nature of all capitals and at the same time it is the real. It produces and penetrates all forms of capital, land ownership, and wage labor. It must develop into the concepts of state, international relation of production, and world market. The capital in general is summed up with the forms of income of social classes in Marx's *Capital*, but it has many premises. The advance of logic from capital in general to others is a process of proof and conceptualization (getting a general idea of the matter) of many preconditions; competition, state, and others. Conceptualization of them is possible only by means of analysis of our idea or presentation of them. In this sense, an advance of logic is going backwards.

Mita pointed out that Uno misunderstood the method of *Capital*, and he tried a logical reconstruction of it in the style of Hegel. It was a self-development of the concept. As a result, not only Uno did separate the principles of universal theory and the theory of particular stages, but he also erased all of historical matters and tendencies of capitalist economy in

Capital and his *Principles*. We can find the separation between the universal and the particular in Uno's theory.

It might appear that the difference between *Principles* and the stage theory in Uno's system depends upon a certain degree of abstraction. But that is to take the wrong view of the matter. Uno denied the concept of abstract universal.[6] For Uno, there must not be a concept of genus in social sciences. The theory of pure capitalism, therefore, is not a universal that could be applied to all stages and histories of capitalist society. The concept of "pure capitalism" was acquired by being idealized from a particular form of capitalism. Thus, the understanding of particular forms could not be acquired by the "pure" concept.

Mita pointed out that it is surprising that the same denial of the concept of genus or universal could be found in the methodology of Max Weber and the dogmatism of orthodox Marxists.

Max Weber thought that genus as a concept of universal was a necessary method in cognition, but a definition by means of genus was useless for cultural concepts of social sciences. On the other hand, Weber denied a dialectic concept of universality in Hegel and Marx. Then Weber created his famous concept of the "ideal type."[7] And many Marxists asserted the difference between dialectic method and analytical method such as abstracting a common feature.

Mita argued that a denial of the concept of genus would fall into self-contradiction because to deny the concept of genus is only to create a new concept of genus. To take an instance, a concept of financial capital in general needs a concept of capital. We cannot use the phrase, mode of production without reducing all modes of production to the common feature.

Uno rejected the concept of universal, on the one hand, and stressed that the concept must develop in itself without an analysis of our intuitions and images of the facts and the objects. This is a mystic and confusing method that is derived from Uno's Hegelian style.

In short, Mita said, Uno's system of political economy, the so-called three levels of study, the theory of a purely capitalist society and a three stage-model of capitalist development was founded on the method of ideal type similar to that of Max Weber. Their concepts do not exist anywhere or at any time. They are not concepts abstracted from any real capitalist economy. So they are speculative and subjective compositions for understanding any real economy. This is a denial of scientific method and a misleading method of dialectic. After setting purity and a model of capitalism as an ideal type, there only remains an empirical and positive study of actual economies. After all, an ideal type and positivism are the essence of

Uno's methodology in spite of his Hegelian style. The word "capitalism" is merely nominal for Uno.

4. BEYOND HEGELISM AND POSITIVISM: RATIONAL DIALECTIC IN THE LOGIC OF *CAPITAL*

The problem comes down to the logical method employed by Marx in *Capital*. More specifically, the point is a relationship between analytical method and dialectic method. I would term it "rational dialectic." Mita has clarified the point in his *Sihonron no Hōhō* (*The Method in Capital*, 1963) and other books, which I will describe below.

4.1. Dialectic Founded on Analytical Method

An analytical method is a common way of scientific thinking and the natural function of human mind. This method, at first, depends on the presentations or its intuitions of the facts and the objects. Next, logical thinking finds the genus, law, substance, cause, force, and factors based on an analysis. These results of thinking are logically named abstract universals. The abstract universal, therefore, does not have, or produce, its own sorts, forms, conditions, and appearances and expression. It only means common nature of the things.

I might give a few examples from Marx's *Capital*. Marx separated use-value in general from the commodity and labor process in general from the capitalist process of production. Then, an analytical method must explain the concrete things only by adding any kind to the genus, an initial condition to the law, a combined condition to the factor, form and cause from outside. This is not the necessary course of object. To give an example, it is not a natural thing that a use-value takes the form of exchange-value, or that a labor process forms into the capitalist process. But extracting common nature from the object is a natural method.

Hegel asserted that an analytical method was the way of empirical science, and it did not meet the requirements of the form of necessity. For Hegel, the philosophical and speculative way of thinking naturally distinguishes itself from an analytical method.[8] The former, dialectic way converts the categories of the latter, formal way. The progress in Hegel's *Logic* is very difficult to understand because he intended to develop the logical category in itself, by itself, without an analysis of the presentation and idea. He intended to show the limitation of categories that had been used in formal logic, and he did it by the self-movement of the concept. Hegel also thought that the concept as a speculative meaning was not an abstract universal, and that the concept as a concrete universal was producing a real world.

But, in fact, Hegel analyzed the images, presentations of objects, and categories of formal logic in his *Logic*. While he said in principle that an analytical method could not be adapted to Philosophy, he tended to clarify the limitation of abstract concepts in formal logic. We, therefore, have to distinguish the surface and the fact in Hegel's *Logic*. Unfortunately, Uno rejected the analysis of the facts and the images of objects, because he accepted Hegel's assertion as a matter of principle just as Hegel did.

Marx was opposed to Hegel's way of thinking. The objective world exists outside the thinking mind, for Marx, and the human brain could only grasp the concept of objects. A concept does not generate a real world, but theoretical thinking goes behind the outward form to grasp the inner meanings of the phenomenon and then conceptualizes the images of objects, the real world.

Marx wrote, "the real subject remains outside the mind and independent of it – that is to say, so long as the mind adopts a purely speculatively, purely theoretical attitude" (Marx, 1857, "Introduction" for *Grundrisse*, *MEGA*, II, Bd. 1, Teil 1, S. 37; Marx, 1986, *Works*, Vol. 28, p. 38).

And Marx noted in his manuscripts of critique of political economy 1861–1863, "criticism and understanding must begin with an analytical method. An analytical method is a necessary prerequisite of genetical presentation, and of understanding of the real, formative process in its different phases" (Marx, 1979, *MEGA*, II, Bd. 3, Teil 4, S. 1498–1499; Marx, 1989, *Works*, Vol. 32, p. 500).

This is not dualism of analytical and generative method. It is not dialectic analysis as Hegel said, either. Marx noticed that without an analytical method it was impossible for us to comprehend the things, and that the concept does not exist for itself. Comprehension or understanding ("begreifen") is premised on an analytical method. Dialectics without analytical method becomes mysterious. It was in this sense that Marx wrote, in the preface to his *Capital* Vol. 1, that Hegel's dialectic was standing on its head.

First, for Marx, analysis does not mean analyzing the notion, but it starts from the facts. Second, analysis separates the essence from the phenomenon by abstraction. By doing so, the phenomena are determined, and the presentation of facts is changed to the notion (concept). Consequently, there are two meanings of the concept of universal. One is abstract universal as commonality, and the other is concrete universal as dialectic meaning.

The latter includes the particular and concrete forms, and develops to their forms.

And, in Marx's theory, the synthesis is a process of moving from the abstract to the concrete, as with the procedure in *Capital*. In synthetic method, there are two kinds of synthesis. The first synthesis is the simple synthesis going up from the abstract concept or common nature to the concrete concept or its form. In this case, the facts are always given. The second synthesis is dialectic synthesis. In this case, transition is necessary, because the notion includes its particular form, just as the value of commodity includes the forms of value, or monetary form. But we must notice in both synthetic methods that the facts or objects are always envisaged, and the process of synthesis proceeds by analyzing concrete things. The synthetic method of Marx necessarily includes analysis.

4.2. Analysis of Representation and Development of the Notion in Capital

Since analyzing the things lengthwise and crosswise is active, cognition is not mere reflection of the object. The following is what was seen in *Capital*, Vol. 1.

Marx did not analyze the concept of commodity; he analyzed the phenomenon of representation of commodity exchange. He separated use-value from exchange-value. After that, Marx analyzed exchange-value and abstracted value as a universal nature from among the commodities. This was done by simple analysis of method. Marx clarified the concept of value as a specific historical form of labor, or reified contents of particular relationships of people. Then the concept of commodity was proved to be a unity of use-value and value itself. The value of commodity is a definition of historical and particular form of the material thing (use-value) and human labor.

The commodity and circulation of money represent merely one side of what is abstracted from the capitalist mode of production by cognition. They are only preconditions of capitalist production, both logically and historically. Orthodox Marxians and Uno both thought that the transformation of money into capital must be a logical/historical process. The orthodox argued that the contradiction between commodity production and monetary economy must produce the capitalist system of production. By contrast, Uno thought that Marx's method was not dialectic and not consistent, so he rewrote the logic of transformation of money into capital, introducing two forms of capital: merchants' capital and moneylenders' capital. In Uno's way of thinking, the concept of commodity as a circulation form must develop to the concept of capital for itself.[9]

However, for Mita, both the orthodox and Uno were mistaken. As Marx wrote, the historical condition for the existence of capital refers not only to the existence of circulation of commodity and money, but also to the existence of free (in a dual sense) laborers. So does Marx have to explain the historical conditions for free labor? No, he does not. What Marx did was to find free laborers around him and grasp them theoretically.

At first, Marx shows the general form of capital, M-C-M'. The form of self-increasing value is mysterious and incompatible with the laws of commodity exchange. Then Marx finds the particular commodity of labor power as a key to the problem and he moves to describe the process of using labor power that is the process of capitalist production. To explain the historical conditions of the existence of labor power, one has to describe the whole process of history. Commodity production and its exchange, money circulation and the existence of labor power (free laborers) are preconditions for the existence of capital. The history of commodity production itself never brought about the commodification of labor power. And merchants' capital and moneylenders' capital were not always, necessarily, converted to industrial capital.

The method in the transformation of money into capital is that Marx analyzed the given condition or the representation of capital, M-C-M', and clarified the logical contradiction between the general form of capital and the laws of commodity exchange. And he could explain why it is possible for self-increasing value to be applied to the laws of commodity exchange. This is a rational way of thinking for the development of concept. The development of the concept in the transformation of commodity and money into capital can be done only by the analysis of the fact (M-C-M') and comparing the fact with already acquired concept (C and M). Marx puts forth a new concept of capital, self-increasing value, which is the first step for the development of capital in general. This way of proceeding is seen throughout the whole of *Capital*.

4.3. Characteristics of Dialectic Method

Mita clarified the essence of dialectic method of *Capital* in his *Hōhō* (Ch. 4). Mita argued that if we talk about the most general character of dialectic method in *Capital*, it is to develop the two sides that reflect each other as the necessary forms of appearance through the nature of capital and from the general concept of capital. For example, monopoly and free competition among capitals are in opposition to each other. In the generative or dialectic method, two particular forms of relationship between capitals are developed by the concept of capital in general.

However, the relationship between the nature and its appearance in dialectic method must be grasped more concretely. For Mita, there are three (concrete) essences in the dialectic method of *Capital*.

First, in general, an organic body as an individual that is countable has several particulars in it. The dialectic universal is not the common nature of all particulars of it. The universal exists as one of the particulars, so it is not a nominal one.[10] The universal concept has its reality, and it coexists with other particulars. Since the universal includes its own particular, there is a contradiction inherent in it. So the universal must develop into an "other" for itself and exist in itself. As the universal is one particular, it can comprehend the whole of a thing. This is how an organic whole exists.

In analyzing capital, Marx separates it into two parts: constant capital and variable capital. They are two particular parts in a capital. Although the common nature of two parts in a capital is self-increasing value, variable capital is the only one that can really increase by itself. That is why variable capital is advanced to the commodity of labor power, and it produces more value than its original amount of value. We must say that capital as capital is variable capital which is the particular part of a capital, and at the same time is the universal capital in a dialectic sense. This is what Marx called the "organic" composition of capital. *Capital in general* as universality originally exists in variable capital as a particular component in it.

We can point out the same in the process of production and the process of circulation of capital. The process of production is particular. Yet, on the other hand, as a comprehensive moment or a universal concept, it comprehends the whole process of capitalist economy. Mita called this first point "the universal as main comprehensive moment" in his *Hōhō*. I think this is an important achievement of Mita.[11]

Mita clarified the second point of dialectic method in *Capital*, which is the universal as an individual. Marx's *Capital* conceptualized the relationship between each of the individual capitals. To give an example, an individual capital includes the relationship between the individual capitals. Marx showed this in his schema of reproduction that analyzed the circulation process of social capital as a whole (*Capital*, Vol. 2, Section 3). This means that an individual capital as a universal concept essentially includes the relationship among all capitals through particular concepts, i.e., two industrial sectors. Two sectors as mediums form a united whole.

Mita called this second point of dialectic method in *Capital* "the dialectic conversion from the universal as an individual to an intertwined relationship between individuals."

He wrote, "if we understand that capital in general exists in the particular and in an individual, then we must grasp the rational character of dialectic method of development. When we scientifically understand the concrete thing as a united whole in which the several sides are premised on each other, the following is the only one and necessary method that first we consider the main, fundamental side of the thing assuming the preconditions, and next we consider the premise. In other case, we separately consider an individual at first, and next consider the relationship between the individuals" (Mita, 1963, *Hōhō*, p. 222).

The third point of dialectic method in *Capital* concerns the logic of contradiction.

In *Capital*, Marx argued that after studying two opposite sides of something, the whole of that thing is newly considered. We can find this at the third volume of *Capital* or at the transition from the second volume to the third of *Capital*. There, a more concrete form of capitalist process is investigated, for example, the conversion of surplus value into profit, the commercial capital, the interest and rent as the form of transition of surplus value.

At the same time, the contradictions of capital stand out clearly. The trend of capital, production for production itself, was studied in the first volume of *Capital*, especially in the section where Marx examines the accumulation process of capital. And production for consumption was studied in the second volume, especially in the third section, where he presents the schema of reproduction. Therefore, Marx comprehends the two essences of capitalist production and he finds the contradiction of capital in the law of profit, where the profit rate has a tendency to fall. It is here, where the two different natures are unified, by considering the process as a whole. The contradiction must be also considered in the third part, after the first study of one side and second study of the other side, because the contradiction is not a mere opposition. The unity of opposite sides is not contradiction. The dialectic meaning of contradiction refers to the antagonism, i.e., the destruction of unity of opposite sides. The consideration of contradiction within the thing itself is different from the transition from one particular to another particular (the first essence as mentioned above), and the conversion from an individual to the relationship between all individuals (the second essence as mentioned above).

Mita called the third point of dialectic method in *Capital* "the progression from two sides of contradiction to the entire, real contradiction."

4.4. Beyond Hegelism, Positivism and Collusion of the Two

As a result, the proceeding of dialectic categories which compose the framework of *Capital* is (1) the progression from the universal as the main moment to the particular as the second moment, (2) the progression from the universal as an individual to an intertwined relationship between the individuals, and (3) the progression from the two sides of contradiction to a real contradiction, or from the two opposite sides to a more concrete notion of totality.

Marx's *Capital* is an anatomy of capitalist economy. The motive power of logical process in it is the precondition of the abstract categories that have to become concrete, and the contradiction between abstract categories and the facts. It means the logical contradiction.

As is shown in Marx's phrase in his early notes ("*Grundrisse*"), "organism as a historical totality," an anatomy of capitalist economy has to be an embryology of it. However, this does not mean that the logical process and the historical process are inherently unified. The orthodox tried to interpret the process of *Capital* as the implicit (*an sich*) unity of logical and historical process. In general, they did not seek to understand the analytical (synthetic) method of *Capital* because they thought that dialectic method should be a system of self-development of the concepts.

Kōzō Uno shared this position with the orthodox. Contrary to the orthodox, however, Uno tried to reconstruct *Capital* in his own manner, in which the logical process might be consistent with historical process. He thought that this method was consistent with the dialectic method of Hegel. This way, however, was limited to Uno's *Principles*. Thus, "pure capitalism" in his *Principles* became a sort of ideal type. He could not apply dialectic method to his stage theory. Instead, he had to rely on the method of ideal types in the stage theory. As a result, there remains nothing except positivist method for the analysis of actual conditions. In Uno's theory he placed his stage theory based on ideal types as the mediation between *Principles* and his analysis of present conditions. In short, from the methodological point of view, Uno's "system" of theory is a mixture or a collusion of Hegelism and positivism in Marxian economics. Acting as an intermediary between Hegelism and positivism was Max Weber's way.

Uno said that Marx not only recognized the object, capitalist society, but also copied its method of abstraction and synthesis. In his opinion, the method is a copy of the object. This phrase of Uno's came from Hegel's *Logic*. Hegel wrote in his *Logic* that the concept analyzes and synthesizes by itself.[12] This is mysterious and irrational and it is what Mita named

Hegelism. Hegelism refers to a way of thinking that denies an analytical method, which abstracts and analyzes the concrete presentation and idea by means of a common sense of understanding, and Hegelism asserts that a dialectic method essentially differs from an analytical method. Because this was a superficial assertion of Hegel, Mita called it Hegelism.

For a common way of understanding, on the other hand, there remains the concrete presentation and idea. Based on Hegel's "introduction to the *Encyclopedia*," it leads to philosophical empiricism and methodological positivism.

The orthodox way of thinking among many Marxian economists had been based on Marx's *Capital* and Lenin's *Imperialism* (1917) and the theory of state-monopoly capitalism as means of analyzing modern capitalism. They tended to place absolute trust in *Capital* and *Imperialism*. It might be called three system of theory in another sense (general theory of capital, particular stage-theory and state-monopoly capitalism). In a sense, both the orthodox and Uno relied upon the authority of Soviet Marxism (Stalinism). Yet, Uno gained a reputation by opposing Soviet Marxism (Stalinism). Uno's theory was a negative exemplum for Soviet Marxism. Both of them had no choice but to rely on positivist method in their analysis of present conditions. Their way of thinking lacked what was most important, a comprehensive method.[13]

Pointing out the limitations of *Capital* and *Imperialism* does not mean to entirely renounce them. The key point is to understand the methodological relationship between the universal and the particular in both a dialectic and analytical sense. It is necessary for us to recall that Marx's plan, the systematic critique of political economy, and *Capital* (*capital in general*) was not only the first part of the system, but also the universal in a dialectic sense. Modern radical political economy is faced with the task of analyzing facts and history on the one hand and the necessity to understand the theoretical potentials in *capital in general* (*Capital*) on the other.[14]

NOTES

1. By way of parenthesis, Munesuke Mita, a sociologist in Japan, is a son of Sekisuke Mita.

2. This paper does not study that Uno affirmed that capitalism since World War I remained an issue for his analysis of current conditions.

3. Uno noticed that his theory of economic policies was similar to Max Weber's ideal types, although he asserted the difference of his stage theory from Max Weber's

ideal types, he only pointed out that Max Weber did not have his "*Principles*". (Uno, Vol. 7, pp. 43–45, and others).

4. See, Masao Maruyama (1962), p. 57.

5. See, Shūichi Kakuta (2005).

6. See, Uno "Kyōkō-ron" (Crisis Theory, 1953, p. 168), (Uno, Vol. 5, p. 131) and others.

7. S. Kakuta (2008), pp. 12–17. Mita pointed out that Uno's methodology depended on Weber in many points including the relationship between theory and praxis, science and partisanship, and science and ideology (Mita, 1968, pp. 68–80).

8. "The real universal should not be confused with what is merely held in common" (Hegel's *Logic*, 1830, Section 163 addition). "We should distinguish what is ordinarily called a notion from notion in the speculative sense" (Section 9). "Analytical and synthetic method is finite cognition. ... Philosophic thought ...evinces itself to be the action of the notion itself" (Section 238 addition). "This very circumstance makes the synthetic method of cognition as little suitable for philosophy as the analytical" (Section 229 addition).

9. Uno rejected the way of simple abstraction. He said that if they abstract simple goods, human labor and desire from the commodities, they could not return to the commodities as a concept. He thought that the categories always have their own power of going up. This thought is mysterious and just Hegelian. *Principles*, Uno, Vol. 1, p. 19, and other pages.

10. Nominalism is the standpoint arguing that the universal does not really exist. On the other hand, Hegel and Marx argued for the realism of the concept (the substantialist view of universal concept).

11. The first point of dialectic method, the universal as main moment and the dialectic relationship between the universal and the particular, had been clarified not only in the study of *Capital*, but also in the study of Hegel's *Logic*.

12. "The method is soul of the object." Hegel wrote this phrase in the final part of his *Science of Logic*, "the absolute Idea."

13. One might ask what Stalinism or Soviet Marxism was. This is a major problem, requiring consideration of the system of thought, history of revolutionary movement, social system of the Soviet Union (USSR) and other countries before and around 1990 and historical processes.

My tentative definition is that Stalinism believed in Marx(ism)-Leninism, and followed the histories and orders of the Soviet Union (USSR). From the methodological point of view, its central themes were the general crisis of capitalism, intensified class conflicts, and the world system of socialism. It had official textbooks like "*Dialectic and Historical Materialism*" published in Stalin's name and "*The Textbook of Political Economy*" issued by the Soviet Academy of Sciences.

I once argued that there were three points in Stalinist political economy. They are monism of property without reification of production relationship, crisis theory without the theory of contradiction, and the theory of class struggle without the theory of human development (Kakuta, 2005, p. 256).

14. Marx not only analyzed the facts of contemporary capitalist society, but also studied theoretical materials of the classical school and other economists. In this way, Marx could conceptualize the real existence, while Hegel thought that his concept and idea (Idee) were realized. Hegel took his idea for the real. If Marx

had not analyzed the real, he would only have analyzed notions as Uno did in his *Principles*. And if Marx had only analyzed the facts, he could not have conceptualized the real.

ACKNOWLEDGMENTS

An earlier version of this paper had been written in the United States, being stimulated by Andrew Barshay, 2004, especially Chapter 4, *Thinking through Capital, Uno Kōzō and Marxian Political Economy*. I thank Professor Barshay (UC Berkeley) for our discussion and his helpful comments. It is my pleasure to acknowledge the help of the following individuals: Duncan Williams, Keiko Hjersman, Kangkook Lee, Sungyun Lim, and Center for Japanese Studies at UC Berkeley. Paul Zarembka and the anonymous reviewers also provided me with valuable remarks.

REFERENCES

Barshay, A. (2004). *The social sciences in modern Japan: The Marxian and modernist traditions.* California: University of California Press.

Hegel, G. W. (1830). *Logic, being part one of the encyclopedia of the philosophical sciences* (translated by W. Wallace, 1873). Oxford: Oxford University Press, 1975.

Kakuta, S. (2005). *"Shihon" no Hōhō to Hegel Ronri-gaku (The method in Capital and Hegel's logic)*. Tokyo: Otsuki Shoten.

Kakuta, S. (2008). *Schomoller to Weber ni-okeru Shakaikagaku to Keizaigaku no Hōhō* (Methodology of Social Science and Political Economy in G. V. Schmoller & M. Weber). In: *"The Ritsumeikan Economic Review,"* Shiga, Vol. 57, No. 1, pp. 1–27.

Maruyama, M. (1962). *Nihon no Shisō (Japanese thought)*. Tokyo: Iwanami Shoten.

Marx, K. (1857). *Ökonomische Manuskripte 1857/58.* In: *Marx Engels Gesamtausgabe* (MEGA), II, 1.1, 1.2, Berlin: Dietz Verlag, 1976, 1981.

Marx, K. (1979). *Zur Kritik der Politischen Ökonomie (Manuskript 1861–1863)*. In: MEGA, II, 3.4, 1979.

Marx, K. (1986). *Collected works* (Vol. 28). Moscow: Progress Publishers, 1986.

Marx, K. (1989). *Collected works* (Vol. 32). Moscow: Progress Publishers, 1989.

Mita, S. (1963). *Shihonron no Hōhō (Marx's method in Capital)*. Tokyo: Kōbundō.

Mita, S. (1968). *Uno Riron to Marukusu-shugi Keizaigaku (Uno theory and Marxist political economy)*. Tokyo: Aoki Shoten.

Uno, K. (1974). *Uno Kōzō chosakushū (Works)*. 10 Volumes plus Suppl. Tokyo: Iwanami Shoten, 1974.

Uno, K. (2008). *Shihonron to Watakushi*. Tokyo: Ochanomizu Shobō.

FURTHER READING

Mita, S. (1977). *Mita Sekisuke chosakushū (Works)* (Vol. 4). Tokyo: Otsuki Shoten, 1977.

Uno, K. (1980). *Principles of political economy, theory of a purely capitalist society* (translated from the Japanese edition, 1964, by Thomas T. Sekine). New Jersey: Harvester/ Humanities Press.